Feminist Locations

I0093605

FEMINIST LOCATIONS

*Global and Local,
Theory and Practice*

edited by
MARIANNE DeKOVEN

RUTGERS UNIVERSITY PRESS
New Brunswick, New Jersey, and London

Library of Congress Calaloging-in-Publication Data

Feminist locations : global and local, theory and practice / edited
by Marianne DeKoven
       p. cm.
    Includes bibliographical references and index.
    ISBN 0-8135-2922-0 (alk. paper)—ISBN 0-8135-2923-9 (pbk. : alk. paper)
    1. Feminist theory. 2. Feminism. I. DeKoven, Marianne, 1948–
    HQ1190 .F4534 2001
    305.42'01—dc21   00-045681

British Cataloging-in-Publication data for this book is available from the British
Library

Copyright © 2001 by Rutgers, the State University
Individual chapters copyright © 2001 in the names of their authors.
For exceptions, please see below.

Grateful acknowledgment is made to the following for permission to reprint:
    Coco Fusco and Nao Bustamante, "Stuff," *TDR/The Drama Review* 41:4 (T156–
winter 1997): 63–82. © 1997 by Coco Fusco and Nao Bustamante, reprinted by permission of the authors. "Introduction," pp. 62–63, © 1997 by The MIT Press Journals,
reprinted by permission of the publisher.
    Radha S. Hegde, "Sons and M(others): Framing the Maternal Body and the Poli-
tics of Reproduction in a South Indian Context," *Women's Studies in Communication*
22:1 (July 1999), reprinted by permission of ORWAC.

All rights reserved
No part of this book may be reproduced or utilized in any form or by any means,
electronic or mechanical, or by any information storage and retrieval system, without written permission from the publisher. Please contact Rutgers University Press,
100 Joyce Kilmer Avenue, Piscataway, NJ 08854–8099. The only exception to this
prohibition is "fair use" as defined by U.S. copyright law.

Contents

Acknowledgments

This collection is based on scholarship presented at the Institute for Research on Women (IRW) at Rutgers University, during my tenure as director, from 1995 to 1998, particularly in the "Thinking about Women" lecture series, and in IRW's 1997–1998 seminar, developed in collaboration with the Institute for Women's Leadership at Rutgers, on Women in the Public Sphere: Power, Practice, Agency. As is evident throughout this collection, the IRW is strongly committed to diversity along all relevant axes of difference, including—in addition to diversity of race, ethnicity, sexuality, and geographical location— disciplinary diversity and diversity of orientation toward scholarship and activism. The interdisciplinarity practiced at the IRW moves beyond appropriation by scholars of one discipline of some objects, methodologies or texts of other disciplines, to work toward a feminist scholarly-activist project that defines, synthesizes, and produces its own multidisciplinary/transdisciplinary objects and methodologies.

Recognition of the various kinds of work that made this collection possible must be both general and specific. The IRW would not exist without the support of the extraordinary and brilliant community of committed women scholars and activists at Rutgers University. This community consists of the dozens of scholars, internal and external, who work in various capacities at the institute every year; of the many hundreds of individuals who constitute the affiliates of the IRW; and also of a diverse array of women's centers, institutes, and programs at Rutgers, including the IRW, brought together organizationally by the Institute for Women's Leadership, under the direction of Mary Hartman. Rutgers has one of the most active, large, diverse, and innovative communities of women scholars and activists in the world, and this community receives invaluable support from the Rutgers University administration. The IRW is greatly indebted, in particular, to the generous, active support of the former dean Richard Foley and the associate dean for the humanities Barry Qualls, both of the Faculty of Arts and Sciences.

Although the affiliates of the IRW number nearly a thousand, all the work of the institute is done by two brilliant, courageous, versatile, resourceful, polymath superwomen: the associate director Beth Hutchison and the office manager Marlene Importico; before Marlene, the superwoman working with the associate director was the administrative assistant Arlene M. Nora. All the usual clichés come to mind, and they all apply: none of the variegated work the IRW does, whoever the director might be, would be possible without Beth, Marlene, and Arlene before her. My gratitude to them is limitless. Marlene and Arlene, in addition to being wonderful people, were crucial organizers, inventors, problem solvers, human relations experts, and facilitators of every kind of IRW activity. Beth, to whom I want to express particular gratitude, shared all my decision making, was remarkably flexible and resourceful in dealing with a mind-boggling array of technical, logistical, and intellectual challenges, and was (and remains) a highly valued friend as well as collaborator. Beth, with the superb assistance of Sharon Kenney, Women's Studies MA candidate, has also been responsible for shepherding this manuscript, efficiently and diligently, through its final stages.

I would like to express my enormous gratitude to Leslie Mitchner, associate director and editor in chief of Rutgers University Press, whose brilliance, expertise, subtle and variegated insight, and gracious patience as editor of this collection have been extraordinary. I would also like to thank Bonnie K. Scott, for her insightful, extremely helpful suggestions for revision of the manuscript, and Debbie Self, the manuscript copyeditor, for her fine work.

As always, I thank my family—my children, Maggie and Daniel Hennefeld; my husband, Julien Hennefeld; my mother, Annabel DeKoven; and my parents-in-law, Lillian and Edmund Hennefeld—for everything in life that makes it worth living and that makes work such as this possible.

Feminist Locations

MARIANNE DEKOVEN

INTRODUCTION

This collection looks toward future locations of feminist theory, scholarship, and practice by undertaking reconfigurations of two key historical binaries: global and local, theory and practice. These reconfigurations are informed by, and hope to have a constructive impact on, the most important current trends in feminist scholarship, particularly those related to interrogations of all classical binary structures by postmodern and postcolonial studies and critical race and ethnicity theories. Contemporary feminist intellectual and activist work has challenged both the concept of the binary itself, structured as hierarchical, self/other dualism, and also many of the particular binary pairs at the heart of Western culture—in addition to global and local, theory and practice, also white and nonwhite, center and margin or periphery (producing "west" and "rest"), universal and particular, and, perhaps most notably for feminism, masculine and feminine itself. The feminist scholarship represented in this collection aims to break apart, disassemble, and reconfigure these binaries into shifting, multiply intersecting, relational fields of difference.

Various categories of difference, most notably race, ethnicity, sexuality, class, and location, as well as gender, have been crucial to the transformation of these binaries by recent feminist scholarship and activism, literally pushing open spaces between their terms. However, binary thinking, particularly as manifest in the pairs global and local and theory and practice, still has a powerful hold on the ways in which we conceptualize our work as feminist scholars and practitioners. Some recent work has been devoted to reconceiving and reinvigorating for feminist theory and practice terms such as *universal*, discredited by postmodern feminism because it is traditionally located on the dominant "self" side of the classic binary of the universal and the particular, with the "othered" terms connected to particularity rather than universality.[1] *Feminist Locations* is interested in understanding the ways in which binary pairs are restructured, refunctioned, resignified: persisting in various forms *through* their deconstruction into relational fields of difference. The binary does not disappear; rather, it is subject to continual interrogation and reconfiguration.

Complex postcolonial transformations—the mutually defining relatedness of local specificity with global and transnational flows of culture and capital—constitute a primary feminist location for pursuing these agendas. Comparable mutualities of theory and practice in new and future feminist scholarship and activism constitute another such location, particularly in relation to investigations of axes of difference such as race, ethnicity, sexuality, nation, region, as well as of questions of equality, rights, participation, citizenship, embodied subjectivity, and other ambiguous legacies of modernity. The interrelation of theory and practice, the local and the global, needs to be addressed in the new studies of gender-race-ethnicity intersectionality that are currently located at the leading edge of feminist studies and in the traditional disciplines so strongly influenced by feminist and other interdisciplinary studies. Reconfigured localisms based on race, ethnicity, and location are deeply implicated in the new economic, political, and cultural globalism. This pervasive connectedness is at once crucial and profoundly undertheorized and underanalyzed. As Homi K. Bhabha says in his essay "On the Irremovable Strangeness of Being Different," "racism, community, blood, and borders haunt the new international and have gained remarkable ideological and affective power."[2] It is a key purpose of *Feminist Locations* to contribute to the project of understanding how a reinvigorated feminist theoretical practice can advance our understanding of these postmodern mutualities of the local and the global.

The simultaneous emphasis this collection places on the terms *feminist* and *location* and the multiplicity of future feminist locations are themselves a gesture toward at once retaining, critiquing, disassembling, and reconfiguring a classic binary. To the extent that feminism implies a dualistic analysis of domination and (in)subordination along a singular axis of gender difference, invoking the term *feminist* retains that binary as a meaningful and in fact crucial gathering point for mobilizing various necessary forms of agency and resistance. But using the term *feminist* as a modifier for the term *locations*, with the emphasis thereby falling on the latter, substantive term, at the same time undoes the homogenizing, difference-suppressing legacy of feminist modernity by dispersing feminist agency and resistance across differential particular locations. The term *locations* also serves to emphasize the concrete situatedness in particular geographical, political, cultural, intellectual, psychic, and subjective domains of the work these essays perform.

Feminist Locations embodies and argues for diversity along all relevant axes of difference, including disciplinary diversity and diversity of orientation toward scholarship and activism and diversity of race, ethnicity, sexuality, and geographical location. This diversity is reflected in the unusual range of intellectual and discursive style, of subject matter, and of approach in this collection and in the range of disciplinary, interdisciplinary, and activist points of view. This collection aims to achieve a genuine interdisciplinarity, or perhaps transdisciplinarity would be a preferable term, that goes beyond appropriation by practitioners of one discipline of some objects, methodologies, or texts of other disciplines, to work toward a feminist scholarly activist project that defines, synthesizes, and produces its own multidisciplinary and transdisciplinary objects and methodologies.[3] At a time when many of the most visible academic feminists lament the exhaustion or even extinction of feminist scholarship, or discuss what Barbara Johnson calls the current "impasse" of feminist theory, the essays in *Feminist Locations* make clear that feminist scholarship can be profoundly germane to the crucial questions of the proper nature and function of intellectual work in our current, highly mediated, dispersed global/local public discourses.[4]

The dual focus of this collection on the reconfiguration of the key binaries theory and practice, global and local, is itself decentered by the three-part structure of the volume. The essays in part 1, "The Practice of Feminist Theory," share an awareness, tacit or overt, of the global dissemination and local differentiation of feminist theory, and the essays in parts 2 and 3, "Global Locations I: Postnational

Politics" and "Global Locations II: Body Politics," are aware of and informed by mutualities of feminist theory and practice. The five authors in part 1, Susan Stanford Friedman, Lynne Segal, Elaine K. Chang, Karen Barad, and Cheryl Johnson-Odim, discuss the current state of feminist theory, in order to assess the feasibility of various possible future directions for a practicing theory, a theorized practice.

Susan Stanford Friedman's "Locational Feminism: Gender, Cultural Geographies, and Geopolitical Literacy," which builds on her recent book *Feminism and the Cultural Geographies of Encounter* and addresses directly, as is evident in the title, the question of feminist locations, is an ideal introductory essay for this volume.[5] "Locational Feminism" takes as its subject the central preoccupation of this collection: the interrelation of current and future feminist theory and practice with the local and global configurations of postmodernity. Friedman argues for a shift in our understanding and naming of feminist theory and practice from "feminisms" to "feminism," not in order to return to the second wave's difference-erasing, falsely monolithic universalism, but in order to represent adequately the feminist location, or locational feminism, of a geographically, locally particular but united (rather than unified) global body of third-wave feminist theory and practice. This locational feminism would be adequate to the profound shift from modernity's temporality, which produced feminist narratives of awakening and transformation, to postmodernity's spatiality, which invites feminist narratives of multiple, shifting, migratory, borderland location. In its large synthetic scope and its powerful lucidity, this essay provides, as Friedman's other essays have provided at key moments in the history of contemporary feminism, an invaluable assessment of the feminist past and present and a call to reassess and redefine our work for the future.

The next two essays in the volume address directly the question of the future of feminist theory and practice. "Only Contradictions on Offer: Anglophone Feminism at the Millennium" is Lynne Segal's pointed, complex set of answers to this question. For every hopeful indicator of feminist success and future potential at the current turn of the century, she finds counterbalancing evidence of powerful backlash, social regression, particularly in the dismantling of the welfare state, and the depoliticization of feminist theory in its preoccupations with the personal and the individual at the expense of the political and the social. Nonetheless, women are positioned to act as agents of future political change precisely by our current location at the site of these contradictions: "Given the continuing strength of traditional gender ideology, it is the daily lives of women which most directly absorb the shocks and contradictions of these mean yet widely disparate times. Hence the continuing potential for women's role in seeking radical social transformation."

Elaine K. Chang's "Last Past the Post: Theory, Futurity, Feminism" addresses the future of feminist theory, and feminist thought about the future, from the perspective of the present as age of the "post-," particularly in postmodernism, postcolonialism, poststructuralism, and, most problematically, so-called postfeminism. Women and feminism are often the location of gaps or absences, or of reified identity, or merely of afterthought, in postmodern, postcolonial, or poststructuralist theory: the site of what Chang calls domesticated alterity. But postfeminism, more dangerously, implies a rigid historical teleology in which feminism can be defeated simply by being marked as superseded. Instead, to avoid collapsing together incommensurable temporalities into a procrustean linear historicism, Chang would rather be a "multi-postal feminist," for whom the future remains malleable and open to feminist agency.

In her meditation on "Re(con)figuring Space, Time, and Matter," Karen Barad addresses the question of spatiality that is at the center of this volume's concerns, but she does it from the perspective of feminist science studies. The other contributors to this collection, as is the case in the overwhelming majority of works of feminist scholarship, are humanists and social scientists. Feminist science studies represent a crucial future direction for feminist scholarship. Given the expanding technological-scientific basis of flows of knowledge, capital, and power, women's presence in science and technology must expand as well in order for there to be a meaningful feminist future. Feminist science studies also have the potential to move scientific thought in a direction more compatible with feminist goals, at the same time that they bring scientific and technological issues and ways of thinking to bear on feminist theory. Barad's agential realism, in particular, complicates the poststructuralist feminist notion that discursive practices produce or construct materiality by linking that notion with a reciprocal notion: in Barad's words, "the possibility of materiality producing discursive consequences." In this linkage, space, or "positionality," must be understood as fluid, shifting, and irreversibly marked: it can never be measured independently of momentum, time, and movement. Agential realism models the ineluctable intertwining of the material, linked to the local, and the discursive, linked to the global.

Cheryl Johnson-Odim's "Who's to Navigate and Who's to Steer? A Consideration of the Role of Theory in Feminist Struggle" outlines some of the limitations of current feminist theoretical practice, particularly to the extent that it has become irrelevant not just to the lives but to the growing activism of women in a multiplicity of global situations. She argues nonetheless that theory is crucial in informing and advancing the development of feminist political practice, as long as practice plays a central role in developing theory, which it must in order for theory to be relevant and politically useful. Johnson-Odim undoes and reconfigures the theory/practice binary in order to understand it instead as a necessary interdependency precisely so that theory and practice can serve the needs of newly reconfigured local and global feminist politics. This chapter therefore serves both as a powerful link between the discursive and the material, the global and the local, and as a pivot between parts 1 and 2 of this collection.

Parts 2 and 3 address the complex mutuality of the local and the global in current and future feminist theory and practice, with part 2 focused primarily on political issues and part 3 on questions of the body. Again, however, as these chapters will make clear, feminist politics should be understood as embodied, and feminist investigations of the body should be understood as having political implications. "Global Locations I: Postnational Politics," consisting of essays by Charlotte Bunch, Leela Fernandes, Debra J. Liebowitz, Cynthia Saltzman, and Rajeswari Sunder Rajan, focuses on cultural and social dimensions of feminist political scholarship. In "Women's Human Rights: The Challenges of Global Feminism and Diversity," Charlotte Bunch, one of the leading activists and theorists in the world in the field of global women's human rights, makes powerfully clear that, under the aegis of the belief that "women's rights are human rights," both local and global feminist political structures, organizations, and ideas are not only mutually implicated, but should be mobilized simultaneously. Emerging global networks of women working to achieve a wide range of advances and reforms must work through local particularity and recognition of cultural diversity in order to be successful. The notion of human rights, seemingly discredited as enlightenment-bound and therefore white, Western, and male, can work to provide "overarching principles to frame visions of justice for women without dictating the precise content of those visions," content which is always constructed and marked by diverse local specificity.

In "Rethinking Globalization: Gender and the Nation in India," Leela Fernandes makes clear how the interaction of globalization and local specificity can be lodged in the articulation of gender difference in a repressive way. In fact, "the global" is itself produced through its particular national location, defined by nationalist narratives, in India. These narratives are constructed around conservative articulations of gender difference, in which national borders are established and policed by establishing and policing the borders of women's subjectivity and sexuality. Understanding this use of nationalist ideologies to control women is a crucial component of the kind of global networking for women's human rights that Bunch discusses.

Debra J. Liebowitz, in "Constructing Cooperation: Feminist Activism and the North American Free Trade Agreement," investigates a particular instance of this border-crossing mode of networking for women's rights. She argues that the efforts of women in North American NGOs (nongovernmental organizations) in particular, in the United States, Canada, and Mexico, to organize transnationally against the adverse impact of NAFTA on economically marginalized communities, show that globalization has a fragmenting, difference-emphasizing effect that exists in tension with its homogenizing, universalizing effect. Careful attention to "differences among the groups in perspective, ideology, political context and their ability to address issues of difference (race, class, nation)" was necessary in order for any degree of effectiveness in this globalized context of women's activism. Transnational activist networking that focuses on particular issues of common concern, such as opposition to NAFTA, therefore deploys a useful strategy for mobilizing a global commonality of feminist purpose that acknowledges and respects local differences.

Focusing on a particular U.S. location, Cynthia Saltzman, in "The Many Faces of Activism," analyzes the 1984–1985 clerical workers' strike at Yale University. The success of Local 34 of the Hotel and Restaurant Employees International Union in organizing clerical

workers at Yale depended on its ability to recognize and appeal
diversely to the very different, primarily female, constituencies, ranging not only across varying class, race, ethnic, and economic positions, but also across a variety of familial and social backgrounds,
levels of education, marital status, and familial obligations. The
union's successful deployment of local "cultures of activism," in
Saltzman's phrase, shows how "a group dynamic may be an expression of class solidarity even as individuals hold onto core identities
that partially contest the group's definition of an oppositional class
dynamic." This often volatile deployment of common interest across
recognized and respected local, particular differences, especially differences of subjective identification, is, again, a key component in
current and future feminist local/global political activism.

In "Feminism and the Politics of the Hindu Goddess," Rajeswari
Sunder Rajan offers a crucial note of caution for feminist theorists
and practitioners at the current intersection of local and global political and cultural discourses and also provides a useful pivot between
parts 2 and 3 of this collection. Sunder Rajan discusses the arguments
on both sides of the debate around the question articulated in her
title, concluding that, despite the progressive ways in which the
Hindu goddess figure can be construed as empowering women, those
symbolic modes of representation can be, and often are, not only divorced from but at odds with the material conditions of women's lives
in contemporary India. In examining the complex intersections and
divergences of representation, belief, and cultural-political materiality, from both local and global feminist points of view, Sunder Rajan
emphasizes the ways in which women's bodies lie at the crossroads
of these intersections and divergences. It is from the knowledges and
modes of agency gained there that feminist theoretical and practical
rearticulations of the local and the global can best proceed.

Part 3, in works by Anne C. Bellows, Coco Fusco and Nao Bustamante,
Radha S. Hegde, and E. Ann Kaplan, investigates the feminist politics of women's embodied experiences. In Anne C. Bellows's "The
Praxis of Food Work in Poland," this connection between politics and
bodies, crucial for the future of local-global feminist theory-practice,
focuses on the food security activism of women in a particular location, post-1989 Poland. She argues for an expansion and redefinition
of conventional notions of the political to include the household-

based work women do. In the context of food scarcity and pollution, by means of spatially and ideologically fluid, shifting, informal affiliations and issue-oriented activism, Polish women work in ingenious, innovative ways to try to guarantee basic food security for their families. Despite its collusion with the reinstatement of traditional gender ideologies in post-communist Eastern Europe, this activism should be recognized as political work, says Bellows, and incorporated into the development of public policy.

In the "Stuff" piece, performance artists Coco Fusco and Nao Bustamante address very similar issues and develop a similar feminist perspective. They use the stereotypical association of Latin women with food to make clear the ways in which the current cultures of consumption in the north literally and figuratively devour the eroticized "raw materials" of women of the south, particularly in the Americas, as "a bit of the Other," suggesting that notions of feminist agency should incorporate the political consciousness made available by these women's subject positions.

Radha S. Hegde, in "Sons and M(others): Framing the Maternal Body and the Politics of Reproduction in a South Indian Context," similarly develops a feminist analysis of the subjectivity and potential agency of women who are controlled and abjected through a particular set of oppressive cultural and political meanings developed around their embodied experiences. She interviewed a number of South Asian women whose maternal bodies had been, in some cases cruelly, disciplined in the cultural-political interest of producing male children. Agendas of cultural meaning and political control had been enforced on and through the bodies of these women at the most literal level. Capitulation to and reproduction of these agendas is inevitable, but, nonetheless, many women are able to find ways to resist this control, through modes of agency that coexist in tension with their inevitable modes of submission. Again, as Hegde, working from Nancy Hartsock's standpoint theory, eloquently argues, "To theorize from the standpoint of those on the margins allows feminist scholarship to examine not only the processes by which women are dominated but also their potential, strength, and resilience for action."

"Trauma, Aging, and Melodrama," by E. Ann Kaplan, brings to bear precisely the interconnections of theory and practice on global locations of embodied feminist political agency that *Feminist Locations* hopes to develop throughout. Focusing on the question of the relationship between narratives of trauma and narratives of women's aging in postmodernity, Kaplan develops a complex argument for women's agency in relation to what Westernized hegemonic global culture considers the trauma of aging. Rather than capitulating to the dominant culture's script for passive consumption of the melodramatic escape from, or false resolution of, the trauma of aging, Kaplan theorizes, in an analysis of a film by Australian aboriginal Tracey Moffatt, *Night Cries,* an alternative mode of feminist agency through witnessing rather than repressing or escaping the trauma of aging. In her carefully argued practices of feminist theory in the context of global locations of politics and bodies, Kaplan admirably articulates and exemplifies the goals of *Feminist Locations.*

NOTES

1. See, for example, *Differences* 7:1 (spring 1995), special issue on "Universalism"; and Jodi Dean, *The Solidarity of Strangers: Feminism after Identity Politics* (Berkeley and Los Angeles: University of California Press, 1996).
2. Homi K. Bhabha, "On the Irremovable Strangeness of Being Different," *PMLA* 113:1 (January 1998): 34–39, 34.
3. For a discussion of transdisciplinarity, see Norma Alarcón, Talk at Institute for Research on Women, Rutgers University, New Brunswick, New Jersey, January 1998.
4. Susan Gubar, for example, in "Who Killed Feminist Criticism?" *Critical Inquiry* 24:4 (summer 1998): 878–902; Barbara Johnson, *The Feminist Difference* (Cambridge: Harvard University Press, 1998).
5. Susan Stanford Friedman, *Feminism and the Cultural Geographies of Encounter* (Princeton, N.J.: Princeton University Press, 1998).

PART ONE

THE PRACTICE OF
FEMINIST THEORY

SUSAN STANFORD FRIEDMAN

LOCATIONAL FEMINISM
Gender, Cultural Geographies, and Geopolitical Literacy

N*ew French Feminisms* (1980) was a path-breaking anthology in American feminist theory. Edited by Elaine Marks and Isabelle de Courtivron, this collection of contemporary French feminist writings did more than introduce American academic feminists to the debates in France and to the speculative possibilities of poststructuralist theory for feminism.[1] In pluralizing the conventionally singular term *feminism*, the volume's title created a grammatical anomaly that perfectly suited the debates and political struggles that more particularly reflected the North American scene of feminist theory and praxis— namely, the important attempt, pioneered especially by women of color, lesbian women, and Jewish feminists, to base an understanding of women and the gender system upon the recognition of differences among women. The feminisms reflected in *New French Feminisms* fell largely into the binarist division between materialist and psychoanalytic/deconstructive theoretical traditions represented by Simone de Beauvoir and Monique Wittig on the one hand and Hélène Cixous, Luce Irigaray, and Julia Kristeva on the other hand. Haunting each were the shadows of Marx and Freud, Sartre, Lacan, and Derrida—intellectuals whose oppositions have long been set into dialogic interplay in Western philosophical and political traditions.

Transplanted to the United States, however, feminisms quickly acquired its own local coloration, much influenced by the way in which the civil rights movement of the 1950s to 1970s along with the general social/political ferment of the 1960s had contributed to the reawakening of feminism and the formation of the gay and lesbian rights movement in the late 1960s and 1970s. Within this context, the *s* added to feminism developed a geographically specific meaning, far more in tune with American political conditions than with French or European intellectual traditions. As Audre Lorde put it, "By and large within the women's movement today, white women focus upon their oppression as women and ignore differences of race, sexual preference, class, and age. There is a pretense to a homogeneity of experience covered by the word *sisterhood* that does not in fact exist."[2] The predominant focus of feminists on the differences between women and men had worked to obscure the difficult and potentially creative differences among women based on other oppressions, Lorde argued. "It is not our differences which separate women," Lorde insisted, "but our reluctance to recognize those differences and to deal effectively with the distortions which have resulted from the ignoring and misnaming of those differences" (122). Lorde's call for direct acknowledgment of differences among women based on multiple oppressions highlighted a process of pluralization into *feminisms* that had already begun in theory and practice with the formation of such organizations as Black Feminism, the caucus structure of the National Women's Studies Association, and anthologies such as *This Bridge Called My Back: Writings by Radical Women of Color,* edited by Cherríe Moraga and Gloria Anzaldúa.[3] In this context, abandonment of the singular term *feminism* and the adoption of the plural *feminisms* signified a theoretical and coalitional praxis that refused any affirmations of a universal sisterhood of women joined together against worldwide patriarchy in the name of WOMAN.

My intention in this chapter is to call—somewhat polemically, I realize—for a reinstitution of *feminism in the singular* and then to examine the spatial/temporal literacy such feminism requires. I do not mean by this re-singularization of feminism a return to a notion of a universal feminist subjectivity or a movement based on an assumption of female homogeneity. Nor do I mean to suggest that the foundational recognition of differences among women based on other systems of stratification such as race, class, or sexuality is no longer necessary (been there, done that). Indeed, I believe that we must remain continuously vigilant to the conditions and effects of such differences. And I accept as a profoundly important advance in feminist theory and praxis that gender can never be fully understood in isolation from other constitutive elements of human identity and the social order. No one register of social organization and no one communal identity sufficiently defines power relations or individual life as negotiated within them—whether gender or race or class or national origin. Moreover, the interactive dynamic among these distinctive systems of stratification requires more than an additive approach to differences. The processes by which race or class or sexuality (and so forth) mediate gender—and vice versa—are themselves key spaces for theoretical reflection and coalitional activism.

What I do mean by feminism in the singular is a locational feminism that is simultaneously situated in a specific locale, global in scope, and constantly in motion through space and time. A locational feminism is one that acknowledges the historically and geographically specific forms in which feminism emerges, takes root, changes, travels, translates, and transplants in different spacio/temporal contexts. The feminism that mandates a quota of representation by lower caste women in village councils of rural India (reported in the *New York Times*, May 3, 1999) is not the same feminism as that which motivates those who demonstrate for reproductive choice outside a beleaguered abortion clinic in the United States. But both feminisms are still political practices informed by theories of gender and social justice that are recognizably a part of a singular entity we can call feminism. Both participate in the notion that the given social order privileges the masculine and distributes power inequitably according to gender (in whatever ways, for whatever reasons, and however differently interactive with other issues of power). Both advocate for a form of gender equity (however equity is conceived or to be achieved). Putting these two locationally different political practices under the same categorical umbrella named *feminism* requires what Gayatri Chakravorty Spivak calls "idiomatic specificity."[4] Reflecting the way in which specific languages are tied to particular places, she uses a linguistic metaphor to insist on feminism's locational particularity. Any given embodiment of feminism is inflected with the overdetermined conditions of its history and geography.

Moreover, any given local instance of feminism can travel to influence others and be influenced in turn by differently inflected forms of feminism. Feminism is global in its widespread indigenous formations, but it is also global in the way that it travels, transplants, and transculturates. I invoke here Edward Said's essay "Traveling Theory," in which he examines how "ideas and theories . . . move from one culture to another."[5] "Such movement into a new environment," he continues, "is never unimpeded. It necessarily involves processes of representation and institutionalization different from those at the point of origin. This complicates any account of the transplantation, transference, circulation, and commerce of theories and ideas" (226). Said's assumption that every traveling idea has an identifiable and presumably single origin from which any transplantation necessarily departs as it localizes needs to be modified, in my view. The notion that a given social order privileges the masculine does not, I believe, have a single origin. Nor does the advocacy of gender equity. Rather, these constitutive components of locational feminism have emerged differently in particular times and places and have traveled from one culture to another, producing hybridic cultural formations of indigenous feminism influenced by other traveling forms of feminism. Such syncretic practices result from ongoing processes of what anthropologists often call transculturation, whereby one culture absorbs and redefines within its own terms what it takes from others as an effect of multiple contact zones.[6]

Feminism in the singular as I have characterized it involves a new emphasis on spatiality evident in the very languages of feminism. Without this locational idiom, feminism would collapse back into misleading and politically regressive forms of universalism.[7] It is this spatiality as an epistemological formation with important implications for praxis that I want to explore in mapping locational feminism. I am in agreement with the postmodern geographer Edward Soja, who suggests "*an overdeveloped historical contextualization of social life and social theory . . . actually submerges and peripheralizes the geographical or spatial imagination* [original emphasis]."[8] Like cultural studies in general, formulation of a locational feminism requires a compensatory emphasis on the spatial over the temporal. Such a provisional privileging of space takes place in the context of an overriding understanding that as interrelated coordinates of human thought, space and time are unthinkable without each other. What the geographer Henri Lefebvre calls the "production of space" is a process that takes place in time, just as the social production of history takes place in a specific geographical location.[9] However, the demand for particularity is still most often posed in terms of historical rather than geographical specificity. An argument or position might well be critiqued as ahistorical, for example, but much less often as ageographical. Consequently, as a compensatory gesture, I want to probe the meanings of spatiality for feminist theory and praxis.

To do so, I will examine the prevailing rhetoric of space in contemporary U.S. feminist theory for the way it reveals a cultural epistemology related to feminist modes of thought and activism especially suited to the conditions of postmodern globalization. In tune with constructivist assumptions, I take as foundational that a given rhetoric reflects how a person or a group of people in a large social setting thinks. The cultural epistemology embedded in feminist theory and praxis potentially provides access to the underlying categories of thought that impact on feminist agencies in the world. Rhetoric is the linguistic *materiale* of consciousness, and, we might add, to what haunts or remains lost to consciousness. For in combination with other determinants, how we think contributes to making us who we are and how we act in the domains of the local and the global.

In this sense rhetoric is more than the garment of thought, more than the figurative arts of language or the communication system within which speech acts take place. Rhetoric also reveals widespread categories of social thought as these in turn shape how we understand human experience. Moreover, as a cultural formation, any given rhetoric has a particular history and location requiring historiographic genealogies and "thick descriptions" of local manifestations. In the spirit of this idiomatic specificity, I will characterize certain feminist rhetorics produced in English largely in the United States in the past thirty years. During this same period, national boundaries have become increasingly porous with the accelerating pace of globalization and transnational cultural traffic. Consequently, my focus on feminist cultural epistemology in the United States takes into account the multiple ways in which rhetorics from outside—particularly those produced by diaspora, immigration, and transnationalism—transform those inside.

SPACE AND TIME IN THE RHETORIC OF FEMINIST CULTURAL EPISTEMOLOGY

Locational feminism by its very terminology invokes notions of space and spatiality. But where does this metaphorics of space come from? Feminist rhetoric in its epistemological register in the United States has shifted dramatically, I want to suggest, from a prevailing temporal rhetoric of awakening, revelation, and rebirth to a spatial rhetoric of location, multipositionality, and migration. Roughly speaking, this shift corresponds to the overlapping but increasingly distinct waves of second-wave feminism in the late 1960s, 1970s, and early 1980s and third-wave feminism in the 1980s and 1990s. Exhibiting the pattern of two, partially superimposed bell curves, the rhetoric of space existed from the beginning but has continued to grow more and more common as the metaphoric of awakening has receded.

These two rhetorics, invoked in the United States particularly in reference to questions of identity and subjectivity, are not arbitrary constructions. Rather, each reflects the more general conditions of its times, its historical moment of emergence. Tied to the social ferment of the 1960s, the rhetoric of awakening reflects the way the struggles and achievements of the first wave of feminism had been largely forgotten in the World War II American culture. The locational rhetoric that prevails in third-wave feminism is linked to a confluence of conditions. First, there has been the rising importance of multiculturalism in the United States under pressure from the civil rights movement and increasing immigration, both of which have helped shape the pioneering work by feminists of color articulating the conditions of multiple oppression, multipositionality, and multiple/ interactive constituents of identity. Second, the discourse of postmodernity in general has heightened the pervasively spatial metaphorics of fluidity, constructivism, and reflexivity. And third, the computer revolution and the related processes of intensified globalization have contributed to a shift from temporal to spatial modes of thought in culture at large as well as cultural studies across the disciplines. As Michel Foucault observed presciently in 1967, "The great obsession of the nineteenth century was, as we know, history. . . . The present epoch will perhaps be above all the epoch of space."[10] I want to sketch in for mainly contrastive purposes the second-wave feminist rhetoric of development and then turn in a more substantive way to the third-wave feminist rhetoric of location.

Time is an overarching category of thought in the early rhetoric of second-wave feminism. The metaphors of awakening, epiphany (the famous feminist "click"), revelation, rebirth, conversion, and initiation are all developmental, even organic in figural form, rooted at the very least in American adaptations of Romanticism's notion of the Self and Modernism's fragmentation of that Self and ironic/nostalgic quest for restoration or redemption. And like both Romanticism and Modernism, they are often specular, emphasizing the role of vision, sight, and consciousness. Consider, for example, a passage from Adrienne Rich's "When We Dead Awaken: Writing as Re-Vision," an essay that acquired canonical status within Anglo-American feminism of the 1970s and early 1980s: "It's exhilarating to be alive in a time of awakening consciousness; it can also be confusing, disorienting, and painful. This awakening of dead or sleeping consciousness has already affected the lives of millions of women. . . . The sleepwalkers are coming awake, and for the first time this awakening has a collective reality; it is no longer such a lonely thing to open one's eyes." "Woman," she concludes, "is becoming her own midwife, creating herself anew."[11]

To some degree, this figural rhetoric implies a "before and after," a narrative of becoming or "coming out."[12] This temporal movement assumes a series of binaries like sleep/awake, blindness/sight, silence/speech, uninitiated/initiated, unborn/reborn, and oppressed/liberated. The predominant narrative of such rhetoric is the story of "consciousness raising," dependent on both the specular economy of epiphany and the oral economy of speech. This in turn presumes a relatively linear series of stages as well as an ultimate hierarchy between the uninitiated and the initiated, between those who belong and those who don't. A secular conversion narrative, the story resonates with powerful and long-standing cultural narratives of quest, liminal passage, initiation, and transformation. The opening poem of Ntozake Shange's widely influential choreopoem and play *for colored girls who have considered suicide/when the rainbow is enuf* (1976) illustrates this confluence of rhetorics in its narrative of becoming:

somebody/anybody
sing a black girl's song
bring her out
to know herself
. . . .

she's been dead so long
closed in silence so long
she doesn't know the sound
of her own voice

. . . .

sing her sighs
sing the song of her possibilities
sing a righteous gospel
the making of a melody
let her be born
let her be born
& handled warmly.[13]

Space serves as the predominant source of metaphor for feminist rhetoric of identity in the third wave. Where the temporal rhetoric of awakening tends to focus on gender in isolation from other systems of stratification, the spatial rhetoric of location emphasizes the interaction of gender with other forms of power relations based on such cultural categories as race, ethnicity, class, sexuality, religion, national origin, age, and so forth. Instead of an underlying linear narrative of progressive development or birth, spatial metaphorics posit dynamic and dialogic motion through socially constructed spaces, what Homi Bhabha calls in *The Location of Culture* "an exploratory, restless movement caught so well in the French rendition of the words *au-delà*—here and there, on all sides, *fort/da,* hither and thither, back and forth."[14] Rather than the *negation* of the awakening metaphor, there is the discourse of *negotiation* built into spatialization.

Space, in these terms, is not a static essence, but rather a location of historical overdetermination. As a mode of thought, spatial rhetoric suggests fluid and flexible ways of being that posit identity as relational, situational, and interactive—the result of an ongoing process of becoming without origin or end. These spatially based notions presume a creative tension within individual and collective identities between agency on the one hand and on the other hand, overdetermination by material and ideological conditions—what Louis Althusser famously refers to as "interpellation" or "hailing."[15] Where the rhetoric of awakening suggests the linear movement from confinement to autonomy, from oppression to liberation (no matter how fraught, doomed, or ironized such a transformation might be), the rhetoric of location assumes an agency that continually negotiates an identity and actions that constitute it within the limits of the social order.

In *Mappings*, I have called this spatial rhetoric the "new geographics of identity." Instead of the individualistic telos of developmental models, the new geographics figures identity as a historically embedded site, a positionality, a standpoint, a terrain, an intersection, a web, a network, a crossroads of multiply situated knowledges. It articulates not the organic unfolding of identity but rather the mapping of territories and boundaries, contours and topographies, the dialectical terrains of inside/outside or center/margin, the axial intersections of different positionalities, and the spaces of dynamic encounter—the "contact zone," the "middle ground," the borderlands, *la frontera*. Moreover, this geographic discourse often emphasizes not the ordered movement of linear growth but the lack of solid ground, the ceaseless change of fluidity, the nomadic wandering of transnational diaspora, the interactive syncretisms of the "global ethnoscape," or the interminable circuitry of cyberspace. Its mobile figurations adapt the landscapes of accelerating change, the technologies of information highways, and the globalization of migratory cultures.

This new geography of identity is polyvocal and often contradictory. Its metaphorics, now sweeping many different fields, has been influenced especially by postcolonial studies, for which the issues of travel, nomadism, diaspora, and the cultural hybridity produced by movement through space have a material reality and political urgency as well as figurative cogency. But the intellectual genealogy of this geographical figuration centers in the different discourses of identity and subjectivity that have developed over the last three decades as effects of late-twentieth-century political and cultural change. These developments have been pioneered frequently by people of color and by people from non-Western countries, those whose daily survival often depends on understanding identity as the product of complex intersections and locations. More generally, the blending and clashing of overlapping or parallel discourses of feminism, multiculturalism, poststructuralism, and postcolonial studies have produced new ways of configuring identity that have moved well beyond the achievements of focusing on a single constituent of identity such as gender.[16]

For North American feminism in particular, this spatial rhetoric has reflected the increasing integration of feminist theory with other domains of discourse based especially in race, ethnicity, sexuality, and national origin.[17] Feminist rhetoric, in short, has increasingly blended with the rhetorics produced in other fields that have developed under the broad rubric of cultural studies. The intensification of globalization as a condition of postmodernity has altered the largely local, regional, and national emphasis of cultural studies in its earliest formations (especially in Britain and the United States). By the 1990s, cultural studies has increasingly taken on an international and transnational scope as it examines the interplay between local and global cultural formations and the circuits of cultural and economic traffic worldwide. Spatial modes of thought have been a marker of this change, for both feminism and cultural studies more generally.

To reflect this shift from temporal to spatial rhetoric, I have called the feminism of the third wave "locational feminism" to emphasize its vigilance to the politics of location.[18] In the space that remains, I will explore the two main areas of spatial rhetoric in contemporary North American feminism: the metaphorics of multipositionality and of the geopolitical. Since I have already written extensively about multipositionality in *Mappings*, I will summarize this discourse fairly rapidly to move on to suggest a grammar for the geopolitical—work that I am still in the process of developing.[19]

THE RHETORIC OF MULTIPOSITIONALITY: A BRIEF SUMMARY

The spatial rhetoric of multipositionality developed in feminism as a way to deal with differences among women based on such factors as race, class, sexuality, religion, and national identity. Black feminists of the 1970s such as Frances Beal, Eleanor Holmes Norton, Alice Walker, Barbara Smith, June Jordan, and Audre Lorde were among the early pioneers of this discourse to which feminists like Gloria Anzaldúa, Cherríe Moraga, Adrienne Rich, Gloria T. Hull, Alice Chai, Amy Ling, Paula Gunn Allen, Chandra Talpade Mohanty, Biddy Martin, Bonnie Zimmerman, Gayatri Spivak, Seyla Benhabib, Nancy Harstock, Teresa de Lauretis, Donna Haraway, Chela Sandoval, Linda Alcoff, Lisa Lowe, Eve Kosofsky Sedgwick, Lata Mani, and many others added to in the 1980s and 1990s. As a result of this work, it is now commonplace in feminist theory to refer to the *position* one occupies, the *standpoint* from which one speaks, and the *location* within which one's agency negotiates. What constitutes this *space* is the interaction of what is often called the *axes of difference* established by the social order. Subjectivity, in other words, takes shape at the intersection or crossroads of different systems of stratification where the circuits of power and privilege are multidirectional and complex. Individuals are constituted at this point of intersection; they cannot be defined by a single identity such as gender or race or religion or nationality or sexuality. Individuals belong to multiple communities—sometimes overlapping, sometimes contradictory. Narratives of interaction and negotiation between these different axes of difference form fluid, situational, and relational subjectivities rather than the "before" and "after" stories of political awakening that characterize earlier feminist rhetorics.

To illustrate this multipositional discourse of identity in *Mappings*, I featured June Jordan's classic personal essay from 1982, "Report from the Bahamas," a theoretical statement that takes narrative form (much as Virginia Woolf's most important theoretical contributions did). Not widely noticed in its first appearance, this essay has by the late 1980s and 1990s acquired canonical status in women's studies classrooms throughout the United States. Its locational rhetoric begins in the very occasion for the essay: Jordan's travel to the Bahamas. This shift in location is what stimulates her to reflect upon the possibilities and difficulties of identification and coalition on the basis of race, class, and gender. Of West Indian descent, she asks herself, for example, what the bond of race and even national origin between herself and the black maid Olive at the Sheraton British Colonial Hotel means in the context of her own (re)location to the United States and her relative privilege as a college professor. This question in turn leads to memories of encounters with various students of different ethnic, racial, and religious backgrounds. Within these landscapes of memory and interaction, power and powerlessness shift relationally and situationally, dependent not on single identifications of race or gender or class but on complex negotiations among these and other constituents of identity. Central to Jordan's theory of feminist coalition across lines of difference is the spatial rhetoric of a dynamic multipositionality.[20]

History, and the temporal mode of thought it represents, of course, is not absent from the locational rhetoric in Jordan's essay or in the general feminist discourse she has so much influenced. The spatial location in which one's identity forms is produced in and changes over time. But the newer feminist metaphorics of identity draws heavily from spatial rather than temporal figuration. The shift I am suggesting is evident in two of Rich's most influential essays: "When We Dead Awaken" from 1971 and "Notes toward a Politics of Location" from 1984. Muting the temporal rhetoric of awakening and birth quoted above from the earlier essay, she emphasizes spatial figuration of location in the later essay. No longer invoking the singular, gender-based identity of *woman,* she speaks in 1984 in the first person as the basis for theorizing identity and defining a politics of location: "I need to understand how a place on the map is also a place in history within which as a woman, a Jew, a lesbian, a feminist I am created and trying to create. Begin, though, not with a continent or a country or a house, but with the geography closest in—the body."[21] Beginning with the body—with the origin of embodiment—requires spatial literacy, a recognition that identity is built upon multiple social locations:

> This body. White, female; or female, white. The first obvious life-long facts. But I was born in the white section of a hospital which separated Black and white women in labor.
>
> The politics of location. Even to begin with my body I have to say that from the outset that body had more than one identity. . . .
>
> The body I was born into was not only female and white, but Jewish—enough for geographic location to have played, in those years, a determining part. (215–216)

TOWARD A GRAMMAR OF GEOPOLITICAL FEMINIST RHETORIC

One of the effects of intensified globalization on feminist spatial rhetoric has been an increased emphasis on the geopolitical. But what does the term *geopolitical* mean for feminists, and how does it enter the emergent rhetoric of feminism? As the term is commonly used, especially by political scientists and others interested in state formations in global context, geopolitical tends to connote intergovernmental relations throughout the world—particularly the relations between nations in an international and transnational landscape. (This meaning reflects the Greek roots of the word in *geo* for earth and the *polis* as the city-state or the *politeia* as government or citizenship.) Geopolitical analysis might therefore involve consideration of the effects of national identity in relation to issues of international conditions, that is, state-to-state power relations as they shape both global and local formations. Feminists, however, have often insisted on a rethinking of the common association of politics with issues of government. At least as far back as Kate Millett's path-breaking *Sexual Politics* (1970), feminists have insisted that the term *politics* refers more broadly to power relations in general, in the private as well as the public sphere, in the relation between the sexes as well as between governmental units.[22] Similarly, I suggest that the term *geopolitical* needs to be rethought within feminist terms. It needs to be removed from an exclusive focus on states in global context, although this dimension remains vitally important to feminism. More broadly conceived, then, in a way that encourages examination of gender in multipositional contexts, a feminist geopolitics can be understood to incorporate an examination of power relations as they are embedded in the earth, in a given location, and as they migrant around the earth locally, regionally, nationally, and transnationally. The geopolitical rhetoric of feminism is fundamentally locational and potentially global in reach.

In defining the geopolitical for feminists in this way, I am not suggesting a return to the much-critiqued category of "global feminism." This term arose in relation to the common second-wave feminist assumption of a universal patriarchy and the promotion of a global sisterhood united in its resistance to worldwide male dominance. Global feminism, often represented by Robin Morgan's anthology *Sisterhood Is Global*, usefully insisted that feminists in the West look beyond their particular national and Western conditions to the status of women in the so-called second and third worlds.[23] It became subject to critique, especially by women in non-Western settings, for isolating gender from the context of other concerns such as colonialism (and its aftereffects), national identity, race, and class, and for assuming a homogeneous sisterhood of women united together against men.

The contemporary geopolitical rhetoric of feminism has to a large extent repudiated notions of monolithic patriarchy and sisterhood in favor of locational heterogeneity and idiomatic particularity in transnational context. This is what Spivak means in her advocacy of "transnational literacy," which assumes multiple agencies and heterogeneities in all locations.[24] This is also what Indepal Grewal and Caren Kaplan call for in their seminal collection, *Scattered Hegemonies: Postmodernity and Transnational Feminist Practices*, where they

theorize the necessity of moving beyond the binaries of center/pe-
riphery, local/global, and first world/third world. Feminism, according to this rhetoric, occurs throughout the globe in different forms
rooted in the particular contexts where it emerges. As feminist ideas
and activism travel from place to place, they take root and translate
into local idioms, each with their own agendas and negotiations
within the context of particular locations. Feminism is global in the
sense that it emerges everywhere in indigenous forms that take shape
through interactions with other feminisms and with its own local conditions. It is also global in the sense that any local formation is shaped
in part by the presence of global forces within it. The acceleration of
intercultural contact in the Global Age has intensified the intercon-
nection of local gender systems worldwide as well as the hybridization of different feminisms. This is what I mean by the geopolitical.

At a metacritical level, the geopolitical rhetoric of feminism as I
have defined it operates according to a transnational grammar with
a number of specific figural formations. I will briefly discuss and illustrate some of the most prevalent forms—namely, the metaphorics
of nation, borders, migration, "glocation," and conjuncture. Geopolitical and transnational literacy for feminists begins, I suggest, in recognizing these five tropic patterns.

First, the discourse of nation and nationalism emerges out of the
impact of colonialism and postcolonialism and resonates most clearly
with the conventional definition of the geopolitical as state-to-state
relations in international context. As the striking essays by Lydia Liu,
Mary Layoun, and others in *Scattered Hegemonies* make so clear, the
relation between gender and nation is fraught with contradictions.[25]
Women often exist in relation to nation in a state of ambivalence,
caught between identification with national aspirations and recognition of men's special privilege within most state formations. The
use of female figures to iconize the nation—as in Britannia, Lady Lib-
erty, Mother India, and so forth—often obscures or even embodies
the inequities of gender relations within the nation where political
power largely resides in the hands of certain types of men. The common feminization of the colonized, as in the tradition of Ireland as
an old hag, often overlaps with a racial hierarchy formulated to ra-
tionalize unequal power relations between peoples or states.

This geopolitical matrix provides the spatial rhetoric for Gish Jen's
postmodern romp through multicultural identity politics in her novel

about a young Chinese American girl who converts to Judaism, morphing from Mona Chang to Mona Changovitz in *Mona and the Promised Land*. Listen to the geopolitical rhetoric of thirteen-year-old Mona as she despairs over the inadequacy of her body, especially as she compares it to that of her Jewish friend, Barbara Gugelstein (who is in turn self-conscious about her Semitic features in other sections of the novel). The issue of girls' and women's body image has been central to American feminism since the 1970s, but the geopolitical rhetoric in this passage represents the new spatial mode of thought about gender and nation, a metaphoric that is so prevalent that it can already be parodied within feminist discourse: "Mona was the first one in her entire grade to get her period. . . . But she doesn't look like, say, Barbara. If her friend is a developed nation, Mona is, sure enough, the third world. Barbara's is the body Mona is still waiting to grow into: her breasts, for example, are veritable colonies of herself, with a distinct tendency toward independence. Whereas Mona's, in contrast, are anything but wayward. A scant handful each, hers are smooth and innocent—the result, you might think, of eating too much ice cream. . . . Oh, to be leggy and buxom like Barbara Gugelstein!"[26]

A second form of geopolitical rhetoric invokes the geographical borders between nations to suggest not only those material conditions as they impact on gender formations but also their figural function to describe psychological, spiritual, and cultural borderlands in between differences of all kinds. As the liminal space in between, the interface of self and other, the interstitial location of syncretic transculturation, borders highlight the paradoxical processes of connection and separation. Regulatory borders are erected to defend against the pollution of the Other or to impose confinements of the Other. But borders are also porous sites of intercultural mixing, cultural hybridization, and creolization. Borders are spaces where murderous acts take place, where identity, particularly in its fundamentalist form, ensures clashing differences and fixed limits. They are also the spaces of desire for connection, utopian longing, and the blending of differences. The multiple meanings and possibilities of border rhetoric are evident in one of the most influential texts in transnational cultural studies, namely the hybridic and autobiographical essay/poem *Borderlands/La Frontera—The New Mestiza* by Gloria Anzaldúa, the self-identified Chicana feminist and lesbian. As I address at greater length in *Mappings,* the complexity of her border talk encompasses a whole range of meanings for material, psychological, spiritual, and sexual *mestizaje,* thus making her creative text a visionary mixing of positions which often remain distinct or even oppositional in cultural theory. Suffice it to quote here briefly from the text to convey a flavor of its spatial epistemology. In the preface, she explains the contradictory subjectivity and materiality of people on the border:

> I am a border woman. I grew up between two cultures, the Mexican (with a heavy Indian influence) and the Anglo (as a member of a colonized people in our own territory). I have been straddling that *tejas*-Mexican border, and others, all my life. It's not a comfortable territory to live in, this place of contradictions. Hatred, anger and exploitation are the prominent features of this landscape.
>
> However, there have been compensations for this *mestiza,* and certain joys. Living on borders and in margins, keeping intact one's shifting and multiple identity and integrity, is like trying to swim in a new element, an "alien" element. There is a certain exhilaration in being a participant in the further evolution of humankind, in being "worked" on. I have the sense that certain "faculties"—not just in me but in every border resident, colored or non-colored—and dormant areas of consciousness are being activated, awakened.[27]

The blending of pain and playful irony near the end of the text restates in poetic form the contradictory meanings of border rhetoric as a geopolitical epistemology:

> To live in the Borderlands means to
> put *chile* in the borscht,
> eat whole wheat *tortillas,*
> speak Tex-Mex with a Brooklyn accent;
> be stopped by *la migra* at the border checkpoints
> . . . .
> To survive the Borderlands
> You must live *sin fronteras*
> Be a crossroads. (194–195)

The third form of geopolitical rhetoric—migration—relies on both the metaphorics of nation and borders but develops them even further to reflect on the meanings of immigration, constant travel back and forth, and diaspora for spatial modes of thinking about identity. As the body moves through space, crossing borders of all kinds, identity acquires sedimented and palimpsestic layers each of which reflects the locations through which the person has moved, each of which exerts some influence on the other layers and on identity as a whole. Thus, in *Black Women, Writing and Identity: Migrations of the Subject* Carol Boyce Davies speaks of her mother's and her own "migratory subjectivity" built out of constant travel back and forth between the Caribbean and the United States, as well as other places:

> My mother's journeys redefine space. Her annual migrations, between the Caribbean and the United States, are ones of persistent re-membering and re-connection. She lives in the Caribbean; she lives in the United States; she lives in America. She also lives in that in-between space that is neither here nor there, locating herself in the communities where her children, grandchildren, family and friends reside. Hers is a deliberate and fundamental migration that defines the sense of specific location that even her children would want to force on her. . . .
>
> I locate myself in the context of migrations, my mother's experience and in the midst of this work as a necessary strategy of concretizing the question of identities. My own path has included migrations to North America, various African and Caribbean countries, Europe and Brazil. Each place shifted, re-defined and reconstituted my identities.[28]

And thus in *The Shock of Arrival: Reflections on Postcolonial Experience,* the poet, novelist, and critic Meena Alexander reflects upon the fluidity of multiple geopolitical embodiments built out of a childhood spent in India and the Sudan, and an adulthood spent in Britain and the United States. What is the meaning of "race" for her in each of the locations she has lived? Just as significantly, what does the relationality of "race" in all its locational meanings signify for her female-embodied self in any one location—from her homeland in Kerala, India, to her second home in Khartoum, where she sometimes "passed" as "black," to her shifting discomfort and comfort in the United States as she faces a crowd of white people or walks through black Harlem?

> I grew up in what might loosely be called the postcolonial Third World. I grew up in two different countries, India and the Sudan. Multiple borders were part of my ordinary reality. In Khartoum as a young girl, I could sometimes pass for Sudanese and this was always a comfort to me. Though deep down inside, borne within me like contraband, was the knowledge I was Indian. . . .

> One is marked by one's body, but how is one marked? . . .
>
> After fifteen years in this country I now have an American passport. . . . With this passport I can travel across borders, enter this country without visa or green card. But what if I don't have the passport on me? And what difference will the passport make to my concern about walking on country roads where no other people of color are to be seen? My fear of coming across men in army camouflage, toting rifles to kill deer, all the xenophobia of America sitting squarely on them, or bikers on Route 23 with big signs pasted to their machines: "500 Years after Columbus, Keep out Foreign Scum!"
>
> In the city, I live close to Harlem. Sometimes when I walk up 125th Street I feel I am in another country, the shouts, the cries, the passing figures, the small shop fronts in the old black neighborhood. I feel quite safe picking out a cap or a pair of overalls. There is no harm here in not being white. But I am not Black either. "Indian?" a man in a khaki vest asks me. I nod. He passes me the clump of green plantains I have paid for. He smiles at me. I can pass here. But what does passing mean? For Asian Americans, multiple ethnic borders are part of the shifting reality we inhabit.[29]

The fourth geopolitical rhetoric of contemporary feminists is "glocational," a term that combines *global* and *local*. I am borrowing from the word current in global and transnational cultural studies to indicate the notion of how the local and the global are co-complicit, each implicated in the other. Cultural theorists like Roland Robertson have themselves borrowed the term from Japanese business, where the concept of products designed in relation to specific locations can be marketed globally.[30] Feminists Inderpal Grewal and Caren Kaplan, among others, have posited this dialogic and co-implicated relationship between the global and the local to argue for a form of transnational feminism that avoids the homogenizing tendencies of "global feminism," respects the material and cultural specificities of local feminist formations, and encourages analysis of how the gender/race/class system in one location is politically and economically linked to that of another. By way of illustrating a glocational mode of thinking, let me turn briefly to Virginia Woolf's classic feminist essay, *A Room of One's Own,* where she figuratively argues that a woman writer needs "500 pounds and a room of one's own" in order to write with independence of mind. Read in gender terms alone, as it often was in the 1970s revival of the text, "500 pounds a year" operates rhetorically for the financial freedom women need to be able to write what they think. Read in glocational terms, however, Woolf's image reveals the implication of an emergent upper-middle-class female subject in the structure of the British Empire and international banking system. This economic and political matrix is woven unconsciously into a passage in which the essay's persona imagines paying her bill at a restaurant:

> I gave the waiter a ten-shilling note in my purse: I noticed it, because it is a fact that still takes my breath away—the power of my purse to breed ten-shilling notes automatically. I open it and there they are. Society gives me chicken and coffee, bed and lodging, in return for a certain number of pieces of paper which were left me by an aunt, for no other reason than that I share her name. My aunt, Mary Beton, I must tell you, died by a fall from her horse when she was riding out to take the night air in Bombay.[31]

The "power of my purse" depends first upon a legacy from her aunt who dies in India as an adjunct to the British Raj and second upon income produced annually from interest on a large capital nest egg. Living on interest from a legacy harks back to the imperial and class structures upon which the upper and upper-middle classes in Britain traditionally relied to fund a leisured way of life, an economic system that underlies the fictional world of Jane Austen, as Edward Said was the first to point out.[32] Thinking glocationally involves understanding how the local, the private, and the domestic are constituted in relation to global systems, and conversely how such systems must be read for their particular locational inflection.

Finally, I will conclude this brief map of a feminist geopolitical grammar with reference to a spatial mode of thinking that replaces traditional comparison/contrast analysis of similarities and differences with what anthropologists often call "conjuncturalism."[33] By this, they mean the juxtaposition of different cultural formations for the light this epistemological juncture sheds on each and for the way in which each discursive system interrupts the other. Borrowing from literary studies, I think of this mode and the geopolitical rhetoric it can engender as *cultural parataxis*. Parataxis is a form of conjuncture or superimposition developed particularly as a part of modernist poetics to describe the radical juxtapositions that poets and artists made with a deliberate suppression of explicit connection.[34] Collage and montage are two forms of parataxis, which then invite the viewer or reader to establish the connections not explicitly expressed by the artist or poet.

Adapting modernist poetics, I suggest that one mode of geopolitical rhetoric that reflects the intensification and acceleration of globalization in the postmodern age is a form of cultural parataxis that performs an imaginative travel from one cultural formation to another for the insight about both that potentially ensues. This strategy and related rhetoric relies upon a spatial epistemology rather than a temporal one. To illustrate what I mean, I want to go back to a canonical second-wave feminist text for an early deployment of cultural parataxis—namely, Alice Walker's riff on *A Room of One's Own* in her 1974 essay "In Search of Our Mothers' Gardens." Here, she radically juxtaposes the sixteenth-century British conditions that made women's writing so difficult in the early modern period as Woolf describes them with the conditions faced by slave women like Phillis Wheatley in colonial, republican, and antebellum America. Her brackets perform in rhetorical terms the cultural parataxis that I find increasingly common in third-wave feminism:

> Virginia Woolf wrote further, speaking of course not of our Phillis, that "any woman born with a great gift in the sixteenth century [insert "black woman," insert "born or made a slave"] would certainly have gone crazed, shot herself, or ended her days in some lonely cottage outside the village, half witch, half wizard [insert "Saint"], feared and mocked at. For it needs little skill and psychology to be sure that a highly gifted girl who had tried to use her gift for poetry would have been so thwarted and hindered by contrary instincts [add "chains, guns, the lash, the ownership of one's body by someone else, submission to an alien religion"], that she must have lost her health and sanity to a certainty."[35] (235, all brackets are in the text)

This conjuncture of different cultural formations is not accusatory, arguing implicitly for a dismissal of Woolf's position as racist. Rather, it illuminates both the race and class privilege implicit in Woolf's analysis of gender oppression at the same time that it draws parallels between the effects of thwarted creativity for enslaved black women and upper-middle-class women alike. The conditions of "Shakespeare's sister" and the achievement of Phillis Wheatley are clarified by the text's rhetorical strategy of cultural parataxis.[36] The fact that Walker produced this form of spatial rhetoric during the heyday of the temporal rhetoric of birth and awakening (to which she herself contributed a great deal) is the exception that proves the rule.[37] Although this passage has been much noted, its pioneering reliance on spatial rhetoric has not, to my knowledge, been pointed out. As feminist studies internationalize, this form of epistemological travel is becoming increasingly common.

FEMINIST GEOPOLITICS

In conclusion, this all-too-rapid excursion through the temporal and spatial rhetorics of second- and third-wave feminism in the United States was not intended to be an exercise in tracking tropes as an end in itself. My hypothesis of a significant shift in feminist rhetoric reflects my belief that feminist rhetoric has an epistemological register that is responsive to changing historical and locational conditions. Paying close attention to what I have called the rhetoric of cultural epistemology provides a window into the interpenetration of language and other cultural formations as products and shapers of their times and places. Such attention potentially constitutes a meta-analysis that allows for interventions in theory and praxis. The explosion of spatial rhetorics throughout many fields of cultural studies, including feminist studies, is part and parcel of the Global Age, a condition of postmodernity in which intensified multiculturalism and the migration of peoples, goods, and cultural practices, along with the invention of cyberspace, are transforming the modes of human thought and expression. The growing emphasis on space is, I believe, a reflection of a transition from print culture to new forms of meaning-making that enhance the visual and spatial and thus compensate for prior privileging of the verbal and temporal. Feminist spatial rhetoric is very much part of this transition in cultural epistemology.

Greater awareness of feminist spatial rhetoric in turn fosters the development of a locational feminism that is geographically inflected and global in scope without the erasure of difference. Supplemented by a recognition that all cultural locations are historically overdetermined, geopolitical literacy requires careful attention to the local idiom of feminist formations, the status of women, and the ways in which particular gender systems interact with other systems of stratification like class, caste, religion, sexuality, race, ethnicity, regional and national identity, and so forth. It asks as well for a recognition

of multiple contact zones and migratory identities that produce intercultural exchange and hybridized combinations of ways of being
and becoming. A feminist geopolitics, in the sense in which I have
(re)defined the term, calls for a re-singularization of feminism as an
umbrella category of theory and praxis, a "thick description" of its
myriad and different local and idiomatic manifestations, attention
to the regional/national/transnational nexus within which local conditions and resistance develop, and tracking of migratory and
transcultural formations whose fluidity is produced by movements
through space.

NOTES

This chapter draws on and extends work initially formulated in chapters 1 to 4 of my *Mappings: Feminism and the Cultural Geographies of Encounter* (Princeton, N.J.: Princeton University Press, 1998) and "Spatial Rhetorics of Feminism in the Age of Globalization," an address delivered at the Symposium of Emerging Rhetorics at Texas Women's University, April 30, 1999. Chapter 1 of *Mappings* was originally delivered at the Institute for Research on Women in 1995 as part of the Thinking about Women lecture series. I am deeply grateful to the lively challenges of audiences at Rutgers University and Texas Women's University for their response to earlier forms of this argument.

1. Elaine Marks and Isabelle de Courtivron, eds., *New French Feminisms: An Anthology* (Amherst, Mass.: University of Massachusetts Press, 1980).
2. Audre Lorde, "Age, Race, Class, and Sex: Women Redefining Difference," *Sister Outsider: Essays and Speeches* (Trumansburg, N.Y.: Crossing Press, 1984), 114–123. Hereafter, page references will be included parenthetically within the text.
3. Cherríe Moraga and Gloria Anzaldúa, eds., *This Bridge Called My Back: Writings by Radical Women of Color* (Watertown, Mass.: Persephone Press, 1981).
4. Gayatri Chakravorty Spivak, Plenary Address, Conference on "Comparative Literacy" in a Global Age: The Question of the Comparative, University of Wisconsin-Madison, March 25–28, 1999.
5. Edward W. Said, "Traveling Theory," *The World, the Text, and the Critic* (Cambridge: Harvard University Press, 1983), 226–247. Hereafter, page references will be included parenthetically within the text.
6. See, for example, Mary Louise Pratt's adaptation of the ethnographic concept of transculturation in which she emphasizes the agency of the colonized: "Ethnographers have used this term [transculturation] to describe how subordinated or marginal groups select and invent from materials transmitted to them by a dominant or metropolitan culture. While subjugated peoples cannot readily control what emanates from the dominant culture, they do determine to varying extents what they absorb into their own, and what they use it for" (*Imperial Eyes: Travel Writing and Transculturation* [London: Routledge, 1992], 6).
7. I am not ready to condemn all forms of universalism as inherently tyrannical, homogenizing, or totalizing. I support in principle the efforts to forge concepts of universal human rights, along with the related movement to define women's rights as human rights. I do not regard such rights as mutually exclusive with locational or idiomatic specificity. The "universal" principles adopted by the 1995 Beijing Women's Conference spell out certain rights in principle but do not spell out the actual forms that such freedoms might take in culturally specific locations. Nor does this global platform mandate how such rights are to be achieved.
8. Edward W. Soja, "Postmodern Geographies: Taking Los Angeles Apart," in *NowHere: Space, Time and Modernity*, ed. Roger Friedland and Deirdre Boden (Berkeley and Los Angeles: University of California Press, 1994), 131.
9. Henri Lefebvre, *The Production of Space*, trans. Donald Nicholson-Smith (Oxford: Basil Blackwell, 1981).

10. Michel Foucault, "Of Other Spaces," *Diacritics* 16 (1986): 22.
11. Adrienne Rich, "When We Dead Awaken: Writing as Re-Vision," in *Adrienne Rich's Poetry*, ed. Barbara Charlesworth Gelpi and Albert Gelpi (New York: Norton, 1975), 98. Spatial rhetoric is also occasionally present in this early essay, as when she alludes to "a whole new psychic geography" (91). In a subsequent version of this essay, the one most commonly reprinted, the final paragraph has been substantially rewritten, with the reference to women's rebirth deleted. For more influential early rhetoric of awakening, see especially Kate Chopin's *The Awakening* (1990), rediscovered by feminists in the 1970s (New York: Signets, 1976), and Sheila Rowbotham's *Woman's Consciousness, Man's World* (Baltimore, Md.: Penguin, 1974), esp. chapter 3.
12. The rhetoric of "coming out," developed by gays and lesbians in the post-Stonewall years, is based upon both temporal and spatial rhetoric—the "before/after" of private or public revelation; the movement from inside to outside the "closet."
13. Ntozake Shange, *for colored girls who have considered suicide/when the rainbow is enuf* (New York: Bantam, 1976), 2–3.
14. Homi K. Bhabha, *The Location of Culture* (London: Routledge, 1994), 1.
15. Louis Althusser, "Ideology and Ideological State Apparatuses (Notes towards an Investigation)," *Lenin and Philosophy* (New York: Monthly Review Press, 1971).
16. See *Mappings*, esp. 17–35.
17. The category of class has not, for the most part, been developed sufficiently, particularly in a way that would take into account the new understanding of globalization (as both a postmodern phenomenon and as a condition that has existed for millennia). As Rita Felski wrote me in a private communication, feminist discussions of class have often been limited to neo-marxist application and debate.
18. For other feminist discussions of the politics of location, see especially Adrienne Rich, "Notes toward a Politics of Location," *Blood, Bread and Poetry: Selected Prose, 1979–1985* (New York: Norton, 1986), 210–232; Caren Kaplan, *Questions of Travel: Postmodern Discourses of Displacement* (Durham, N.C.: Duke University Press, 1996); Chandra Mohanty, "Feminist Encounters: Locating the Politics of Experience," *Copyright* 1 (fall 1987): 30–44; Elspeth Probyn, "Travels in the Postmodern: Making Sense of the Local," in *Feminism/Postmodernism*, ed. Linda Nicholson (London: Routledge, 1990), 176–189; Lata Mani, "Multiple Mediations: Feminist Scholarship in the Age of Multinational Reception," *Inscriptions* 5 (1989): 1–24; Kathleen M. Kirby, *Indifferent Boundaries: Spatial Concepts of Human Subjectivity* (New York: Guilford Press, 1996); Neil Smith and Cindi Katz, "Grounding Metaphor: Towards a Spatialized Politics," *Place and the Politics of Identity* (London: Routledge, 1993), 67–83; Vivek Dhareshwar, "Marxism, Location Politics, and the Possibility of Critique," *Public Culture* 6:1 (1993): 41–54; and James Clifford, "Notes on Travel and Theory," *Inscriptions* 5 (1989): 177–188.
19. See *Mappings*, esp. chapters 1 to 3 for discussions of multipositionality and feminism. For earlier formulations of what I called "geopolitical literacy," see chapter 4. For other formulations of third-wave feminism, see especially Devoney Looser and E. Ann Kaplan, eds., *Generations: Academic Feminists in Dialogue* (Minneapolis: University of Minnesota Press, 1997); Leslie Heywood and Jennifer Drake, eds., *Third Wave Agenda: Being Feminist/Doing Feminism* (Minneapolis: University of Minnesota Press, 1997); Deborah Siegel, "The Legacy of the Personal: Generating Theory in Feminism's Third Wave," *Hypatia* 12:3 (summer 1997): 46–75; Rebecca Walker, ed., *To Be Real: Telling the Truth and Changing the Face of Feminism* (New York: Anchor Books, 1995); and Barbara Findler, ed., *Listen Up: Voices from the Next Feminist Generation* (Seattle, Wash.: Seal Press, 1995).
20. June Jordan, "Report from the Bahamas," *On Call: Personal Essays* (Boston: South End Press, 1985), 39–50. See extended discussion in *Mappings*, 48–50.
21. Adrienne Rich, "Notes toward a Politics of Location," 212. Hereafter, page references will be included parenthetically within the text.
22. Kate Millett, *Sexual Politics* (New York: Avon, 1970), esp. 1–39.
23. See Robin Morgan, ed., *Sisterhood Is Global: The International Women's Movement Anthology* (New York: Anchor, 1984); for critiques of "global feminism," see Gayatri Chakravorty Spivak, "French Feminism in an International Frame," in *Other Worlds: Essays in Cultural Politics* (New York: Methuen, 1987), 134–153; Chandra Talpade Mohanty, Ann Russo, and Lourdes Torres, eds., *Third World Women and the Politics of Feminism* (Bloomington: Indiana University Press, 1991); and Inderpal Grewal and Caren Kaplan,

"Introduction," in their collection, *Scattered Hegemonies: Postmodernity and Transnational Feminist Practices* (Minneapolis: University of Minnesota Press, 1994), 1–33.

24. Gayatri Chakravorty Spivak, "Scattered Speculations on the Question of Cultural Studies," *Outside in the Teaching Machine* (London: Routledge, 1993), 255–284.

25. See Lydia Liu, "The Female Body and Nationalist Discourse: *The Field of Life and Death Revisited*," in Grewal and Kaplan, *Scattered Hegemonies*, 37–62; Mary Layoun, "The Female Body and 'Transnational' Reproduction; or, Rape by Any Other Name?" in Grewal and Kaplan, 63–75; Nalini Natarajan, "Woman, Nation, and Narration in *Midnight's Children*," in Grewal and Kaplan, 76–89; and Norma Alarcón, "Traddutora, Traditora: A Paradigmatic Figure of Chicana Feminism," in Grewal and Kaplan, 110–136. See also Anne McClintock, "No Longer in a Future Heaven: Nationalism, Gender, and Race," *Imperial Leather* (London: Routledge, 1995), 352–390; Andrew Parker, Mary Russo, Doris Sommer, and Patricia Yaeger, eds., *Nationalisms and Sexualities* (London: Routledge, 1992); and R. Radhakrishnan, "Feminist Historiography and Poststructuralist Thought," in *The Difference Within: Feminism and Critical Theory*, ed. Elizabeth Meese and Alice Parker (Philadelphia: John Benjamins, 1989), 189–205.

26. Gish Jen, *Mona in the Promised Land* (New York: Knopf, 1996), 76–77.

27. Gloria Anzaldúa, *Borderlands/La Frontera—The New Mestiza* (San Francisco, Calif.: Spinsters/Aunt Lute Press, 1987), n.p. Hereafter, page references will be included parenthetically within the text.

28. Carole Boyce Davies, *Black Women, Writing and Identity: Migrations of the Subject* (London: Routledge, 1994), 1–2. See also *Nomadic Subjects*, in which Rosi Braidotti represents linguistically and philosophically the multiple languages and locations (Italy, Asia, France, the Netherlands) that have influenced her migratory mode of thinking (New York: Columbia University Press, 1994).

29. Meena Alexander, *The Shock of Arrival: Reflections on Postcolonial Experience* (Boston: South End Press, 1996), 68–69, 64–65.

30. See Roland Robertson, "Glocalization: Time—Space and Homogeneity—Heterogeneity," in *Global Modernities*, ed. Mike Featherstone, Scott Lash, and Roland Robertson (London: Sage, 1995), 25–44.

31. Virginia Woolf, *A Room of One's Own* (New York: Harcourt Brace Jovanovich, 1957), 37.

32. Edward W. Said, "Jane Austen and Empire," *Culture and Imperialism* (New York: Anchor, 1993), 80–96.

33. See, for example, the feminist anthropologist Kamala Visweswaran, *Fictions of Feminist Ethnography* (Minneapolis: University of Minnesota Press, 1994), esp. 11, 13–14, 139; and the discussions of conjuncturalism in *Mappings*, esp. 9–10, 129–130, 178, 244n9.

34. Ezra Pound's "In the Station of the Metro" is one of the best-known examples of modernist parataxis: "The apparition of these faces in the crowd; / Petals on a wet, black bough" (*Selected Poems* [New York: New Directions, 1957], 35).

35. Alice Walker, "In Search of Our Mothers' Gardens," *In Search of Our Mothers' Gardens: Womanist Prose* (New York: Harcourt Brace Jovanovich, 1983), 235. All brackets are in the text.

36. Without having yet formulated the term *cultural parataxis*, I nonetheless use this form of conjuncture in juxtaposing the town porch in Eatonville, Florida, in Zora Neale Hurston's *Their Eyes Were Watching God*, Woolf's "room of one's own," and the potential response of Mamphela Ramphele, a South African feminist/anti-Apartheid activist and writer. See *Mappings*, 126–130.

37. See, for example, her "One Child of One's Own," *In Search of Our Mothers' Gardens*, 361–383.

LYNNE SEGAL

ONLY CONTRADICTIONS ON OFFER
Anglophone Feminism at the Millennium

Can feminism still inspire a broadly transformative and confrontational politics and culture, or is it nowadays better seen as merely a blip in the march of economic neoliberalism? It's hard, of course, to avoid either idealizing or else trashing one's own past—thereby feeding the unruly envy among and within political generations. It's harder still, and obviously foolhardy, given inflated narratives of the death of grand narrative, to engage in any form of futurology—especially if we believe, like Joan Scott, that feminism has "Only Paradoxes to Offer."[1] In any political movement, once the excitement of finding a new collective identity begins to ebb, everyday politics becomes a far more discouraging, even tedious affair, a matter of competing interests and conflicting alliances. It never remains the transformative revelation which first inspired new levels of self-confidence and hope, as it was when women's liberation erupted into the lives of many women at the close of the 1960s. Yesterday's visionaries are today's scapegoats: if not newly tamed and domesticated.

The declining passion for politics evident in many veteran feminists, accompanying the frank rejection of feminism by many young women, is obviously part of the wider "exhaustion of utopian energies" in the last two decades, in an era everywhere described as postsocialist, if not postpolitical.[2] There existed a solid orthodoxy at the close of the last century that little, if anything, now remains of a socialist left capable of winning popular support for its vision of a more egalitarian future. The consensus on feminism, and its now many differing aspirations, remains more ambivalent. Feminism's promotion of women's interests is usually officially endorsed in mainstream politics, even while anxiously traduced on every side. But the inequalities and divisions among women themselves have dramatically deepened, even though so many of the worries and dilemmas that energized feminists in the 1970s everywhere persist. This is both despite, and also because of, the many gains of women throughout the century: some consciously fought for, others the more ambiguous, unintended consequences of maneuvers of capital—pushing women "into the future first," as exemplary low-paid, flexible workers.[3] Indeed, public debate today is obsessed with gender contrasts and conflicts. This is often packaged as slanging matches between feminists; pitting movement feminists, like British old-timer Bea Campbell, against American celebrity feminists/antifeminists, like Camille Paglia. Here women's political differences can be made to service misogynist expectation. However, despite the dubious delivery, there is no doubting the continuing centrality of gender anxieties— whether triggered by family breakdown, new "laddism," teen-age pregnancy, or some other form of sexual panic. This means that as feminists it is hard to remain completely detached from the political arena, whether or not we feel able to preserve, or refashion, our political visions, or, harder still, our collective engagements.

SNAPSHOTS OF GENDER

The Janus face of feminism in the media reflects competing aspects of women's lives today. Depending on our framing, we can contemplate two deeply contrasting pictures. The first is gloomy. In line with unevenly manifest global trends in economic restructuring and the promotion of a pro-scarcity culture arising from the spread of economic neoliberalism over the last two decades, there has been a huge expansion in low-waged, insecure jobs in Britain, the United States, and elsewhere, accompanying continuing attacks on all welfare benefits (from disability to old-age pensions), and the specific targeting of state assistance for single mothers. This goes along with renewed emphasis on the importance of traditional family life and, in particular, fathers' rights and responsibilities. Women not only suffer specifically, or disproportionately, from the cruelties of welfare cutbacks, deepening inequalities, and paternalistic rhetorics, but they serve to undermine precisely those goals for which the women's movement in the 1970s fought so vigorously. It is startling that there has so far been so little organized response from feminists to these attacks—either in the United Kingdom or the United States. Moreover, political assaults on anything coded as feminist scholarship in the American academy (Harold Bloom's denunciation of the "rabblement" of "inchoate would-be Parisians"), have grown more vicious of late, with the conservative "culture wars" reaching out beyond their U.S. birthplace acquiring, as we shall see, some unlikely followers along their way.[4] At the same time, when absorbed into mainstream political agendas, feminist discourses have as often as not been twisted into conservative moral crusades waged in the name of women and children's intrinsic need for protection from predatory male sexuality (although radical feminist analysis bears some responsibility for this appropriation).[5] Returning to basics, in the United Kingdom, from where I write, even women's pay as a percentage of men's (despite an upward surge in the early 1970s) has remained stable—between 56 and 60 percent—for most of this century, and housework and child care are still primarily seen as women's responsibility in the overwhelming majority of households, including dual-income families.[6] Some might well wonder, some do wonder, has feminism been on a hiding to nowhere?

Yet, tilt the frame just a little, and the second picture to emerge seems much more cheerful. Welfare reform, new policies for single mothers, and an emphasis on paternal responsibilities, are characteristically couched in the language of autonomy and responsibility which was at the heart of seventies' feminist rhetoric. Indeed, as others have noticed—and the mourning of Princess Diana in Britain encapsulated—the espousal of a new type of "feminized," personalized, or therapeutic rhetoric abounds today on radio, television, and in the plethora of self-help books, borrowing the feminist consciousness-raising discourses of disclosure and shared pain. Moreover, the choices open to women appear to have increased steadily in recent decades: many women now delay motherhood, more of them recently giving birth in their thirties than their twenties in Britain; more women cohabit and marry later; more divorce and separate; more remain childless; more raise children on their own.[7] Meanwhile, the once

near-invisible domain of women's lives has moved nearer the forefront of international politics—one which has become more, rather
than less, blind to class, and more equivocal about race. Why else
did more than fifty thousand people (mostly women) attend the
United Nations Fourth World Conference on Women in 1995 in
Beijing, and the associated Non-Governmental Organization (NGO)
Forum held nearby? The consequent Beijing Declaration and Platform
for Action, built upon twenty years of planning, debates, and action,
really is an impressive statement urging the promotion of women's
interests worldwide.[8] "The energy, the activity of Beijing, has not gone
away," Charlotte Bunch recently declared, from her Center for Global Leadership at Rutgers University, in agreement with other feminists assessing its impact on government actions internationally, over
two years later.[9]

What are we to make of these clashing configurations? How we
respond will depend upon the type of feminism we espouse. There
have always been, and inexhaustibly continue to be, differing versions of what feminism is all about, with the new or latest trajectories invariably keen to mark their distance from the old. We must
"stop looking at all our problems through men's eyes and discussing
them in men's phraseology," one self-defined "new feminist" writes:
"At last we have done with the boring business of measuring everything that women want, or that is offered them, by men's standards."
This particular advocate of a difference-based feminism was determined to distance her vision and goals from, in her words, "old feminist" campaigns for equal pay and open access to men's jobs, or for
labor market reforms which could not answer the needs of unwaged
women. However, she was *not* picking up on poststructuralist theorizing, phallogocentrism, or on women's nomadic, multifarious but
ineluctable "otherness" (the bedrock of those young women now "Doing Feminism, Being Feminist" in the 1990s, some of whom call themselves "the third wave").[10] Rather, Eleanor Rathbone, for it was she,
represented the "new" feminist vision of over eighty years ago, against
the "old" feminism of the previous decades in the last fin de siècle.
Her distance from our own new feminism of the 1990s, which also
likes to distinguish itself from the old equal-rights feminism of the
1970s, is easily detectable in her very next comment on the occasion
of that particular address. Only "state intervention" and "welfare reforms," she continued, could end women's economic dependence

through the "endowment of motherhood," thereby freeing women from men's control.[11] How her "old statist rhetoric" betrays her!

THE SUBJECT OF DEPENDENCY

Today, in Britain as in the United States, the preeminent political usage of the term *dependency* has itself been refashioned through repeated discursive shifts. Via successive Atlantic crossings, the very notion of "dependency" is becoming synonymous with "welfare beneficiary," prefigured in the words of the American Democrat, Daniel Moynihan, twenty-five years ago: "the issue of welfare is the issue of dependency." Tracing this genealogical transformation, Nancy Fraser and Linda Gordon note its conjunction with a flourishing, deceptively feminist-sounding, self-help literature on autonomy which, by mystifying the link between the psychological and the political, inflates "welfare dependency" into a personality syndrome, one testifying to inadequacy.[12] This is why single mothers can be demonized if they don't work, even while married women with young children can be demonized if they do. Shifting a mother from dependence on the state to reliance on a man for economic support, in this troubling slippage, supposedly removes a woman from the pathologies of dependence.

The truth is otherwise. The continuing offensive against welfare provides, perhaps, the single most general threat to Western women's interests at present—at least insofar as most women still take the major responsibility for caring work in the home. As feminists in the 1970s made so clear, and sought so hard to transform, women are most vulnerable to the very worst pathologies of dependence, when they are most at the mercy of husbands, or male partners, especially during and after pregnancy and childbirth. Indeed, midwives in Britain have recently been asked to look for signs of abuse in just such women, following alarming reports from midwives in the United States examining the bruised bodies of pregnant women and those who have recently become mothers.[13] Similar antitheses exist in relation to needy children. Carolyn Steedman, among others, has written of how the expansion of welfare in the late 1940s gave a particular confidence to working-class children like herself: "I think I would be a different person now if orange juice and milk and dinners at school hadn't told me, in a covert way, that I had a right to exist, was worth something . . . its central benefit being that, unlike my mother, the state asked for nothing in return. Psychic structures are shaped by these huge historical labels: 'charity,' 'philanthropy,' 'state intervention.'" Although, like Steedman herself, well aware of the limitations of such services—their largely unaccountable, undemocratic delivery making them vulnerable to subsequent attack—Liz Heron echoes these sentiments. Introducing her anthology of autobiographical writings by girls growing up in Britain in the fifties, Heron writes: "Along with the orange juice and the cod-liver oil, the malt supplement and the free school milk, we may also have absorbed a certain sense of our own worth and the sense of a future that would get better and better, as if history were on our side."[14] Not anymore!

FAMILY VALUES

Such knowledge is deliberately occluded by the latest shifts in the meaning of dependence. The disavowal of the possible pathologies of women's and children's traditional familial dependency has been strenuously cultivated by the surge of family values campaigners over the last two decades. Pro-family movements first arose in the 1970s as part of the explicit new right backlash against feminism and sexual liberation (soon to be underwritten by Reagan and Thatcher). Two decades later, however, this neoconservative rhetoric is ubiquitous across the political spectrum. "Strengthening the family has to be a number-one social priority," Tony Blair announced at the Labour Party Conference in Britain in 1995, embracing the double-dealing Communitarian Agenda of the American sociologist Amitai Etzioni, and echoing the sentiments of that other traditional patriarch, Bill Clinton (a married man, of course, can hardly be more sexually conservative than to solicit sexual favors from his young employees!). This new family rhetoric, so powerfully promoted in the United States, is no longer explicitly antifeminist, but hovers somewhere between postfeminist and antifeminist agendas.

Meanwhile, the knowledge that the heterosexual married couple can create a living hell of cruelty and physical and sexual neglect and abuse is beaten back by what the American sociologist Judith Stacey calls the "virtual social science" of continual media dissemination of distorted data about the perils of fatherless, divorced, or lone-parent families.[15] This encourages the continuing denials of lesbian and gay rights of all sorts, as in campaigns to restrict custody and adoption rights to married heterosexuals, and obstructs official recognition of any same-sex relationships. Furthermore, it dismisses the often invaluable role of non-family friendships and wider structures of social support which may be all that many individuals can rely upon to keep them sane, when most dependent on the family: like those for whom childhood is, at the very best, a time of gritting the teeth and enduring. Most biographical narratives, attention to clinical literature, if not serious self-reflection, can swiftly trounce the supposedly caring values of pro-family warriors: yet such is the symbolic geography of that place we call "home," they continue to flourish.[16]

Even the evils of paternal incest and domestic violence (recently once again deemed epidemic in U.S. society by no less an authority than the cautious and conservative American Medical Association) are discarded for the evils of fatherlessness in the tendentious social science discourses of David Popenoe or David Blakenhorn, in books like *Rebuilding the Nest and Fatherless America: Confronting Our Most Urgent Social Problem.*[17] Mysteriously, these pathologies of abuse, which feminists identified as part of the warp and weave of traditional, male-dominated family patterns, have been rethreaded to appear as *themselves* the product of family breakdown. Thus, when he lists the all-encompassing personal and social harms of "fatherlessness," Blakenhorn moves on from citing "crime" and "adolescent pregnancy" to include "child sexual abuse [and] domestic violence against women."[18] We are clearly not meant to unscramble the twisted appropriation of what were once solely feminist concerns now placed in the service of a traditional patriarchal orthodoxy.[19]

SWEEPING ANTISTATISM

The once explicit, but nowadays more often disguised or disavowed, antifeminist, antigay, sentiments expressed in family values crusades are all of a piece with a sweeping antistatist rhetoric—increasingly as prevalent on the left as the right, at least in the United States. I was dismayingly alerted to further potential political reversals which may well lie ahead for antiquated socialist feminists, such as myself, by recent thoughts about the state expressed by that once enduringly hopeful and combative feminist radical (and longtime friend of mine), Barbara Ehrenreich. In her "Confessions of a Recovering Statist," she publicly renounces any hopes for progressive social reforms in the United States, whether around child care or parental leave (or environmental reform). "For the time being," she declares, "we're not going to get anywhere with a progressive agenda consisting of . . . government initiatives. *Believe me, I have tried.*"[20] And she certainly has.

Ehrenreich contrasts the situation in the United States with the kinds of universal state provision she believes is taken for granted in Western Europe. In the United States, she argues, there is now no combating the right's antistate propaganda: after two decades of radical conservative pressure, and after Clinton's welfare reform which removes federal responsibility for assisting children in poverty, while at the same time authorizing millions of dollars to be spent not on sex education or contraception or to prevent violence against women, but rather on a puritanical morality which consigns single mothers to courses in abstinence education. Other feminist political scientists, based in the United States, such as Zillah Eisenstein and Anna Marie Smith, also express their increasing suspicions of the costs of what they call the insider strategy. They believe that feminist support for Clinton facilitated his successful presentation of feminine and feminist signifiers, making women's votes decisive in his reelection in 1996 (with the largest gender gap in the history of U.S. presidential voting), but ultimately helping to neutralize opposition to his welfare cuts.[21] Even some of the current, most sophisticated and cautious theoretical works, like Wendy Brown's *States of Injury*, while skillfully exposing both the logic of victimhood and the theoretical incoherence in feminist rhetorics like that of Catharine MacKinnon demanding state protection from "pornographic" imagery, retain a near exclusive focus on "the state as a negative domain for democratic political transformation," stressing the "perils" attending all feminist appeals to it for gender justice.[22] Without wanting to deny the oppressive role of the modern state (not only in its official policing and militaristic role, but also in its protection of already dominant groups via normative regimes regulating access to welfare and social resources), it seems to me that those seeking a better world for all women can hardly afford to abandon struggles in and against it.

Meanwhile, although terminally pessimistic about feminists having any progressive alignment with mainstream politics in the United States, Ehrenreich herself is perhaps too optimistic about Europe. There too, welfare reform is underway, with some feminists in Britain now asking themselves how long the Anglo-American contrasts will hold. For in Blair's new Britain, again with rhetoric borrowed from old conservative voices, it is precisely the notion of universal entitlements (as opposed to the provision of meager welfare for the poor) which is being transformed. This serves to undermine the whole heritage and rationale of the British welfare state: one which relied upon progressive taxation attempting to deliver social services to all its members. Using the defense that poorer welfare recipients can be financially assisted by removing benefits from more affluent ones, progressive legislation involving general entitlements to maternity provision, child benefits, disability, or old-age pensions are now all under threat in Britain. This means that ever more people will have increasingly less reason to support a national insurance system from which they will, in principle, be excluded, feeding the destructively antisocial, anti-government feelings now so dominant in the United States: the sense that people get nothing in return for the taxes they pay—since they must take out private insurance for everything anyway. Comparing the failure of U.S. rationing with the success of austerity measures in Britain during World War II, Harvey Levenstein concluded that the British, unlike Americans, still had "faith in their government."[23] In this age of socially regulated austerity, that faith may crumble.

SWITCHING TO THE SUBJECT

Welfare struggles were central to what is now seen as seventies' equality feminism: a democratizing, egalitarian, and essentially modernist reformist movement, with many utopian overtones. Back then, when "reform or revolution" was the dominant rhetorical binary, most feminists stubbornly refused to choose, twisting and turning around it. Exchanging old binaries for new, "equality versus difference" is now articulated as the central conundrum within more recent feminist thought, the latter embracing both identity and, increasingly important in academic feminism, anti-identity politics: the joys and sorrows of subjectivity and the question of its dismantling—each, at different times, harnessed to affirmations of a "postmodernist" kind. Clashes over this conceptual divide continue to reverberate, nowadays feeding into the most futile and unhealthy of divisions within the left: between class-based and cultural politics.

On its own, it is now no secret that the theorizing of "difference" paradigms in feminism, rightly suspicious of the chauvinisms, gaps, and silences in old emancipatory rhetorics and practices of class, have tended to overshadow material differences within oppressed subject groups. Inside the Western academy, the prestige of poststructuralism and deconstruction directed prominent feminist theoreticians to focus upon the discursive formations of selfhood, or identity, via logics of exclusion and repudiation. Centrally concerned with ways of displacing or subverting the negation or subordination of the feminine in language, or the silencing of women's voices in culture, the emphasis on identities, and their affirmations and negations, has been far less engaged with tackling questions of redistributive justice and social restructuring, which were once central to socialist feminism—that current now most often excised from feminist texts as it is abridged into the subsequently labeled "equality" paradigm.

In a widely rehearsed debate in Italian feminism, for example, a minority, like Adrianna Cavarero and Patrizia Romito, complain of the "mamismo" in its mainstream movement, which has so exalted the maternal that it plays into the hands of conservative forces violently hostile to change in traditional gender arrangements.[24] Such an emphasis certainly has little purchase on the reason Italian women have the lowest birthrate in the developed world—mamismo notwithstanding. More ironically, the tension between identitarian struggles (affirming, or deconstructing, hitherto demeaned or abjected subjectivities) and other political struggles prioritizing social equality and material need (which have often challenged or denied inherent subjective differences) have only deepened as the meanings of the "difference" paradigm expanded to include the multiply diverse, internally fragmented, postcolonial, antiheterosexist, queer, in-between subject positions women occupy.[25]

It is now more than a decade since Juliet Mitchell argued that feminism had unwittingly eased the way for new developments in capitalism, in an article assessing the effects of the first two decades of second-wave feminism.[26] With its theorizing of the "free play of multifarious differences," feminism had helped construct an ideology which could disregard class and side-line socioeconomic comparisons to focus almost exclusively upon the all-embracing opposition between men and women. It is easier now, she correctly noted, to get statistics on gender differences in educational achievement than on class comparisons—twenty years ago the situation was completely the reverse.[27] Misleadingly, in my view, Mitchell attributed far too much agency to feminism in assisting capitalist market forces, rather than seeing women as ensnared within them.[28] Her words foreshadow those of many an incorrigible old chauvinist, like Norman Mailer, announcing that feminism was so successful because it "was perfect for the corporation," promoting women as its "gilt-edged peons."[29] More usefully, however, Mitchell highlighted, as others soon would, the way in which feminist rhetoric and goals could be appropriated to legitimate technological, economic, and legislative changes, which were not in themselves what feminists had been fighting for (again we could look at Judith Stacey's work, in particular her study of women working for the Silicon Valley corporations, in *Brave New Families*).[30] The crucial point, and one often displaced in the feminist turn to theorizing subjectivities in the 1980s, is the need to pay very careful attention to the relationship between feminist discourses and practices, as they at times contest, and at others serve more to reflect, shifting economic and social change which has little to do with eliminating social injustice. If feminists are not to hide away in the largely misleading romance of women's ineluctable "otherness," we will need to turn outwards more often: observing the centrality of some women in the new professional and managerial world, even as others are pushed more securely to the margins.

ACTIVIST CHALLENGES

Do not misunderstand me. I am well aware that studies of identities and differences were and are important in their attention to the limitations of previously uncontested universalisms and in their focus on the diversity of subordinated and excluded positionings of people in language and culture. These hierarchically gendered, sexualized, racialized, or hybridized productions of identity are all material in their injurious effects, and usually, though not necessarily and in differing ways, tied up with the structuring of economic disadvantage and marginalization. Indeed, it is identity-based politics which have so often inspired the cultures of activism which, in the best of times, form part of, or in other ways service, class-based trade-union and community struggles for better lives.[31] As most feminists were once well aware, the really difficult challenge remains that of building culture and class coalitions, where sexism and racism are always on the agenda. This is still the only way "to prevent white male interests from dominating class politics and middle class interests from dominating cultural politics," as Andrew Ross recently noted.[32] If the left is ever to reconstitute itself as a popular movement, it can only do so by embracing the greatest possible diversity of progressive cultural alignments, while attending to the volatilities of class itself, as it is culturally produced and experienced.

Moreover, the ethnic and racialist provincialism of some earlier incarnations of feminism have themselves needed to be challenged by the insights of those theorists now emphasizing the intrinsic instabilities of being positioned as a woman. Whether mapping the discourses, or studying their modes of normalization, developments in feminist theory have usefully stressed the cultural particularities and psychic complexities of women's subjectivities (at least, when not submitting themselves to the dogged singularity of Lacan's law). However, for feminists moving forward in the academy, it was never likely to be easy to return from the austere individual pleasures (or torments) of abstract thought to the heated exchanges of collective confrontation and strategic coalition.

As Jane Gallop, one of the most provocative and passionate defenders of feminist pedagogy, has mused: "We don't seem very able to theorize about how we speak, as feminists *wanting social change,* from within our positions in the academy."[33] Much more bitterly, the African Americanist Hazel Carby points out that the new scholarly recognition of diversity and difference, and the inclusion of black writers in the syllabus of women's studies and literature departments in the United States over the last decade, has accompanied the significant and steady decline in the percentage of black students reaching college. Observing how few alliances have been forged in recent times between the academy and the black working class and urban poor, Carby concludes (understandably, if somewhat harshly, and echoing the thoughts of Paul Gilroy and Anthony Appiah): "Black cultural texts have become fictional substitutes for the lack of any sustained social and political relationships with black people in a society that retains many of its historical practices of apartheid in housing and schooling."[34] The problem, according to left critics of multiculturalism, is not that it politicizes the academy (to the horror of its right-wing critics), but that it constitutes politics as primarily academic.

In a particularly painful debate on the links between theory and action published in *Signs*, in 1996, some of the best-known feminist activists in the United States, all of whom are in or close to the academy, maintain that they no longer read feminist theory. Rightly or wrongly, they argue that it bears little relation to the empirical complexities of analyzing the demands of the women in ongoing struggles to whom they are committed—most often women fighting for what they see as basic human rights (rather than specifically women's concerns) for health, housing, better educational or other welfare resources, as well as an end to poverty.[35] One problem is that the struggles these activists refer to require an overall vision of a radically egalitarian society, in considerable tension with the positioning of much recent feminist theory as antihumanist, post-enlightenment, and post–nation-state.

The form of feminist activism involving solidarity with women in struggle worldwide is thus one which harks back to the so-called equality feminism of the 1970s. Theorizing subjectivities and differences rarely inspires engaged rapport with those who, in Temma Kaplan's words, are most "Crazy for Democracy": women leading human rights campaigns against the very worst exploitation and abuses, whether in Southern or Northern hemispheres. For where women are most actively engaged in grass-roots struggles today, as Kaplan's research illustrates, is also where leaders are blurring rather than affirming differences between groups in favor of reclaiming, on their own terms, a rhetoric of *universal* human rights: for example, that "all human beings are entitled to safe housing and a clean environment and that sometimes only women can secure them."[36] Patricia Williams, in *The Alchemy of Race and Rights*, argues rather similarly that rights rhetoric has been and remains important for black struggles, even though, and in part, just because, rights are historically "unstable and shifting."[37] On the one hand, then, it has been essential for feminists to dismantle notions of the disembodied, abstract universal, hitherto operating to exclude them in their particularity. On the other hand, the paradoxical empowerment of rights rhetoric is precisely that its universal ideal can never be fixed, once and for all, but remains an abiding source of conflict and struggle (as Etienne Balibar, among others, forcefully argues).[38]

DISCIPLINING FEMINISM

Meanwhile, whatever the political potential of appeals to "ambiguous universalities," the grass roots movements for social justice which women are leading today require a variety of types of scholarly servicing, some of which are less visible in feminist theorizing, as it has moved from its earlier location in sociology and the social sciences into English and the humanities. Such servicing would need to encompass theories of world markets, and seek to explain why increasing globalization has gone hand in hand with the rolling back of welfare rights, even in developed capitalist countries such as Britain (though not, like Mitchell, in order to impugn feminist complicity). Without such theory, it is hard to know the possibilities and limits of effective resistance, especially when we are faced with the partially unjustified alarmism that nation states have become powerless in the face of such globalization.[39] Feminist studies, like cultural studies, began as a genuinely interdisciplinary field of knowledge. But the current pressures of the academy are such that it is almost impossible to maintain genuinely cross-disciplinary interests, so harnessed are we to ever narrower channels of disciplinary career routes and publication. Attending feminist conferences seemed once to promise access to areas of knowledge far removed from one's own, but the disciplining of feminism within the academy makes that much less likely today.

Indicatively, the well-attended and well-received *At the Millennium* conference organized by *Woman: A Cultural Review*, although "interdisciplinary" in conception and subtitle, reflected the predominance of English and cultural studies in the vanguard of academic feminism today (indeed, I was the sole speaker from the social sciences). This stimulated distinctive modes of gender interrogation which, although certainly diverse, thoughtful, and creative, authorized specific but mostly narrowly conceived visions of futurity: many of them in search of the most enabling metaphors for feminists to work with. One, for example, offered the "trickster," as postmodern shape-shifter, who can be both man and woman, hence paying no deference to single categories like that of gender or sexuality. While helping us explore the instabilities of gender, however, its champion on this occasion (Gillian Beer) was careful to caution us that her particular future-oriented, feminist figurine has little concern for others, indeed performs her/his tricks at the expense of others. Another (Elizabeth Bronfen) suggested the "hysteric" as futuristic feminist icon. Once we depathologize her, we were told, she offers a strategy for questioning and teasing the master's narrative, revealing its fraudulence.

These playful, transgressive emissaries of change or resistance can help us address the agonies and duplicities of subjectivities and encourage us to see that there are potentially mutually contradictory descriptions of reality. But, they cannot provide the theoretical resources most useful for women hoping for a stake in the future while positioned at the sharpest edge of struggles for justice and survival, wherever located. That requires more, rather than less, attention to actually existing social relations and their discursive boundaries. I notice just the same disciplinary dominance when perusing the recent U.S. publication, *Generations: Academic Feminists in Dialogue,* with nineteen of the twenty-one voices speaking from literature departments. Distinguishing what she sees as the personal and political strands of feminism from the intellectual, one contributor sums up her view of the intellectual dimension of feminism through an exclusively disciplinary lens: "Intellectual feminism is analytical; it concerns itself with 'reading' the representations of women in culture and its texts and artifacts."[40] Academic feminism has taken a very particular route here, one which might seem strange indeed to that poet whom feminist literary scholars once interviewed and studied, Grace Paley: "Feminism means political consciousness. It means that you see the relationship between the life of women and the political life and power around her. From there you can take any route you want."[41]

But can we take any route as feminists within the academy today? There is an important connection between the last two problems I have been addressing: the academization of feminist politics and the logic of a narrow disciplinarity. Many feminists have worked very hard to keep open a space for interdisciplinary work in the academy (which is not the same thing as renouncing scholarly expertise and academic specialization). Yet, the harsh irony is, the more strict disciplinarity has been undermined by philosophical and political critique of its founding assumptions (those grand narratives rejected by the late and influential Jean-François Lyotard), the more competing pressures inside the academy have forced disciplinary boundaries to tighten up in fiscally contracting times for higher education.[42] Meanwhile, the move in academic fashions from sociology and the social sciences to English and the humanities was itself at least partly a sign of the decline of left politics after the close of the 1970s. There has been a corresponding change in the character of cultural studies, away from the sociology and cultural history of literature—manifest in Raymond Williams and his ex-students, like Francis Mulhern and Terry Eagleton, or Stuart Hall and Birmingham Cultural Studies—toward more ahistorical and nonsociological theories of representation.[43] Whether mourning the move away from the historicizing and contextualizing of culture, or castigating its analysis as "recycled semiotics," a number of scholars, like Cary Nelson in the United States, have begun arguing for the repolitization of cultural studies and its opening up to other disciplinary resources: "Recognizing how fragile and contingent both moral and historical consensus is," Nelson argues, "only increases the need for advocacy and interpretation."[44] Similarly, among feminist scholars, even such a radical deconstructionist as Barbara Johnson has recently admitted: "I think it's true that in order for certain things to happen, sites have to be occupied blindly or out of a passion for justice." The most intellectually productive thing, she now concludes, is to be both politically committed at the same time as retaining "skepticism toward the authority of existing cultural arrangements, [and] toward the supposed 'universality' or 'impartiality' of existing 'truths.'"[45]

CULTURAL IMPERATIVES

Although desiring greater crossdisciplinary communication in feminist forums, I am not endorsing those academics now making a name for themselves through an antitheoretical populism. Least of all am I trying to jettison cultural analysis for what is often falsely posed against it as "material" analysis. Any feminism still seeking to overturn the indignities many women face (whether gender specific or not, though the two are unlikely to be easily unraveled) needs to work to overcome the rifts which repeatedly arise between those positioning cultural and economic analysis as opposing priorities. For it is precisely cultural analysis of the pivotal place of sexual difference in the formation of subjectivity, combined with the coercive centrality of gender in structuring wider social relations, that remains at the heart of gender politics around the globe: past, present, and future. Whatever general rights and pragmatic distinctions need to be called upon in mobilizing support for women fighting for better lives, feminists can in no way afford to retreat to reductive positions which would definitively demarcate the economic and political terrain from those some would like to marginalize, if not dismiss, as the discursive or the "merely cultural" (as Judith Butler recently described such dismissals).[46] Indeed, few intellectual efforts are less politically productive, or more symptomatic of morbidity, than the attempts of left offshoots of the culture wars in the United States (now making their appearance in Europe) to defend the supposedly real left against a phony cultural left—most egregiously expressed in the hoaxing of *Social Text* by the physicist Alan Sokal, with the assistance of two well-known feminist scholars and to the applause of many others.[47]

Economic realities, and the shifting, uneven fortunes of women worldwide are, everywhere, enmeshed within cultural understandings of sexual difference, which still, on all sides, help to promote male paranoia, misogyny, homophobia, and related violence against women, gays, and other subordinated or dissident men. How else, for example, could we seriously understand the increasingly promoted sense that women in the West are now the winners, and men the losers, in an ongoing battle of the sexes?[48] It is time for "the winners" to help "the losers," that seasoned conservative ideologue Ferdinand Mount proclaimed recently in the British press. Such sentiments are heard on all sides, even emanating from former feminists—and I don't just mean mavericks like the British novelist Fay Weldon or American liberals like Betty Friedan. Approaching the millennium there is a deluge of publications warning us of boys' and men's heightened intellectual, emotional, and physical anxieties, degeneration, and deep sense of failure (with ample statistics, and personal testimony, to back them up). And men's suffering is undoubtedly real, even though, worldwide, the general preservation of men's power over women—politically, economically, and culturally— has nowhere been overturned, least of all at elite levels: whatever personal freedoms, privileges, and autonomy some women have gained, and some men have lost. We will never even begin to understand what is at stake here, for either men or women, without attention to the cultural.

Men suffer as men because of the ways in which masculinity symbolizes power: a power secured only relationally, through its dominance over, and repudiation of, femininity.[49] This is why it is only when women appear to be in any way ahead of men that talk of men's gender crisis makes headlines. And that is why the fact that almost every other social difference (especially of class and race) is of overwhelmingly greater significance than gender in throwing light on what lies behind the "losing out" of certain boys and men, and is obliterated in talk of gender crisis: usefully for governments and ruling elites who would have us ignore socioeconomic issues. (In fact, of course, there is nothing remotely new about working-class and black male youth faring particularly badly in school, resorting to crime, and generally being seen as threatening.) Men's predicament is that power and authority are still everywhere the symbolic attributes of masculinity, yet many men, faced with low pay, job insecurities, and unemployment, have less and less secure access to either. Women, although the primary and continuing targets of men's sense of failure and aggression, have very little to do with their problems. The specter haunting men is—abidingly—"masculinity" itself, with its policing of boys and men who do not look and act like winners.

FEMINISM WITHOUT POLITICS

Meanwhile, the notion of gender crisis generates its own type of therapeutic solutions. From a host of mainstream psychological texts and mediations to Bly's mythopoetic men's movement, we see attempts to reform or refashion masculinity, in ways seen as more in tune with changing demands upon men. Ironically, they all draw upon many of the resources of early feminist consciousness-raising, while discarding its accompanying confrontational mode, stressing the need for men collectively to express and share their feelings, vulnerabilities and anxieties. This returns us to the expedient accommodation of mainstream culture to feminism, which I mentioned at the beginning. Feminist rhetoric has been widely accepted insofar as it applauds a gentle type of care-based ethic, the affirmation of a benevolent femininity, open and sensitive to the needs and vulnerabilities of others (for example, in the media-friendly, widely promoted work of Carol Gilligan or Jean Bethke Elsthain), but distanced from any radical or threatening challenges: either of thought or action.

The continuing dissemination of just such a feminist into feminizing personal ethos seems to offer a feminism without an oppositional culture or politics, one which has encouraged some feminists to replace what they now describe as their former "hardened" language of politics, with a "cozier" language of feelings. (These sentiments were expressed by several feminists interviewed recently in the British newspaper, the *Observer*.)[50] Such a therapeutic version of feminism can easily slide into, or at least be used in the service of, a wider culture of blandness and denial: one collapsing the political into the personal, the collective into the individual. Such a culture can accommodate governments which pretend that they cannot change what it is *only* in their power to change, while demanding that individuals— whether parents, teachers, or simply as luckless souls—*can* change what they have little hope of changing (given socially generated scarcity, deepening levels of inequality, and ever-growing competitiveness).

POLITICAL FUTURES OF FEMINISM

The last fin de siècle was seen as an optimistic era by many first-wave feminists. This time around, despite the continuous murmuring of backlash voices, despite its internal conflicts and ambivalence, and despite co-option by commercial, conservative, or gender normalizing forces, feminism remains a powerful cultural force. Indeed, in Britain at present, widespread publicity recently accompanied the appearance of a book declaring the dawn of a "new feminism": this time as a mainstream, majority movement in which women—from the Spice Girls to Cherie Blair and her husband's hundred new women MPs— can celebrate their own sudden power and achievements (partly thanks to Margaret Thatcher for normalizing female success). Its author, the journalist Natasha Walter (like Naomi Wolf before her), offers a maverick form of power-feminism, emptied of political theory and largely destitute of political strategy for combating the many obstacles which confront women far removed from where Walter likes to see them: lined up "in the corridors of power." Indeed, it is free from collective political formations or affiliations of any kind.

Although symptomatic of many women's good will toward a feminism they feel free to fashion, it is hardly politically serious.

Surveying the multifarious voices of feminism today, I find not so much paradoxes on offer, as full-blown contradictions. The more porous, flexible, and volatile our identities, bodies, and lives are conceived to be in academic discourses deconstructing genders and sexualities, the more social constraints, pressures, and the compulsions become apparent in the lives of many women (and men). Symptomatically, the subjective fluidities being revealed, as deconstruction continues to hegemonize progressive literary theory, are mocked by the rigidities being recycled, as Darwinian reductionism returns to become the new science for popular consumption. A mere decade ago, there was still a debate in the British and American media on the future of the nuclear family. Today the superiority of that family structure over all possible alternatives is once again heard everywhere. Only a decade ago, feminists still hoped to transform the relations between employment and family lives. Today, Blair's new Victorian Britain installs an old and punishing work ethic which, despite three decades of feminist attention to the "labors of love," remains incapable of questioning any of the old terms—whether that of "labor" or "love."

In the most technologically innovative of times, as some feminists write of women's particular affinity with the supposed freedoms offered by the networks of cyberspace (despite men's dominance of 90 percent of its highways), many women face a future where we are leading the most comprehensively conservative of lives: less politically engaged, less utopian in vision, less time, even, for friends and family.[51] Writing of the unexpected decline of leisure in the United States, Juliet Schor points out that for the last three decades there has been a steady increase in the number of hours on the job put in by fully employed workers, while the same alarms about ever-expanding working hours are sounding in the United Kingdom.[52] It is primarily women who are still somehow expected to make up for the hours lost from creating loving homes and healthy communities, while simultaneously applauded for how far they have come in gaining equality with men. Given the persisting strength of traditional gender ideology, it is, as always, the daily lives of women which most directly absorb the shocks and contradictions of these mean yet widely disparate times. Hence the continuing potential for women's role in seeking radical social transformation.

Time, one might think, for a renaissance of feminist politics. But few women have the time, even if they had the inclination (in these days when only instrumentalized self-serving is applauded), to sift through the potentialities and perils of differing versions of feminism. This leaves only a contentious minority of women attempting to map out and assess which different pieces in the jigsaw of feminism get picked up, leaving us to ask just who is selecting the fragments, and whose particular interests their delivery serves. Given the diversity of reformist, identitarian, deconstructive, activist, therapeutic, and power feminisms, it is true that we can indeed take any route we want as feminists leaving the twentieth century. But it is only by finding creative ways to combine forces, and by learning from one another's journeys, that feminists can still hope to open spaces for more women to flaunt the diverse pleasures, entitlements, and self-questioning to which recent feminist thinking has encouraged us to aspire (often, disconcertingly, in line with late capitalist consumerism).

NOTES

1. Joan Scott, *Only Paradoxes to Offer: French Feminists and the Rights of Man* (Cambridge: Harvard University Press, 1996).
2. Jürgen Habermas, "The New Obscurity and the Exhaustion of Utopian Energies," in *Observations on the Spiritual Situation of the Age*, ed. Jürgen Habermas (Cambridge, Mass.: MIT Press, 1984).
3. Juliet Mitchell, "Reflections on Twenty Years of Feminism," in *What Is Feminism?* ed. Juliet Mitchell and Ann Oakley (Oxford: Basil Blackwell, 1986), 34–48.
4. Quoted in Sandra M. Gilbert, "Presidential Address 1996: Shadows of Futurity: The Literary Imagination, the MLA, and the Twenty-first Century," *PMLA* 112:3 (May 1997).
5. See Lynne Segal, *Straight Sex: The Politics of Pleasure* (Berkeley and Los Angeles: University of California Press, 1994).
6. B. Bagilhole, *Women, Work and Equal Opportunity* (Aldershot: Avebury, 1994), 1.
7. Information from *Social Focus on Women* quoted in Ann Oakley and Juliet Mitchell, eds. *Who's Afraid of Feminism Seeing through the Backlash* (London: Penguin, 1997), 7.
8. The declaration condemns violence against women, especially systemic rape in warfare, and encourages assistance for female victims of violence; recommends enactment of legislation to guarantee the right of women and men to equal pay for equal work; supports the promotion of businesses run by women and women's media networks; calls for women's equal participation in governments; promotes research on women's health, and so on. See a variety of reports from the Beijing conference in *Signs: Journal of Women in Culture and Society* 22:1(1996): 181–226.
9. Barbara Crossette, "Women See Key Gains since Talks in Beijing," *New York Times*, March 8, 1998.
10. For example, Leslie Heywood and Jennifer Drake, eds., *Third Wave Agenda: Doing Feminism, Being Feminist* (Minneapolis: University of Minnesota Press, 1997); Special Issue: Third Wave Feminisms, J. Zita, ed., *Hypatia: A Journal of Feminist Philosophy* (summer 1997).
11. Quoted in Susan Pedersen, "The Failure of Feminism in the Making of the British Welfare State," *Radical History Review: The Women's Story* 43 (winter 198): 86–110, 86.
12. Nancy Fraser and Linda Gordon, "A Genealogy of 'Dependency': Tracing a Keyword of the U.S. Welfare State," in *Justice Interruptus: Critical Reflections on the "Postsocialist" Condition*, ed. Nancy Fraser (London: Routledge, 1997). Moynihan quote, in Fraser and Gordon, ibid., 138.

13. News in Brief, "Midwives to Look for Abuse of Women," *Guardian*, December 29, 1997, 8: "There seems to be evidence of violence starting or being exacerbated when a woman is pregnant or post-natally, with the violence directed towards her stomach, breasts and genitals."

14. Liz Heron, *Truth, Dare or Promise: Girls Growing Up in the Sixties* (London: Virago, 1985), 6.

15. Judith Stacey, "Families against the Family," *Radical Philosophy* 89 (May/June 1998); *In the Name of the Family: Rethinking Family Values in the Postmodern Age* (Boston: Beacon Press, 1996), ch. 4.

16. Lillian Rubin, *The Transcendent Child: Tales of Triumph over the Past* (New York: Harper Collins, 1997).

17. Quoted in Carol Gilligan, "Getting Civilized," in Oakley and Mitchell, eds., *What Is Feminism*, 15.

18. David Blakenhorn, Jean Bethke Elsthain, and Steven Bayme, eds., *Rebuilding the Nest: A New Commitment to the American Family* (Milwaukee, Wis.: Family Service American, 1991); David Blakenhorn, *Fatherless America: Confronting Our Most Urgent Social Problem* (New York: Basic Books, 1995); David Blakenhorn, *American Family Dilemmas*.

19. In fact, as analyses of the last U.S. presidential election illustrate, familial rhetoric encouraged a continuous appeal to American women via the latest media fiction of the "soccer Mom" (the middle-class, married, white mother, concerned primarily for her children and their fitness and success), thereby enabling an actual erasure of most women's interests (whether for child care, job prospects, personal safety, reproductive control, or racial justice) even as they were being targeted for votes. Susan Carroll, "'My Kids Play Soccer and I Vote': The Production of the Soccer Mom in the 1996 Elections," unpub. (scarroll@rci.rutgers.edu).

20. Barbara Ehrenreich, "When Government Gets Mean: Confessions of a Recovering Statist," *Nation*, November 17, 1997, 12.

21. See Anna Marie Smith, "Feminist Activism and Presidential Politics: Theorizing the Costs of the 'Insider Strategy,'" *Radical Philosophy* (May/June 1997).

22. Wendy Brown, *States of Injury Power and Freedom in Late Modernity* (Princeton, N.J.: Princeton University Press, 1995), x. In this chapter I do not address the influential strand of anti-pornography feminism, though I have done so frequently elsewhere, because I believe it has served primarily to reinvigorate the moral right, rather than any progressive left politics. See Segal, *Straight Sex*; Segal and McIntosh, eds., *Sex Exposed: Sexuality and the Pornography Debates* (New Brunswick, N.J.: Rutgers University Press, 1994).

23. Harvey Levenstein, *Paradoxes of Plenty: A Social History of Eating in Modern America* (New York: Oxford University Press, 1993), 81.

24. Patrizia Romito, "'Damned if You Do and Damned if You Don't': Psychological and Social Constraints on Motherhood in Contemporary Europe," in Oakley and Mitchell; Adrianna Cavarero, "The Politics of Sexual Difference," presented at the Radical Philosophy Conference: *Torn Halves: Theory and Politics in Contemporary Feminism*, School of Oriental and African Studies, University of London, November 9, 1996.

25. See Rita Felski, "The Doxa of Difference," *Signs* 23:1 (autumn 1997): 162–186.

26. A point which Cora Kaplan made in her talk delivered during the *At the Millennium: Interrogating Gender* conference, London, January 9, 2000.

27. Juliet Mitchell, "Reflections on Twenty Years of Feminism," in Mitchell and Oakley, 47, 48, 45.

28. For example, speaking of equal pay legislation, Mitchell suggested that "a tragic effect of our achievement was to . . . erode conditions of employment, to help lower expectations of social security, state benefits, trade union support etc." (43)

29. David Denby, "The Contender," *New Yorker*, April 20, 1998, 70.

30. See, for example, Judith Stacey, *Brave New Families: Stories of Domestic Upheaval in the Late Twentieth Century* (New York: Basic Books, 1990).

31. Cynthia Saltzman, *In the Shadows of Privilege: Women and Unions at Yale*, forthcoming; Hank Johnson and Bert Klandermans, eds., *Social Movements and Culture (Social Movements, Protest, and Contention*, Vol. 4) (Minneapolis: University of Minnesota Press, 1995).

32. Andrew Ross, *Real Love: In Pursuit of Cultural Justice* (New York: New York University Press, 1998), 5, 216.

33. Jane Gallop, *Around 1981: Academic Feminist Literary Theory* (London: Routledge, 1992), 4.

34. Hazel V. Carby, "The Multicultural Wars," *Radical History Review* 54 (1992): 7–18.
35. "I do not see the feminist theory discourse in this country addressing the practical prob-
    lems of how to bring women back together so they strengthen each other," Charlotte
    Bunch mourns, from her position heading up the Center for Women's Global Leadership
    at Rutgers University, "There needs to be more dialogue between those engaged in trying
    to make change in the world and those writing those theories." Charlotte Bunch in Heidi
    Hartmann et al., "Bringing Together Feminist Theory and Practice: A Collective Inter-
    view," *Signs* 21:41 (1996).
36. Temma Kaplan, *Crazy for Democracy: Women in Grass-roots Movements* (London:
    Routledge, 1997), 1.
37. "The vocabulary of rights speaks to an establishment that values the guise of stability,
    and from whom social change for the better must come (whether it is given, taken or
    smuggled). [But] Changes argued for in the sheep's clothing of stability ("rights") can be
    effective, even as it destabilizes certain other establishment values (segregation)." Patricia
    Williams, *The Alchemy of Race and Rights* (Cambridge: Harvard University Press, 1991),
    149. See also John Anner, ed., *Beyond Identity Politics: Emerging Social Justice Move-
    ments in Communities of Color* (Boston: South End Press, 1996). Reporting on the wave
    of black and immigrant-based struggles in the United States over the last decade, in all of
    which women have played a critical role, John Anner similarly points to the need for
    shared political ideals to forge bonds between diverse identities and communities of
    interest.
38. See Etienne Balibar, "Ambiguous Universality," *Differences: A Journal of Feminist Cultural
    Studies* 7:1 (1995): 48–74.
39. See Paul Hirst and Grahame Thompson, *Globalization in Question* (Cambridge: Polity
    Press, 1996); Simon Bromley, "Globalization," *Radical Philosophy* 80 (November/De-
    cember 1996): 76–93.
40. Theresa Ann Sears, "Feminist Misogyny; or, What Kind of Feminist Are You?" in *Genera-
    tions: Academic Feminists in Dialogue*, Devoney Looser and E. Ann Kaplan, ed. (Minne-
    apolis: University of Minnesota Press, 1997), 269.
41. Kathleen Hulley, "Interview with Grace Paley," *Delta: Grace Paley* 14 (May 1982): 32.
42. Jean-François Lyotard, *The Postmodern Condition: A Report on Knowledge*, trans. Geoff
    Bennington and Brian Massumi (Minneapolis: University of Minnesota Press, 1984).
43. See the many interesting essays along these lines in Elizabeth Long, ed., *From Sociology
    to Cultural Studies* (Oxford: Basil Blackwell, 1997).
44. Cary Nelson, *Manifesto of a Tenured Radical* (New York: New York University Press,
    1997), 51. See also Peter Osborne and Lynne Segal, "Culture and Power: Interview with
    Stuart Hall," *Radical Philosophy* 86 (November/December 1997).
45. Barbara Johnson, *The Wake of Deconstruction* (Oxford: Basil Blackwell, 1995), 94, 85.
46. See Judith Butler, "Merely Cultural," *Social Text* 15:3–4 (fall/winter 1997): 52–53.
47. Alan D. Sokal, "Transgressing the Boundaries: Towards a Transformative Hermeneutics
    of Quantum Gravity," *Social Text* 46 (spring/summer 1996). The feminists assisting
    Sokal were Barbara Epstein and Ruth Rosen; for insightful discussion, see Ellen Willis,
    "My Sokaled Life," *Village Voice* 25 (June 1996): 22–23.
48. Ferdinand Mount, "Death and Burial of the Utopian Feminist," *London Sunday Times*,
    December 14, 1997, 15.
49. See Lynne Segal, *Slow Motion: Changing Masculinities, Changing Men* (New Brunswick,
    N.J.: Rutgers University Press, 1997).
50. However, this particular structure of feeling, although frequently attributed to the effects
    of pain and suffering, is one which is always seen as adjustable, not the intractable
    terrors of paranoia, sadism, or terminal despair: "I suppose I am more interested in
    average grief, inner grief, the grief most of us feel," one such newly retrained psycho-
    therapist reflected. It is interesting that at a time when the air is full of therapeutic
    reskilling, the man who provided the seedbed from which such diversified trainings have
    grown is everywhere denounced for his "fraudulence" and "fakery": Freud offered a far
    bleaker, more pessimistic vision.
51. For example, Sadie Plant, *Zeroes and Ones: Digital Women and the New Technoculture*
    (London: Fourth Estate, 1997).
52. Juliet Schor, *The Overworked American: The Unexpected Decline of Leisure* (New York:
    Basic Books, 1991); WFD/Management Today survey, London, published May 1998.

ELAINE K. CHANG

LAST PAST THE POST
Theory, Futurity, Feminism

In her critique of selected late-1980s examples of critical race and gender studies, Sara Suleri gives momentary voice to her "belief" that had
she "any veto power over prefixes, *post-* would be the first to go."[1]
This expression of resistance and resignation comes after the writer's
apparently voluntary application of the term *postfeminism* to one of
several aspects of Trinh T. Minh-ha's *Woman, Native, Other: Writing
Postcoloniality and Feminism* that she finds objectionable. Suleri deploys the "post" at one moment in a particularized, descriptive form—
while the precise significance attributed to postfeminism is opaque,
that it is a pejorative term is clear in the context of her usage—and
immediately thereafter questions and disowns the prefix, detached
from its referent, in general terms.[2] This double-edged gesture, of re-
luctant reutterance, seems to have borne repeating in many encounters with the post. I for my part apprehend the term "postfeminism"
with some dread, am uncertain to whom or what it might apply, but
confirm its provisional currency, at least, in order to reckon with
Suleri's reference to it as the "inevitable territory" on which Trinh's
attempts to "represent the categories of 'woman' and 'race' at the
same time" are said to founder.[3] As I endeavor to decipher the "post"
in this and other, also perplexing, instances, I would be suggesting
that the prefix could stay. Or so might run my belief, different from

Suleri's but, to again reiterate her terms, no less "futile" or "tangential to the issue at hand."[4]

When feminist thinkers polarize over the post, questions may arise as to whether the four-letter prefix has inscribed itself indelibly into the very axes of power, identification, space, and time that shape and shift relations between culture and politics, between power and knowledge, and without which analysis of these relations is impossible; and whether the already ambiguous post might invite the ambivalent signifying intentions of irony, sarcasm, passive aggression, flippancy, and wistfulness that different users speak through it. Yet for all the time I, for one, have spent wondering what inherent properties of the post might be identified and held accountable for tensions among feminists—that frequently struck between "theory" and "activism," for instance—I've hit upon nothing that will stick, no compelling or satisfactory way to circumvent the post, or to pretend it isn't there. Rather than denigrate or celebrate the post, then, and rather than attempt to collect a representative assortment of post words and explicate them, en masse or in their discreteness, this brief essay offers selected sightings and readings of the post at or near certain persistent problems for contemporary feminists, particularly as regards questions of temporality, history, difference, and futurity.

The author of a 1996 editorial in the *Nation* wondered why the phrase "going postal" had entered into the lexicon and come so widely to signify a dramatic rise in workplace mass assaults—when the homicide rate among postal service employees was actually much lower than that among industrial workers as a whole.[5] Had the "post's" cachet in popular and critical discourse carried over, metonymically and by virtue of homonym and pun, to what the *Nation's* editorialist described as "random attacks by uncommonly angry individuals"?[6] To borrow from some critics of postcolonialism and postmodernism, perhaps going postal serves both to contain and to render marginal or insignificant the activities named by the phrase. From a different perspective, going postal may resonate with the critical insights of, for example, poststructuralism—insofar as murderous postal workers, and their re-creation of the post office as a space of danger and unpredictability, might be said to make grossly, materially explicit the mediation of meaning between senders and recipients of discourse occluded by structuralists and liberal humanists.

Going postal may furthermore, or alternatively, be read as an appall-ing symptom of postindustrial (or disorganized) capitalism and/as postmodernity: workers in the center, rendered surplus and dispos-able in an era of transnational corporations and flexible accumula-tion, engage in a particularly violent form of self-extermination, and take others with them. Inasmuch as going postal has this connota-tion of desperate protest, against the elimination of "earlier" politi-cal forms such as labor unions, employment security, and health care, the *Nation*'s editorialist appropriately turned the phrase back on the state governors who had cut their budgets for public mental health services in the face of this "lethal boom."[7]

Where complex problems defy yet demand solutions and expla-nations, the post can make an appearance to order. This capacity as both a place holder and a displacement or deferral of explanation con-stitutes part of the peril, and part of the appeal, of the nefarious prepo-sition. The post designates dislocations and liminalities in space that are often simultaneously convolutions and interruptions in time: when Homi Bhabha describes the post in terms of a move "to touch the future on its hither side," or when Anne McClintock identifies in the sheer ubiquity of post words "a widespread, epochal crisis in the idea of linear, historical 'progress,'" time is being transposed, or is perceived as being transposed, into space, and vice versa.[8] The im-plication of the post in the compressions and crises of time and space suggests several ways in which the discourses of postmodernism, poststructuralism, and postcolonialism have informed and been in-formed by feminist conceptions of the future.

Challenges confronted by contemporary feminists have included that of deconstructing "woman" as a transhistorical, homogenizing category while at the same time bringing women more fully into the scope of the universal—whether by "universal" one means the inter-national human rights and social justice disproportionately denied to women, the global division of labor in which women are dispro-portionately exploited, and/or the economies of artistic and political representation in which women are overvalued and undervalued at once. A related challenge has emerged in the framework of coalition politics, committed to decentralizing feminist movements by situat-ing the subject of feminism in terms of multiple determinations (by race, class, gender, age, and sexuality, for example), but a framework in which inequality has persisted along these very lines, and prior

notions of feminist unity and progress have been recentered. As Judith
Butler has argued: "Despite the clearly democratizing impulse that
motivates coalition building, the coalitional theorist can inadvertently
reinsert herself as sovereign of the process by trying to assert an ideal
form for coalitional structures in advance, one that will effectively
guarantee unity as the outcome."[9]

Butler asks whether feminist movement can conceive—both
imagine and produce—a future in which its political outcome is neither dictated or knowable in advance nor postulated from a fixed or
idealized subject position. At stake is one version of a general problem that materializes amidst the traffic of post signifiers: the problem of conceptualizing and narrating history—as either continuist,
teleological and singular, or discontinuous and multiple, or as some
combination or collision of these alternatives. That coalition politics
has rendered feminism more inclusive and diverse than it formerly
had been cannot and need not be disputed; what has been and remains contested, and to be more fully historicized, is the valorization of inclusion and diversity as principles for feminist movement
and unity. The multiculturalist model of inclusivity—and diversifi-
cation-by-*addition*, whereby categories of identity proliferate potentially indefinitely and as if in abstract equivalence with all other
categories, has been critiqued from various quarters. Butler contributes to this discussion a careful interior critique of the multiculturalist
paradigm, reading in the failure of this model for feminist politics
the potential for a new one:

> The theories of feminist identity that elaborate predicates of color,
> sexuality, ethnicity, class, and able-bodiedness invariably close with
> an embarrassed "etc." at the end of the list. Through this horizon-
> tal trajectory of adjectives, these positions strive to encompass a
> situated subject, but invariably fail to be complete. This failure, how-
> ever, is instructive: what political impetus is to be derived from the
> exasperated "etc." that so often occurs at the end of such lines?
> This is a sign of exhaustion as well of the illimitable process of sig-
> nification itself. It is the supplement, the excess that necessarily
> accompanies any effort to posit identity once and for all. This illim-
> itable et cetera, however, offers itself as a new departure for femi-
> nist political theorizing.[10]

Butler's "new departure" is self-consciously deconstructivist in its
conceptualization: signification grounds and proliferates difference,

the supplement—in this case the "illimitable et cetera"—exceeds attempts to generate positivist categories. Although I cannot elaborate here several, as-yet unsettled debates concerning the applicability of poststructuralist theory toward feminist ends, I wish to emphasize the specificity of the situation in which Butler theorizes the et cetera of feminist coalition politics.[11] This supplement, "the sign of exhaustion," enacts the illimitable play of signification within certain, circumscribed conditions of forced labor. That is, insofar as the et cetera can be said to provisionally designate "she" or "they" who are as yet unidentifiable according to the available categories—who are thus invisible, incognito, external and unknown to the governing representational system—the et cetera is enlisted to perform the hard work of coalition, to hold the place for any "other" body that coalition aspires to include, and to hold in place all the extant identificatory categories in the interim. The et cetera stands both for the principle of coherence and unity in coalition, which is deferred, and for the ongoing and anterior prospect or menace of incoherence and noncoalescence: in short, of difference.

The deconstructivist critic, to quote Barbara Johnson, begins to assume the impossible but necessary task of "set[ting] oneself up to be surprised by otherness," in part "by indulging in some judicious time-wasting with what one does not know how to use or what has fallen into disrepute."[12] Reading in the "embarrassed 'etc.'" an opening for otherness, other constructions of agency, and other projects, Butler takes feminist theories of identity precisely to this contradictory task. The political implications of this act of renunciation and resuscitation might emerge more clearly when read alongside Homi Bhabha's theorization of the contrast between cultural diversity (of which coalition politics might be one example) and cultural difference (perhaps analogous in operation to the work and play of Butler's "etc."):

> Cultural diversity is an epistemological object—culture as an object of empirical knowledge—whereas cultural difference is the process of the *enunciation* of culture as "knowledge*able*," authoritative, adequate to the construction of cultural identification. If cultural diversity is a category of comparative ethics, aesthetics or ethnology, cultural difference is a process of signification through which statements *of* culture or *on* culture differentiate, discriminate and authorize the production of fields of force, reference, applicability and

capacity. Cultural diversity is the recognition of pre-given cultural contents and customs; held in a time-frame of relativism it gives rise to liberal notions of multiculturalism, cultural exchange or the culture of humanity. Cultural diversity is also the representation of a radical rhetoric of the separation of totalized cultures that live unsullied by the intertextuality of their historical locations, safe in the Utopianism of a mythic memory of a unique collective identity.[13]

Counter to liberalism's well-intentioned but ineffectual moral polemics against racism and stereotypes, and counter to strategies of binary division and negation characteristic of standard theory/practice debates, Bhabha offers the enunciation of cultural difference and strategies of ambivalence and negotiation as means by which to address historical, material, and political process and specificity.[14] Invoking Frantz Fanon's famous representation of the time of national liberation—"the zone of occult instability where the people dwell"— as an example of negotiation in struggle, and as a present not bound in a binary division with a past, Bhabha construes temporality in terms of contestation within political and cultural theory: "The struggle is often between the historicist teleological or mythical time and narrative of traditionalism—of the right or the left—and the shifting, strategically displaced time of the articulation of a historical politics of negotiation."[15]

As the above excerpts from Bhabha and Butler would suggest, time itself, the location of the present in the production of past and future, varies both within and across polemical and discursive registers. The lack of consensus on the "before and after" relations designated by the post is perhaps symptomatic of this temporal-conceptual variance. Itself a subject or object of negotiation in struggle, the post can thus be read, not so as to determine "for all time" its bankruptcy or validity, but rather for its context-specific dis- and re-articulations of posterity and futurity in political and cultural discussion. Both Butler and Bhabha call attention to the heterogeneity of practices, commitments, and agents that can disappear in binarisms of theory and politics and in the presumed self-evidence or transparency of relations between past, present, and future.

Along these lines, I would like to comment on the representation of women and of feminism in the substance of Bhabha's argument and perhaps in (postmodern, postcolonial) theory more generally. Referring to the miners' strike in Britain of 1984–1985,

Bhabha attempts to restore the women miners to their rightful place in histories of industrial struggle too often narrated as composite stories of working-class men. Bhabha describes, as "startlingly different" from and "more complex" than the experiences of the male strikers, the process during which the women who participated in the strike came to question their positions within the family and the community: "two central institutions which articulated the meanings . . . of the *tradition* of the labouring classes around which ideological battle was enjoined."[16] Rejecting as "simplistic" attempts to explain the women's role in the struggle in the terms of either class politics or feminism, Bhabha perceives in these women's stories the multiple and discontinuous nature of political agency and an example of "the hybrid moment of political change."[17]

Feminists may have good reason to meet this representation of women's time and women's movement with a certain degree of skepticism. Male theorists of the postmodern and the postcolonial have often responded to the surprise of women's otherness in one of several ways: (1) by ignoring women and their historical agency altogether, in some instances by rendering them in time-worn and untimely traditional poses; (2) by momentarily disbanding or interrupting otherwise systematic and consistent analytical programs to "make room" for women, who appear in the resulting gaps as at times too singular, too heroic, too victimized, or too glamorous; and/or (3) by simply getting stuck on questions of the difference of women, and how their difference mediates and obstructs the relations under investigation between the global and the local, the general and the particular. (One could argue that, of these tendencies, the last has the comparative advantage of failing or refusing to represent, to domesticate, the alterity of women.)

Andreas Huyssen's groundbreaking essay, "Mapping the Postmodern"—the only male-authored piece, incidentally, to be included in Linda J. Nicholson's 1990 anthology, *Feminism/Postmodernism*—stresses the importance of feminist movements to the historical and cultural condition of postmodernity, particularly to what he defines as an oppositional postmodernism, or an emergent "postmodernism of resistance."[18] Yet despite his close attention to and demonstrated knowledge and admiration of second-wave Western feminism, Huyssen may be assigning it a subordinate status vis-à-vis an otherwise autonomous if exhausted artistic, political, and critical culture. A reader (admittedly, an unimaginative or an overly imaginative one) could be led to think that the task of renewal and rejuvenation has been the historical project of second-wave feminism, that women and feminism (of the first wave, for example) have had negligible or at any rate retroactive impact on modernism, and that women—and other "others"—do not significantly affect culture and politics on either side of the Atlantic until the 1960s and 1970s. What difference does gender make? Are women's movements to be seen in adjunct or corrective relation to the movements of Anglo-American and European men, "prior" both in time and in comparative importance? Or is gender a difference which emerges in historical process, reorganizing and reorganized by the specific terms and positions of struggle? To juxtapose Huyssen's and Bhabha's gestures toward women's alterity is not so much to contemplate a choice between options—to determine which might be "better" or "worse" for women in the transhistorical abstract—but to highlight practices of conceptualizing difference, of articulating heterogeneity and historical conflict, within theory.

That specific conceptualizations of difference evoke or entail specific conceptualizations of time can be seen in the temporal contradictions of two additional works: one ostensibly "for," the other "against," postcolonial theory. Linda Hutcheon—whose important work has included analyses of the intersections between postmodernism and postcolonialism, and reflections on the possibilities of a distinctively Canadian postmodernism/postcolonialism—has described temporal discontinuities among the "posts" in these terms:

> The current post-structuralist/postmodern challenges to the coherent, autonomous subject have to be put on hold in feminist and post-colonial discourses, for both must work first to assert and affirm a denied or alienated subjectivity: those radical postmodern challenges are in many ways the luxury of the dominant order which can afford to challenge that which it securely possesses.[19]

Disentangling postmodern, postcolonial, and feminist theories and histories, Hutcheon argues that certain poststructuralist and postmodernist declarations of the death of the subject, and of the obsolescence of Enlightenment humanism, are reminders of material inequalities and in many senses are premature. Yet this crucial apprehension of political and methodological difference is accomplished through a problematic trope of historical representation: that of suspended or arrested development, whereby women, minorities, the colonized, "et cetera" (in Butler's sense of the term)—who put someone else's itineraries for them "on hold," and "work first" toward securing for themselves the otherwise outmoded privileges of "modernist" subjectivity—are represented as the perennial children or teenagers of the world order.

A teleological model of historical progress thus makes its often habitual reappearance, and with it, an equation of "development" with technological and philosophical modernization. The post, despite Hutcheon's success in demonstrating the heterogeneity of its application, designates "anti-" and "after" within a temporal scheme in which the difference and specificity of political and cultural opposition and resistance must be measured against a single developmental standard. The implication is that to differ or to oppose, those excluded from or marginalized in dominant geopolitical and discursive formations may need nevertheless to hurry up, catch up, and grow up according to a unitary logic of historical progression.

The "post" in this way can attest to traditional temporal models' enduring power, even amidst efforts to challenge or supplant them. In contrast to Hutcheon, Anne McClintock argues that postcolonial theory actively cultivates close affinities with postmodernism and poststructuralism, and grafts a binary axis of power (between colonizer and colonized) onto a binary axis of time. Reading the post as the reified and reductive signal of a future which has not arrived—and postcolonialism as presuming the end or aftermath of colonialism—McClintock attacks the dominant, progressivist notion of time, in which history is identified with the itinerary of power and figured as a succession of finished moments.[20] Yet in the course of her critique of postcolonialism's false or prematurely declared victories—a critique which restricts its textual attention to the coauthored survey, *The Empire Writes Back*—McClintock manages, or so it would seem, to reinscribe precisely this teleological definition of history and its corresponding assumption of "homogeneous, empty time."[21]

The essay begins by mapping a concatenation of posts—one that includes the usual suspects, and also post-Marxism, post-Fordism, post–cold war, postfeminism, and "postcontemporary"—to which a unifying project is attributed as "a reluctance to surrender the privilege of seeing the world in terms of a singular and ahistorical abstraction."[22] It is against the monolithic abstraction of the post that the critic offers a powerful analysis of the geopolitical divisions created and exacerbated by third-world development policy, the Gulf War, and other issues and moments—banished, she argues, together with women and feminism from postcolonial literary and critical concerns. (The discrepancy between Hutcheon's perception of an alliance between feminism and postcolonialism and McClintock's notion of an imbalance of power and prestige may illuminate some of the risks and idiosyncrasies of relativist/counterrelativist arguments about or around the post. Feminism appears across such accounts as something of the odd theory, either in or out: a tendency which might be productively submitted to feminist critique.) According to McClintock, it is the post that effaces division, difference, and historical particularity, but additional differences are razed in the process of opposing this great leveler.

McClintock rehearses a familiar derogation of postcolonial theory when she comments on the "academic clout and professional marketability" of the post: "the term [postcolonialism] borrows . . . on the dazzling marketing success of the term 'post-modernism.'"[23] I would suggest that such observations, however accurate or persuasive, should serve as points of departure for further reflection. For "borrowed" authority is a complex and contradictory relationship of power. The pairings set up around the post—of poststructuralism/structuralism, postmodernism/modernism, and postcolonialism/colonialism—are not, to refer back to Hutcheon's argument, binary in one and the same way. Colonialism, for instance, fails to designate a historically developed body of knowledge or texts, so labeled, so defined, or so disseminated; rather, colonialist and colonizing literary and cultural traditions, canons, and institutions have become objects of study and critique largely by virtue of "postcolonial" theoretical intervention. The sheer range of anticolonialist strategies provisionally labeled as postcolonial or postcolonialist in current academic discourse would further tend to refute readings of the "post" as strictly synonymous with "after." By eliding the differential development of postcolonial, poststructuralist, postmodern, and feminist theoretical preoccupations, McClintock may reconceal the very multiplicity and unevenness of history to which her analysis is dedicated.

Is postcolonialism "prematurely celebratory," as McClintock contends?[24] If the post in postcolonial is indeed the same post that has modified modernism, structuralism, Marxism, and so forth, and if that post inflexibly and inexorably designates "after" or "beyond" in a uniform temporal scheme, one would have to answer in the affirmative. But postcolonialism may name a more complicated array of relations among colonialism, anticolonialism, decolonization, and neocolonialism—relations which, as Homi Bhabha suggests, enact forms of "shifting, strategically displaced time" that interrogate the assumptions of traditional historical narratives.[25] Given the very geopolitical and historical dislocations and discontinuities that McClintock describes, and the contradictions of institutional history that she largely ignores, the work of postcolonial theory may be at this stage too underdeveloped to be thrown onto the same rubbish heap with possibly more well-established academic post words. McClintock occupies her own negative, and negating, temporal concept of the post when she issues the call to get over and beyond it: the verdict on a prematurely celebratory postcolonialism may itself be premature, a premature postmortem on a field of inquiry that has yet to grow into, much less outlive, the times and places of its tentative articulation.

McClintock ends her essay by rendering Benjamin's Angel of History (now "the Angel of Progress") in a curiously static pose: "We face being becalmed in an historically empty space in which our sole direction is found by gazing back, spellbound, at the epoch behind us, in a perpetual present marked only as 'post.'"[26] Neglecting the dynamic negotiation of time and space in Benjamin's metaphor—the "state of emergency" and "moment of danger" between a past which continues catastrophically to accumulate before one's eyes and a future toward which one is irresistibly propelled, between the impulse to stay and the imperative to go—McClintock reinstates (and inexplicably attributes to Benjamin) the linear, progressivist concept of history and futurity that is the crux of her disagreement with postcolonialism.[27] The future cannot or should not be held up, she suggests, by the "backward" longings of the post in the present; and "the need for innovative theories of history" is to be answered elsewhere than in a present well-nigh colonized by the post, a present seen to stagnate in its mesmerism by the past.[28]

But just as the backward glance of Benjamin's Angel does not freeze the past, settle it as if for once and for all, the temporality of the post may be more complex, ambivalent, and multiple than the phrase "perpetual present" might imply. The Angel of History inhabits the present as an impermanent dislocation between past and future, and the only vantage from which history can be theorized, the ideology of progress resisted, and the future forecast. Then, now, later; forwardness, backwardness, stasis: these coordinates and relations shift as the wreckage of the past "grows skyward" before the Angel's eyes, and as the storm carries him ever farther from the debris. The Angel's eye view—of hindsight oriented toward a different future—could be thought that to which the post aspires: an aspiration which many would seem to have neither the time nor the patience to investigate. To conflate all posts into a single catastrophe of progress may be to assume the predicament of the Angel of History, only to abandon the project of historical materialist reflection that such a predicament demands.

I return in closing to a particularly slippery post word, slippery because it has tended to operate more in the breach than in the observance: "postfeminism." The reference to Sara Suleri with which this essay began suggests the term's predominantly derisive application: as a label by which one can abject some nebulous, dubious kind of feminism from the vicinity of one's own critical and political concerns.[29] "Post" in this polemical context refers to the perception, conferral, and denial of legitimacy in a present moment of struggle and negotiation, of history-in-the-making. Given differences among the posts, and the persistence of the temporal and developmental paradigms with which posts both clash and comply, to be a multi-postal feminist, but not necessarily a postfeminist, may be to assume one kind of ambivalent position amidst the contradictory exigencies of the here and now. I would suggest that it might be about time that feminists began to historicize and make critical distinctions between the "posts."

To continue to oppose theory with politics, or to regard one's task as beginning and ending with programmatic forms of etymological purism, may be to discard, yet again, that already and categorically excluded from dominant epistemological and political models: the unknown, the uncertain, the unrepresented, the different. As Gillian Rose has argued, in one of her own, highly particularized interventions into a "freighted and fraught agglomeration of terms":

> [P]olitics does not happen when you act on behalf of your own dam-
> aged good, but when you act, *without guarantees*, for the good of
> all—this is to take *the risk* of the *universal* interest. Politics in this
> sense requires representation, the critique of representation, and
> the critique of the critique of representation.[30]

A feminism which continually rethinks, rather than presumes, its central terms, claims, allies, and resources acknowledges and takes up
the *risk* of acting and theorizing on behalf of "all women": a constituency which history shows cannot be mastered in advance. Perhaps arrested development and prematurity can suggest for feminists
modes of anticipating and mobilizing toward a future over which we
can nevertheless claim no prior understanding or sovereign control.
Perhaps, for now, we need not consider our time injudiciously wasted
if we have yet to move past the post.

NOTES

I would like to express my appreciation to participants of the IRW toward 2000 seminar
and discussion series for their thoughtful responses to an earlier version of this paper,
presented on February 14, 1996; and especially to Marianne DeKoven, Sandra Gun-
ning, and Brian Rourke for their detailed comments and encouragement.

1. Sara Suleri, "Woman Skin Deep: Feminism and the Postcolonial Condition," *Critical Inquiry* 18 (1992): 756–769; rpt. in *Colonial Discourse and Post-Colonial Theory: A Reader,*
ed. Patrick Williams and Laura Chrisman (New York: Columbia University Press, 1994),
244–256, 248.

2. Throughout this chapter, I refrain from hyphenating the term *post* when it appears in my
own prose as a noun and/or nounless qualifier. This device, employed for the sake of
consistency, serves both to occlude and to emphasize the inconsistency and instability of
the "post-signifier," and cannot and is not intended to foreclose several important debates regarding the semantic, symbolic and polemical operations of the hyphen, its
absence, or its implicit intervention between otherwise typographically unmediated terms
in critical discussion. For a reading of the difference hyphens can make in post(-)colonial
textual and theoretical investigation, see Vijay Mishra and Bob Hodge, "What Is Post(-)
Colonialism?" *Textual Practice* 5:3 (1991): 399–414; rpt. in Williams and Chrisman,
Colonial Discourse and Post-Colonial Theory, 276–290. For relevant discussions in another context, see David Leiwei Li's argument for the historical emergence of an emphatically unhyphenated "Asian America(n)" in *Imagining the Nation: Asian American
Literature and Cultural Consent* (Stanford, Calif.: Stanford University Press, 1998), 6–8;
and Trinh T. Minh-ha's articulation of "the challenge of the hyphenated reality . . . : the
becoming Asian-American," in *When the Moon Waxes Red: Representation, Gender and
Cultural Politics* (London: Routledge, 1991), 157.

3. Suleri, "Woman Skin Deep: Feminism and the Postcolonial Condition," 247–248. Exactly
why race and gender cannot be historicized and thought together is a question the critic
seems herself to defer onto "the inevitable territory of postfeminism," conjured out of
perceived contentions among feminist and postcolonial theoretical "pietisms" (247). Speculations regarding individual authorial "desire," "obsessive attention," and "will to subjectivity" serve, I think, to weaken Suleri's arguments against Trinh and also Chandra Talpade
Mohanty and bell hooks, and to render "postfeminism" principally a term of abuse.

4. Suleri, "Woman Skin Deep: Feminism and the Postcolonial Condition," 248.

5. "Going Postal," *The Nation*, January 23, 1996, 3.

6. "Going Postal."

7. "Going Postal."
8. Homi K. Bhabha, *The Location of Culture* (London: Routledge, 1994), 18; Anne McClintock, "The Angel of Progress: Pitfalls of the Term 'Post-Colonialism,'" *Social Text* (spring 1992): 1–15; rpt. in Williams and Chrisman, *Colonial Discourse and Post-Colonial Theory*, 291–304, 292.
9. Judith Butler, *Gender Trouble: Feminism and the Subversion of Identity* (London: Routledge, 1990), 14.
10. Butler, *Gender Trouble*, 143.
11. I have attempted elsewhere to demonstrate that the "poststructuralist controversy" in feminism—for instance, as regards the opposition between "real world" and "text," materiality and textuality—can itself productively ground and initiate feminist inquiry ("Run through the Borders: Feminism, Postmodernism, and Runaway Subjectivity," in *Border Theory: The Limits of Cultural Politics*, ed. Scott Michaelsen and David E. Johnson [Minneapolis: University of Minnesota Press, 1997], 169–194). The extent to which such controversy remains topical for feminist analysis and activism has been suggested by Martha C. Nussbaum's indictment of Judith Butler in the *New Republic*, and the rejoinders by feminist critics such as Gayatri Chakravorty Spivak, Nancy Fraser, and Joan W. Scott. See Martha C. Nussbaum, "The Professor of Parody: The Hip Defeatism of Judith Butler," *New Republic*, February 23, 1999, 37–45; and "Martha C. Nussbaum and Her Critics: An Exchange," *New Republic*, April 19, 1999, 43–44.
12. Barbara Johnson, *A World of Difference* (Baltimore: Johns Hopkins University Press, 1987), 15, 16.
13. Bhabha, *The Location of Culture*, 34.
14. The theoretical enterprise, according to Bhabha, distinguishes its *politics* from that posited or presumed by traditional and current forms of ethical and ideological critique, in part via an alternative conception of "the true": "The 'true' is always marked and informed by the ambivalence of the process of emergence itself, the productivity of meanings that construct counter-knowledges *in medias res*, in the very act of agonism, within the terms of a negotiation (rather than a negation) of oppositional and antagonistic elements. Political positions are not simply identifiable as progressive or reactionary, bourgeois or radical, prior to the act of *critique engagée*, or outside the terms and conditions of their discursive address" (22).
15. Bhabha, *The Location of Culture*, 35.
16. Bhabha, 27.
17. Bhabha, 27, 28; Andreas Huyssen, *After the Great Divide: Modernism, Mass Culture, Postmodernism* (Bloomington: University of Indiana Press, 1986), 178–221; Linda J. Nicholson, ed., *Feminism/Postmodernism* (London: Routledge, 1990).
18. Huyssen, *After the Great Divide*, 219–220. Very abbreviated reference to feminism is made toward the essay's conclusion, as one of "four recent phenomena" (219) demanding reevaluation of tired "aesthetics vs. politics" approaches to questions of modernity and postmodernity.
19. Linda Hutcheon, "Circling the Downspout of Empire: Post-Colonialism and Postmodernism," *Ariel* 20 (October 1989): 151; quoted in Mishra and Hodge, "What Is Post(-)Colonialism?" 281.
20. Hutcheon has articulated the broader, "emblematic" significance of this temporal interpretation of the post in "Colonialism and the Postcolonial Condition: Complexities Abounding," *PMLA* 110 (1995): 10.
21. Bill Ashcroft, Gareth Griffiths, and Helen Tiffin, *The Empire Writes Back: Theory and Practice in Post-Colonial Literatures* (London: Routledge, 1989).
22. McClintock, "The Angel of Progress: Pitfalls of the Term 'Post-Colonialism,'" 293.
23. McClintock, "The Angel of Progress: Pitfalls of the Term 'Post-Colonialism,'" 293, 299. For a similar criticism, albeit one offered from a vastly different political-institutional perspective, see Ihab Hassan, "Queries for Postcolonial Studies," *Philosophy and Literature* 22:2 (1998): 328–342.
24. McClintock, "The Angel of Progress: Pitfalls of the Term 'Post-Colonialism,'" 294.
25. For possibly the definitive argument for the primarily relational significance of the post in postmodernism, see Huyssen, *After the Great Divide*, esp. 207.
26. McClintock, "The Angel of Progress: Pitfalls of the Term 'Post-Colonialism,'" 303.
27. Walter Benjamin, "Theses on the Philosophy of History," *Illuminations*, trans. Harry Zohn (New York: Schocken, 1969), 253–267.

28. McClintock, "The Angel of Progress: Pitfalls of the Term 'Post-Colonialism,'" 302.

29. Ann Brookes's *Postfeminisms: Feminism, Cultural Theory and Cultural Forms* (London: Routledge, 1997) is a noteworthy exception to this tendency.

30. Gillian Rose, *Mourning Becomes the Law* (Cambridge, U.K.: Cambridge University Press, 1996), 62.

KAREN BARAD

RE(CON)FIGURING SPACE, TIME, AND MATTER

During a transatlantic flight from New York to London, at a cruising altitude of 35,000 feet, a communications link between an Intel-based notebook computer, perched on a tray in front of the passenger in seat 3A of the Boeing 747, and a SUN workstation on the twentieth floor in a Merrill Lynch brokerage house in Sydney, initiates the transfer of investment capital from a Swiss bank account to a corporate venture involving a Zhejiang textile mill. The event produces an ambiguity of scale that defies geometrical analysis. Proximity and location become ineffective measures of spatiality. Distance loses its objectivity—its edge—to pressing questions of boundary and connectivity. Geometry gives way to changing topologies as the transfer of a specific pattern of 0s and 1s, represented as so many pixels on a screen, induces the flow of capital and a consequent change in the material conditions of the Zhejiang mill and surrounding community. With the click of a mouse, space, time, and matter are mutually reconfigured in this cyborg "trans-action" that violates the boundaries between human and machine, nature and culture, and economic and discursive practices.[1]

The view from somewhere, social location, positionality, standpoint, embodiment, contextuality, intersectionality, local knowledges, and global capital are notions that line many a feminist toolbox for good reasons. And yet, however thoughtfully modified, whatever caveats are offered to mitigate the limitations of these metaphors, these effective and useful tools are constrained by a Euclidean geometric imaginary.[2] The view of space as container/context for matter in motion—spatial coordinates mapped via projections along axes that set up a metric for tracking the locations of the inhabitants of the container, and time divided up in evenly spaced increments marking a progression of events—pervades much of Western epistemology. As the geographer Edward Soja points out,

> From the materialist perspective, whether mechanistic or dialectical, time and space in the general or abstract sense represent the objective form of matter. Time, space, and matter are inextricably connected, with the nature of this relationship being a central theme in the history of the philosophy of science. This essentially physical view of space has deeply influenced all forms of spatial analysis, whether philosophical, theoretical or empirical, whether applied to the movement of heavenly bodies or to the history and landscape of human society. It has also tended to imbue all things spatial with a lingering sense of primordiality and physical composition, an aura of objectivity, inevitability, and reification.[3]

Following Ruth Wilson Gilmore's suggestion that we replace the "politics of location" with a "politics of possibilities," in this chapter I aim to dislocate the Euclidean geometric frame of reference by reconceptualizing the notions of space, time, and matter using an alternative framework that shakes loose the foundational character of notions such as location and opens up a space in which indeterminacies, contingencies, and ambiguities coexist with causality.[4] The space of possibilities that is freed up using this nondeterministic notion of causality, and a postobjectivist notion of objectivity, allows for normative analyses crucial to critical political practices.[5]

"Agential realism" is an epistemological and ontological framework that cuts across many of the well-worn oppositions that circulate in traditional realism versus constructivism, agency versus structure, idealism versus materialism, and poststructuralism versus Marxism debates.[6] In its reformulation of agency and its analysis of the productive, constraining, and exclusionary nature of practices (including their crucial role in the materialization of the body), agential realism goes beyond performativity theories by providing a framework for taking account of the discursive and material nature of social practices.[7] For example, it provides a way to incorporate material constraints and conditions and the material dimensions of agency into poststructuralist analyses. In this important sense it diverges from feminist postmodern and poststructuralist theories that acknowledge materiality solely as an effect or consequence of discursive practices. Lacking an account of materiality as an active and productive factor in its own right, these theories reinscribe the active-culture/passive-nature dichotomy. Additionally, they leave untheorized a host of pressing questions: What is meant by the claim that discourses have material consequences? What is the relationship between discourse and materiality such that discourse can work its effects? Is there any sense in which materiality might be said to constrain discourses? If so, how? Do material reconfigurations have discursive consequences? What is it about our current material and discursive conditions that questions concerning the material consequences of discourses and the discursive consequences of materiality seem to preclude one another? This is not to say that such theories do not provide crucial philosophical and political insights. However, they prove inadequate in the face of one of the litmus tests of viable critical social theories: "to *explain* the relation between economic forces—like the formation of new markets through colonization, shifting centers of production, or the development of new technologies—and the reformation of subjectivities."[8]

Leela Fernandes's work makes significant inroads in this regard, advancing our understanding of social reality in her theorization of the relationship between structural and discursive forces. For Fernandes, as well as for other feminist theorists, like Rosemary Hennessy and Ruth Wilson Gilmore, poststructuralism is emphatically not an antidote to Marxism, but rather is usefully appropriated as a corrective elaboration of orthodox forms of structural analysis. As such, understanding class as a dynamic variable with integral cultural, ideological, and discursive dimensions does not diminish, but indeed is necessary, to a thorough-going analysis of economic capital in its materiality. Likewise, it is important to recognize the material dimensions of cultural economies.

In this chapter, I work Fernandes's notion of the "structural-discursive" relations of power and an agential realist understanding of "material-discursive" relations of power through one another, thus providing a deeper understanding of the nature of structures and of

materiality and their relationship to discourses, and a new understanding of the dynamics of power relations. It will also suggest a need
for remilling some of our most important feminist tools.

PRODUCING WORKERS/PRODUCING STRUCTURES: THE SHOP FLOOR AS A MATERIAL-DISCURSIVE APPARATUS OF BODILY PRODUCTION

> The 'structural' dimension of class can be thought of as the
> ways in which workers are positioned on the factory floor,
> through recruitment practices and a particular division of la-
> bor. This positioning of workers is contingent on the politics
> of gender and community, since such identities are instru-
> mental in decisions regarding the positioning of workers; thus,
> gender and community are integral to the class 'structure.'
> Meanwhile, the gendering of space signifies particular kinds
> of class hierarchies between workers and managers and be-
> tween male and female workers.
> —Leela Fernandes, *Producing Workers*

Issues of political economy and cultural identity are inseparable.
Leela Fernandes's analysis of the structural and ideological workings
of power in a Calcutta jute mill gives strong empirical support for
this claim. In her groundbreaking book, *Producing Workers*, Fernandes
employs analytical tools from poststructuralist and Marxist schools
of thought, meshing and shifting the gears of these heavy machin-
eries, to obtain an understanding of the multiple technologies
through which the working class is produced. Disassembling the long-
standing assumption in research on labor that "class structure is a
uniform, objective 'purity' while other forms of social identity such
as gender, religion, and ethnicity are symbolic or ideological forces
that either divide or intersect with class identity" (59), Fernandes exposes the manifold connections and detailed inter-(re)workings of
identity categories through an examination of shop-floor dynamics
as they unfold in the course of the everyday life of the workers. Ongoing contests over space, time, and movement in the life of the factory are analyzed in terms of the iterative production of its spatiality,
and the shiftings of the differential material constraints on the movement of different socially positioned personnel are read in terms of
the dynamics of structural relations. For example, Fernandes analyzes
the structural dimensions of class in terms of the differential positioning of workers on the factory floor through gendered recruitment

practices and gendered divisions of labor. She uses this examination of the gendering of space to argue that "gender and community are integral to class 'structure'" (59). That is, class itself needs to be understood as "a product of dynamic and contested political processes at the local level of shop-floor politics" (58).

It is important not to mistake this claim as a demotion of class to the realm of the merely ideological-cultural-discursive. A potential misunderstanding of this nature rests on at least two false assumptions which Fernandes calls into question: (1) that economic categories alone are material, and social categories are not; and (2) that identity categories such as class, gender, nationality, caste, and religion are separable and that an understanding of social dynamics is a matter of knowing how they interact or intersect. For Fernandes, class is about economic capital, and at the same time the economic is not merely about class (i.e., the working class is discursively and structurally produced through class, gender, and community). Her shift from a traditional conception of class that assumes that capitalist production is experienced the same by all workers all over the world to an understanding of class structures as dynamic and local products goes hand in hand with her insistence that "gender represents a structural force and is not limited to a discursive or symbolic category" (11–12). The gears of the capitalist machinery—which must be understood as different local and contested forms of the global political economy—are simultaneously materially and discursively produced. Fernandes rejects assembly line notions of identities as analytically identical and interchangeable parts, and she eschews the notion that identities work in lockstep as parallel gears in a single assemblage. The dynamics, as Fernandes describes it, is perhaps more akin to a differential gear assemblage in which the gear operations literally work through one another and yet the uneven distribution of forces results in and is the enabling condition for different potentials and performances among the gears.

Fernandes appropriates and extends Foucault's analysis of the important productive effects of disciplinary regimes of power that "partitions as closely as possible time, space, and movement."[9] She argues that "structures" should be understood "as the codification of power through movement, space, and position" (175) and that "the system of codification that controls time, disciplines movement and partitions space codes workers' bodies through meanings of gender, caste, and ethnicity. If, as Foucault asserts, 'discipline organizes an analytical space' (1979 [*sic*], 143), such techniques of power are in effect employed in the task of producing particular analytical and material borders between class, gender, and community."[10]

I read Fernandes as saying that while disciplinary regimes of power operate through the production of individual subjects this mode of operation destabilizes, reconfigures, and stabilizes new structural relations of power in reconfiguring the material borders between class, gender, and community that mark these very bodies in their materializing subjectivities. In contrast to those who would interpret Foucault's microphysics of power as a refutation of the importance, indeed the very existence of structural relations, Fernandes takes Foucault's formulation as an opportunity to rethink the structural dynamics of power. According to Fernandes, "structure does not represent a set of transcendental, objective determinants but is shaped by modes of representation and meanings that social actors . . . give to their positions and activities."[11] In other words, structures are not only productive, they are themselves produced.

How is such a claim to be understood? In what sense are structures produced? What is the nature of the processes which "shape" structures? What is the relationship between the material and discursive dimensions of power? How are we to understand the nature of power dynamics? of materiality? These are some of the questions that I want to explore in reading Fernandes's powerful insights concerning the structural-discursive relations of power and agential realism through one another.

I begin by outlining the framework of agential realism in the next two sections. I propose that the shop floor be understood in agential realist terms as a "material-discursive apparatus of bodily production"—an instrument of power through which particular meanings and bodies and material-discursive boundaries are produced.[12] I then turn to the agential realist understanding of apparatuses as being themselves produced and reworked through a dynamics of "iterative intra-activity" and "enfolding." This dynamics entails a rethinking of the nature of causality and the role of exclusions in creating the conditions for the possibility of contesting and remaking apparatuses themselves. Furthermore, I will argue that this dynamics requires a rethinking of the nature of space, time, and matter, and agency. Agency—rather than being thought in opposition to structures as forms of subjective intentionality and the potential for individual action—is about changing topologies, about reconfiguring the structural relations of power, about the possibilities and accountability entailed in reconfiguring material-discursive apparatuses of bodily production, including the boundary articulations and exclusions that are marked by those practices. Agential realist analyses insist on the examination of the production of and the very nature of the materiality of nonhuman beings alongside their human counterparts as well as the processes by which these distinctions are produced. It also brings to the fore consideration of the possibilities of nonhuman and cyborgian forms of agency.

MACHINE LABOR: TOWARD A POLITICAL ECONOMY OF APPARATUSES OR HOW APPARATUSES WORK

How do machines work? What is their relationship to humans? What do they produce and how are they themselves produced?

The historian of science Norton Wise claims that machines mediate societal values in the production of knowledge. He argues, for example, that the steam engine "simultaneously instantiates 'labor value' in political economy and 'work' in engineering mechanics, thereby identifying the two concepts in the region of their common reference." This "partial identification," he claims, "carries with it a structural analogy between a network of concepts from political economy and a similar network in natural philosophy, providing a potent heuristic for the reformulation and further development of dynamics."[13] By way of example, Wise begins by pointing to the fact that in 1845, prior to the development of his work-centered perspective on dynamics (1845–1862), William Thomson (Lord Kelvin) began to "regard the idea of natural agency—electric, magnetic, thermal, etc.—as an expression of the capacity to produce work, and thus to regard natural systems as engines."[14]

The productive role of apparatuses in linking issues of social and cultural values, political economy, and human and nonhuman forms of agency is one of the central themes of this chapter. However, the analysis offered here rejects the notion that machines and apparatuses more generally play a mediating role. Indeed, the proposed shift in understanding can be viewed in terms of a corresponding shift in the epistemological economy of natural philosophy. William Thomson

and his contemporary Karl Marx were both immersed in an equilib-
rium heatbath in which Newtonian conceptions of the notions of
forces and causality were part of the cultural background. However,
approximately half a century later the Newtonian worldview would
start to dissipate. Ultimately, a phase transition, a discontinuous
change of rule, would occur in the world of physics: Newtonian mechanics would find a successor in quantum mechanics.[15] A key contributor to this scientific revolution was physicist Niels Bohr. Bohr
brings to light a very different understanding of the nature of forces
and causality. And I will argue here that this important shift leads to
a very different understanding of the notion of dynamics and the role
of apparatuses.

I begin with a presentation of Bohr's analysis of the epistemological significance of measuring apparauses.[16] Bohr's careful analysis of the process of observation led him to conclude that two implicit
assumptions needed to support the Newtonian framework, and its
notion of the transparency of observations, were flawed: (1) the assumption that observation-independent objects have well-defined
intrinsic properties that are representable as abstract universal concepts, and (2) the assumption that the measurement interactions between the objects and the agencies of observation are continuous and
determinable, ensuring that the values of the properties obtained reflect those of the observation-independent objects, as separate from
the agencies of observation. In contrast to these Newtonian assumptions, Bohr argued that *theoretical concepts are defined by the circumstances required for their measurement.* It follows from this fact, and the
fact that there is an empirically verifiable discontinuity in measurement interactions, that there is no unambiguous way to differenti-
ate between the "object" and the "agencies of observation." As no
inherent cut exists between "object" and "agencies of observation,"
measured values cannot be attributed to observation-independent
objects. In fact, he concluded that observation-independent objects
do not possess well-defined inherent properties.[17]

Bohr constructs his post-Newtonian framework on the basis of
quantum wholeness, the lack of an inherent distinction between the
"object" and the "agencies of observation." He uses the term *phenomenon,* in a very specific sense, to designate particular instances of
wholeness: "While, within the scope of classical physics, the interaction between object and apparatus can be neglected or, if necessary,

compensated for, in quantum physics *this interaction thus forms an inseparable part of the phenomenon*. Accordingly, the unambiguous account of proper quantum phenomena must, in principle, include a description of all relevant features of the experimental arrangement" (emphasis mine).[18]

Bohr's insight concerning the intertwining of the conceptual and physical dimensions of measurement processes is central to his epistemological framework. The physical apparatus marks the conceptual subject-object distinction: the physical and conceptual apparatuses form a nondualistic whole. That is, descriptive concepts obtain their meaning by reference to a particular physical apparatus which in turn marks the placement of a constructed cut between the "object" and the "agencies of observation." For example, instruments with fixed parts are required to understand what we might mean by the concept "position." However, any such apparatus necessarily excludes other concepts, such as "momentum," from having meaning during this set of measurements, since these other variables require an instrument with movable parts for their definition. Physical and conceptual constraints and exclusions are co-constitutive.

Since there is no inherent cut delineating the "object" from the "agencies of observation" the following question emerges: What sense, if any, should we attribute to the notion of observation? Bohr suggests that "by an experiment we simply understand an event about which we are able in an unambiguous way to state the conditions necessary for the reproduction of the phenomena."[19] This is possible on the condition that the experimenter introduces a constructed cut between an "object" and the "agencies of observation."[20] That is, in contrast to the Newtonian worldview, Bohr argues that no inherent distinction preexists the measurement process, that every measurement involves a particular choice of apparatus, providing the conditions necessary to give definition to a particular set of classical variables, at the exclusion of other equally essential variables, and thereby embodying a particular constructed cut delineating the "object" from the "agencies of observation." This particular constructed cut resolves the ambiguities only for a given context; it marks off and is part of a particular instance of wholeness (i.e., the phenomenon).[21]

Especially in his later writings, Bohr insists that quantum mechanical measurements are "objective." Since he also emphasizes the inseparability of objects and agencies of observation, he cannot possibly mean by "objective" that measurements reveal inherent properties of independent objects. But Bohr does not reject objectivity out of hand, he simply reformulates it. For Bohr, objectivity is a matter of "permanent marks—such as a spot on a photographic plate, caused by the impact of an electron—left on the bodies which define the experimental conditions."[22] Objectivity is defined in reference to bodies and, as we have seen, reference must be made to bodies in order for concepts to have meaning. Clearly, Bohr's notion of objectivity, which is not predicated on an inherent distinction between objects and agencies of observation, stands in stark contrast to a Newtonian sense of objectivity denoting observer independence.

The question remains: What is the referent of any particular objective property? Since there is no inherent distinction between object and apparatus, the property in question cannot be meaningfully attributed to either an abstracted object or an abstracted measuring instrument. That is, the measured quantities in a given experiment are not values of properties which belong to an observation-independent object, nor are they purely artifactual values created by the act of measurement (which would belie any sensible meaning of the word *measurement*). My reading is that the measured properties refer to phenomena, remembering that phenomena are physical-conceptual "intra-actions" whose unambiguous account requires "a description of all relevant features of the experimental arrangement." I use intra-actions to signify *the inseparability of "objects" and "agencies of observation"* (rather than "interactions" which reinscribes the contested dichotomy).

While Newtonian physics is well known for its strict determinism, its widely acclaimed ability to predict and retrodict the full set of physical states of a system for all times, based upon the simultaneous specification of two particular variables at any one instant of time, Bohr's general epistemological framework proposes a radical revision of such an understanding of causality.[23] He explains that the inseparability of the object from the apparatus "entails ... the necessity of a final renunciation of the classical ideal of causality and a radical revision of our attitude towards the problem of physical reality."[24] While claiming that his analysis forces him to issue a final renunciation of the classical ideal of causality, that is, of strict determinism, Bohr does not presume that this entails overarching disorder, lawlessness, or an outright rejection of the cause and effect relationship. Rather, he suggests that our understanding of the terms of that relationship must be reworked: "The feeling of volition and the demand for causality are equally indispensable elements in the relation between subject and object which forms the core of the problem of knowledge."[25] In short, he rejects both poles of the usual dualist thinking about causality—freedom and determinism—and proposes a third possibility.

Bohr's epistemological framework deviates in an important fashion from classical correspondence or mirroring theories of science. For example, consider the wave-particle duality paradox originating from early twentieth-century observations conducted by experimenters who reported seemingly contradictory evidence about the nature of light: under certain experimental circumstances light manifests particle-like properties and under an experimentally incompatible set of circumstances light manifests wave-like properties. This situation is paradoxical to the classical realist mindset because the true ontological nature of light is in question: Either light is a wave or it is particle, it can't be both. Bohr resolved the wave-particle duality paradox as follows: wave and particle are classical descriptive concepts that refer to different mutually exclusive phenomena, and not to independent physical objects. He emphasized that this saved quantum theory from inconsistencies because it was impossible to observe particle and wave behaviors simultaneously since mutually exclusive experimental arrangements are required. To put the point in a more modern context, according to Bohr's general epistemological framework referentiality must be reconceptualized: the referent is not an observation-independent object, but a phenomenon. This shift in referentiality is a condition for the possibility of objective knowledge. That is, a condition for objective knowledge is that the referent is a phenomenon (and not an observation-independent object).

AGENTIAL REALISM: PRODUCING APPARATUSES OF BODILY PRODUCTION

Apparatuses, in Bohr's sense, are not passive observing instruments. On the contrary, they are productive of (and part of) phenomena. However, Bohr does not give a complete account of apparatuses. He does insist that what constitutes an apparatus emerges within specific observational practices. But while focusing on the lack of an inherent distinction between the apparatus and the object, Bohr doesn't directly address the question of where the apparatus ends. Is the outside boundary of the apparatus coincident with the visual terminus of the instrumentation? What if an infrared interface (i.e., a wireless connection) exists between the measuring instrument and a computer that collects the data? Does the apparatus include the computer? the scientist performing the experiment? the scientific community that judges the value of the research and decides upon its funding? What precisely constitutes the limits of the apparatus that gives meaning to certain concepts at the exclusion of others?

A central focus in Bohr's discussion of objectivity is the possibility of "unambiguous communication" which can only take place in reference to "bodies which define the experimental conditions" and which embody particular concepts, to the exclusion of others. This seems to indicate Bohr's recognition of the social nature of scientific practices: making meanings involves the interrelationship of complex discursive and material practices. What is needed is an articulation of the notion of apparatuses—beyond that of merely observation instruments—that acknowledges this complexity.

In "Getting Real" I further elaborate upon the notion of material-discursive apparatuses by reading Bohr's insights through those of Michel Foucault and Judith Butler.[26] In particular, I combine Bohr's notion of apparatuses as physical-conceptual devices that are productive of (and part of) phenomena with Foucault's post-Althusserian notion of apparatuses as technologies of subjectivation through which power acts, and with Butler's theory of gender performativity which links subject formation as an iterative and contingent process to the materialization of sexed bodies. I argue that the fact that Foucault and Butler leave the materiality of nonhuman beings untheorized ultimately contributes to an imbalance in the accounting of material and discursive, and spatial and temporal, factors in their respective works.[27] For example, in *Discipline and Punish* Foucault insists that the specific material arrangement of the prison sustains particular discourses and is the basis for its efficacy as an instrument of power (30). However, while Foucault interrogates the processes which shape the human body, he does not examine the nature of the materiality of the *prison* nor does he theorize the sense in which materiality provides a "support" for discourses. In her work *Bodies That Matter,* Judith Butler insists on the temporality of the matter of human bodies but her theory of performativity focuses exclusively on the discursive/ citational nature of the iterative process of materialization, and she leaves unexamined the material dimensions of regulatory practices, including the productive and enabling aspects of *material* constraints and exclusions and the *material* dimensions of agency. Indeed, it is far from obvious how to take account of material constraints and exclusions and other "active" dimensions of matter, if materiality itself is theorized as a "dissimulated effect of power." However, the power of refiguring materiality as materialization is diluted if we limit its role to be simply an effect of the reiterative power of discourses or a mere support for discursive practices. In a related fashion, her focus is on the temporality of the process of materialization, and she ignores its spatiality. In contrast, the search for an adequate understanding of the relationship between the material and the discursive will here entail a reconceptualization of space, time, and matter, and, indeed, of the very nature of reality itself.

Taking a cue from Bohr I suggest that *phenomena constitute "agential reality."* It is important to note that the elaboration and extension of Bohr's analysis from observation instruments as physical-conceptual devices to the notion of material-discursive apparatuses requires that the notion of phenomena be reevaluated as well. According to the framework of "agential realism," *phenomena are produced through complex intra-actions of multiple material-discursive apparatuses of bodily production, where apparatuses are not mere observing instruments, but rather are specific interventions/practices involving humans and nonhumans.* (Indeed, such practices are implicated in differentially demarcating the "human" from the "nonhuman.") Agential reality is not a fixed ontology that is independent of epistemic practices; rather it is sedimented out of the process of making the world intelligible through certain practices and not others. Agential reality is continually reconstituted through our material-discursive intra-actions. Therefore, we are not only responsible for the knowledge that we seek, but in part, for what exists. Shifting our understanding of the ontologically real from that "which stands outside the sphere of cultural influence and historical change" to agential reality allows a new formulation of realism (and truth) that is not premised on the representational nature of knowledge.[28] Agential realism offers the possibility of providing accurate descriptions of agential reality—that reality within which we intra-act and have our being. Not all practices are equally efficacious partners in the production of phenomena, that is, in the iterative processes of materialization (simply saying something is so will not cause its materialization); and explanations of various phenomena and events that do not take account of material, as well as discursive, constraints will fail to provide empirically adequate accounts (not any story will do).

Matter is not little bits of Nature, or a blank slate, surface, or site passively awaiting signification, nor is it an uncontested ground for scientific, feminist, or Marxist theories. Neither is it simply "a kind of citationality," nor a support for discourses which are the ultimate delimiting factors in the shaping of human bodies.[29] According to agential realism, *matter is a stabilizing and destabilizing process of iterative intra-activity.* Matter refers to the materiality/materialization of phenomena, not to some assumed inherent fixed property of the abstracted objects of Newtonian physics; material constraints and exclusions and the material dimensions of regulatory practices are important factors in the process of materialization.

Advocates of empiricism and many of its challengers share in the presupposition of a Newtonian conception of matter: the point of contention between them is generally framed in terms of whether or not one takes the mediation of matter by language, the social, power, or other intermediaries to be benign or not; but the underlying ontology is generally not questioned. In contrast, according to agential realism, it is not necessary (or correct) to secure matter as a fixed substance with inherent properties in order to take into account how matter comes to matter. On the contrary, to attempt to reinstate materiality as natural—as simple brute positivity—is to assign materiality to the realm of nonbeing, to a space outside of the real (i.e., it misses the objective referent). Within the framework of agential realism, reference to the material constraints and exclusions and the material dimensions of power is both imperative and possible without naturalizing matter because materiality refers to the objective referent—to agential reality—which is explicitly not nature-outside-of-culture.

In contrast to Foucault and Butler's more singular focus on the materialization of human bodies, the framework of agential realism calls for a critical examination of the very practices by which the differential boundaries of the human and the nonhuman are drawn, for these very same practices are always already implicated in particular materializations. If matter as a process of materialization can be retheorized beyond the realm of the human, then it becomes possible to provide a richer, more complete, and more complex understanding of the nature of regulatory (power/knowledge) practices and their participatory role in the production of bodies. To put it bluntly, if not crudely, the material dimension of regulatory apparatuses, which is indissociable from its discursive dimension, is to be understood in terms of the materiality of phenomena.[30] Apparatuses have a physical presence or an ontological there-ness as phenomena in the process of becoming; there is no fixed metaphysical outside. This framework provides a way to understand both the temporality and spatiality of regulatory practices and their effectiveness (and lack thereof) in intra-actively producing particular bodies (human and nonhuman) that also have a physical presence. In essence, agential realism theorizes the material dimension of regulatory apparatuses in terms of the materiality of phenomena; it thereby provides an account of regulatory practices and their causal (but nondeterministic) materializing effects in the intra-active production of material-discursive bodies. Hence, materialization is not only a matter of how discourse comes to matter but *how matter comes to matter.* Or to put it more precisely, *materialization is an (open but nonarbitrary) iteratively intra-active process whereby material-discursive bodies are sedimented out of the intra-action of multiple material-discursive apparatuses through which these phenomena (bodies) become intelligible.*

Key to this understanding of the nature of the material dimension of regulatory practices is the fact that *apparatuses are themselves phenomena.* Indeed, they are made up of specific intra-actions of humans and nonhumans (where the differential constitutions human and nonhuman designate particular phenomena which are enfolded and reworked in the shifting of apparatuses and the reconstitution of boundaries), and what gets defined as subject and object and what gets defined as an apparatus is intra-actively constituted within specific practices. In other words, apparatuses are not preexisting or fixed entities; they are themselves constituted through particular practices that are perpetually open to rearrangements, rearticulations, and other reworkings. Furthermore, any particular apparatus is always in the process of intra-acting with other apparatuses, and the enfolding of

phenomena into subsequent iterations of particular practices constitute important shifts in the particular apparatuses in question and
therefore in the nature of the intra-actions that result in the production of new phenomena and so on. The materialization of an apparatus is an open (but nonarbitrary) ongoing process: apparatuses do
not simply change in time, they materialize through time and space.

SHIFTING GEARS/SHIFTING DYNAMICS: RETHINKING SPACE, TIME, AND MATTER

Feminists and other theorists commonly invoke the notion of a power
dynamics. In doing so they often worry about what is meant by power
and how it operates, but assume that the notion of "dynamics" is a
settled and unproblematic concept. Dynamics, as it is generally conceptualized within the natural sciences, is concerned with how the
values of particular variables change over time as a result of the interaction of different forces, where time is presumed to march along
as an external parameter. But an agential realist notion of dynamics
differs in many ways from the traditional one: intra-actions are caus-
ally constrained but nondeterministic irreversible enactments through
which matter-in-the-process-of-becoming is sedimented out and becomes an enfolded ingredient in the further materialization of human, nonhuman, and cyborgian bodies; such a dynamics is not
marked by an exterior parameter called time, nor does it take place
in a container called space, but rather iterative intra-actions are the
dynamics through which temporality and spatiality are produced and
reconfigured in the (re)making of material-discursive boundaries and
their constitutive exclusions. Exclusions introduce indeterminacies
and open up a space of agency; they are the conditions of possibility
of new possibilities. In what follows, I elaborate upon these claims.

As discussed in the previous section, according to agential realism materialization is not the end product or simply a succession of
intermediary effects of purely discursive practices. Materiality itself
is a factor in materialization. As such, the iterative enfolding of phenomena comes to matter. Temporality is produced through the iterative enfolding of material-discursive phenomena just as rings of
trees mark the sedimented history of their intra-actions within the
world. Matter carries the sedimented histories of the practices in

which it is rooted and nourished deep within it—it is engrained in its becoming, while it simultaneously plays a role in and is a part of other materializations and sedimenting histories. *Time has a history.* Therefore, it doesn't make sense to construe time as a succession of evenly spaced moments or as an external parameter that tracks the motion of matter in some preexisting space. Intra-actions are temporal not in the sense that the values of properties change in time, but rather *the properties themselves are redefined through time*—through the shifting of apparatuses in the very making/marking of time. *Temporality is constituted through iterative intra-actions.*

A common point of departure for Judith Butler and Niels Bohr is the fact that exclusions constitute the defining limit of the domain of intelligibility.

> This exclusionary matrix by which subjects are formed thus requires the simultaneous production of a domain of abject beings, those who are not yet "subjects," but who form the constitutive outside to the domain of the subject. The abject designates here precisely those "unlivable" and "uninhabitable" zones of social life which are nevertheless densely populated by those who do not enjoy the status of the subject, but whose living under the sign of the "unlivable" is required to circumscribe the domain of the subject.[31]

Material-discursive practices are boundary drawing practices: intra-actions entail the making of boundaries, the specification of the domains of interiority and exteriority that differentially separate the intelligible from the unintelligible.

Through the enfolding of phenomena and the dynamics of iterative intra-activity the domains of interior and exterior lose their prior designations. Agential reworkings of apparatuses, made possible by the indeterminacies inherent in exclusions, entail transgressions relative to the prior distinctions and the constitution of new boundaries and exclusions. The "cuts" that are made in the process of defining different categories do not merely exist in some abstract space, they are indeed material. (Recall Bohr's starting point: descriptive concepts require particular material circumstances for their definition.) Space is not a container in which objects assume their respective places at a given moment in time. *Spatiality is an ongoing process of (re)structuring through the (re)making of boundaries which depends upon and plays a productive role in the materialization of phenomena.* The iterative enfolding of phenomena and the shifting of boundaries entails an iterative reworking of the domains of interiority and exteriority thereby reconfiguring space itself, changing its topology. Hence, spatiality is defined not only in terms of boundaries but also in terms of exclusions.

Furthermore, the notions of "position" and "trajectory" lose their status as sacred variables characterizing the dynamics that is presumed to occur within the "container" of space. As Bohr points out, particular material conditions have to exist in order for the concept of position to be meaningful. And if such conditions exist they materially exclude the notion of momentum from being intelligible. Hence, not only is the notion of position understood to be contingent, but the mutual exclusivity of position and momentum—the two quantities that Newtonian mechanics enlists in the specification of deterministic trajectories—represents a failure of the Newtonian framework along with its traditional notions of trajectory and causality. Additionally, an agential realist dynamics is not reversible, as is its Newtonian counterpart, for intra-actions produce marks on bodies in their sedimenting historicity.

The philosopher of science Isabelle Stengers writes:

> Einstein is often credited with the audacity of having envisaged time as a fourth dimension. But Lagrange, and also d'Alembert in the *Encyclopédie,* had already proposed that duration and the three spatial dimensions formed a unity of four dimensions. In fact to affirm that time is nothing other than the geometrical parameter that allows calculation from the exterior, and as such, negates the becoming of all natural beings, has been almost a constant of the tradition of physics for the last three centuries. Thus, Emile Meyerson was able to describe the history of modern science as the progressive realization of what he regarded as a constitutive basis of human reason: the need for an explanation that reduces the diverse and the changing to the identical and the permanent, and as a result *eliminates time.*[32]

But according to agential realism, any claim to the effect that time is the fourth dimension of space cannot be understood as an elimination of time, that is, as the demotion of time to a "geometrical parameter that allows calculation from the exterior, and as such, negates the becoming of natural beings."[33] Time is not eliminated. "Spacetime" is a matter of the co-constitution of spatiality and temporality through the dynamics of iterative intra-activity. Spacetime manifolds are configured in terms of how material-discursive practices come to matter. The spacetime manifold is iteratively reconfigured through the dynamics of enfolding involving the reworking of the connectivity of the manifold itself, rather than a mere change in the shape or the size of the bounded domain. Agency is the space of possibilities opened up by the indeterminacies entailed in exclusions. The reworking of exclusions entail changes in the topology of spacetime. Interior and exterior, past and future, are iteratively enfolded and reworked, but never eliminated. The boundary between interiority and exteriority is what makes the past and the future possible.

Causality is neither a matter of strict determinism nor unconstrained freedom. The exclusions that are necessarily associated with the drawing of particular boundaries foreclose the possibility of determinism. Exclusions are the conditions for the possibility of an open future. Material-discursive apparatuses offer constraints on what is produced, but they also always produce particular exclusions. Therefore, intra-actions are constraining but not determining. *The notion of intra-actions reformulates the traditional notion of causality and opens up a space for material-discursive forms of agency.*

Agency is a matter of intra-acting; it is an enactment, not something that someone or something has. Agency cannot be designated as an attribute of subjects or objects (as they do not preexist as such). Agency is a matter of iterative changes to particular practices through the dynamics of intra-activity and enfolding. Agency is about the possibilities and accountability entailed in refiguring material-discursive apparatuses of bodily production, including the boundary articulations and exclusions that are marked by those practices.

Agential realism highlights the importance of taking account of human, nonhuman, and cyborgian forms of agency, of recognizing that there is a sense in which the world "kicks back." This is both possible and necessary because agency is a matter of changes in the apparatuses of bodily production, and such changes take place in various intra-actions, some of which remake the boundaries that delineate the differential constitution of the human. Holding the category "human" fixed excludes an entire range of possibilities in advance and freezes out important dimensions of the analysis of the workings of power.

WHEN MACHINES DON'T WORK: MATERIALIZING STRUCTURES/ PRODUCING WORKERS AND THE MANIFOLD POSSIBILITIES FOR RE(CON)FIGURATION

> "[C]lass is not this or that part of the machine, but *the way the machine works* . . . the friction of interests—the movement itself, the heat, the thundering noise. . . . class itself is not a thing, it is a happening."
>
> —E. P. Thompson, *The Poverty of Theory and Other Essays*

> "The shop floor tends to be crowded, for machines have been added at various stages in order to increase productivity . . . The spatial concentration of workers and machines allows workers to talk to each other on the shop floor and has led to numerous complaints by managers that workers tend to gossip and loiter. Such . . . everyday acts of resistance . . . point to the contested nature of the production process and demonstrate that the control of time and movement through the production process represents a political and conflicted terrain."
>
> —Leela Fernandes, *Producing Workers*

Fernandes's book, *Producing Workers,* is a detailed study of the structural relations of power as they are iteratively (re)produced and contested on the shop floor of a Calcutta jute mill. Fernandes makes use of the spatial positioning of workers on the shop floor as a material marker of the structural dimensions of class. She cleverly focuses on the material constraints that restrict the positioning and constrain the movement of workers throughout the factory, rather than attempting to capture a single deterministic trajectory of power. Indeed, such an idealized trajectory would be meaningless since it misses the important role that multiple intra-actions, exclusions, and agency play in the dynamics of power.[34]

In reading Fernandes's work it is important to notice that material constraints cannot be understood as immutable obstacles in an otherwise unlimited space of freedom. Furthermore, they are not to be interpreted as being completely independent of discursive practices, nor reducible to them, nor as the mere endpoints of such practices. Rather, I read Fernandes's analysis of the dynamics of structural relations in terms of the contingent materialization of the shop floor: the politics of space of the jute mill not only produces workers as appropriately disciplined subjects in intra-action with the ever-changing relations of power, but the spatiality of capitalism is itself produced through the politics of gender, community, and class and daily contests over the relations of power by those very subjects. For example, Fernandes argues that "[w]hen unions and male workers engage in this reproduction of asymmetrical gender relations, they in fact produce a scattered array of local practices and discourses that maintain the national hegemonic construction of class. In this process, they do not merely use pre-existing gendered ideologies but also actively manufacture gender through the creation of particular notions of masculinity and femininity" that wind up reinforcing the powers of management and undermining attempts by the unions to successfully intervene in certain class-based—always already-gendered—practices of management.[35] In other words, Fernandes maintains that the spatiality of capitalism is not merely produced through actions of managers who carve up the production process, but through the workers' own exclusionary practices as well. That is, while the mill is perhaps most obviously an ongoing process of the materialization of capital, importantly, the iterative materialization of the mill is also the outcome of the exclusionary practices of the workers themselves, but not via some linear additive dynamics. Rather, the exclusionary practices of the workers need to be understood to be part of the technologies of capitalism. The intra-action of these material-discursive apparatuses, which includes the practices of the workers as well as the managers, produces a space/structure marked by the topological enfolding of gender, community, and class. In other words, the spatiality of the mill is produced through the dynamics of intra-activity and the reconfiguration and enfolding of structural relations. Structures are apparatuses that contribute to the production of phenomena, but they also must be understood as thoroughly implicated in the dynamics of power: *structures are themselves material-discursive phenomena* which are produced through the intra-action of specific apparatuses of bodily production marked by exclusions.[36]

Hence, using the framework of agential realism, the jute mill can be understood as a material-discursive apparatus of bodily production which is itself a phenomenon materializing through iterative intra-actions among workers, management, machines, and other materials and beings which are enfolded into these apparatuses. Accordingly, materiality is rethought as a contingent and contested, constrained but nondetermining, process of iterative intra-activity through which material-discursive practices come to matter, rather than as mere brute positivity or some purified notion of the economic.

It is not the case that economic practices are material while the presumably separate set of social matters (such as gender and community identity) are merely ideological. The very nature of *production* is refigured as iterative intra-activity; production is not merely a process of making commodities, but also of making subjects, and remaking structures.[37]

Production should not be thought of as the repetition of some fixed set of processes (despite the pervasiveness of the Fordist assembly line image it often connotes). Rather, the nature of production processes are continually reworked as a result of human, nonhuman, and cyborgian forms of agency. Indeed, as Fernandes points out, when a machine refuses to work it may initiate a series of events: lost wages for a weaver, a fight between the weaver and the mechanic who was late fixing the machine, the intervention of management to resolve the conflict, union charges against management for mishandling the conflict, a union strike that leads to the restructuring of relations between management and workers, a reconfiguration of machines and workers on the shop floor, or a day off. Fernandes opens her book with just such an example, analyzing the events in terms of contests over the boundaries between social categories as they are constructed through and placed in conflict with other identities:

> The incident reveals the manner in which worker resistance, such as a strike, may arise out of conflicts and social hierarchies between groups of workers. In this case the caste allegiance of the weaver shaped the union's participation and occurred at the expense of the mechanic. However, once the conflict involved a union-management confrontation, it acquired a different meaning for the participants and the workers in general. The wildcat strike rested on a link between the workers' caste positions and union mobilization. However, the meaning of the strike was not limited to this caste relationship. To many workers not involved in the conflict, the strike represented a challenge to an unfair system of authority, that is, within the capitalist system in the factory. In short, there was continual slippage between the politics of caste and class through this sequence of events.[38]

An elaboration and extension of the differential gear assemblage metaphor that I invoked earlier may provide a way of envisioning this new understanding of the nature of production, structures, and dynamics. The extension that I have in mind is designed to focus attention on the fact that apparatuses are themselves phenomena. Imagine a differential gear assemblage (i.e., a gear assemblage in which the gear operations literally work through one another and in which an uneven distribution of forces results in and is the enabling condition for different potentials and performances among the gears) which in an ongoing fashion is being (re)configured/(re)assembled while it is itself in the process of producing other differential gear assemblages. Gears are remilled through intra-actions with other gears, and some gears are in the process of being enfolded into the assemblage as part of its ongoing process of reconfiguration. The assemblages are marked by these processes of (re)assembly. The accumulating marks of time do not correspond to the history of any individual gear, but rather are integrally tied to the genealogy of the assemblage and its changing topology, that is, to the processes of inclusion and exclusion in the reworking of the boundaries of the assemblages. Imagine further that the differential gear assemblages involve specific configurations of humans and nonhumans, where the differential constitution of human and nonhuman change during the reconfiguration processes.[39]

I have engaged this all-too-mechanistic analogy, playing off against the most pedestrian metaphor of production, in an attempt to highlight some of the shortcomings of common (mis)conceptions of production processes. For example, all too often the focus is either exclusively on the human dimensions of production, distribution, and consumption practices, narrowly conceived as that which occurs in the formal sector of the economy, or on the material culture of these practices in ways that assume separability and stable divisions between the human and the nonhuman.[40] Furthermore, notice that this proposed mutating variant of the machine metaphor for production entails a different understanding of the nature of *dynamics*—a dynamics in which there is an ongoing reworking of the nature of the production of the very technologies of production themselves. The dynamics of intra-activity is explicitly nonlinear, causal, and nondeterministic. Enfolding is not an arbitrary, random, automatic, or continuous process; enfolding changes the topology of spacetime as the connectivity of the spacetime manifold and the boundaries between interior and exterior are reworked. The reconstitution of boundaries and exclusions are agential processes. The apparatuses of production are themselves (re)produced (as is the very notion of production). Agential realism disassembles the notion that structures are Althusserian apparatuses—rigidified and separable formations of power that operate from the outside to constrain the processes of subject formation. On the contrary, structures are to be understood as material-discursive phenomena that are iteratively (re)produced through ongoing material-discursive intra-actions.[41]

This machine is not a Euclidean device, nor is it merely a static instrument with a non-Euclidean geometry. It is a topological animal which mutates through a dynamics of intra-activity. Questions of connectivity, boundary formation, and exclusion (topological concerns) must supplement and inform concerns about positionality and location (too often figured in geometrical terms). As an example, consider the notion of "intersectionality" as introduced by feminists of color. Feminists of color who fought/fight hard to displace hegemonic discourses that insist/ed on the reductive equation women = gender clearly appreciate/d the importance of a topological dynamics and warn/ed against geometrical interpretations of social location and identity formation.[42] Ironically, however, hegemonic invocations of the term *intersectionality* continue to suffer from a Euclideanization pathology—most likely due to their dis-ease with questions of race—in their misappropriations of the term. That is, these misappropriations completely neglect the topological dynamics and figure intersectionality in Euclidean geometrical terms as a mutually perpendicular set of axes of identification within which marked bodies can be positioned. This Euclideanization of the much more complex topological notion of intersectionality uses the common Euclidean imagery of intersection to its maximum advantage in trying to combat its own dis-ease. The following set of misunderstandings seem axiomatic to this pathology, a belief that (1) gender, race, class, sexuality, et cetera, are separate characteristics of individual human beings (i.e., that the axes of identity are at right angles to one another—that the axes themselves are independent and do not intersect—and that they measure inherent characteristics of individuals); (2) it is only important to pay attention to the ways in which these multiple identities intersect in certain specifically marked bodies, as if gender only matters for women, race only matters for people of color, et cetera (i.e., that the dimensionality of the coordinate system is determined by the degree of multiplicity, which is equal to the number of categories that are thought to apply to a specific individual if and only if that individual is seen as marked by the category in question); and (3) that the situation of people "with multiple identities" ought to be understood in terms of the intersection of "their" gender, race, et cetera (i.e., (3) is thought to logically follow by geometrical theorem directly from (1) and (2) above).

The dynamics of iterative intra-activity tears a hole in the fabric of this geometrical metaphor. Identities are not separable, they do not intersect. Rather, identity formation must be understood in terms of the topological dynamics of iterative intra-activity. Particular material-discursive circumstances constrain and enable the specific intra-action of multiple structural apparatuses of bodily production. Consequently, identity formation must be understood as a (contingent and contested ongoing) material process through which different identity categories are formed and reformed through one another. Instead of attempting to trace the presumed trajectories of identity formation, what is needed are genealogies of the changing topologies of the contingent structural relations of power which materialize in intra-action with one another (i.e., the re(con)figurations of the spacetime manifold).

Fernandes provides multiple illustrations of this topological dynamics. In the example above of the union-management conflict in the factory, the "unions produced a form of working-class politics that was constructed through caste politics. The boundaries of class interests thus became contingent on caste hierarchies through a specifically political process that involved the participation of workers, unions, and managers in the factory." But caste hierarchies are themselves produced: "[C]ommunity identity is created through a conflicted dynamic of hegemony and resistance, a process in which community simultaneously produces and is manufactured through narratives of class and gender within a contested symbolic terrain."[43] Caste, gender, and class materialize through and are enfolded into one another. The nature of this enfolding matters to the changing topology. Structures are constraining and enabling, not determining. Furthermore, structures are iteratively enfolded and materialize in intra-action with other apparatuses of bodily production. Agential reconfigurations of the apparatuses of bodily production are implicated in the changing topology of the spacetime manifold, making clear the need for responsibility and accountability in material-discursive practices.

SUMMARY

"How we represent space and time in theory matters, because
it affects how we and others interpret and then act with respect to the world."
—David Harvey, *The Condition of Postmodernity*

The shop floor is not a neutral observing device or a Euclidean frame
of reference that allows managers and social scientists to track the
trajectories of individual workers; the apparatuses that lend "position"
its intelligibility are implicated in the iterative (re)production of particular material-discursive boundaries among workers. Not only is the
notion of position itself a produced, contingent, and contested category that changes through time (not simply whose value changes
with time), but also, "worker" is not a fixed and unitary property of
individual human beings, but rather is an actively contested and
disunified—but nonetheless objective—category which refers to particular material-discursive beings (phenomena), that is, subjects in
intra-action with and iteratively (re)produced through changing relations of power. Consequently, it would be inappropriate to view
workers as pawns occupying different, but uniform, spaces on the
chessboard of an overarching static structure called capitalism; rather,
the spatiality of capitalism is itself a contested and ever-changing
topology that is iteratively (re)produced through the dynamics of
intra-activity and enfolding. The nature of the category "class," its
intelligibility and its materiality, depends upon this changing dynamics including intra-actions with particular material-discursive practices
that locally define gender and "community." "Thus, 'the working
class' does not represent a singular unit but is constituted by status
differences." Likewise, gender, which "represents a type of 'structuring' category, a form of 'habitus' that produces and negotiates patterns within social and cultural life," is itself a contested category
whose intelligibility depends in part upon the specifics of materializing structural relations (including, for example, ones that might
commonly be labeled "economic").[44] In particular, gender is constituted through class and community and other structural relations of
power. Gender, class, and community are enfolded into and produced
through one another. The claim that class is discursively produced is
not a denial of its materiality; likewise, gender and community are
no less material and no more discursive than class.

Material conditions matter, not because they "support" particular discourses which are the actual generative factors in the formation of subjects, but rather because both discourses and matter comes to matter through processes of materialization and the iterative enfolding of phenomena into apparatuses of bodily production. The relationship between materiality and discourse is not one of "support" or "mediation," but rather the material and the discursive are intertwined through the dynamics of intra-activity and enfolding. Material and discursive constraints and exclusions are similarly intertwined, thereby limiting the validity of analyses that attempt to determine individual effects of material or discursive factors. Furthermore, the conceptualization of materiality offered by agential realism makes it possible to take account of material constraints and conditions once again without reinscribing traditional empiricist assumptions concerning the transparent or immediate given-ness of the world and without falling into the analytical stalemate that simply calls for a recognition of the mediation of the world and then rests its case. The ubiquitous pronouncements proclaiming that experience or the material world are "mediated" have offered precious little guidance about how to proceed. The metaphor of mediation has for too long stood in the way of a more thoroughgoing accounting of the empirical. While incorporating some of the most important insights of poststructuralism, feminist science studies, and other critical reconsiderations of the body, of matter, and of nature, the reconceptualization of materiality offered here makes it possible to take the empirical world seriously once again in the construction and testing of theories, but this time with the understanding that the objective referent is phenomena, not the seeming "immediately given-ness" of the world.

In the opening vignette, I suggest that geometrical analyses are insufficient for a thorough-going account of complex events such as the one described. What is the intrinsic metric in this example? What feature unambiguously defines the sense of proximity, of location, of distance or scale that determines its geometry? Understanding the dynamics of this cyborg "trans-action"—which involves not merely the transgression of spatial and other material-discursive boundaries, but a re(con)figuration of the spacetime manifold itself—requires topological analysis. Questions of size and shape (geometrical concerns) must be supplemented by and reevaluated in terms of questions of boundary, connectivity, interiority, and exteriority (topological concerns).

Analyzing the multidimensional heterogeneous geopolitical-economic-social-cultural landscape on the basis of geometrical considerations won't suffice. Not even if what is meant by geometry is retrofitted for postmodern sensibilities by insisting on the relative and socially constructed nature of presumably geometrical terms (e.g., scale). Nor is it sufficient to figure responsibility in terms of positionality or other efforts to locate oneself within the relevant social horizon. The inadequacy of geometrical analysis in isolation from topological considerations lies in the very nature of "construction." Spatiality is always an exclusionary process and those exclusions are of agential significance.

For example, in contrast to some unfortunate geometrical readings of the notion of scale (whereby the nesting relationship local $\subset$ national $\subset$ global is presumed to hold), the geographer Neil Smith explicitly explores the exclusionary nature of the production of scale. He notes that "scale is produced in and through societal activity which in turn produces and is produced by geographical structures of social interaction." This insight can be understood in terms of the fact that "scale" refers to a property of spatial phenomena intra-actively produced, contested, and reproduced, and furthermore, that it is "an active progenitor of specific social processes" as a result of becoming enfolded into various material-discursive apparatuses of production. As Smith emphasizes "it is precisely the active social connectedness of scales that is vital." This "connectedness" should not be understood as linkages among pre-existing discrete nested scales but rather as the agential enfolding of different scales through one another (so that, for example, the different scales of individual bodies, homes, communities, regions, nations, and the global are not seen as geometrically nested in accordance with some physical notion of size, but rather are understood as being intra-actively produced through one another). That is, Smith's notion of "jumping scales" can be elaborated as an element of a topological dynamics in terms of agential enfoldings that reconfigure the connectivity of the spacetime manifold.[45]

Boundary transgressions are another instance where geometrical considerations won't suffice. Boundary transgressions should not be equated with the dissolution of traversed boundaries (as some authors have suggested), but rather with their reconfiguration. For example, information technologies are often touted as the neutrino of the geo-political-economic-social-cultural landscape, passing through matter as if it were transparent, innocently traversing all borders whether those of nation-states or different computer platforms with undis-criminating ease and disregard for obstacles—the great democratizer, the realization of a mobility and reach that knows no bounds. But information technologies do not reconfigure spacetime into a flat manifold, a level playing field; on the contrary, in some cases they exacerbate the unevenness of the distribution of material goods, fur-ther stabilizing constraints that place restrictions on the everyday lives of those who experience this so-called "expansion of opportunity" as a diminishing of possibilities.[46] Similarly, as Fernandes (this vol-ume) makes clear, trans/nationalism does not make the notion of the nation-state obsolete. The relationship between the local, the regional, the national, and the global is not a geometrical nesting. "Local," "re-gional," "national," "global" are topological matters, intra-actively produced through one another, so that an increase in the flow of in-formation and goods across national boundaries does not in and of itself constitute the obsolescence of the nation-state.

What is needed are genealogies of the material-discursive appa-ratuses of production which take account of the intra-active topologi-cal dynamics that reconfigure the spacetime manifold. In particular, it is important that they include an analysis of the connectivity of phenomena at different scales.[47] As Ruth Wilson Gilmore points out, it is crucial to trace the "frictions of distance, to do analyses that move through the range of scales of injustice, not by pointing out similari-ties between one place or event and another, but by understanding how those places or events are made through one another."[48]

The topological dynamics of space, time, and matter are an agen-tial matter and as such require an ethics of knowing and being: Intra-actions have the potential to do more than participate in the constitution of the geometries of power, they open up possibilities for changes in its topology, and as such, interventions in the mani-fold possibilities made available reconfigure both what will be and what will be possible. The space of possibilities does not represent a fixed event horizon within which the social location of knowers can be mapped, nor a homogenous fixed uniform container of choices.

Rather, the dynamics of the spacetime manifold is produced by agential interventions made possible in its very re(con)figuration. The "politics of identity" and the "politics of location," however useful, have been circumscribed by a geometrical conception of power that arrests and flattens important features of its dynamics. Perhaps what is needed is a "politics of possibilities": ways of responsibly imagining and intervening in the re(con)figurations of power.

NOTES

I would like to thank Laura Liu and Rupal Oza for comments on an earlier draft. I would also like to thank the students in my spring 2000 senior seminar on "Feminist and Queer Theories" at Mount Holyoke College for wonderful conversations about poststructuralist conceptions of structures. Thanks as well to Mary Renda for a great conversation about some of the ideas presented here. My deepest gratitude to Leela Fernandes and Ruth Wilson Gilmore for their helpful comments, support, and the inspiration of their respective phenomenally important contributions.

1. I wrote this vignette for this chapter. I return to the issues that it raises in the conclusion.
2. I thank Laura Liu for bringing to my attention a paper by Neil Smith and Cindi Katz that similarly cautions against the uncritical embrace of spatial metaphors, particularly when many of the spatial metaphors that feminist and other theorists rely upon are rooted in a modernist (Euclidean) representation of space as absolute; Neil Smith and Cindi Katz, "Grounding Metaphor: Towards a Spatialized Politics," in *Place and the Politics of Identity*, ed. Michael Keith and Steve Pile (London: Routledge, 1993). Presenting a very interesting sketch of the history of its modernist conception, they argue that "this space is quite literally the space of capitalist patriarchy and racist imperialism." (79) There are other interesting essays in the collection, *Place and the Politics of Identity*, in which the Smith and Katz piece appear, and several of them express similar concerns. In her article in this same collection, Doreen Massey offers a very thoughtful and imaginative reconceptualization of spatiality. Like my own analysis offered here, Massey's approach uses physics as a point of departure. Ultimately, however, I found her reformulation to be inconsistent due to its reliance on an unfortunate elision between the epistemological lessons of quantum mechanics and special relativity. A wonderful January faculty seminar at Smith College on postcolonial feminisms brought Caren Kaplan's "Postmodern Geographies" to my attention. In this chapter of her book *Questions of Travel*, Kaplan addresses similar issues but gives a different justification for feminist reliance on spatial metaphors by tracing the history of its theoretical purchase within feminist discourses. Ultimately, she argues that feminists should not abandon the notion of location, but rather reconsider its meaning; she encourages us to think of location as "an axis rather than a place" (183) and suggests that location be understood as a frame for investigating the production of different identities. Unfortunately then, the notion of location that Kaplan winds up embracing reinscribes the Euclidean container model of space, rather than providing the needed understanding of the dynamic production of spacetime. I thank Caren for her gracious engagement with my critique and some other wonderful conversation during her visit.
3. Edward W. Soja, *Postmodern Geographies: The Reassertion of Space in Critical Social Theory* (New York: Verso, 1989).
4. Ruth Wilson Gilmore, "Queer Publics: Transforming Policy, Scholarship, and Politics," Opening Plenary, Local Politics and Global Change: Activists and Academics Thinking about a Queer Future Conference, Center for Lesbian and Gay Studies, City University of New York, April 1999.
5. Of course, a crucial ingredient of critical politics/praxis is the ongoing contestation of those very norms, but this is not to deny their relevance to such practices.
6. Admittedly, the metaphor of a framework harkens back once again to the image of a Euclidean geometrical structure. The pervasiveness of the Euclidean imaginary haunts even its possible reimaginings. But the point here is not the banishment of all such

conceptualizations as a matter of principle, but to think critically about the implicit reliance of contemporary theories on this taken-for-granted understanding of spatiality and the constraints it poses on theorizing. (See references to Barad.)

7. On performativity see Judith Butler, *Bodies That Matter: On the Discursive Limits of "Sex"* (London: Routledge, 1993).

8. Rosemary Hennessy, *Materialist Feminism and the Politics of Discourse* (London: Routledge, 1993), 25.

9. Michel Foucault, trans., *Discipline and Punish: The Birth of the Prison* (New York: Vintage Books, 1977), 137.

10. Leela Fernandes, *Producing Workers: The Politics of Gender, Class, and Culture in the Calcutta Jute Mills* (Philadelphia: University of Pennsylvania Press, 1997), 59.

11. Ibid., 137.

12. More accurately, the shop floor should be understood in terms of the intra-action of multiple apparatuses. (Note: the neologism "intra-action" and the hyphenated structure "material-discursive" are explained in the next section.) There are no singular apparatuses. All apparatuses are multiply intra-acting, implicated in processes of enfolding, and dynamically made and remade through different kinds of boundary-making practices. Indeed, the articulation of a given apparatus is always already a boundary-making practice. At the same time, genealogies of the most important apparatuses and their intra-actions are needed for thorough-going political analyses; see Karen Barad, "Reconceiving Scientific Literacy as Agential Literacy, or Learning How to Intra-act Responsibly within the World," in *Doing Science + Culture*, ed. Roddey Reid and Sharon Traweek (London: Routledge, 2000). "What constitutes an apparatus of bodily production cannot be known in advance of engaging in the always messy projects of description, narration, intervention, inhabiting, conversing, exchanging, and building. The point is to get at how worlds are made and unmade, in order to participate in the process, in order to foster some forms of life and not others"; Donna Haraway, "A Game of Cat's Cradle: Science Studies, Feminist Theory, Cultural Studies," *Configurations: A Journal of Literature and Science* 1 (1994): 63.

13. M. Norton Wise, "Mediating Machines," *Science in Context* 2:1 (1988): 77–113, 77.

14. Ibid., 80.

15. Note that what is at stake is not simply a change of rulers, but a change in the nature of rule analogous to a Foucaultian shift from sovereign power to a microphysics of power.

16. Much of this presentation is excerpted from Karen Barad, "Agential Realism: Feminist Interventions in Understanding Scientific Practices," in *The Science Studies Reader*, ed. Mario Biagioli (London: Routledge, 1998). Karen Barad, "Meeting the Universe Halfway: Realism and Social Constructivism without Contradiction," in *Feminism, Science, and the Philosophy of Science*, ed. Lynn Hankinson Nelson and Jack Nelson (Dordrecht, Holland: Kluwer Press, 1996), gives a more detailed account.

17. For more details, see Barad, "Meeting the Universe Halfway: Realism and Social Constructivism without Contradiction." (Note: "Agencies of observation" is Bohr's term, which he seems to use interchangeably with "apparatus." Because of the usual association of agency with subjectivity, "agencies of observation" hints at an ambiguity in what precisely constitutes an apparatus for Bohr. For further discussion, see Barad, "Getting Real: Technoscientific Practices and the Materialization of Reality."

18. Niels Bohr, *The Philosophical Writings of Niels Bohr, Vol. III: Essays 1958–1962 on Atomic Physics and Human Knowledge* (Woodbridge, Conn.: Ox Bow Press, 1963), 4.

19. Bohr quoted in Henry Folse, *The Philosophy of Niels Bohr: The Framework of Complementarity* (New York: North Holland Physics Publishing, 1985), 124.

20. Bohr called this cut "arbitrary" to distinguish it from an "inherent" cut. But the cut isn't completely arbitrary (see Barad, forthcoming) and so I have used "constructed" as a contrast to "inherent."

21. Since wholeness takes on a particular set of connotations within feminist theory, it is probably worth mentioning some of the ways in which wholeness is being reconceptualized here. "Wholeness, according to agential realism, does not signify the dissolution of boundaries. On the contrary, boundaries are necessary for making meanings. Theoretical concepts are only defined within a given context, as specified by constructed boundaries. Wholeness is not about the prioritizing of the innocent whole over the sum of the parts; wholeness signifies the inseparability of the material and the [discursive]. Wholeness requires that delineations, differentiations, distinctions be drawn; differentness is required

of wholeness. Utopian dreams of dissolving boundaries are pure illusion since by definition there is no agential reality without constructed boundaries." Barad, "Meeting the
Universe Halfway: Realism and Social Constructivism without Contradiction," 182.

22. Bohr, *The Philosophical Writings of Niels Bohr, Vol. III: Essays 1958–1962 on Atomic
Physics and Human Knowledge,* 3.

23. According to Newtonian physics, the two variables that need to be specified simultaneously are position and momentum. Bohr argued that an understanding of causality as
strict determinism must be revised because mutually exclusive apparatuses are required
to define position and momentum.

24. Niels Bohr, *The Philosophical Writings of Niels Bohr, Vol. II: Essays 1932–1957 on
Atomic Physics and Human Knowledge* (Woodbridge, Conn.: Ox Bow Press, 1963), 59–
60.

25. Niels Bohr, *The Philosophical Writings of Niels Bohr, Vol. I: Atomic Theory and the Description of Nature* (Woodbridge, Conn.: Ox Bow Press, 1963), 117.

26. Karen Barad, "Getting Real: Technoscientific Practices and the Materialization of Reality," *Differences: A Journal of Feminist Cultural Studies* 10:2 (summer 1998).

27. David Harvey and Gayatri Spivak are among those that critique Foucault for his limited
conception of space. Harvey characterizes Foucault's conception of space as a "container of power"; David Harvey, *The Condition of Postmodernity* (Oxford: Basil Blackwell,
1990). Spivak writes that "Foucault is a brilliant thinker of power-in-spacing, but the
awareness of the topographical reinscription of imperialism does not inform his presup-
positions"; Gayatri Chakravorty Spivak, "Can the Subaltern Speak?" in *Marxism and the
Interpretation of Culture,* ed. L. Grossberg and C. Nelson (Urbana: University of Illinois
Press, 1988), 292. Soja discusses Foucault's "ambivalent spatiality"; Soja, *Postmodern
Geographies: The Reassertion of Space in Critical Social Theory.*

28. Diana Fuss, *Essentially Speaking: Feminism, Nature, Difference* (London: Routledge, 1989),
3.

29. Butler, *Bodies That Matter: On the Discursive Limits of "Sex,"* 15.

30. To put the point even more crudely, but in a way that is perhaps helpful for some, the
effectiveness of particular discourses in processes of materialization depends upon the
materiality through which they are "mobilized." (A key point in getting some mileage out of
this metaphor is the notion of enfolding, discussed below.)

31. Butler, *Bodies That Matter: On the Discursive Limits of "Sex,"* 3

32. Isabelle Stengers, trans., *Power and Invention* (Minneapolis: University of Minnesota
Press, 1997), 40.

33. Ibid.

34. Fernandes, *Producing Workers,* 63.

35. Ibid., 74.

36. Apparatuses are clearly not pure entities since they are always already implicated in
ongoing intra-actions and enfoldings. Traditionally, however, they have been treated as
separable: for example, some have been labeled "economic" and some (mis)identified as
"merely cultural" (that is, as having to do with the "politics of recognition," as opposed to
the "politics of redistribution"). Interestingly, in *Justice Interruptus,* Nancy Fraser argues
against making "an either/or choice between the politics of redistribution and the politics
of recognition" (4), yet her starting point is to set up redistribution and recognition as
perpendicular—that is entirely separate—axes of a coordinate system of injustices (the
metaphor is hers). This analytical boundary cut (draws a line around the economic as
singularly a matter of class, contra Fernandes, which Fraser herself readily admits is
artificial, limits her attempt at synthesizing the very elements she insists on separating at
the outset. As Judith Butler argues, Fraser's analysis reinscribes the problematic conception of social identities as merely cultural; Judith Butler, "Merely Cultural," *Social Text*
52–53 (1997): 265–277. (See also Fraser's response to Butler in the same volume.)
Indeed, Fraser's conception of materiality is limited to the merely economic. This stands
in contrast to the alternative conception of materiality offered here. I want to thank
Nancy Fraser for an interesting interchange about this point during an IRW faculty seminar at Rutgers in the fall of 1997.

37. Miranda Joseph argues for an expanded understanding of production which includes the
productivity of performativity (where performativity is understood by Joseph in an expanded sense of its own as a form of production) in a similar effort to dislodge the taken-
for-granted opposition between the economic and the social; Miranda Joseph, "The

Performace of Production and Consumption," *Social Text* 54 (spring 1998). In "Getting Real" I argue for a revised understanding of performativity from iterative citationality to iterative intra-activity; the latter differs from the former in its inclusion of material dimensions, ignored in the former conception, that are indeed crucial to understanding the nature of production. This is related to an expanded understanding of materiality itself in terms of iterative intra-activity (and not as mere brute matter or as the economic understood as merely an issue of class). Additionally, I argue here that these material dimensions are crucial to understanding the nature of structures and their dynamics.

38. Fernandes, *Producing Workers*, 3–4.
39. Production processes involving information and biotechnologies are instances where the shifting of boundaries between human and nonhuman are perhaps most evident and most thoroughly analyzed, though they are not the only ones. The literature on this is extensive; see, for example, Donna Haraway, *Modest Witness@Second Millennium. FemaleMan© Meets OncoMouse™: Feminism and Technoscience* (London: Routledge, 1997); and Chris Gray, ed., *The Cyborg Handbook* (London: Routledge, 1995).
40. My critique of their assumed separability should not be misunderstood as a suggestion that these categories ought to be collapsed.
41. The poststructuralist response to Althusser's inadequate theorizing of the workings of power through a rigidified, separable, and constraining conception of apparatuses of power—a formulation which lacks many important dimensions of the productive effects of power—has itself produced an aversion to the notion of apparatuses (and structures) in toto. However, it may be that maintaining some notion of apparatus—albeit one that contests many of its structuralist features—at minimum serves the purpose of keeping track of the very production of that which does the producing. For example, a full accounting of the workings of power requires that we understand how matter comes to matter and not simply how discourses come to matter. An analysis of these features requires a genealogy of apparatuses (Barad,"Getting Real"; Barad, "Reconceiving Scientific Literacy as Agential Literacy, or Learning How to Intra-act Responsibly within the World."
42. The literature on intersectionality is extensive. See, for example, Gloria Anzaldúa, ed., *Making Face, Making Soul/Haciendo Caras: Creative and Critical Perspectives by Women of Color* (San Francisco: An Aunt Lute Foundation Book, 1990). The term *intersectionality* is often attributed to Kimberlé Crenshaw, "Demarginalizing the Intersection of Race and Sex: A Black Critique of Antidiscrimination Doctrine, Feminist Theory and Antiracist Politics," *University of Chicago Legal Forum* (1989): 139–167.
43. Fernandes, *Producing Workers*, 4, 89.
44. Ibid., 10, 11.
45. Neil Smith, "Contours of a Spatialized Politics: Homeless Vehicles and the Production of Geographical Scale," *Social Text* 33 (1992): 55–81, 62, 66.
46. According to Marx, uneven development is intrinsic to capitalism. For contemporary analyses of uneven development, see, for example, Neil Smith, *Uneven Development: Nature, Capital, and the Production of Space* (Oxford: Basil Blackwell, 1991); and Doreen Massey, "Politics and Space/Time," in *Place and the Politics of Identity*, ed. Michael Keith and Steve Pile (London: Routledge, 1993).
47. This important work has already begun. See, for example, the groundbreaking work on "Corporate Genealogies" being done by Barbara Harlow, Punima Bose, Laura Lyons, and Rachel Gennings (panel at the Rethinking Marxism Conference, September 23, 2000, Amherst, Mass.).
48. Panel at the Rethinking Marxism Conference, "Rosa and Ruth/Terror and Truth—Dialogue" with Ruth Wilson Gilmore and Barbara Harlow, September 24, 2000, Amherst, Mass.

REFERENCES

Anzaldúa, Gloria (ed). *Making Face, Making Soul/Haciendo Caras: Creative and Critical Perspectives by Women of Color.* San Francisco: An Aunt Lute Foundation Book, 1990.
Barad, Karen. *Meeting the Universe Halfway.* (forthcoming)
———. "Agential Realism." In *Encyclopedia of Feminist Theories,* edited by Lorraine Code. London: Routledge, 2000.
———. "Reconceiving Scientific Literacy as Agential Literacy, or Learning How to Intra-act

Responsibly within the World." In *Doing Science + Culture*, edited by Roddey Reid and Sharon Traweek. London: Routledge, 2000.

———. "Agential Realism: Feminist Interventions in Understanding Scientific Practices." In *The Science Studies Reader*, edited by Mario Biagioli. London: Routledge, 1998.

———. "Getting Real: Technoscientific Practices and the Materialization of Reality." *Differences: A Journal of Feminist Cultural Studies* 10: 2 (summer 1998).

———. "Meeting the Universe Halfway: Realism and Social Constructivism without Contradiction." In *Feminism, Science, and the Philosophy of Science*, edited by Lynn Hankinson Nelson and Jack Nelson. Dordrecht, Holland: Kluwer Press, 1996.

Bohr, Niels. *The Philosophical Writings of Niels Bohr, Vol. I: Atomic Theory and the Description of Nature*. Woodbridge, Conn.: Ox Bow Press, 1963.

———. *The Philosophical Writings of Niels Bohr, Vol. II: Essays 1932–1957 on Atomic Physics and Human Knowledge*. Woodbridge, Conn.: Ox Bow Press, 1963.

———. *The Philosophical Writings of Niels Bohr, Vol. III: Essays 1958–1962 on Atomic Physics and Human Knowledge*. Woodbridge, Conn.: Ox Bow Press, 1963.

Butler, Judith. "Merely Cultural." *Social Text* 52–53 (1997): 265–277.

———. *Bodies That Matter: On the Discursive Limits of "Sex."* London: Routledge, 1993.

Crenshaw, Kimberlé. "Demarginalizing the Intersection of Race and Sex: A Black Feminist Critique of Antidiscrimination Doctrine, Feminist Theory and Antiracist Politics." In *University of Chicago Legal Forum* (1989): 139–167.

Fernandes, Leela. "Rethinking Globalization: Gender and Nation in India." *Feminist Locations*, 2001.

———. *Producing Workers: The Politics of Gender, Class, and Culture in the Calcutta Jute Mills*. Philadelphia: University of Pennsylvania Press, 1997.

Folse, Henry. *The Philosophy of Niels Bohr: The Framework of Complementarity*. New York: North Holland Physics Publishing, 1985.

Foucault, Michel. *Discipline and Punish: The Birth of the Prison*. New York: Vintage Books, 1977.

Fraser, Nancy. *Justice Interruptus: Critical Reflections on the "Postsocialist" Condition*. London: Routledge, 1997.

Fuss, Diana. *Essentially Speaking: Feminism, Nature, Difference*. London: Routledge, 1989.

Gilmore, Ruth Wilson. "Queer Publics: Transforming Policy, Scholarship, and Politics," Opening Plenary, Local Politics and Global Change: Activists and Academics Thinking about a Queer Future Conference, Center for Lesbian and Gay Studies, City University of New York, April,1999.

Gray, Chris, ed. T*he Cyborg Handbook*. London: Routledge, 1995.

Haraway, Donna. *Modest_Witness@Second_Millennium.FemaleMan©_Meets_OncoMouse™: Feminism and Technoscience*. London: Routledge, 1997.

———. "A Game of Cat's Cradle: Science Studies, Feminist Theory, Cultural Studies." *Configurations: A Journal of Literature and Science* 1 (1994): 59–71.

Harvey, David. *The Condition of Postmodernity*. Oxford: Blackwell, 1990.

Hennessy, Rosemary. *Materialist Feminism and the Politics of Discourse*. London: Routledge, 1993.

Joseph, Miranda. 1998. "The Performance of Production and Consumption." *Social Text* 54:16 (spring 1998).

Kaplan, Caren. *Questions of Travel*. Durham: Duke University Press, 1996.

Massey, Doreen. "Politics and Space/Time." In *Place and the Politics of Identity*, edited by Michael Keith and Steve Pile. London: Routledge, 1993.

———. *Spatial Divisions of Labor: Social Structures and the Geography of Production*. New York: Methuen, 1984.

Smith, Neil, and Cindi Katz. "Grounding Metaphor: Towards a Spatialized Politics." In *Place and the Politics of Identity*, edited by Michael Keith and Steve Pile. London: Routledge, 1993.

Smith, Neil. "Contours of a Spatialized Politics: Homeless Vehicles and the Production of Geographical Scale." *Social Text* 33 (1992): 55–81.

———. *Uneven Development: Nature, Capital, and the Production of Space*. Oxford: Basil Blackwell, 1991.

Soja, Edward W. *Postmodern Geographies: The Reassertion of Space in Critical Social Theory*. New York: Verso, 1989.

Spivak, Gayatri Chakravorty. "Can the Subaltern Speak?" In *Marxism and the Interpretation of*

Culture, edited by L. Grossberg and C. Nelson, 271–313. Urbana: University of Illinois Press, 1988.

Stengers, Isabelle, trans. *Power and Invention.* Minneapolis: University of Minnesota Press, 1997.

Thompson, E. P. *The Poverty of Theory and Other Essays.* London: Merlin, 1978.

Wise, M. Norton. "Mediating Machines." *Science in Context* 2:1 (1988): 77–113.

CHERYL JOHNSON-ODIM

WHO'S TO NAVIGATE AND WHO'S TO STEER?
A Consideration of the Role of Theory in Feminist Struggle

This chapter is intended as a think piece about feminist theory. I intend to be constructively provocative. I do not propose to synthesize past or present feminist theory. Rather, I propose to query the uses, abuses, definitions of, and creation of theory itself. In doing so, I suppose I am actually proposing a theory about theory. In fact, this is one of the major trajectories in which feminist theory is now traveling—that is, questioning the development of theory. This is a process which really commences, for what in the past I have called Euro-American feminism, at the very beginning of the second wave, in the 1960s. It began with African American women, and some radical white women, debating what the new feminism said about issues of race and class, and lesbian women interrogating it for what it said about sexual orientation. In the early 1970s the chorus of voices asking "Whose feminism for whom?" grows to include Latina and Asian American diaspora communities and Native American women, and, toward the middle of that decade, mostly at international fora, African, Asian, Caribbean, Latin American, Middle Eastern, and Pacific Islander women. By the middle 1980s what many had referred to as Euro-American feminism, or even white feminism, becomes bifurcated itself into European and Anglo-American feminism. Of course, one of the primary things that this suggests to us is that location, both geopolitical and historical, not surprisingly, is a primary component of identity and worldview, therefore, an explicator not only of who and where we are situationally, but also relationally. More about this later.

My point here is that it has been the involvement of a multiplicity of women's voices that has forced feminist theorists over the last thirty years to begin to deconstruct feminism, feminist theory, and feminist struggle even while it was being constructed. This simultaneous process of construction and deconstruction, this dialectical process if you will, has led logically to a discussion of a theory about theory, which is the focus of this essay.

Let me begin by raising some critical issues. Certainly, the following is not an exhaustive list, but has been chosen as representative of what I think are some of the most important questions in this process: What are our reasons for engaging in the creation of theory? How has the reality of current global power relations influenced the development of feminist theory? What qualifies as theory? What is the relationship between theory and praxis? How do we find what women *qua* women have in common for a struggle against the oppression of women while not losing sight of the role of class and/or race privilege in the lives of some women and class and/or race oppression in the lives of other women, especially when they are systemically related? How do we deal with gender issues in the context of women's oppression? If I can even suggest ways of thinking about these questions, not even to say posing solutions to them, I will feel that I have made some contribution to the debate.

And lastly, by way of introduction, let me say that I am deeply interested in these questions not merely as a matter of academic enterprise and contribution to the discourse, but as a matter of considering myself an activist-scholar, and thus as a matter of what I hope to *do* (continue to engage in antiracist, antisexist, and class struggle) as well as what I hope to think. Even my role as an academician emerges out of struggle, because I know that, but for certain struggles, I would not be positioned in the way which I am in the academy or in the discussion. So that the question of the relationship between theory and struggle is a part of the pattern of my life as I have lived it and as I continue to choose to live it in the future. And, my position as an activist scholar means that among those things about which I am most concerned regarding theory are its accessibility and its relevance. I think that we need to be concerned with such things as whether the language of feminist theory renders it not only inaccessible to most women but even inaccessible to political struggle itself.

What the function of theory is, is not a simple question with one answer, because theory has multiple functions. Let me focus on some of the functions, or uses, of theory. One of the functions of theory is to develop explanatory models, for often theoretical models postulate replicable causality; that is, if condition *a* results in condition *b*, will it do that again and again? A second function of theory is to explicate relationships; that is, the nature of the relationship between *a* and *b* is what keeps *a*, *a* and keeps *b*, *b*, or even, what constructs *a* as *a*, and *b* as *b*. A third function of theory is to guide praxis. In my view, theory and praxis are interrelated processes, and thus should be in a constant state of interaction.

My greatest interest in theory is its ability to inform praxis. It is that, the protean relationship between theory and struggle, on which I will concentrate.

Theory is a necessity for revolution. Amilcar Cabral, an African male theorist of the anticolonial struggle in Guinea Bissau, in an essay entitled "The Weapon of Theory," wrote: "If it is true that revolution can fail, even though it be nurtured on perfectly conceived theories, nobody has yet successfully practiced revolution without a revolutionary theory."[1]

Among the most important ways that theory informs feminist praxis is by leading to the development of strategies for struggle, and to the delineation of end goals of struggle. In this process theory looks to history, to the present, and into the future. It looks to history to root itself in evidence and to establish context. Thus, an accurate historical framework derived from an investigative process that is neither myopic nor incestuous, is critical if we are committed to a struggle aimed at simultaneously transforming the gendered nature of power relations in a variety of locations, and, especially, in looking at overlapping systemic constructions of power (which also have implications for intra gender power relations). It is, in fact, due to such an investigative process that second-wave feminist theory has become more refined not least from the integration of analyses of race, class, and sexual orientation, but also geopolitics and historical experience, even when race and class remain constant. I refer, for instance, to some of the work on European feminist theory (particularly that on France and Germany by scholars such as Louise Tilly and Amy Hackett) as distinct from what is more and more being referred to as Anglo-American feminist theory. Amy Hackett, for instance, in writing on German feminist theory of the very late nineteenth- and early twentieth-century remarks: "The American bias [in feminist scholarship] is particularly evident in the frequent assumption that equality of rights is the essence of feminism."[2] Another example of the refinement in second-wave feminist theory is third-world feminist theory. I should say here that I agree with what some have suggested about the need to problematize terminology such as third world. It needs to be problematized primarily because it refers to such a diversity of people and places, and tends to buy into the binary opposition of "them" and "us." Still, in certain contexts, I find it a useful term. What the so-called third world has in common is a similar set of historical experiences with the West in which colonialism and imperialism economically underdeveloped certain areas of the world and theorized their populations as inferior "others" needing to be made over in the image of the West. We must understand imperialism and colonialism not merely as politico-economic systems of domination but as systems of social domination as well. Neocolonialism, or if you prefer, neoimperialism, often in partnership with internal indigenous elements who depend for their privilege on that very partnership, continues to export Western systems of domination. Thus, the third world continues to have that in common. In the context of feminism one finds that women from these areas of the world say many similar things, particularly they articulate a women's struggle that while fighting sex discrimination internally and globally, recognizes that many of those things that oppress them are part of an inequitable and exploitative global order which the elimination of sex-based discrimination will not eradicate. I have delineated this much more fully elsewhere but it is in this context that I use the term *third-world* feminism.[3]

To go back, theory also looks to the present to inform praxis. In the present it assesses the situation. But whose situation does it assess? Is there a universal category "woman"? Or even, a universalizable category "woman"? In some ways I would argue that there is, in a limited, descriptive way. That is, biologically, there is woman. And this, in no small measure, is important to feminist struggle. Biological women are diverse in their sexuality and include lesbians and women who are bisexual and who are transvestites.[4] I'm going to put the discussion that might logically follow here, that of the utility of identity politics, aside for the moment, but I'll come back to it. For all the angst and debate that my attribution of biological characteristics calls forth in defining woman, what other basis, at least in the first instance, through space and time, can we employ for defining woman?

Biology is certainly not destiny, and I do not mean to imply that it determines one's life. As simplistic as it may sound, I mean to say that being biologically a woman establishes something in common, delineates some bond. When it comes to such issues as medical research and reproductive freedom and technologies, biology can be of critical importance. And for what it's worth recognizing biology as some kind of bond also establishes that women are a little more than half the population of the world—hardly a numerical minority. It may seem exceedingly simplistic to start out here, with biological woman, but it is that simple assumption that gives a unifying principle even to the discourse on gender and difference. More on this when I discuss identity politics below.

I said previously that theory also looks to the future in informing praxis. This is among the most important things that theory does in relationship to feminist struggle, because here it posits what should be in contradistinction to what is. This is, also, the hardest question, because it debates not only the relationship between women and men, but between women and women, in fact, between people. It is at this level that we generate a vision for the future, and, it is largely because of underdevelopment and inadequacy in the first two levels—that is, the historicizing of women's experience and definitions of women beyond the biological—that this level is so problematic.

Earlier on I said I would come back to a discussion of third-world feminist theory. Third-world feminists are particularly interested in questions of feminist theory, for what and for whom? The realities of women in the third world, women in third-world communities in their diasporas in the West, and poor women in general, require that feminist theory be informed by multiple perspectives and that it be informed by praxis. What do I mean by realities? I mean that women struggling for survival want to embrace a feminism that speaks to an improvement in their concrete material conditions, one that proposes an organized political process to make change that enhances the material quality of their lives and those of their loved ones (including men), and one that they see as having relevance to their lives. If theory is not going to explicitly serve the function of leading to, or at least proposing, a transformation in their lives as they live them, how is it relevant to them? Women need to be able to recognize themselves and their lives in theory. Somehow, a second-wave feminist theorizing that started out questioning power relationships and their consequences has often become dominated by a discourse on the genesis and process of female subordination primarily along a Western historical trajectory.

Many third-world women view the disposition of some Western feminist theory to regard male power as the primary, and sometimes the sole locus of women's oppression, as a view which is unable to locate and describe the interstices of women's oppression. Since, as Gerda Lerner once stated, the master of a black woman is as likely to be a white woman as a white man, and as Gloria Joseph put differently, black women have as much in common with black men as they do with white women when it comes to their oppression, what are we to make of feminist theory that singly proposes an end goal of equality between men and women? Which women are to be equal to which men? Are women to be equal to their cohort men—that is, men with whom they share race, class, and location (such as residence in the West)? That is a sure formula for entrenching privilege in the name of feminism.

The end goals of feminism are, in fact, perhaps the most contested terrain and the least explicitly discussed in many recent theoretical treatises on feminism. When it comes to the end goals of feminism, as women who are members of dispossessed communities argue for clean water, affordable health care, decent education for their children, reproductive freedom as opposed to population control, et cetera—it becomes clear that this is a vision for the future that goes beyond male/female equality. In fact, this is a vision that proposes a global re-ordering that is bound to have implications for the privilege of women in the so-called Northern centers of the world. It is a vision that requires investigating the relationship between the relative privilege of some men and women and the deprivation of others.

Maria Lugones, in her essay written with Elizabeth Spellman, "Have We Got a Theory for You! Feminist Theory, Cultural Imperialism, and the Demand for Woman's Voice," asks if feminist theorists are clear about whom they are accountable to, the profession, or those about whom they theorize?[5] This line of inquiry proposes that we theorize, for instance, about the relationship between *maquilladoras* (export manufacturing plants in places such as Mexico and the Philippines) and consumption patterns in North America and Europe, consumption patterns over which some women in these wealthier centers could exercise power. Or, that we emphasize the importance of clean, piped water to women's health in Africa where its absence poses an even more serious threat of death and illness than female circumcision/genital mutilation. But the relationship between maquilladoras and consumption patterns, between clean water and an exploitative economic order that privileges places like the United States, requires a willingness to confront women's oppression that cannot be ascribed to internal male domination or patriarchy alone, and which does not have as its solution only the end goal of female/male equality. It insists that we recognize the role that our privilege plays in the exploitation of women elsewhere in the world. In other words, is the production of feminist theory becoming more and more an academic exercise rather than being clearly related to a political struggle with delineated outcomes?

It is, in fact, a focus on outcome rather than on theory as an academic exercise, that most clearly problematizes the globalization of feminism. What do feminists mean when we talk about women's liberation? In 1990 Gloria Joseph posed the question "[W]ho remains exploited in the process of other [women] being liberated?"[6] One of the key goal-oriented differences between women's rights and feminism has to be systemic transformation—so we don't merely change the sex of the oppressor. But systemic transformation will be revolutionary. In an important and frequently cited article Karen Offen objected to calling feminism revolutionary, preferring, she said, to call it transformational, because the latter word carried "fewer connotations of physical violence."[7] In the same article she goes on to posit feminism as fundamentally a struggle against male domination, and, in arguing for a more inclusive historical basis for feminist analysis; that is, a more comparative study, says many feminist theorists in focusing on the individualism she sees as inherent in much Anglo-American feminism, have been blinded "to the range of effective arguments used to combat male privilege in the western world . . . and

even to arguments put forth today by women and men in economically less-privileged countries where women's aspirations to self-
sovereignty are often subordinated to pressing short-term political and
socioeconomic necessities."[8] In all fairness, I'm speculating here as
to what Offen means by "short-term political and economic necessities," but it seems to allude to anything outside of "women's aspirations to self-sovereignty"—that is, anything that does not take as its
fundamental premise achieving equality with men. So what does
equality with men mean? In its most easily understood definition,
the prohibition of discrimination based upon sex, equality with men
is important to all women everywhere. But in a deeper sense of defining women's liberation as freedom from those things which oppress them, shorten their lives and make their lives harder, kill and
circumscribe their dreams—is equality with men as the ultimate feminist goal merely a prescription for "transforming" the lives of women
privileged by class, race, and/or location? Is the revolutionary aspect
of women's liberation, as the liberation of over half the people of the
world, a world in which the majority of women are oppressed by race,
class, and location, too systemically broad an outcome for feminism
to embrace? Alice Walker once wrote, "Choosing revolution is not
about being willing to give up your life, but being willing to give up
your comfort."[9]

Why is it that so many third-world women, in particular, are re-
luctant to call themselves feminists? One major reason is because their
lived experiences are ones of not only domination by cohort men,
but also of a domination (that they share with cohort men) by a global and often racialized class order. Thus, they do not position men
as the sole enemy, as the lone impediment to their freedom from
want and poverty, or the sole deniers of their freedom to have autonomy over their lives. In an article titled "Cultural Feminism versus Post-Structuralism: The Identity Crisis in Feminist Theory," Linda
Alcoff wrote, "I have simply not found writings by feminists who are
oppressed also by race and/or class that place or position maleness
as wholly other."[10] She is remarking on the fact that, as explicated
in much of third-world feminist theory, women of color recognize
the salience of race and class oppression in their subordination as
women.

In fact, as stated above, the critique of feminism by third-world
women resulted in a dramatic shift in Anglo-American feminist

theory. Whether that theory was lesbian or queer theory, socialist feminist or Marxist feminist, cultural or relational feminist, classic liberal feminist, standpoint theory, or a number of the other varieties of feminist theory that have surfaced in the last several decades, all of it began to incorporate what I will call difference theory into the context of its articulation. Simultaneously the rise of poststructuralist, postmodernist, and postcolonial theory provided space, so to speak, in which to theorize difference. Moreover, the increasing discourse on pluralism and multiculturalism were additional stimuli for theorizing difference.

Poststructuralists and postmodernists often problematized differences to, I will say, a fault. (I know that what I say next is not going to do justice to these very complex theories, but I'm striving to make a particular point about the uses of certain aspects of these theories.) As radical as the premises of these theories appear to be—that is, that we are each uniquely positioned in relative space, contesting relative truths—their applications to political struggle can amount to a prescription for thrashing about in a nihilistic fashion. Their promise, that perspective is important, is a progressive one, except where it allows perspective to be construed as only individualistic or predetermined by a social order absent agency, and therefore boomerangs back to classic, liberal, bourgeois individualism. There are important ways in which the perspective analysis of poststructuralist and postmodernist theories can provide insight for feminist theory, not the least being a demand that we incorporate difference into the theories and agendas of feminist struggle, but aimed toward an end goal of power sharing rather than allowing examination of difference to trap us in the paralysis of analysis.

Similar to poststructuralist and postmodernist theories, standpoint theory has provided important insights for feminist theory. A 1997 article by Susan Hekman critiqued standpoint theory.[11] Replies to Hekman's critique by four of the best-known feminist standpoint theorists, Nancy Hartsock, Patricia Hill Collins, Sandra Harding, and Dorothy Smith, were pointedly critical of what they saw as Hekman's wrong-headed reading of standpoint theory. Hekman takes standpoint theory to task primarily because she sees the multiplicity of feminist standpoints "making coherent analyses . . . impossible, because we have too many axes of analysis."[12] However, standpoint theory is not just talking about axes of analysis, but about dominance and power sharing. Standpoint theory is concerned with the *relations* between axes of analysis. Hartsock and Hill Collins provide the most important response to Hekman's critique by reminding her that she reads standpoint theories, in Hartsock's words, "through a kind of American pluralism that prefers to speak not about power or justice, but rather about knowledge and epistemology."[13] Hill Collins says that Hekman misses the point of standpoint theory overall and that "by decontextualizing standpoint theory from its initial moorings in a knowledge/power framework, while simultaneously recontextualizing it in an apolitical discussion of feminist truth and method" Hekman depoliticizes standpoint theory.[14]

This discussion is the crux of the problem of some feminist theory. How interesting that as the need to problematize difference in feminist theory as a method of understanding power relations, and as related to a political process seeking more equitable distribution of power (justice) surfaces, it is nearly immediately challenged by theories assuming difference as individualistic, unrelated to political outcomes, but rather as ways of knowing. Difference becomes understood as individual uniqueness, not really related to practical theory— that is, theory with delineated outcomes—but to epistemology. Implicitly, we are back to the root of Western philosophy, self—the individual, and equally implicitly back to a binary explanation of the universe, self/other. There is a universal, same as before, only this time the universal is *difference* itself, and it is too diffuse to explain any notion of power relations, in fact, it belies a notion of power relations at all.

This, in fact, is what multiculturalism and pluralism are rapidly turning into, at least in their implementation—difference that is apolitical. A sleight of hand that depoliticizes the inherently political. In 1990 Gerda Lerner wrote of the "advance" from theories of the "melting pot" to theories of the "salad bowl" for theorizing difference in U.S. history.[15] She opined that the "salad bowl mode of analysis was still insufficient as a model of reality because . . . it ignores power, dominance, hegemony. It assumes that the process of doing justice to 'differences' is additive."[16] That is, we allow for difference without analyzing it relationally. I'm a slave, you're my owner, we're different, we have different perspectives on the world. If I write a history of slavery it will be different than the history of slavery that you write. Both histories, on their own, are equally explanatory of slavery,

and where does that get us?—right where we started vis-à-vis our relationship: me still slave, you still owner, our power relations undis-
turbed by analysis.

The real question here is, how do we keep difference politicized,
discuss it relationally, and do so such that rather than being trapped
in the binary paralysis of difference/universality, local/global, we see
difference in and through connection and connection in and through
difference? In a summer 1989 special issue of *Signs* on "Race, Ethnicity
and Class in Women's Lives," Elsa Barkley Brown, in an article titled
"African-American Women's Quilting: A Framework for Conceptualizing and Teaching African-American Women's History," wrote,

> What my mother teaches me are the essential lessons of the quilt:
> that people and actions do move in multiple directions at once. If
> we analyze these people and actions by linear models, we will cre-
> ate dichotomies, ambiguities, cognitive dissonance, disorientation,
> and confusion in places where none exists. If, however . . . we can
> allow the way in which they saw and constructed their own lives to
> provide framework by which we attempt to understand their expe-
> riences and their world . . . [it will] provide [a] structural framework.[17]

This is standpoint theory at its best. People have an understanding
of their location and the more we know about the locations of others, the more we understand our own location in relationship to
theirs, and, more and more, to continue the metaphor, the quilt
comes into sight. Though a quilt can be seen as a whole piece when
it is together, it is actually made up of other, whole pieces, each of
which has a pattern that stands alone, but the quilt is the final unit
of analysis. The whole quilt pattern only comes into view through
seeing the relationship of its parts.

Because at its best standpoint theory provides us insight into the
shared perspectives of those who have conditions and/or characteristics in common, it brings me again to the issue of identity politics.
Identity politics has been critiqued in the name of attacking negative essentialisms. Establishing identity has been a formidable political tool. It has been used by the powerful to delimit those who,
defined as others, are less deserving than themselves, and thus ac-
ceptably, even naturally, exploitable. But it has also been used by the
powerless, as a tool for identifying those who, because they share a
set of similar circumstances, constitute a logical group to organize to
struggle for justice. If people are exploited because of identity it makes

sense for them to use that identity to organize against such exploitation. For instance, if there are de jure or de facto laws/conventions against black people being able to do certain things, should they not organize as black people to challenge such proscriptions? Identity politics may begin to lose some of its salience as the multiple identities (class, gender, etc.) of black people surface in the context of struggle, but as long as there are proscriptions based on that even un-deconstructed identity of being black, it never loses all of its salience. Of course, the efficacy of identity politics depends on a certain degree of self-selection—of recognizing one's identity of interest (and not all one's interests need be shared) with a particular group. And of course, recognizing the utility, even the common sense, of identity politics does not preclude joining in struggle with allies who do not share that identity.

In a recent collection of essays on critical race theory edited by Kimberle Crenshaw et al., Crenshaw discusses what she calls the construction of "vulgar anti-essentialism" by those who want to argue that race simply isn't real and who therefore propose a color-blind public policy that flies in the face of the reality that black people are still disadvantaged as measured by where the majority of them are located economically, politically, educationally, and socially compared to those defined as white.[18] Thus, this color-blind proposal, under the guise of helping blacks and ridding the society of racism, conflates race consciousness with racism, and in a wicked and masterful sleight of hand, blacks who argue for the continuation of ameliorative race-based policies are, in this formulation, construed as racists themselves.

Critical legal theorists such as Alan Freeman argue that, in fact, the legal system has joined hands with such pseudo-logic by increasing emphasis in the judicial system on interpreting anti-discrimination suits based on a perpetrator perspective rather than a victim perspective.[19] The perpetrator perspective places the burden on an individual plaintiff to show discriminatory intent by an individual person or institution. The victim perspective, while still carrying the need to show proof, interprets discrimination as a discriminatory result. Thus, if women and men of color, and white women, have not had their positions measurably improved by legislation to end discrimination, then discrimination is presumed to be still taking place and there is the need to continue ameliorative action. Thus the theory of the law as being neutral, unless testable against a result of neutrality on the ground (a measurable outcome) is meaningless, and in fact can retard justice.

Similarly, theory that does not have a political and real-life application that is testable for providing a measurable outcome on the ground is useless for struggle. Theory that does not even propose a real life application can retard struggle. But second-wave feminism began as a political struggle aimed at making real changes in the lives of real women, and we cannot lose sight of that purpose. We need to be able to see, transparently, in much of feminist theory, an explicit political purpose, a demonstrable political purpose.

Perhaps one of the things we need to return to in developing feminist theory is the connection between theory and practice, not merely in the way in which we construct theory, but in the ways in which we live it. The historian and activist Barbara Ransby recently gave a talk on the renowned late African American civil rights activist Ella Baker in which she posited, "Praxis in concrete struggle transforms not only the world, but the activist herself."[20] Can we create practical theory in the absence of praxis? And in fact, what counts as theory? While there may legitimately be theoreticians who engage in a little praxis to inform their theory, there are minions of practitioners who in the process of practice create theory but who go uninterviewed, unconsulted, uninvolved in our creation of theory because we don't recognize action as a kind of theory itself.[21] As feminists we must be certain that we do not, even implicitly, draw false dichotomies between intellectuals and activists. That does not mean that some feminists might not spend the majority of their time in intellectual production, and others might not spend the majority of their time in active organizational work. What it does mean is that we must actively promote both and actively delineate the relationship between the two. We cannot do this merely by providing lip service to it. Grassroots activists do not always have the tools and the resources to translate their activity, in an available way, to the theoretical level. Theoreticians often end up talking to one another, advancing careers and celebrity status, but doing little that really effects change. Each has resources to bring to the other, because those struggling on the ground also think, debate, critique, and strategize— and more often than not, in relation to real conditions. Those who write do so, one presumes, from a perspective of questioning the justice, utility, morality, and righteousness of what exists. Moreover, many of us do some of both. Yet we need to be more pro-active in providing space and resources where we all debate theory as it relates to action, where we record, video, publish, and analyze things that are actually happening on the ground.

In my metaphor of the quilt, borrowed from Elsa Barkley Brown, I see an analogy with a current trajectory in feminist theory. That trajectory, as mentioned, is an acknowledgment of difference. People now mostly speak of feminisms. In an acknowledgment of the variety of emphases among various feminist constituencies, a theory of feminisms creates the space for political articulation of difference. But the question is, are we striving for representing different perspectives of different women in feminist theory as an end goal? Or, do we still wish feminist theory to provide an analysis of power relations, in the words of Gerda Lerner quoted earlier, to explicate dominance and hegemony for the purpose of seeking a more equitably ordered world for women and men? It is the latter that will illuminate the systematic structure of dominance and its construction not only in intersecting and overlapping pieces, but interdependent pieces, such that white women see how antiracist work is germane to the antisexist struggle, and heterosexuals understand why antihomophobia is their struggle.

There are many women, locally, regionally, nationally, and internationally, who are doing work to better women's lives and also men's lives, and they may not be found in organizations or enterprises that call themselves feminist or that even have the word *woman* in their titles. The work that they do, for instance, in exposing the underbelly of structural adjustment programs, or in attacking regimes that violate human rights, even when women are in the leadership and among the primary beneficiaries, often goes unclaimed as feminist work because it doesn't fit neatly under a rubric of working toward equality with men. We have to look to where women actually are in struggle to be able to relate theory to practice. And, though I don't wish to go into this issue here, a related critical question is the role of men in feminist struggle. In many of these kinds of concrete struggles in real communities around the world, men and women are engaged, therefore, feminist theory needs to deal more explicitly and complexly with men in the struggle, that is, as other than some pure opposition.

Maybe there can be no grand theory, no meta-theory of feminism. But do we believe that feminism can be successful, even in its most narrow construction as women's equality with even cohort men, without challenging the construction of interdependent systems of dominance? Gender will have to be re-configured for even that narrow success, and the configuration of gender has been interdependent with the configuration of race and class for the modern period. In the modern world they cannot be understood independently or extrapolated from one another systemically. So, while there may be, legitimately, different feminisms for different feminist constituencies simultaneously working toward a new world order, somewhere, these multiple routes will converge in challenge to a sexist, racialized, and class-ordered international system of dominance. At each level in that struggle where we achieve some form of success for some women, success becomes problematized when we ignore issues such as race and class oppression. For instance, the decision rendered by the U.S. Supreme Court in *Roe v. Wade* was a dramatic and very real victory that provided freedom of choice and control over their own bodies to all women in the United States. However, within a few years, the Hyde amendment, which disallowed the use of federal funds for abortion, meant that poor women, whose ranks were disproportionately populated by women of color, effectively had that right rescinded. Thus, issues of race and class were just as important as issues of sex and gender in securing certain freedoms and rights for millions of women. The revolution necessary to bring justice to the lives of most women of the world (oppressed by class, and many by race) may be far too disturbing of their own privilege for some feminists and women's rights advocates.

In Mozambique, in the context of struggling against the Portuguese for independence, Mozambicans used to say, "A luta continua, vitoría e certa" ("The struggle continues, victory is certain"). After they achieved independence, victory in armed struggle was clearly seen as a steppingstone to economic, social, and political justice for the Mozambican population, and they said, "Vitoría continua, la Luta e certa" ("Victory continues, the struggle is certain").

The title of this chapter, "Who's to Navigate and Who's to Steer," is meant as an allusion to what I see as a dangerously incipient dichotomy among feminists—that is, some of us create theory, set agenda, decide direction, and choose and rank women's issues, for others to get on board with, others who are sometimes in distant places and spaces both figuratively and literally. Conversely, some of us go about struggling to change practices we define as inimical to the interests of women, eschewing any idea that we are feminists and in fact, sometimes claiming the contrary.

Amilcar Cabral once said that we must pay adequate attention to our own weaknesses as we draw up the list of our enemies.[22] And as such the left, and other progressive feminists, must look within our own ranks and question not merely our anodes of analysis, but our modes of organization and action—and the relationship between the two.

Among our major, emerging challenges as feminists are the following imperatives:

1. The need to more concretely integrate theory with praxis.
2. The need to recognize various modes of articulating theory.
3. The need to identify remaining connections in the process of deconstruction, but also to more concretely develop a discourse on outcomes which will require us to understand differences relationally and not merely as an abstract mode of analysis.
4. The need to better explicate the interdependence of systems of dominance so that the multiplicity of women's standpoints informs even short-term feminist goals.
5. And the need to act on the fact that the discourse about difference is not meant merely as a mode of analysis, but is centrally meant as a discourse about power relations.

A luta continua.

NOTES

1. Amilcar Cabral, "The Weapon of Theory," *Return to the Source* (New York: Monthly Review Press, 1973).
2. Amy Hackett, "The Politics of Feminism in Wilhelmine, Germany, 1890–1920," 2 vols. Ph.D. dissertation, Columbia University, New York, 1976.
3. Cheryl Johnson-Odim, "Common Themes and Different Contexts: Third World Women and Feminism," in *Third World Women and the Politics of Feminism*, ed. Chandra Mohanty et al. (Bloomington: Indiana University Press, 1991).
4. I have not included transsexuals here because it is unclear what role biology (e.g., hormones, etc., *before* surgery) plays in rendering them "biological" women. For instance, when it comes to medical research, which would apply more to transsexual women who were formerly men—results from research on male heart attack victims or female heart attack victims? Thus I am not sure they can be claimed as women in more than a gender sense.
5. Maria Lugones and Elizabeth Spellman, "Have We Got a Theory for You! Feminist Theory, Cultural Imperialism, and the Demand for Woman's Voice," in *Feminism and Philosophy: Essential Readings in Theory, Reinterpretation, and Application*, ed. Nancy Twana and Rosemarie Toing (Boulder, Colo.: Westview Press, 1995).

6. Gloria Joseph, *News and Letters*, June 1990.

7. Karen Offen, "Defining Feminism: A Historical Approach," *Signs* 14:1 (1988): 152.

8. Ibid., 138.

9. Alice Walker, *Goodnight, Willie Lee, I'll See You in the Mornin'*.

10. Linda Alcoff, "Cultural Feminism versus Post-Structuralism: The Identity Crisis in Feminist Theory," *Signs* 13:3 (1988): 412.

11. Susan Hekman, "Truth and Method: Feminist Standpoint Theory Revisited," *Signs* 22:2 (winter 1997): 341–365.

12. Ibid., 367–398.

13. Ibid., 367.

14. Ibid.

15. Gerda Lerner, "Reconceptualizing Differences among Women," *Journal of Women's History* (winter 1990): 106–122.

16. Ibid.

17. Elsa Barkley Brown, "African-American Women's Quilting: A Framework for Conceptualizing and Teaching African-American Women's History," *Signs* 14:4 (summer 1989): 929.

18. Kimberle Crenshaw et al., *Critical Race Theory* (1995).

19. Alan Freeman, in *Critical Legal Studies*, ed. Allan C. Hutchinson (1989).

20. In a talk at Loyola University, Chicago, in March 1997.

21. For a discussion of this idea, see Cheryl Johnson-Odim, "Actions Louder Than Words: The Historical Task of Defining Feminist Consciousness in Colonial West Africa," in *Nation, Empire, Colony: Historicizing Gender and Race*, ed. Ruth Roach Pierson and Nupur Chaudhuri (Bloomington: Indiana University Press, 1999), 77–93.

22. Cabral, "The Weapon of Theory."

PART TWO

GLOBAL LOCATIONS
Postnational Politics

CHARLOTTE BUNCH

WOMEN'S HUMAN RIGHTS
The Challenges of Global
Feminism and Diversity

I want to start with a story from the first African Women's Leadership Institute that I attended in Uganda (February 1997) because it illustrates issues I want to discuss and conveys the sense of possibility that I feel about what I call global feminism. While the term *global feminism* is problematic, it still has resonance for many as a way of describing the growth of feminism(s) around the world over the past two decades. The African Women's Leadership Institute was organized by four young women from different countries in Africa who had attended the global leadership institutes sponsored by the Center for Women's Global Leadership each year and who have been active in the Global Campaign for Women's Human Rights.

They brought twenty-five women, ages twenty-five to forty, from eighteen countries in Africa for three weeks of intensive training in a program that was explicitly dealing with feminism and leadership for the twenty-first century. The fact that over three hundred women applied to spend three weeks there speaks volumes about both the growth of feminism in the region and the seriousness of women's commitments to it. The participants were diverse in terms of country, ethnic identity, and class. Some worked in the public sector in politics and government; many came from nongovernmental organizations (NGOs) and grass-roots women's projects; and a few worked in private corporations or in universities. Their backgrounds were diverse as were their issues of primary concern. Yet as so often happens in events like this, there was also a commonality in the stories that they told about the discrimination and violence that they faced as women that brought them together in spite of their differences.

In one of the opening lectures, Patricia McFadden, a feminist theorist from Swaziland, wove together the themes of feminism in Africa with analysis of colonialism and the ways in which Western patriarchy had imposed itself on the continent. At the same time, she talked about how this should not blind women to the indigenous forms of patriarchy that they also had to confront. She ended her analysis of the intersection of race, class, gender, and sexuality in Africa with a participatory exercise in which she asked women to list on the board names that feminists get called in their country. A multitude of words spewed forth from bra burners to unfeminine to promiscuous to frigid to lesbian to Western/white-identified to women who can't get a man to women who want to be a man to women who are ugly to women who read too much (and "lose contact with their roots") to the "know-alls" and even "Beijing Women," referring to the Fourth World Conference on Women held in Beijing in 1995. Even though these names were expressed in various local languages often reflecting particular cultural concepts, the same accusations that women have experienced in other parts of the world kept appearing on the list. It reminded me that one of the universalities of the feminist struggle is the commonality of our opposition.

McFadden also asked participants to say why they do or don't call themselves feminists. Many replied that before they came to the institute, they didn't or weren't sure whether to call themselves a feminist for various reasons. But many added that after this lecture they would do so because now they understood that was who they were and how the term had been used against women. It was a transforming process that I have seen happen in different ways and arenas around the world. Yet it is still powerful to see how demystifying this word and understanding the way in which it has been used against women enables many to recognize its political nature and reinforces their ability to stand up to those who put women down.

WOMEN'S GLOBAL NETWORKING

The struggle to reclaim and broaden feminism is central to working for women's human rights. Someone once asked if we say "women's human rights" because it's easier for people to accept than feminism. The intention of this movement has not been to avoid the word feminism, but rather to take feminist analysis into the arena of human rights and use it to make women's claims more indisputable by defining them as human rights. By applying feminist concepts and gender analysis to human rights theory and practice, we seek to transform a major body of work and its related institutions that have enormous influence, both practically and theoretically, in the world, and make them more inclusive of women's lives and experiences. Looking at human rights from a gender-conscious point of view has already begun to challenge the limited parameters of what was previously defined as human rights and opened new avenues of government accountability to women.

The growth of women's movements around the world since the 1970s and the United Nations Decade for Women (1975–1985) with its world conferences on women provided the context and background for the movement for women's human rights to emerge in the 1990s. The four UN world conferences on women held from 1975 to 1995 became places where women at the regional and global levels got to know one another and to exchange information, ideas, and strategies. While there have been many other women's international events where such exchange took place as well, the UN conferences played a particularly important role because they provided resources for and a legitimacy to what women were doing that was critical to many women's ability to participate. This global feminist discussion has often been rocky with important contentious debates, but it also has enabled networks and groups of women to see where they share common goals and can build linkages across differences. The irony is that the United Nations certainly never intended to facilitate global feminist networking, but it has helped to create the conditions and sometimes the context from which many women have developed a greater understanding of one another and found ways to work together.

When I speak of the "global" in global feminism, I do not see it in opposition to the "local." This is one of those false dualisms that we must transcend. The greatest strength of women's movements in every region of the world, including the United States, is in the wide diversity of particularized local activity that women do. Most of what feminism has achieved in the last three decades has been through fairly small, specific, local organizations or projects of a million different sorts. These are often competing and debating with one another how to describe various women's experiences and what changes women should seek. In this process, women have developed their own analyses of the reality of women in their particular setting and built strategies responsive to their own specific struggles. It is the richness of this very particularized and local experience that makes it possible to imagine global networking that is reflective of women's diversity. Through the process of development by each specific group of women of their own priority issues and identities the feminist discourse has remained vital and evolved over time. This attention to diversity should also provide the basis for creating more inclusive strategies and visions for the future. These diverse, local, and particularized women's movements are the ground upon which any global activity must build and where it must always return to check out its viability.

Nevertheless, over the past decade, many women have come to feel that working in thousands of small separate projects is not enough. The changes feminists seek demand addressing global forces that are affecting so much of local life today. More women are understanding that their particularized concerns and projects cannot be viewed in isolation from this larger context. For example, the global economy is transforming the conditions of women's work both in the paid economy and at home; organizing in this sector must take this into account. Feminist analysis of the global economy is growing as women examine how their lives are affected by trends like the privatization policies that go by many different names: structural adjustment in the third world, the downsizing of employees and services in the United States, and ending the service sector and job guarantees in Eastern Europe.

Global culture and media also have significant impacts on women's lives and on our efforts to organize. To take an example from that list of things that feminists in Africa get called, one stereotype that has been created by the media and spread through global culture is feminists as "bra burners." Even though, as Patricia McFadden pointed out, the bra was a Western invention with no roots in African culture, nonetheless, feminists there get accused of being West-ern because they're "bra burners." Some of the women at the Afri-can Institute asked, "Where did this term come from?" In the ensuing discussion it was noted that media-created stereotypes spread rapidly from continent to continent. Further, even men who otherwise oppose each other politically will often eagerly use the same media-generated concepts when it comes to what's wrong with feminists.

One of the most damaging and persistent stereotypes used by men everywhere and reinforced by the media is to say that feminism is only Western (white) and middle class (bourgeois). Many feminist leaders and groups have certainly made mistakes and taken actions that reflected these biases, and this must be continuously challenged as we work to create concepts and strategies that are inclusive of women's diversity. However, the continual litany that this is what feminism is and who defines it is a profound insult to the millions of diverse women worldwide, including in the United States, whose ideas and lives have given shape to feminism not only in the past few decades but also over centuries. There have been vibrant femi-nist movements in many countries of Asia, Africa, and Latin America at various points during this century and certainly since the 1970s. Yet, the media systematically neglects reporting on them and usu-ally focuses only on the terrible problems women there face—if it notices them at all. Thus, the feminisms and movements of women in the rest of the world remain unknown to most. Similarly, there is not one Western feminism but rather quite a diverse range of femi-nisms expressed by different groups of women living in Western countries. Yet most of these faces of feminism are rarely if ever ac-knowledged in the media. Thus, even to speak of global feminism requires reclaiming the term *feminism* and recognizing how distor-tions of it have been systematically used to exacerbate differences among women.

Perhaps the greatest challenge feminists face locally is that at the same time a global phenomena is on the rise of different kinds of fundamentalisms and backlash, both religious and secular. Religious fundamentalism—whether Christian, Muslim, Hindu, Jewish, or Bud-dhist—and secular fundamentalism like nationalism in the former Yugoslavia, all force women to identify with the particular narrow identity of their group and to disavow "the other." Most of these fun-damentalisms also demand that women be the carriers of the cultural purity of their particular group. When women are identified with culture—as reproducers and bearers of tradition—their freedom is usually circumscribed by the male leaders of their group, and they are often also used as the front line against feminism. The ability of competing fundamentalisms to unite as a global force against feminists was made clear at the Women's Conference in Beijing when right-wing Republican U.S. congressmen were in agreement with the Vatican, the Islamic mullahs, and the secular Chinese Communist government in their opposition to the inclusion of gender, sexuality, and reproductive rights in the Platform for Action.

Growing recognition of the global forces affecting women's lives has fueled women's efforts at global networking during the 1990s—including within the women's human rights movement. And this is where the UN world conferences have come to play a key role. Prior to the World Conference on Women in Nairobi in 1985, most of what went on in the name of global feminism or international women's work was information sharing or solidarity work supporting another group's needs. But the global networking that has emerged in the nineties goes beyond solidarity—though that continues to be important—to a more integrated understanding of the connection between what's happening in one country and another. Thus, not only do women care about what's happening to other women in Afghanistan or Rwanda, but also we understand that the advance of fundamentalism anywhere has implications for its growth in other countries and the instability and violence of armed conflicts spill over many borders. Feminists of course still need to act out of solidarity but also to understand that events in diverse parts of the world affect each other. Global networks that have the capacity to respond with a greater international effort can thus strengthen local work.

Understanding the need for more global connections among women gained considerable ground at the time of the third UN World Conference on Women in Nairobi. In 1975, at the first UN World Conference on Women in Mexico City, the debates were generally divided along the lines of the three prevailing UN blocs and the slogan for the UN Decade symbolized this: "Equality, Development, and Peace." These terms reflected what was understood as central to the "woman question" in each of the three blocs. Thus, Equality was seen primarily as a feminist issue coming from Western industrialized countries; Peace was included at the request of the Eastern Socialist bloc; and Development was perceived as key to the improvement of women's lives in third-world countries. At the end of the decade conference in Nairobi by contrast, many women had rejected this division into separate areas and were calling for an understanding of the intersection of these issues. The seeds of several future global networks were sown in Nairobi. One of the groups leading in this effort was DAWN—Development Alternatives with Women for a New Era—a group of women from the South who worked together to produce a book for Nairobi that was a feminist analysis of development and international capitalism and their impact on women. To respond to the challenges posed by the global economy, they called for strategies that crossed North and South lines, with leadership from Southern feminists. They saw no hope of achieving the kind of changes women sought nationally without building alliances that moved both South-South and North-South. Alliances like these played a key role in beginning to shift the discussion of development in the international community to take greater account of women and gender analysis.

The UN world conferences in the 1990s became the occasion for many of these nascent networks to emerge in a more public arena. Women were already sharing strategies and information around development, health, the environment, violence, et cetera. What the world conferences provided was an opportunity to make more visible women's experiences and to showcase feminist/gender-aware perspectives on major global issues. Throughout the eighties many women had been involved in significant efforts to redefine development, and witnessed how the United Nations and some other development agencies began to reflect some of women's concerns in what came to be called human development, a concept that went beyond the prevailing economic development theories. Similar work to redefine society's major paradigms became the focus of women's global networking around the UN world conferences: The Earth Summit on the Environment in Rio in 1992; the World Conference on Human Rights in Vienna in 1993; the International Conference on Population and Development in Cairo in 1994; the World Summit for Social Development in Copenhagen in 1995; the World Conference on Women in Beijing in 1995; the Habitat World Conference on Human Settlement in Istanbul in 1996; and the World Food Summit in Rome in 1997.

Feminist analysis and practice moved into these global public spaces as women brought work done on issues concerning violence, reproductive rights, pay equity, women's political participation, et cetera, to the agendas of the world conferences. The women demonstrated what a gender analysis means in terms of global public policy. While there were of course many differences and debates among women about what should be done at the conferences and how to define a gendered approach, these were generally political differences, not ones based primarily on identity and geography. Women found themselves agreeing with some of the women from different countries and as often disagreeing with some of the women from their own identity groups. While women drew on the insights gained in identity politics, they also recognized the need to move beyond that in order to create a global political force.

These global networks are still emerging, but their experience points to the possibility of organizing that builds on the specificity that women have developed around particular identities and takes account of diversity but also creates a broader political analysis from that place. This is an effort to take the best of identity politics and its grounding in the particulars of differences according to race, class, sexuality, nationality, and other factors and move from that knowledge toward a common political analysis of the larger forces at work. It assumes that diverse experiences can help build broader strategies and more effective next steps. An example of how this works can be seen in the women's human rights movement that has grown out of this impetus for global feminist networking.

The international movement for women's human rights crystallized around the second United Nations World Conference on Human Rights held in Vienna in 1993. It emerged in response to numerous concerns and reflected women's collaborative efforts in diverse contexts. In particular, many women in different regions believed that the issues they were organizing against—especially various forms of gender-based violence such as battery, rape, female genital mutilation, female infanticide, or trafficking—were human rights crises that were not being taken seriously as human rights violations. Thus, despite the many differences among the women organizing for the Vienna conference, women were able to articulate, develop, and act upon a common agenda that took as its focal point the issue of gender-based violence against women.

One of the major expressions of this movement at the international level has been the Global Campaign for Women's Human Rights—a loose coalition of groups and individuals worldwide formed in preparation for the Vienna conference. Several organizations and regional networks worked together to launch the Global Campaign, and they used networking as a primary mode of mobilizing women. This coalition pursued a number of diverse strategies and advanced various issues under the broad umbrella of demanding that women be put on the agenda in Vienna and that violence against women be recognized as a human rights violation. Having gained recognition of women's rights as human rights in Vienna, the Global Campaign then coordinated a series of actions that included workshops, strategic planning meetings, human rights caucuses, and hearings on women's human rights at the International Conference on Population and Development in Cairo, the World Summit for Social Development in Copenhagen, and the Fourth World Conference on Women in Beijing.

Since these conferences, one of the ongoing tasks of the Global Campaign for Women's Human Rights has been pushing for implementation of the various UN world conference commitments to women. Activists have coordinated efforts globally to lobby the various human rights mechanisms of the UN to fulfill their commitment to the full integration of gender concerns and awareness into their work. Similarly, much effort has gone into working with regional and national bodies, both governmental and nongovernmental, for the full incorporation of gender consciousness and women's human rights into their agendas. In 1998, the Global Campaign utilized this same method of networking in putting forth several broad themes under the slogan Celebrate and Demand Women's Human Rights. This effort sought to bring women's perspectives into commemorations of the fiftieth anniversary of the Universal Declaration of Human Rights at the global level and to encourage diverse but coordinated expressions of this theme locally.

Another ongoing initiative of the women's human rights movement that embodies this approach is the "16 Days of Activism against Gender Violence," an international campaign which links November 25 (International Day against Violence against Women) to December 10 (International Human Rights Day). The 16 Days Campaign aims to provide a global umbrella for local activities that promote public awareness about gender-based violence as a human rights concern and that seek specific commitments to women's human rights at all levels. Groups participating in the campaign select their own particularized objectives and determine their own local activities, but all are done with a sense of being part of this larger global focus.

The driving force of these campaigns has been commitment to action-oriented networking and to building linkages among women across multiple boundaries including class, race, ethnicity, religion, and sexual orientation, both within local and national-level communities and across geopolitical divides. In these activities, the women's human rights movement has utilized human rights approaches to strengthen local mobilization efforts and to advance local objectives, while at the same time linking them to a larger international movement with broad common goals. It has thus incorporated a wide range of particularized women's issues into an overall international framework for action and change.

WHY HUMAN RIGHTS?

One of the first questions that the women's human rights movement has had to address is why feminists should use the human rights concepts and framework for our concerns at all? The limitations in the origins of modern human rights practice are real: it's Western, it's male, it's individualistic, its emphasis has been on political and not economic rights. However, looking beyond its origins to the particular movements for change in the twentieth century that have taken up this concept, we see that the idea that all people have fundamental human rights has become one of the most powerful concepts that disenfranchised groups have used to legitimize their struggles. In the anticolonial independence movements in Asia and Africa, in struggles against dictatorships in Latin America, in movements for the rights of the indigenous, in the African American movement in the United States, human rights language has given voice to claims to be included in the human community as equal citizens. As each group that has been excluded from mainstream power and political discourse stakes their claim to human rights, the term and the practice that derives from it has also been revitalized and expanded in its meaning—taking it further from those limited origins and closer to the ideal of universal human rights for all. The whole body of human rights literature as well as the UN treaties and mechanisms to enforce them established in the last fifty years has had to change and grow as each group has laid out its claims.

Women are following this historical precedent in demanding full recognition of our humanity and posing challenges that are already beginning to transform human rights concepts and practice to be more responsive to women's lives. Human rights language creates a space in which different accounts of women's lives and new ways of demanding change can be developed. Women from many different countries have used it to articulate diverse demands in relation to a broad array of issues. Human rights also provides overarching principles to frame visions of justice for women without dictating the precise content of those visions. As an ethical concept, human rights speaks to values and principles that are not tied to any one religion and can be useful to feminists in answering conservative or fundamentalist attacks.

Human rights is a powerful term that transforms the discussion from being about something that is a good idea to that which ought to be the birthright of every person. Thus it provides a powerful vocabulary for naming gender-based violations and impediments to the exercise of women's full equality and citizenship that legitimizes the demand that these be taken seriously. For many women, it has been empowering to realize that abuses they endure or have endured such as rape, battery, forced marriage, or bodily mutilations are recognized as violations of their humanity. Further, by interpreting abuses of women as human rights violations, women gain greater access to the large body of international and regional human rights treaties, covenants, and agreements that make up international human rights law and practice.

Human rights is as close as we have in the world today to an agreement about what is crucial to human dignity. It is at the center of debates over what every person should have the right to and what no person or state should be able to violate. The Universal Declaration of Human Rights adopted by all the governments in the United Nations in 1948 remains the core document for human rights deliberations. It defines human rights as universal, inalienable, and indivisible. All of these defining characteristics are important for women.

The idea of human rights as *inalienable* means that no one can voluntarily abdicate her/his human rights since those are rights which we have by virtue of being human. This also means that no person or group can deprive another individual of her/his human rights. Thus, for example, debts incurred by migrant workers or by women caught up in sex-trafficking can never justify indentured servitude (slavery), or the deprivation of food, of freedom of movement, or of compensation. Human rights cannot be sold, ransomed, or forfeited for any reason. In theory, then, these are not rights which a country gives or can take away from anyone since they inhere in each person. Further, if governments do deprive citizens of these rights or fail to protect them, they are in violation of their obligation as a state to promote and protect their citizen's rights.

The *universality* of human rights means that human rights should apply to every single person equally, for everyone is equal in simply being human. While such an interpretation of universality may seem simple, this egalitarian premise has a radical edge that makes it one of the most challenged issues in human rights. By invoking the universality of human rights, women have demanded the incorporation of women- and gender-aware perspectives into all of the ideas and institutions that are already committed to the promotion and protection of human rights. Further, universality challenges the contention that the human rights of women (or any group) can be limited by religious or culturally specific definitions of their role.

It is important to note that the concept of universality in human rights does not mean that everyone is or should be the same, but rather that all are equal in their rights by virtue of their humanity. Further, it demands that these rights not be culturally circumscribed and denied to any one group of humans. Of course interpretations of human rights are not static but represent what the prevailing forces in the human community decide are the fundamentals of what is acceptable for the treatment of people. The question then is, who decides what are these agreed-upon human rights? Women are demanding both an end to the double standard of who has human rights and, perhaps even more important, the right to be engaged in their ongoing definition and interpretation. In cultures where there is debate about whether the concept of human rights is being imposed from the outside, women have argued that the concept of universality means that they have the right to be part of those deciding how to interpret human rights principles in their context and that their interpretation must apply equally to men and women.

The *indivisibility* of human rights means that none of the rights that are considered to be fundamental is supposed to be seen as more important than any of the others and that they are interrelated. Moreover, since human rights encompass civil, political, social, economic, and cultural facets of human existence, the indivisibility premise highlights that the ability of people to live their lives in dignity and to exercise their human rights fully depends on the recognition that these aspects are interdependent. The fact that human rights are indivisible is important for women, since their civil and political rights historically have been compromised by their economic status, by social and cultural limitations placed on their activities, and by the ever-present threat of violence that often constitutes an insurmountable obstacle to women's participation in public and political life.

Indivisibility also challenges the historic Western bias in favor of civil and political rights over social and economic rights. Many people in the United States don't even realize that the Universal Declaration of Human Rights includes social and economic rights. However, many groups throughout the world have spent a great deal of time working on how to demand and realize rights to things like development, housing, and employment. Women's human rights activists have rejected a human rights hierarchy which places either political and civil rights or socioeconomic rights as primary. Instead, women have charged that political stability cannot be realized unless women's social and economic rights are also addressed; that sustainable development is impossible without the simultaneous respect for, and incorporation into the policy process of women's cultural and social roles in the daily reproduction of life; and that social equity cannot be generated without economic justice and women's participation in all levels of political decision making.

While indivisibility has not yet been realized in human rights practice, it reinforces what feminists have called intersectionality or the interrelatedness of factors like race, class, age, gender, and sexuality. A person's rights or experience of violation cannot often be divided out according to one of these factors alone, for how one experiences each of these is affected by the others. The everyday reality of this principle was reiterated in most of the testimonies presented in the hearings and tribunals organized by the Global Campaign for Women's Human Rights at the UN world conferences. As women told the story of how they were violated in one area of their lives such as domestic violence, it was evident how this was exacerbated by other factors such as race or their lack of economic or political rights in other areas. Further, indivisibility of human rights reminds us that human rights are not for some while others can be left on the margins. As long as the rights of some are denied—whether on the basis of race, gender, culture, sexual orientation, or other factors—the human rights of all are undermined.

These basic concepts reflect the ideals of human rights while the considerable body of human rights standards, treaties and mechanisms that have evolved over the past fifty years are intended to translate those ideals into reality. These are particularly useful to establishing governmental accountability for protecting and promoting the human rights of women. While governments may not fulfill these obligations, most claim to care about human rights and are sensitive to both internal and external pressure to live up to the treaties they have signed. These have sometimes provided the basis for legal challenges to national law. For example, a woman in Botswana sued her government for the right to give her children her own nationality under the terms of the Convention on the Elimination of All Forms of Discrimination against Women (CEDAW). She won her suit on the grounds that this was sex discrimination that violated CEDAW, which her country had ratified. Since a number of countries do not allow women to pass on their nationality to their children, who must take that of the father, her victory had implications beyond Botswana.

In the effort to bring the issue of rape and forced pregnancy in war and conflict onto the international human rights agenda, women have successfully utilized human rights arenas such as the Vienna World Conference on Human Rights and mechanisms such as the International Criminal Tribunals for the former Yugoslavia and Rwanda. The United Nations is currently engaged in setting up an international criminal court, which can have a significant impact on how such crimes against women are pursued in the future. They are debating the terms of the court: what will be the definition of war crimes? Will rape, sexual slavery, forced pregnancy, and other violations of women be war crimes and under what conditions? Will crimes against women outside of warfare be included in the jurisdiction of an international criminal court? Will individuals be able to bring crimes before the international court, or will it only be governments who can do so? The decisions made now will determine what kind of access women will have to this international justice system in the future. Women's human rights activists from all regions of the world have operated for several years as an ongoing international group called the Women's Caucus for Gender Justice in the International Criminal Court to inject a gender perspective and to influence such decisions from the inception of the court rather than having to add gender later on, as women must do in so many of the existing human rights bodies.

There are a number of other treaties, standards, and mechanisms that the United Nations and regional organizations have developed for realizing human rights which women are now seeking to address from a gender-conscious perspective. But for people in the United States, we face a particular problem because our government claims to be a big defender of human rights internationally yet has refused to ratify many human rights treaties. It has refused to do so precisely because it is afraid that people in this country will use them to address abuses of human rights within the United States. The Convention on the Elimination of All Forms of Discrimination against Women, for example, is much more progressive than anything in the U.S. Constitution, even than the ERA, which was defeated. There are a number of provisions in the Convention on the Rights of the Child as well that cover human rights in the family that have been useful to women elsewhere, but the U.S. Government is the only industrialized country that has ratified neither of these treaties. The United States has also refused to ratify the Covenant on Social, Economic, and Cultural Rights, because it might become the basis for challenging economic policies here. Indeed, some welfare rights organizations are now doing just that—utilizing human rights principles and covenants to challenge U.S. welfare policy.

One of the most important future potential uses of human rights is to be the basis for establishing standards by which international financial institutions and multinational corporations can be held accountable for the impact of their policies. In the trend toward privatization in recent years, many governments find themselves relatively helpless in the face of violations by multinational corporations or in relation to the World Trade Organization. The question is, do we as a human community believe there should be checks on these transnational forces? Some people are beginning to look at whether the human rights system can be utilized to establish standards of what is expected from the private sector in the world today. Women's human rights advocates must be present from the beginning of this important exploration or once more, gender-aware perspectives on the responsibilities of global economic forces and the rights of women workers may be left out.

Another demonstration of the power of talking about women's rights as human rights could be seen at the Fourth World Conference on Women in Beijing as women articulated the various issues of the agenda as questions of the human right to education, to political participation, to health care, to a life free of violence, et cetera. Many governments became nervous and began to talk about how the conference must not "create any new rights." However, the expanding interpretation of human rights principles from the perspective of previously excluded groups like women always brings with it the articulation of "new"—that is, not previously recognized—rights. The clearest example of this for women has been the rapid acceptance in the nineties of violence against women as a violation of human rights; the greatest resistance to this expansion has been the reluctance of many to recognize sexual rights as human rights. Further, it was clear in Beijing that many governments recognized that women's increasing use of human rights language implied a greater demand for government accountability to the promises that were being made. Identifying these issues as human rights does not automatically provide ways of holding governments accountable, but it does open wider the doors of the human rights system for women to take steps toward more effective measures for such accountability.

SUMMARY

The success and extent of women's human rights networking globally is all the more significant in light of critiques that suggest that the effort to find a common articulation of women's concerns or a common basis for women's organizing is seriously flawed. Some argue that to do so is to universalize the category of woman and to impose a limited agenda on all women on the basis of the experience of some women—usually white, middle class, and living in the north. Given the ways in which geography, ethnicity, race, culture, sexuality, class, and tradition shape what it means to be a woman and the specificities of local and national politics, it is important not to conceive of women or the women's movement as singular and coherent entities. Nevertheless, the experience of the women's human rights movement suggests that a global feminism driven by international feminist networking is also possible. Such networking does not require homogeneity of experience or perspective, or even ongoing consensus across a range of issues. Rather it can be built around acknowledging diversity while also finding common moments at the intersection of diverse paths.

Even as women have worked to recognize, admit, and incorporate diverse perspectives in their thinking and work, they have also struggled to create alliances and to work together in solidarity across differences in the face of conservative and fundamentalist backlashes against feminism occurring in many parts of both the North and the South. Through an understanding of the exercise of power as global and interconnected (that is, universally experienced, though different in its effects) universal human rights can be seen as a system of accountability required by the way power is exercised. In this way, the idea of universal human rights serves as a regulative principle which informs the articulation of women's local demands and strengthens their resistance to abuses of power.

When local women's groups use human rights thinking and practice, especially in the context of international networking, they actively demonstrate the complementary links between universal ideals and local struggles for justice. The Global Campaigns for Women's Human Rights can be seen as one example of the kind of mobilization that is necessary to translate international human rights standards into local social and political practice. Although it is difficult to find a common framework through which to analyze women's lives and organize for change without falling into the trap of false universalization, the international movement for women's human rights has consciously strived to challenge the idea that we must choose between universality and particularity. The movement began with the central operating principle that its concepts and activities should be developed through a process of networking with women who work and organize at the local, national, and international levels in all regions of the world. Similar types of networking have been taken up as a method of organizing by tens of thousands of women from all over the world, and they have successfully linked together women from diverse backgrounds to work on common projects.

The experiences that women gained in networking nationally, regionally, and internationally around the UN world conferences have provided the basis of trust for many to now seek to work on common and diverse projects in collaboration and solidarity on a regular basis. As this work gets translated into local and global expressions, the ability of women's networking to provide a model for affirming the universality of human rights while respecting the diversity of our particular experiences will grow. This can then lead us to take more effective action on behalf of all human rights in a time when the need for common action globally based on ethical principles is greatly needed.

NOTE

This essay is based on "Women's Rights Are Human Rights: Discourses of Universality and Particularlity," a presentation given as part of the Thinking about Women Series at the Institute for Research on Women at Rutgers University in 1997.

I would like to acknowledge in particular the collaboration of Samantha Frost and Niamh Reilly in the development of some of these ideas for an earlier essay.

LEELA FERNANDES

RETHINKING GLOBALIZATION
Gender and the Nation in India

In recent years, the paradigm of globalization has sought to demonstrate and explain the limits and decline of the nation-state in the face of transnational cultural and economic formations.[1] In his essay on recent intellectual deployments of the concept of diaspora, James Clifford notes that "An unruly crowd of descriptive/interpretive terms now jostle and converse in an effort to characterize the contact zones of nations, cultures and regions: terms such as 'border,' 'travel,' 'creolization,' 'transculturation,' 'hybridity,' and 'diaspora.'"[2] This catalogue of concepts signifies the emergence of a growing body of scholarship that has attempted to interpret and explain the transnational flows of people, capital, and culture of various historically specific forms of globalization.[3] One of the central theoretical foundations, in this endeavor, has been the notion that such global flows fundamentally center on the crossing of boundaries and borders. The question of territoriality thus occupies a critical location in context of debates regarding the implications of contemporary processes of globalization. In particular, scholars have argued that globalization is marked by processes of deterritorialization which transcend or destabilize the territorial boundaries of the modern nation-state.[4]

In this chapter, my aim is to shift the terms of this debate from the question of how the nation is being reformed through processes

of globalization to the question of how the production of "the global" occurs within the space of the nation-state and through nationalist narratives. The foundation for such a shift rests on a paradoxical
assumption of territoriality which marks contemporary discussions
of globalization. Such arguments are often implicitly based on a geographic imagination which assumes that "the global" (or geographically speaking, the globe) can only encompass "the national" (the
territorially bounded nation-state). In other words, the paradigm of
globalization assumes that processes within the larger territorial unit
(the global field) can impact on and destabilize the smaller territorial unit of the nation-state. However, such an approach does not interrogate the ways in which different forms of globality, "the terms
in which the world-as-a-whole is defined," are produced within the
territorial and cultural space of the nation-state.[5] In such approaches,
globalization, then, by a tautological definition must be marked by
cultural, economic, and political processes which transcend the nation and provide the foundation for the possibility of a postnational
era.[6]

The invention of conceptions of globality occurs within the context of both the economic and cultural particularities of specific national contexts as nation-states interpret, respond to and manage the
transnational movement of capital, people, and cultural forms. This
process of producing a form of globality in conjunction with nationalism in fact can be traced to older historical processes. Benedict
Anderson, for instance, has demonstrated that the naturalization of
European dynasties in the nineteenth century occurred in conjunction with the development of "official nationalisms" in a process that
he terms the "willed merger of nation and dynastic empire."[7] Such
comparative historical instances serve as reminders that globalization
is not a historically new process that has replaced the nation. On the
contrary, older conceptions of globality have in fact historically developed in conjunction with nationalism. The task at hand, then, is
to locate conceptions of globality within specific historical, cultural,
and material contexts.

Globalization in India has occurred within the context of the
"new economic policies" of liberalization initiated in the 1990s. This
process of liberalization has been characterized by an increased pace
and in an appearance of public acceptance of India's transition to a
free market economy. Both television and print media images increas-

ingly seem to contribute to the reproduction of a new public culture, one that has discarded the last remnants of a state-dominated planned economy. This public culture becomes a critical site in which the politics of economic liberalization are negotiated through the articulation of a new relationship between the national and the global. Such a relationship between the national and the global rests on an emerging paradigm that attempts to manage the disjunctures of India's accelerated integration into the global economy through a continual interplay between a fetishization of hybridity and a politics of purity. On the one hand, public cultural representations increasingly depict India's shifting relationship with the world economy through images of a productive hybrid relation between the national and the global. On the other hand, unsettling configurations of power which may suggest that globalizing forces are overwhelming the Indian nation are displaced onto the territory of women's sexuality. The purity of sexuality, then, marks and maintains the borders of "Indianness" in the context of the hybridized relationship between the national and the global.

A study of the cultural politics of globalization in India presents a striking exemplar of the ways in which "globality" is invented through the deployment of nationalist narratives. As I have demonstrated elsewhere, such an analysis calls into question three central components of the postnational thesis of the globalization paradigm.[8] The first component consists of the notion that "the work of the imagination" is a central feature of modern subjectivity and is primarily constituted through the globalizing forces of media and migration.[9] I demonstrate that the imagined form of the "global" is itself produced through cultural signs and symbols that rest on the deployment of nationalist narratives; semiotic spaces in the media created through globalization thus do not in this context necessarily lead to a weakening of the nationalist imagination. Second, hybridity, a social category which has been represented as a central marker of transnationalism, provides a means for a reworking of the national imagination in response to movements of economic and cultural capital.[10]

Here, I will focus on the ways in which globalization in the Indian context has not led to a form of deterritorialization but instead has produced a form of reterritorialization which centers around the politicization of gender and sexuality in contemporary India.[11] In this context, the potential destabilization of social codes which might arise from cultural products traveling across national borders is managed through attempts to police the border of women's activities. The "cartographic anxiety" of the postcolonial nation-state produces a link between the protection of the territorial borders of the nation and the protection of women.[12] Such a conception entails once again moving away from a geographic conception of globalization which identifies processes of deterritorialization with the movement of people and commodities across the territorial units of nation-states to an approach which conceptualizes globalization in terms of the "changing forms of the spatial organization of social relations."[13] As we will see, this analysis provides the basis for a reconceptualization of the relationship between space and territory. Local spatial practices are technologies for the production of the nation. Contemporary globalization, in effect, allows for the reterritorialization of the nation through forms of socio-spatial reorganization which occur within the nation-state rather than merely at its official territorial borders and build on and produce internal social inequalities such as gender, class, and ethnicity. Such a reconceptualization of notions of space and territory must, then, follow Stuart Hall's call to move away from simple binary oppositions between the local and the global and turn instead to an analysis of the ways in which linkages between the local, national, and global are articulated in the context of specific historical, cultural, and material circumstances.[14]

I explore this gendered relationship between the national and the global through an analysis of cultural representations in the public sphere in contemporary India. My aim in this chapter is not merely to dispute the postnational thesis of globalization through an analysis of processes associated with the traditional political domain of the nation-state but to analyze the ways in which the very public cultural sites marked as the signifiers of postnationalism delineate meanings of globality constructed within the terrain of nationalist discourses. Arjun Appadurai, for instance, has argued that it is "the micronarratives of film, television, music and other expressive forms, which allow modernity to be rewritten more as vernacular globalization and less as a concession to large-scale national and international politics."[15] My methodological approach thus draws on an analysis which rests on a foundation not of a quantitative content analysis of advertisements nor on a deconstructive or psychoanalytical study of the effects of particular media images but on an interpretive approach that crosses genres (film, state legislation, social activism, and media representations) in its analysis. In this endeavor, I treat such genres as the signs and symbols which constitute the "webs of significance" which are used to interpret, manage, and produce conceptions of globality.[16] My analysis demonstrates that, on the contrary, such cultural sites provide the means for the vernacular mobilization that leads to the consolidation of rather than a withering away of the nation-state. Such an endeavor necessitates a move away from geographic conceptions of the local, national and global as expanding levels of scale to an interrogation of the ways in which "the global" is imagined within the constraints of an actually existing cartography of national polities and economies. The analysis draws on nine months of fieldwork which I conducted in Bombay in 1996 and 1998. The fieldwork included the documentation of public representations in the print and television media, twenty-five formal interviews with representatives in the advertising industry and journalists and editors in the print media, fifty interviews with individuals documenting the actual experiences and responses of middle classes to the effects of economic reform, ethnographic observations and numerous informal conversations.

GLOBALIZING THE NATION, NATIONALIZING THE GLOBAL

The invention of contemporary meanings of globality occurs through displays of commodities and nations produced in cultural sites such as print and visual media images.[17] This exhibition of the world in the context of late twentieth-century capitalism occurs within the space of the modern nation-state in a process which intricately intertwines the idea of the global with the nationalist imagination. Contemporary globalization does not in this context pose a self-evident challenge to the form of the nation-state. On the contrary, the case of India demonstrates a dialectical relationship in which globalization produces a refashioning of the Indian nation while the global is simultaneously invented through national discourses. The specific material conditions of globalization in India, manifested in policies of economic liberalization, result in the production of a national political culture which centers on a culture of consumption; such newly available commodities, in effect, serve as signifiers that assimilate globalization to the Indian nation-state.[18]

The transformation of the Indian nation through processes of globalization can be seen in the transition in national political culture from the early years of the Nehruvian regime in the 1950s to the contemporary moment of liberalization in India. The early decades of economic policy in post-independence India were focused on the development of large-scale industrial units; the emphasis of economic development was on production in heavy industries rather than on the production of consumer-oriented commodities. Political rhetoric ranging from speeches of politicians to popular films such as *Mother India* produced linkages between modernist ideologies of development, the reduction of poverty, and the Indian nation; the urban middle classes were relatively invisible in this visual political culture. This vision of the Indian nation has undergone a striking shift in the context of contemporary globalization. The accelerated economic reform process which was unfolding in India in the 1990s has brought to the forefront an intensified manifestation of the image of the Indian nation which Rajiv Gandhi imagined through his policies and rhetoric in the second half of the 1980s. Rajiv Gandhi's vision substantially rested on the role of the middle classes. If the tenets of Nehruvian development could be captured by symbols of dams and mass-based factories, the markers of Rajiv Gandhi's shifted to the possibility of commodities that would tap into the tastes and consumption practices of the urban middle classes.[19] This possibility has, to a large extent, been realized in the 1990s. As Rajiv Gandhi envisioned, the commodities available through multinational corporations and through joint production ventures by Indian and multinational capital signify the production of a national cultural standard associated with the urban middle and upper classes.

Representations of such newly available commodities in advertising in the print media provide a lens through which we can view the ways in which meanings attached to such commodities weave together narratives of nationhood and development with the production of middle-class identity. If the historical emergence of modern nationalism has been linked to the rise of what Benedict Anderson has called "print capitalism," the imagination of the nation in the more recent historical past is inextricably bound to capitalist technologies of vision.[20] Images of newly available commodities in contemporary urban India are inextricably linked to the deployment of nationalist narratives. The contest between both Indian companies and multinational brands is played out through their attempts to associate their products with symbols of Indian nationhood. Businesses have increasingly attempted to consciously address social criticisms of the negative cultural effects of multinational products. Marketing strategies which now commonly involve the sponsorship of cultural events and the deployment of culturally specific symbols are thus constitutive of systemic shifts in business practices. In the process, this contest begins to transform the nation form. The fetishized hybridity of the national and the global begins to rewrite the Indian nation in the context of India's changing relationship with the global economy.[21] The aesthetic of the commodity in this context does not merely serve as a passive reflector of wider social and cultural processes but instead becomes a central site in which the Indian nation is reimagined within the context of a globalizing economy.

W. F. Haug has explored the ways in which the aesthetic of the commodity form (the types of meanings which surround the commodity) intervenes in the collective imagination of the society in question and the ways in which such aesthetics react with already existing social and cultural forms.[22] In his conception, this involves a circular process which place the capitalist commodity, aesthetics, and social relations in an inextricable, mutually constitutive relation. He argues that while commodities first borrow their aesthetic language from human relations, as the circulation of the commodity is consolidated, people then begin to borrow their aesthetic expression from the world of the commodity. I am suggesting, following Haug's argument, that the cultural politics of globalization in India has produced a relationship between the commodity, aesthetics, and the nation. The result then is that the language of the nation in this process begins to borrow its aesthetic expression from the world of the commodity. The intervention of the commodity form into the collective imagination then represents a critical intervention into the way in which the nation is imagined. The nation is imagined not just through the conventional sites and symbols of nationalism such as war memorials or Independence Day celebrations but through the aesthetic of the commodity form.

Meanwhile, the nation form in India also undergoes a process of transformation as it is aestheticized through the newly available commodities. In this process, the desire for the nation, like the desire for the commodity, becomes linked to the aesthetic promise of use value.[23] The markers of the progress of the Indian nation no longer rest on the mass-based factories of the Nehruvian vision or the physical labor of grass-roots self-reliance which marked Gandhi's conception of village development. Hence, there is a significant shift in the ways in which the material progress of the Indian nation must now be measured. Such progress can now no longer be limited to the desire for the physical quantity of production but must confront the quality of the commodities. The aesthetic promise of the use value of newly available commodities then provides a critical rationale for the accumulation of foreign capital within the Indian nation-state.[24] Hence, it is an aestheticized vision of the Indian nation-state rather than a transnational cultural identity that attempts to manage India's integration into the global economy. This rewriting of the Indian nation centers around the role of the middle classes and the articulation of a new cultural standard associated with the production of a middle-class urban lifestyle in globalizing India.

The invention of a hybridized form of globality, one which is dialectically linked to the nationalist imagination in liberalizing India, provides the foundation for an empirical and theoretical conception of the social category of hybridity as an identity which does not transcend but is intricately connected to processes of capital formation within the boundaries of the modern nation-state. As Pheng Cheah, in his critique of metropolitan conceptions of hybridity, has cautioned, "New cosmopolitanisms cannot explain why globalization has paradoxically led to the intensification of nationalism in the postcolonial South without resorting to the knee-jerk dismissal of the national/local as an ideological form."[25] My point is not to make a case for the ideological form of the nation-state but to suggest that the apparent paradox between globalization and nationalism stems from the territorially based assumption that globalization is a wider process that must transcend or dislodge the nation-state. The subversive potential of hybridity and diaspora rests on an identification between a cultural form of hybridity and the crossing of territorial national boundaries.[26] Such an identification does not, however, interrogate the ideological and material conditions that constitute the production of conceptions of hybridity. Thus, in existing conceptions while the nation-state is conceptualized as an ideological form rather than an empirical sociological fact, hybridity is often constructed as a given social location which transcends the material conditions and territorial boundaries of the nation-state. On the contrary, an analysis of the cultural politics of liberalization in India demonstrates that hybridity is linked both to the reproduction of territorial nationalism as well as to the production of specific forms of materially based class cultures which are linked to the global circulation of capital and commodities. Such processes, in the Indian context, have been centrally linked to the production of public cultural images of the urban middle classes, images which attempt to re-imagine the Indian nation in conjunction with the politics of globalization. This delineation of linkages between middle-class respectability and commodity consumption was echoed in interviews which I conducted with journalists and advertisers in the print media.

Images of consumption constitute part of the technologies of visions which begin to define the aesthetic and cultural standards of what counts as ideal individual, family, and community cultural and social practices. This mediation between the national and the global unfolds through the reworking and reproduction of particular gendered social codes. If newly available commodities such as cellular phones and pagers denote status symbols for the middle class they are also cast as the tools to keep families together, or as the text of one ad reads, "If you were told that a pager ties you down, well, it does bind your family together." A central category of images which dominate the print media attempts to associate domestic commodities such as automobiles and refrigerators with particular forms of class and gender identity. Such images are rife with scenes of idealized heterosexual domesticity. For instance, a series of automobile advertisements "Man Woman and Child and Car" appear to reproduce a sense of order that may quell the anxieties of forms of cultural, social, and economic disorder associated with economic liberalization. Such images implicitly invoke older messages of state family planning rhetoric which have promoted smaller, nuclear families. However, the austere warnings about the ills of large families which characterized earlier state-sponsored advertisements now give way to an association between an idealized tranquillity of the nuclear family with status, and material comfort. Meanwhile, the four members of the state-sponsored family model (man, woman, son, and daughter) have been replaced by man, woman, child, and car. In this vision of the modern Indian family, the commodity once again while seeming to displace the nation-state in fact reworks and underlines older ideological narratives which have been deployed by the state. Such images of the urban middle classes begin to outline the contours of a new bourgeois public sphere for it is the urban middle classes which are delineated as the consumers not just of the newly available commodities in liberalizing India but consumers of the new India produced through the meanings attached to these commodities. Central to this vision is the re/articulation of narratives of gender which can both mark and manage the disruptions which lie beneath the sanitized images of the comfort and satisfaction of the middle classes.

RETERRITORIALIZING THE NATION: GENDER SEXUALITY AND THE NATIONAL BODY POLITIC

In the context of contemporary globalization, the politics of gender serves as a central ideological site for the production of a new script which can manage the contradictions of liberalization and mark the boundaries of the future of the globalizing Indian nation. The sense of shared temporality through "the steady onward clocking of homogeneous, empty time" serves as a constitutive basis for nation formation not merely as a synchronic moment but as a diachronic progression which rests both on the invention of a shared past as well as a vision of futurity.[27] The imagination of a national future unfolds through a set of contradictory and contested gendered politics. The trajectory of a globalizing India has produced images of "the new Indian woman," one who "must attend her national identity as well as her modernity; she is Indian as well as new."[28] "The New Indian Woman" as the publicity release for a contemporary women's magazine puts it is "the tough as nails career woman who finds it easy to indulge in the occasional superstition. Her outlook is global, but her values would make her grandma proud." As the publisher of this women's magazine argued, "Our values remain, they don't leave a certain framework which is still the Indian value system . . . I think we respect that and we function and address women within that framework. Of course she's urban, she's contemporary, she travels . . . but that framework still exists."[29]

Images of the "new Indian woman" attempt to negotiate the contradictions inherent in the politics of globalization. Gender, in this context, serves as the sociosymbolic site which attempts to manage the destabilizing contradictions which globalization produces in the

Indian nation. The intermeshing of nationalist narratives with images of global economic and cultural flows rest in uneasy tension with global configurations of power. The remapping of the Indian nation and the production of urban public culture occurs in conjunction with external constraints posed by International Monetary Fund and World Bank loans and economic restructuring programs; nationalized constructions of foreign commodities rest alongside an intensified economic dependence on foreign capital investment in India. Such systemic hierarchies which potentially unsettle the boundaries of the nation then serve to transform the cultural politics of globalization into the potential threat of Westernization; the lure of hybridity in this context holds within it the dangers of impurity. The potential disruption is managed through a remapping of the nation's boundaries through a politics of gender which centers around conflicts over the preservation of the purity of women's sexuality, a process which once again conflates the preservation of nationness with the protection of women.[30] This form of gendered politics signifies a form of reterritorialization of the nation; the borders of the national body politic are, then, policed through the regulation of women's bodies. Such a conception entails once again moving away from a geographic conception of globalization which identifies processes of deterritorialization with the movement of people and commodities across the territorial units of nation-states to an approach which conceptualizes globalization in terms of the "changing forms of the spatial organization of social relations."[31] These spatial practices are technologies for the production of the nation. Contemporary globalization, in effect, allows for the reterritorialization of the nation through forms of socio-spatial reorganization which occur within the nation-state. Thus, conceptions of the relationship between globalization and territorialization cannot rest on a focus on the crossing of the official territorial borders of the nation-state but must interrogate the ways in which the technologies of territorialization re/produce the boundaries of internal social inequalities such as gender, class, and ethnicity within the nation-state.[32]

Consider the events following the 1996 national elections in India when the Bharatiya Janata Party (BJP), one of the central opposition parties and proponents of a form of economic nationalism (swadeshi), was asked to form a government.[33] During this initial tenure in government, the party whose anti-consumerism election slogan on the new economic policies had been "computer chips not potato chips," appointed a finance minister well known for his pro-liberalization policies in a critical move signaling that the BJP would not reverse the existing direction of economic reforms initiated by the previous Congress party government.[34] However, during the BJP's rule, the central force of the government's anti-reform rhetoric was concentrated on the cultural sphere, particularly in relation to television and advertising. The focus on obscenity and calls for increased censorship of film and media images have comprised a significant and consistent component of the BJP's political rhetoric and activities.[35] During the BJP's early stint in power in 1996, for instance, the information and broadcasting minister, Sushma Swaraj, launched a series of attacks on supposed sexualized representations within the media ranging from advertisements for contraception which she directed were not to be aired during times when young children might view television, to a television advertisement which depicted a woman with a billowing skirt (modeled on the well-known Marilyn Monroe scene), to Swaraj's reported comments that Doordarshan (state television) announcers needed to refrain from wearing revealing clothes during newscasts. Such events are exemplary of a broader pattern of the ways in which such resistance to the new economic policies of liberalization is displaced from the realm of concrete economic policy to a confrontation with a gendered cultural politics of globalization; nationalist resistance in the form of BJP's swadeshi platform was concentrated on the supposed contamination of the purity of Indian culture, embodied in this context by the potential threat to the purity of women's sexuality.

Let us further examine this process through a consideration of two additional situations which stage a similar attempt to manage the disjunctures of globalization through the invocation of a politics of purity.[36] On July 10, 1996, thousands of women workers who were employed as waitresses and dancers marched to the Maharashtra state government's office in Bombay in protest against state laws that would prohibit them from working in bars and restaurants after 8:30 P.M.[37] The law, which represented a reactivation of a 1948 act that barred the employment of women from working in establishments such as shops and restaurants before 6 A.M. and after 8:30 P.M., was part of a morality drive launched by the conservative Shiv Sena government in Bombay.[38] The Maharashtra Government's Cultural Affairs Ministry, which spearheaded this endeavor, began to revoke the licenses of establishments that held late-night dance shows.[39] The clubs and bars that cater to middle-class men (ranging from "regular" middle-class constituencies to "VIP" rooms that cater to wealthy businessmen) are concentrated mainly in the suburban areas around Bombay.[40] In the context of the creation of the urban public culture that I have outlined, such local state strategies provide a clear attempt to redefine the boundaries of Indianness, boundaries which rest on the purification of Indian cultural life. Government officials, for example, argued that the offending establishments had distorted accepted cultural norms as they had obtained licenses by classifying the dances as classical dances; according to local officials, dances set to popular film songs did not fit the category of legitimate cultural activities.

The state's move to police the boundaries of cultural life was fundamentally dependent on the deployment of a set of gendered discourses. Public rhetoric of government officials and some newspaper reports centrally located the rationale for this middle-class morality drive in terms of the protection and purification of women's sexuality. On the one hand, officials indicated that the 1948 law was being reactivated in the name of the safety of women. Indeed, this act is related to wider protective labor legislation, which has also prohibited women from working in night shifts in factories. As in the case of factory employment where such night-shift regulations have threatened the employment of women workers, women protesting the law in Bombay argued that such restrictions would cause significant losses in wages as a substantial portion of their earnings were comprised of tips earned in later hours of the evening (when businessmen visit the bars after work). This politics of protection, which has been a central ideological strategy of state policy in comparative contexts, has provided the symbolic capital for the state government's efforts to displace the disjunctures of globalization onto a gendered terrain of public cultural life. This process of displacement is highlighted by the paradoxical situation where the government was imposing restrictions on women workers in bars and restaurants whereas the export-oriented jewelry and electronics industries (which are in line with the export-oriented growth strategies of the new economic policies) was recently successfully able to modify the Factories Act weakening national labor law which has prohibited the employment of women workers in factory night-shift work. As Kapur and Cossman have argued, a central component of Hindu nationalist discourses "has become one of constituting the identity of 'modern but not western.'"[41] The production of this identity, then, is able to negotiate the tensions between globalization and the nation-state; potential social contradictions resulting from the entry of women in the paid work force necessary in the context of contemporary global capitalism are managed through the cultural purity of the "new Indian woman."

Such processes are not, moreover, limited to the official realm of state discourses. Consider, for instance, various public discourses on the barmaids in the print media. Newspapers simultaneously began to contribute to this discursive transformation of women's labor rights into a problem of protection. Newspapers began reporting numerous rapes of women working in bars. However, such reports focused on women's vulnerability to assaults during late-night hours rather than on violence against women as a social problem. The incidents of rape were recast as evidence of the dangers of women traveling from work at night rather than in terms of patriarchal domestic ideologies that attempt to confine women to the home. Such media representations converge with national patterns of judicial discourses on rape which, as Veena Das has argued, "mediate the everyday categories of sexuality and sexual violence, sorting and classifying the normal and the pathological in terms of marriage and alliance."[42] Hence, both state and civil discourses contributed to the transformation of working women into deviant figures implicitly displacing the responsibility of sexual violence to the socio-spatial transgressions of the women in question. This transgressive quality to women's nighttime employment was underlined by a second trope deployed by government officials and news commentators who speculated on the link between women employed in bars and restaurants and the supposed spread of prostitution.[43] Thus, the state government's attempt to rescue Indian cultural life rested on both the protection and purification of women's sexuality, a project which revealed the persistent links between the politics of sexuality, culture, and morality and the significance of the social enforcement of such links in the context of wider social and economic transitions.

Such events are not merely deviant occurrences in a local conservative state government but they represent also instances of a wider set of processes associated with the politics of globalization in India.

Rupal Oza, for instance, has analyzed the ways in which widespread protests over the "Miss World" contest held in Bangalore were framed through a set of gendered nationalist discourses. Organizations from a wide ideological spectrum ranging from women's wings of the Communist Party of India to the Bharatiya Janata Party protested the pageant on the grounds that it represented a threat to the Indian nation; while the BJP depicted this threat as an assault on Indian national culture and womanhood, organizations from the ideological left argued that the contest encouraged the entry of foreign capital into the country.[44]

Let us turn to another cultural text, a "socially progressive" film, *Aastha,* which further demonstrates the ways in which recent economic and cultural shifts in postcolonial India across the ideological spectrum have been articulated in terms of the problem of the purity of women's sexuality.[45] In contrast to popular commercial Hindi cinematic representations which increasingly contribute to the imagination of a globalizing India and the rejection of Nehruvian state socialism, *Aastha* is firmly grounded in a critical analysis of transnational capitalism and the effects of consumerism and commodification of the new economic policies on the urban middle classes in India.[46] The story, set in Bombay, focuses on the lives of Amar, a professor who teaches English literature, his wife, Maansi, and their daughter; the plot of the film centers on the ways in which the production of desire for newly available brand-name commodities disrupts their comfortable middle-class family life; Maansi, without her husband's knowledge, becomes a high-class prostitute in order to earn money to buy goods which they cannot afford on their middle-class income. The central event which produces this disruption occurs when their daughter breaks her shoe. The incident causes a significant problem for Maansi as her daughter wants Nike or Adidas shoes, both of which are foreign brands and are significantly outside the reach of their family income. Maansi is then drawn into prostitution by Reena, a woman she meets in the store who offers to purchase the shoes for her. Her first act of prostitution presents an ambiguous synthesis of consent and coercion—she is unaware that Reena has brought her to a luxury hotel in order to service a client; however, the event is presented as an act of seduction as Maansi is captivated by the splendor of the hotel, the plush surrounding of the suite, and the delicate soaps in the bathroom. While she initially appears to resist the man's advances, the film projects her submission in terms of a form of consensual acquiescence which rests on the intermingling of sexual pleasure and materialistic desire; during the course of the film she continues her relations with this man, using the money to purchase commodities for her family and herself. The film, by calling into question the boundaries between sexual desire and Maansi's prostitution, attempts to point to the links between commodity desire and India's economic prostitution within the global economy—as Amar comments in one scene when his students ask him how he came to Bombay, "Bombay imports everything."

Aastha's representation of the conflation between commodity desire and sexual desire departs in many ways from the state government's morality drive which I have discussed above. The depiction of Amar as an English professor (with scenes of discussions of Shakespeare's plays) disrupts a clear-cut categorization of the film as anti-Western; on the contrary, the film clearly focuses its social criticism on a (Western) multinational capitalism and its links to commodification. Meanwhile, the film's depiction of the heroine involved in extramarital sexual relations is atypical both in its graphic visual representation of such relations as well as in the fact that Maansi's relations do not inevitably lead to the breakup of her marriage.[47] However, the film inadvertently produces a cultural text, which, as with the case of the Shiv Sena government's drive for moral purification, designates the terrain of women's sexuality as the site for the production of a cultural critique of the globalization (particularly in relation to India's shifting relationship with the global economy). In this process, I want to suggest that gender is not merely a symbolic or metaphorical code of the contamination of India's social and cultural order, rather women's sexuality becomes the actual material site for this interplay between contamination and purification. For instance, Maansi's prostitution begins to affect her lovemaking with her husband as she becomes more sexually aggressive. In a striking scene, Amar asks her where she has learned this, and she responds by saying she has watched a video. Although he admits to liking her new sexual identity, he tells her that there is no need to learn any more—she has learned enough. It is Maansi's sexuality which must now be controlled as she is in danger of transgressing acceptable middle-class (patriarchal) codes of behavior. Her transgression of acceptable boundaries shifts from the question of an economically based relationship of exploitation which has induced her to have sexual relations in return for money to a context where her viola- tion of social codes centers on the quality of her own sexual prac- tices outside of this economic relationship. It is here that the critique of multinational capitalism shifts subtly from a focus on an economi- cally based form of consumerism to a gendered, culturally based form of sexual transgression. Thus, throughout the film, it is Amar who stands as the voice of critical reason which rejects rampant consum- erism, while Maansi is captured within a spiraling cycle of pleasure, power, and desire (Foucault, 1978). The possibility of the film pre- senting a critique which traces links between the commodification of goods and the commodification of women in the context of transnational capitalism is curtailed by this shift to a conflation be- tween commodity desire and women's sexual desire. This socially progressive economically based critique of consumerism and multi- national capitalism inadvertently converges with the Shiv Sena's cul- turally based drive for the preservation of moral standards in Bombay. The threat to the purity of women's sexuality becomes a central trope which places these two ideologically disparate instances of cultural critique of globalization within a shared discursive space. Such a poli- tics of purity thus emerges as a means for the management of the disruptions that arise from a hybridized construction of the national and the global as India continues its accelerated integration into the global capitalist-cultural economy.

SUMMARY

I have argued that the social and cultural disruptions stemming from India's new economic policies of liberalization are being negotiated through the delineation of a new relationship between the national and the global. This form of contemporary globalization in India calls into question the central components of paradigms which argue that globalization leads to the decline of the nation-state central com- ponents of the postnational thesis: the workings of a postnationalist imagination, transnational processes of hybridization, and of deterri- torialization. The unsettling danger of power relations immanent in the system of international relations which may allow globalizing forces to overwhelm the Indian nation are displaced onto the terrain of women's sexuality. In this process, the hybridized version of the

national and the global, which bring together within a single space
the master narratives of global capitalism and nationalism, attempts
to produce a gendered cultural economy which can temporarily resolve the dislocations of the age of globalization and its specific manifestations through the economic policies of liberalization in India.

NOTES

1. I am grateful to Benedict Anderson, Cavidad Souza, and Arvind Rajagopal for comments
   on an earlier version of this essay. Thanks go to Lloyd Rudolph for pointing me to an
   analysis of Rajiv Gandhi's policies. The framing of the argument benefited from Bob
   Goldman's comments on a presentation of this research at the Association for Asian
   Studies, 1998. Thanks go to Rupal Oza and Susanne Rudolph for their support. Fieldwork for this essay was conducted with the support of an American Institute for Indian
   Studies Senior Research Fellowship, 1995–1996 and by an American Council of Learned
   Societies/Social Science Research Council, 1998–1999.
2. James Clifford, *Routes: Travel and Translation in the Late Twentieth Century* (Cambridge:
   Harvard University Press, 1997).
3. See, for example, Arjun Appadurai, *Modernity at Large: Cultural Dimensions of Globaliza-
   tion* (Minneapolis: University of Minnesota Press, 1996); Homi Bhabha, *The Location of
   Culture* (London: Routledge, 1994); Anthony King, ed., *Culture, Globalization and the
   World System: Contemporary Conditions for the Representation of Identity* (Minneapolis:
   University of Minnesota Press, 1997).
4. See Appadurai, *Modernity at Large*; J. M. Guehenno, *The End of the Nation-State*, trans.
   V. Elliott (Minneapolis: University of Minnesota Press, 1995); Jürgen Habermas, "The
   European Nation-State: On the Past and Future of Sovereignty and Citizenship," *Public
   Culture* 10 (2): 397–416; K. Omae, *The End of the Nation-State: The Rise of Regional
   Economies* (New York: Free Press, 1995).
5. Roland Robertson, "Social Theory, Cultural Relativity and the Problem of Globality," in
   King, *Culture, Globalization and the World System*, 88.
6. Appadurai, *Modernity at Large*, 159.
7. Benedict Anderson, *Imagined Communities: Reflections on the Origin and Spread of
   Nationalism* (New York: Verso, 1983), 83.
8. My concern in this essay is with this particular paradigm of globalization. In particular, my
   argument engages with theoretical approaches that explicitly deal with postcolonial contexts as my research concentrates on postcolonial India. For a critique of liberal and
   marxist versions of the postnational thesis of globalization, see Anthony Smith, *Nations
   and Nationalism in a Global Era* (Cambridge, Mass.: Polity Press, 1995).
9. Appadurai, *Modernity at Large*, 9.
10. See, for example. Bhabha, *The Location of Culture*; Clifford, *Routes*.
11. See Appadurai, *Modernity at Large*, for an elaboration of this notion of deterritorialization.
12. Sankaran Krishna, "Cartographic Anxiety: Mapping the Body Politic in India," *Alternatives*
    19 (1994): 507–521.
13. Doreen Massey, *Space, Place and Gender* (Minneapolis: University of Minnesota Press,
    1994).
14. Stuart Hall, "The Local and the Global: Globalization and Ethnicity," in King, *Culture, Glo-
    balization and the World System*.
15. Appadurai, *Modernity at Large*, 9.
16. Clifford Geertz, *The Interpretation of Cultures* (New York: Basic Books, 1973), 5.
17. This section summarizes a more extensive theoretical discussion and presentation of
    empirical research which I have developed in "Media Images, Cultural Politics and the
    Middle Class in India," *Media, Culture and Society* 22:5 (2000): 611–628.
18. My point throughout this discussion is not to suggest that this shift in political culture is
    a finished or uncontested process but to examine the making of this culture.
19. Rajiv Gandhi formally announced his new economic policies in 1986. The policies pro-
    vided an initial phase of liberalization which rested to a great extent on the expansion of
    the consumer goods industries (soft drinks, cosmetics, VCRs, automobiles).

20. Such processes are also critical in the case of television. S. C. Bhatt points out that even in state-owned television (Doordarshan) in 1992 four of the top five advertisers were multinational corporations (accounting for 21 percent of total advertising revenue). However, the expenditure share of the advertising industry is still highest in the print media (67 percent for print media and 20 percent for television in 1992). See S. C. Bhatt, *Satellite Invasion of India* (New Delhi: Gyan Publishing House, 1994).

21. My discussions of the fetishization of hybridity draws on a Marxian rather than a psychoanalytical conception of fetishism. I am suggesting that hybridity is transformed into a commodity that embodies the relationship between the Indian nation and transnational capitalism. See Karl Marx, "The Fetishism of Commodities and the Secret Thereof," in *Capital*, Vol. 1, Unabridged Version, ed. Frederick Engels (New York: International Publishers, 1975 [1887]).

22. See W. F. Haug, *Critique of Commodity Aesthetics: Appearance, Sexuality and Advertising in Capitalist Society* (Minneapolis: University of Minnesota Press, 1986).

23. Haug, *Critique of Commodity Aesthetics*, 17.

24. I am building here on Haug's discussion of the ways in which the aesthetic promise of use value is linked to the accumulation of capital; within the context of global capitalism and its specific manifestation in the form of economic liberalization, the aesthetic promise of use value is linked not just to capital accumulation in the general sense but also to the accumulation of foreign capital. The lure of foreign brands being produced and distributed in India can thus be linked to the opening up to foreign investment multinational companies and the loosening of import restrictions.

25. Pheng Cheah, "Given Culture: Rethinking Cosmopolitical Freedom in Transnationalism," *Boundary* 24:2 (summer 1997): 70.

26. See Bhabha, *The Location of Culture*.

27. Anderson, *Imagined Communities*, 37.

28. Rajeswari Sunder Rajan, *Real and Imagined Women: Gender, Culture and Postcolonialism* (London: Routledge, 1993).

29. Interview with author, September 17, 1998.

30. Such processes are also evident in other national contexts. See, for example, Jacqui Alexander, "Not Just (Any)Body Can Be a Citizen: The Politics of Law, Sexuality and Postcoloniality in Trinidad and Tobago and the Bahamas," *Feminist Review* 48 (1994): 5–23; and Anne McClintock, *Imperial Leather: Race, Gender and Sexuality in the Colonial Context* (London: Routledge, 1995).

31. Massey, *Space, Place and Gender*, 168.

32. I develop this theoretical argument regarding the boundaries of categories in *Producing Workers: The Politics of Gender, Class and Culture in the Calcutta Jute Mills* (Philadelphia: University of Pennsylvania Press, 1997).

33. The election results failed to produce a clear parliamentary victory for the leading national political parties and the president asked the Bharatiya Janata Party, now the single largest party in parliament to form a government, to prove its majority in parliament within two weeks. The BJP-led government failed to gain enough allies to prove a majority, and the government lasted only twelve days. However, the recent national elections have returned the BJP to power as the leading party of a new coalition government. Limits of space prevent a full discussion of the role of communalism and Hindutva. For a discussion of the relationship between the media and the Hindutva movement, see Arvind Rajagopal, *Politics after Television: Religious Nationalism and the Making of a "Hindu" Public* (Cambridge, U.K.: Cambridge University Press, forthcoming).

34. This has also characterized the new BJP-led government. While the BJP continues to espouse a policy of swadeshi, the government has also made assurances that foreign investors will not be affected. Note also that the Hindutva movement in general and the BJP party are not a homogeneous unit and are comprised of both pro- and anti-economic-reform wings.

35. See Ratna Kapur and Brenda Cossman, *Subversive Sites: Feminist Engagements with the Law in India* (New Delhi: Sage Publications, 1996), 253, for an analysis of the legal ramifications of this trend.

36. Such gendered effects are not unitary. New television shows are also producing middle-class spaces for the discussion of issues of gender and sexuality. My point here is to analyze the ways in which a politics of purity is serving a critical site for the management of the disjunctures of globalization.

37. Note that the law only applies to the service industry. The march was organized by the Maharashtra Bar and Restaurant Ladies' Employees' Union. According to one estimate, 500 bars in the Bombay area employ over 30,000 waitresses. See Shameem Akthar, "Barred Maids," *Indian Express*, May 14, 1995. Note also that the restrictions were eventually withdrawn.

38. The Shiv Sena represents a Maharashtrian party which has been known for its conservative regional nativism and has been a long-standing political ally of the BJP in national and state politics. For a discussion of the Shiv Sena, see Jayant Lele, "Saffronisation of Shiv Sena: Political Economy of City, State and Nation," *Economic and Political Weekly* (June 1995): 1520–1528.

39. The shows that involve women dancing to the latest popular Hindi film songs do not, in general, involve any form of public nudity.

40. In addition, the morality drive required restaurants to close at 12:30 A.M. Note, however, that five-star hotels catering to transnational businessmen were exempted from this legislation.

41. Kapur and Cossman, *Subversive Sites*, 267.

42. Veena Das, "Sexual Violence Discursive for Matron and the State," *Economic and Political Weekly* 42 (September 1996): 2411–2423.

43. Similar discourses operate in relation to women employed in factories, author's work 1997.

44. See Rupal Oza, "Showcasing India: Anxiety, Nation and Sexuality" (Paper presented at the Association for Asian Studies, 1998). Note, in contrast, the Shiv Sena sponsored a highly publicized Michael Jackson concert: A Western cultural event that did not threaten hegemonic gender codes was clearly acceptable to the Shiv Sena's code of cultural and national purity.

45. The film departs from commercial popular films in its attempt to present a serious critical commentary on social transitions which have occurred in the contexts of the new economic policies; the film does not contain any scenes of violence or regular popular film song and dance sequences.

46. See Tejaswini Niranjana, "Integrating Whose Nation? Tourists and Terrorists in Roja," *Economic and Political Weekly* 29 (1994): 79–82.

47. The film does not present the audience with closure on this subject; it ends with Maansi and her husband discussing the events in terms of a hypothetical situation. The final scene presents Maansi asking Amar what he would do if she were the woman; in response, he embraces her and the film ends.

REFERENCES

Alexander, Jacqui. "Not Just (Any)Body Can Be a Citizen: The Politics of Law, Sexuality and Postcoloniality in Trinidad and Tobago and the Bahamas." *Feminist Review* 48 (1994): 5–23.

Anderson, Benedict. *Imagined Communities: Reflections on the Origin and Spread of Nationalism.* New York: Verso, 1983.

Aneja, Rajendra. "Marketing and Selling in India in the Year 2000." *Economic and Political Weekly* (May 1996): M26–M30.

Appadurai, Arjun. *Modernity at Large: Cultural Dimensions of Globalization.* Minneapolis: University of Minnesota Press, 1996.

———. and Carol Breckenridge. "Introduction." In *Consuming Modernity: Public Culture in a South Asian World,* ed. Carol Breckenridge. Minneapolis: University of Minnesota Press, 1995.

Berger, Suzanne, and Robert Dole, eds. *National Diversity and Global Capitalism.* Ithaca, N.Y.: Cornell University Press, 1996.

Bhabha, Homi. *The Location of Culture.* London: Routledge, 1994.

Bhatt, S. C. *Satellite Invasion of India.* New Delhi: Gyan Publishing House, 1994.

Bourdieu, Pierre. *Distinction: A Social Critique of the Judgement of Taste.* Trans. Richard Nice. Cambridge: Harvard University Press, 1984.

Chatterji, Partha. "The Nationalist Resolution of the Women's Question." In *Recasting Women: Essays in Indian Colonial History,* ed. Kum Kum Sangari and Sudesh Vaid. New Brunswick, N.J.: Rutgers University Press, 1990.

———. *The Nation and Its Fragments: Colonial and Postcolonial Histories.* Princeton, N.J.: Princeton University Press, 1993.

Cheah, Pheng. "Given Culture: Rethinking Cosmopolitical Freedom in Transnationalism." *Boundary* 24:2 (summer 1997): 157–197.

Clifford, James. *Routes: Travel and Translation in the Late Twentieth Century.* Cambridge: Harvard University Press, 1997.

Dubey, Suman. "The Middle Class." In *India Briefing,* ed. Philip Oldenberg. Boulder, Colo.: Westview Press, 1991.

Featherstone, Mike, ed. *Global Culture: Nationalism, Globalization and Modernity.* London: Sage Publications, 1990.

Fernandes, Leela. *Producing Workers: The Politics of Gender, Class and Culture in the Calcutta Jute Mills.* Philadelphia: University of Pennsylvania Press, 1997.

———. "Beyond Public Spaces and Private Spheres: Gender, Family and Working-Class Politics in India." *Feminist Studies* 23:3 (fall 1997): 525–547.

———. 1999. "Reading 'India's Bandit Queen': A Trans/National Perspective on the Discrepancies of Representation." *Signs: A Journal of Women, Culture and Society* (autumn 1999).

———. "Media Images, Cultural Politics and the Middle Class in India," *Media, Culture and Society* 22:5 (2000): 611–628.

Habermas, Jürgen. "The European Nation-State: On the Past and Future of Sovereignty and Citizenship." *Public Culture* 10:2 (1998): 397–416.

Hall, Stuart. "The Local and the Global: Globalization and Ethnicity." In *Culture, Globalization and the World System,* ed. Anthony King. Minneapolis: University of Minnesota Press, 1997.

Haug, W. F. *Critique of Commodity Aesthetics: Appearance, Sexuality and Advertising in Capitalist Society.* Minneapolis: University of Minnesota Press, 1986.

Khilnani, Sunil. *The Idea of India.* New York: Farrar, Straus and Giroux, 1997.

King, Anthony, ed. *Culture, Globalization and the World-System: Contemporary Conditions for the Representation of Identity.* Minneapolis: University of Minnesota Press, 1997.

Kothari, Rajni. *Growing Amnesia: An Essay on Poverty and Human Consciousness.* New Delhi: Viking, 1993.

Krishna, Sankaran. "Cartographic Anxiety: Mapping the Body Politic in India." *Alternatives* 19 (1994): 507–521.

Marx, Karl. *Capital* Vol. 1. Unabridged Version (1887). Edited by Frederick Engels. New York: International Publishers, 1975.

Massey, Doreen. *Space, Place and Gender.* Minneapolis: University of Minnesota Press, 1994.

McClintock, Anne. *Imperial Leather: Race, Gender and Sexuality in the Colonial Contest.* London: Routledge, 1995.

Mitchell, Timothy. *Colonizing Egypt.* Berkeley and Los Angeles: University of California Press, 1991.

National Council of Applied Economic Research, Indian Society of Advertisers. *Socioeconomic Effects of Advertising.* New Delhi: National Council of Applied Economic Research, 1992.

Ninan, T. N. "Rise of the Middle Class." *India Today,* December 3, 1985.

Oza, Rupal. "Showcasing India: Anxiety, Nation and Sexuality." Paper presented at the Association for Asian Studies Conference, Washington, D.C., 1998

Rajagopal, Arvind. "The Uses of the Past: The Televisual Broadcast of an Ancient Epic and its Reception in Indian Society." Ph.D. Dissertation. University of California, Berkeley, 1992.

Rajan, Rajeswari Sunder. *Real and Imagined Women: Gender, Culture and Postcolonialism.* London: Routledge, 1993.

———. "The Rise of National Programming: The Case of Indian Television." *Media, Culture and Society* 15:1 (1993): 91–112.

Robertson, Ronald. "Social Theory, Cultural Relativity and the Problem of Globality." In *Culture, Globalization and the World System,* ed. Anthony King. Minneapolis: University of Minnesota Press, 1997.

Robison, Richard, and David Goodman. *The New Rich in Asia: Mobile Phones, McDonalds and Middle-Class Revolution.* London: Routledge, 1996.

Rudolph, Lloyd. "The Faltering Novitiate: Rajiv at Home and Abroad in 1988." In *India Briefing,* ed. Marshall Bouton and Philip Oldenburg. Boulder, Colo.: Westview Press, 1989.

Smith, Anthony. "Towards a Global Culture?" In *Global Culture: Nationalism, Globalization and Modernity,* ed. Mike Featherstone. London: Sage Publications, 1990.

———. *Nations and Nationalism in a Global Era.* Cambridge, Mass.: Polity Press, 1995.

Vasavi, A. R. "Co-opting Culture: Managerialism in Age of Consumer Capitalism," *Economic and Political Weekly* (May 1996): M22–M25.

Williamson, Judith. *Decoding Advertisements: Ideology and Meaning in Advertising.* New York: Boyars, 1978.

DEBRA J. LIEBOWITZ

CONSTRUCTING COOPERATION
Feminist Activism and NAFTA

The collective power of people to shape the future is greater
now than ever before, and the need to exercise it is more
compelling. Mobilizing that power to make life in the twenty-
first century more democratic, more secure, and more sustainable is the foremost challenge of this generation. The world
needs a new vision that can galvanize people everywhere to
achieve higher levels of co-operation in areas of common concern and shared destiny.
                          —The Commission on Global Governance, *Our Global
                                                  Neighborhood*, 1995

We need to turn the process around and you can't do that by
yourself. You have to be connected to other people or
groups . . . especially because the process itself is global. We
need to have globalization empower women and not just harm
them. . . . This is an optimistic vision for how we can develop
global strategies for changing the situation of women.
                          —Patricia Fernández, January 12, 1996

GLOBALIZATION AND FEMINIST TRANSNATIONAL ORGANIZING

The North American Free Trade Agreement (NAFTA), which came into
effect in 1994, created the single largest trade bloc in the world with
a combined annual GNP of over $6 trillion and a labor market of more
than 362 million people. Nongovernmental organizations (NGOs) responded to their governments' call to create a "borderless" North
America by crossing those very same borders. They strategized, developed, and collectively articulated numerous critiques of the proposed agreement. Among them, they pointed out that the state
boundaries of the "new" North America were selectively porous: the
holes would be large enough to let capital investment, manufactured
goods, commodities, and pollution through, at the same time that

they slowed the flow of people (read illegal Mexican immigrants) into the United States. Unlike the terms of European integration, the free flow of citizens was not part of the bargain. However, somewhat unexpectedly, nongovernmental political organizers found their own ways of breaking down the national borders dividing the three countries by working to critique, reframe, and challenge the proposed agreement. My focus is on feminist transnational organizing in these efforts.[1]

As the case of North American economic integration demonstrates, transnational political organizing has developed in direct response to the increasingly global economy. Cross-border political organizing plays an important role in shaping economic integration by contesting a version of globalization and economic restructuring that does not adequately address the needs of economically marginal populations. Undergirding these efforts is the belief that the process of globalization is not inexorable and instead is constituted through political resistance and engagement. Indeed, as feminist political contestation of NAFTA shows, structural economic and political changes have an impact on the relations between and among citizens and states. In other words, the "logic of collective action" has been altered by international economic restructuring.[2] And, consequently, the terms of the debate over trade policy and globalization more generally have been reconfigured.[3] Economic integration at the governmental level reshapes the public sphere since the processes of policy formation and decision making do not inhere within national borders. For my purposes this process of reconfiguring the politics of resistance in light of globalization is a critical part of the story of NAFTA's birth. Governmental negotiation about North American integration was occurring at the regional level and in order to maximize their influence NGO activists sought to operate regionally as well.

In this chapter, I examine the transnational connections made among women in Mexico, Canada, and the United States in response to the North American Free Trade Agreement.[4] Examining the response to NAFTA by feminist organizers highlights the difficulties attendant to, and possibilities of, international collaboration to address gender issues. Given the gendered and racialized nature of political, economic, and social restructuring, feminist cross-border organizing must be understood in greater depth and theorized more precisely.

We need to understand the impact that globalization has on the ability of NGOs to create and sustain cross-border organizing networks and hence the reconfiguration of political contestation as we enter the twenty-first century.

The discourse and processes of globalization are important because they help to define contemporary political problems as well as the political resistance and engagement which addresses these problems.[5] In this way, globalization represents a convergence of forces that together are shrinking the global sphere. It refers to a growing sense of global community and to policy convergence on the international level.[6] The discourse of globalization makes clear that the issues confronted by individuals, organizations, and nations in one locale are intricately connected to those in other parts of the world. Yet, I am not suggesting that globalization has created a singular global culture, economy, religion, or polity. While globalization may increase people's awareness of each other, of different cultural practices, lifestyles, and forms of political participation and repression, it has not erased difference. To the contrary, globalization has, in some respects, made people more aware of difference(s) between them and "others" and serves to create and recreate "others" within and between groups. Indeed, economic integration contributes to social, cultural, and political (dis)integration and as such, globalization must be understood as a simultaneously homogenizing and fragmenting force.[7] The tensions between the homogenizing impulse of globalization, and the fragmentation or difference that globalization brings into sharp relief, are clearly evident in the struggles of NGOs to organize transnationally in response to NAFTA.

TRANSNATIONAL ADVOCACY NETWORKS

A wide variety of NGOs worked across borders to contest NAFTA: labor, environment, development, human rights, women's, and consumer groups. They worked to contest the agreement and to pressure the Mexican, Canadian, and U.S. governments to change some of the policy's provisions. The form of this cross-border collaboration can be described as a transnational advocacy network.[8] Transnational advocacy networks are *"communicative structures* for political exchange."[9] They bring together a group of political actors—individuals and organizations—working across national borders on a particular issue.[10]

The networks are often loosely structured. They help to frame issues in new ways and to bring political messages to the venues where they are most likely to be heard. In this way they blur traditional boundaries between domestic and international politics.[11] Transnational advocacy networks in response to NAFTA functioned as mechanisms for communication, strategy coordination, and more general political exchange. I use the plural "networks" to highlight that multiple and overlapping transnational advocacy networks were operating. The broad-based umbrella network included those organizations represented by the anti-NAFTA coordinating bodies in each country—in Canada, *Réseau Canadien d'Action,* the Action Canada Network, and Common Frontiers; in Mexico, La Red Mexicana de Acción Frente al Libre Comercio; and in the United States, the Alliance for Responsible Trade and the Citizens' Trade Campaign.[12] At times, women's transnational advocacy efforts intersected with those of the broader network. At other times, this subgroup of women functioned relatively autonomously from the broader anti-NAFTA network.

Feminists mobilized in order to bring the needs of economically marginal communities to the table. The historic economic and political marginalization of women in each of the three nations served as the basis for articulating a set of common interests with regard to the proposed agreement. Organizers exchanged experiences in order to articulate a common ground from which they could coordinate transnationally. Furthermore, these activists worked transnationally in order to bring more women into conversations about issues of international economic import—conversations in which women have not traditionally participated and in which gender is usually rendered invisible.

The network of women organizing around NAFTA consisted primarily of professional, career activists working in NGOs, who came together to share information as a means to understand the needs and interests of women in the three signatory nations. They were interested in collectively articulating gender issues associated with globalization. This was seen as the first step toward substantively affecting the agenda of the broader anti-NAFTA advocacy network and of challenging the gender-neutral assumptions of the debate over globalization more generally.

While transnational NGO organizing efforts were quite remarkable in response to NAFTA, differences among the groups in perspective, ideology, political context, and their ability to address issues of difference (race, class, nation) were evident. Indeed, the construction and sustenance of these organizing efforts required attention to the differences among those who are participating. Healy and Macdonald adeptly point out that in "each attempt to articulate a common platform, there are unspoken diverse and even contradictory ontological assumptions" undergirding a group's shared rhetoric.[13] In this chapter, I argue that differences among participants—differences of race, gender, nation, and class—create underlying contradictory interests and approaches even within the bounds of shared rhetoric and political strategy.

While the problem of identity is always an issue in political organizing, transnational networks face the additional pressure of cross-border work in an era of globalization. Globalization—or the pressure for economic, cultural, and political convergence—brings questions of difference to the foreground. Yet, the pressure of globalization also serves to flatten, ignore, and downplay those very same differences. As a result, understanding the politics of identity and difference in an era of globalization is crucial to theorizing transnational political organizing as it highlights both the commonalities and the fissures between groups that facilitate or militate against the success of their efforts. While globalization and the politics of identity set the stage for cross-border coalitions, the heterogeneity of women's identities and the way that globalization paradoxically highlights difference serve to complicate cross-border advocacy work.

The use of the category "women" to initiate political activism has been very important but has also drawn a significant amount of criticism from the very constituency that the category seeks to cohere.[14] The women's movement in many parts of the world has been criticized by both internal and external sources for the construction of a hegemonic movement which excludes by not adequately taking differences among women into account. More generally, this critique is an important part of women's history, feminist theory, and scholarship, and is both theoretical and practical in origin. Feminists have criticized an understanding of women's interests and identity which is too unidimensional and have proposed alternative theoretical paradigms which highlight the mutual constitution of gender, race, class, sexuality, and ethnicity in formulating identity and in contributing to an individual's social and political power and position. For instance, bell hooks calls for a resistance based on "radical post-modernism" where "those shared sensibilities which cross the boundaries of class, gender, race, etc. . . . would promote recognition of common commitments, and serve as a base for solidarity and coalition."[15] Here, hooks argues that the way to address difference in the context of political struggle is to recognize "common interests."

The goal of women's transnational advocacy networking in response to NAFTA was to articulate common interests which could serve as the basis for cross-border organizing. As Chandra Mohanty suggests, this does not imply a search for common experiences, since the quest for sameness necessarily obscures the historical and cultural specificity of women's lives.[16] Instead, political organizing that is based on the mutuality of interests takes its strength from the common context of political struggles.[17]

Inserting a gender analysis into the NAFTA debate required a concerted effort to develop the analysis and concepts necessary to construct appropriate organizing strategies. As a result, feminists participated in the broad anti–free trade networks and simultaneously created a separate transnational advocacy network. In doing so, they faced not only the difficulty of bringing women's issues and a gender analysis to debates about free trade and the creation of a restructured North America, they also confronted the challenges of addressing issues of identity, race, class, and nation among women in their own organizations and in the women's transnational advocacy network.

LEADERS OF THE ANTI–FREE TRADE FIGHT: THE WOMEN'S MOVEMENT IN CANADA

While the story of anti–free trade organizing by nongovernmental actors begins with NAFTA in the United States and Mexico, in Canada it began nearly ten years earlier. Signed in 1988, after three years of debate and negotiation, Canadian prime minister Brian Mulroney and U.S. president Ronald Reagan committed the two countries to lowering tariff and nontariff barriers to trade in a free trade agreement (the FTA). The specter of a free trade agreement between the United States and Canada led to opposition organizing in nearly all sectors of Canadian civil society. Emphasizing this point, Marjorie Griffin Cohen writes, "Coalitions developed in unprecedented ways and people and groups which had never worked together before began to identify their common interests in opposition to free trade."[18] Indeed, the fight against the FTA in Canada was hard fought and touched most nongovernmental organizations in the country. The first anti–free trade group in Toronto was initiated by Laurell Ritchie, a member of the trade union movement who was then on the executive governing body of the largest women's organization in Canada—the National Action Committee on the Status of Women (NAC). Formed in 1972, the NAC is an umbrella organization for hundreds of women's organizations in Canada. It represents over five hundred groups with a membership of more than three million.[19]

From her position with the NAC, Ritchie had members of all groups—women's, native, poverty, trade unions, arts, and religious organizations come to the NAC office to discuss the issue of free trade. As a result, the national Canadian women's organization became the catalyst for anti–free trade organizing. For many of the groups who came to this and subsequent meetings, it was important that they were meeting on the NAC's turf. While mistrust between the various trade unionists was significant, all the groups were comfortable with the NAC. Meeting on neutral ground helped them to develop trust among themselves.[20] The group met monthly at the NAC offices for about three years and was called the Coalition against Free Trade.

During the debate over the FTA, women's organizations, supported by the NAC's initiatives, developed a relatively sophisticated analysis of the impact that the agreement would have on women in Canada. One of the primary tasks was to analyze what such an agreement would mean and educate the NAC's constituency using that information.[21] At first, they focused on what the implications would be for industrial labor. However they soon came to realize that it would also have a significant effect on the service sector.[22] This was the first trade agreement that included trade in services in such a significant way. Marjorie Cohen, a feminist economist at York University who was also a vice president of the National Action Committee on the Status of Women and very active with NAC in these efforts, said in an interview, "When we saw the draft of the first agreement, we realized how far it was going to go in services and this was going to be the real issue for women. Later on we focused on what the implications were going to be on public services and later on indeed, we focused on what they were going to mean around issues of democracy for women."[23] Cohen's analysis of the FTA provided a critical basis for movement organizing.

ESTABLISHING CROSS-BORDER LINKAGES FROM CANADA TO MEXICO TO THE UNITED STATES

The centrality of the Canadian women's movement to the debate over the FTA set the stage for the cross-border outreach that they initiated during the subsequent NAFTA debate. Once the Canadian government announced its intention to join the United States in expanding the FTA to include Mexico, creating a North American free trade zone, opposition groups in Canada began looking at expanding their anti–free trade organizing to include groups in Mexico and the United States. Working with organizations in the United States and Mexico required some changes in the work of NAC since their work had been primarily focused on domestic issues.[24] Transnational organizing also required a slight reframing of the nationalist rhetoric of the anti-FTA fight.

The Canadian women's movement was among the first to begin promoting strategies of cross-border solidarity in their work against NAFTA. In order to integrate international work into NAC's mission, a Global Strategies Committee was established in 1991. The purpose of the committee was to "strengthen NAC's commitment to international solidarity; . . . deepen NAC's understanding of how global restructuring is affecting women's lives and struggles in Canada and other countries; identify more effective ways of working together internationally."[25] This committee, and its coordinator Lynda Yanz, was instrumental in building linkages between women in Canada and Mexico around the proposed North American Free Trade Agreement.

Given the likely consequences of capital mobility throughout the hemisphere, women in Canada believed that they shared common interests with women in Mexico and the United States to fight the proposed agreement. Assumptions about common interests were based on the gendered divisions of labor in the international political economy and the ways that poverty and labor are structured along race and gender lines. While they knew that NAFTA was going to affect women in the three countries differently, they believed that "there were common interests among women in limiting the strength and mobility of capital."[26] Furthermore, they believed that "[n]ew and creative collective organizing initiatives and solidarity are essential to ensure that women are not left to bear the brunt of governments' and corporations' actions to restructure our economies."[27] This articulation of shared interests based on their identity as women was the impetus to commence transnational networking efforts. However, as the rest of this story shows, a shared identity must be constructed, cannot be assumed, and many obstacles exist to articulating a shared identity strong enough to sustain transnational organizing efforts.

One of the groups that Yanz and the NAC Global Strategies Committee worked most closely with in Mexico was Mujer a Mujer (Woman to Woman). Founded in 1985 by a small group of U.S. activists, Mujer a Mujer began by connecting Mexican and U.S. grass-roots women activists. Mujer a Mujer was established with the explicit purpose of making transnational linkages between activists in the United States and Mexican women's movements. The organization's goal was to help activists gain international access to people with similar interests and concerns. Mujer a Mujer became the most important women's organization working against NAFTA in Mexico. Importantly, the group was started by white women from the United States who lived in Mexico. (I will return to this point as who these organizers were affected how they operated and what issues they confronted in their organizing efforts.)

One of the first projects of Mujer a Mujer was to organize a number of worker-to-worker exchanges between Mexican and U.S. women and set up similar exchanges between political activists in the two countries. Their work promoted women's leadership using popular education and grass-roots cross-cultural exchange as their primary tools. The unique organizing helped women to understand the broader economic context of their own work by highlighting the connections between gender and economic change. Although Mujer a Mujer addressed a range of women's issues—women in the urban popular movement, domestic violence, lesbian rights, the rights of women workers—their work always addressed the connections between gender and the economy. In particular, Mujer a Mujer worked with the national coordinating council of urban popular movements called the *Coordinadora Nacional del Movimiento Urbano Popular* (CONAMUP).

Connections between gender and economic issues had been

especially important to organizing in Mexico's urban popular movements.[28] These *movimientos populares* blossomed during the economic
crisis of the late 1970s and the early 1980s in a context in which social movements have had a long history of responding to issues of
economic crisis. Popular movements (or grass-roots movements) demanded that services—education, housing, sewage, health care, nutrition—be provided in poor urban areas. Historically, popular
movements have played a significant role in Mexican politics and are
generally recognized as "one of the most significant political developments of the past twenty years."[29] While they are not women's
organizations in the Northern sense of the term, women have been
central to their work.[30] By 1983, women had created the Women's
Regional Council (*Consejo Regional de Mujeres* or CRM) within
CONAMUP to increase their voice and political power.[31] Mujer a Mujer
worked extensively with the Women's Council of the CONAMUP by
arranging exchanges with U.S. organizations for their members. Eventually, women working with CONAMUP began participating in the
Mujer a Mujer collective.

Mujer a Mujer's interest in working on issues of gender and the
economy with activists in the United States and Canada came from
their realization that the economic crisis in Mexico was not, according to one of the organization's founders, "a whim of Salinas, but
was an economic package that was being implemented all over the
world. It has an internal coherence that women needed to understand."[32] The main question driving their work was "how did these
structural adjustment policies impact women's ability to realize their
rights?"[33] Mujer a Mujer refocused its energies due to concern about
the impact and logic of structural adjustment policies in Mexico. It
reduced its direct exchange work with groups in the United States in
order to devote more time and energy to studying and analyzing the
gendered implications of free trade, structural adjustment, and the
economic model of globalization. In large part, this shift to looking
at the impact that the proposed North American Free Trade Agreement would have on women in Mexico was the result of connections
made between women's organizations in Canada and the women of
Mujer a Mujer in Mexico. They began using what was happening in
Canada as part of their popular education and organizing work and
began working with women in Canada to establish a Canadian branch
of the organization.[34] Importantly, Mujer a Mujer became a place for

people to meet across organizations and borders to examine "an issue which was impacting all of them."[35]

This coordinated work was initiated because the women in Canada and Mexico believed that they had common interests in defeating the agreement. Seeing NAFTA as an extension of the Canada-U.S. Free Trade Agreement, Canadian activists worked with Mexican organizers to help them resist and reshape the agreement.[36] After two years of monitoring the impact of the FTA in Canada, many argued that the agreement was not working in the interest of most Canadians. A 1992 report issued by the Canadian Centre for Policy Alternatives articulates this sentiment: "Canadians were falsely promised much in the original Free Trade Agreement with the United States—jobs, prosperity, protection. Now, our experience with more than three years of the Free Trade Agenda has convinced the majority of Canadians that this vision/agenda is not in our interests—nor in the interests of the peoples of the Americas."[37] From the perspective of Canadian feminists, NAFTA was designed to benefit corporate interests in the United States and was especially problematic since it further entrenched the principles of the FTA. An awareness of the similarities of the situation of women in Mexico and women in Canada with regard to NAFTA led activists to use Mujer a Mujer as a vehicle to coordinate resistance to the proposed agreement. As Lynda Yanz stated in my interview with her, "People in Mujer a Mujer were really sort of visionary in thinking that there could be some networking around the free trade stuff. I was centrally involved in some of the anti-free trade organizing taking place here [in Canada] so when I got involved in Mujer a Mujer I helped to bring those issues into the focus of the organization's work."[38]

Indeed, Mujer a Mujer's role in transnational organizing in response to NAFTA was critically important. In 1992 they sponsored the First Tri-National Conference of Women Workers on Economic Integration and Free Trade. This conference, held in February 1992 in Valle de Bravo, Mexico, brought together 120 women to cooperatively analyze the impact of the proposed North American Free Trade Agreement on women in the region.[39] As Elaine Burns, one of the founders of Mujer a Mujer in Mexico, said during my interview, "With NAFTA it became obvious to us that we had to get to know each other across borders to try and influence the process of regional integration rather than just accepting the negative effects that it was going to have on women. The question was how could we develop new forms of working together given the ways that globalization was . . . changing the nature of all three economies."[40] This conference was a place for women in Mexico, Canada, and the United States to strategize about how to actively shape the process of North American political and economic integration. How could they work to redirect the process and reduce the harm that globalization would have on women?

The conference participants examined the impact of economic restructuring in Mexico, Canada, and the United States. As a political strategy, they shared experiences about the consequences of economic and political change as a way to establish common ground across national, racial, ethnic, and class differences. For example, they explored ways that "'restructuring,' 'integration' and 'modernisation' are words that have real effects on the lives of women" especially on women's role in the work force.[41] Women from the United States, like Mary McGinn of Labor Notes in Detroit (who also lived in Mexico and worked with Mujer a Mujer until 1991), talked about the ways that transnational corporations push for "concessions from labour" and then "blam[e] it on international competition."[42] As McGinn underscored, transnational corporations (TNCs) are reticent to take full responsibility for their business and financial strategies. Instead, they blame their decisions on the larger "invisible forces" of globalization.[43] However, conference participants argued that globalization is not an exogenous force over which states and NGOs have little or no control. Instead, they hoped that sharing these experiences would demystify the rhetoric of globalization. As a result, they aspired to build strategies that demand accountability on the part of transnational capital and individual states.

The Valle de Bravo meeting provided an opportunity for Canadian women to discuss their experiences under the first few years of the Canadian-U.S. Free Trade Agreement. They did so in order to explicate women's interests with regard to NAFTA. For example, Mary Shortell of the Canadian Auto Workers Union/Women's Committee explained that "many of our social programs were redefined by the U.S. as 'unfair advantage' and are being destroyed."[44] The concerns of women in Mexico, however, were slightly different. As NAFTA would increase United States and Canadian investment in Mexico, employment opportunities for women were expected to grow. While it was clear that North American economic integration would create jobs for young Mexican women, participants at the Valle de Bravo meeting noted that these jobs are only hiring "at a fraction of the wages of traditional industries in Mexico."[45] As Rosaura Davila of CAM pointed out, "There are 80 *maquiladora* plants in Matamoros, providing jobs for 32,000 women. These plants have brought hope for women who had no other means of livelihood. But they have also resulted in a worsening of our city's problems, such as public safety.... Some of the *maquiladoras* are highly polluting ... Children are born with mental retardation because their mothers worked with PVC's while they were pregnant."[46] As these women and many others noted during the conference, women are affected in particular ways by economic integration. Thus, the activists argued, the gendered nature of globalization must be made visible and such insights must consistently inform the policy process.

This tri-national conference on gender and NAFTA generated a set of demands and joint organizing strategies that focused on ensuring that integration proceeds with the upward harmonization of workplace health and safety standards, increased training for women workers, full democratic participation of women in the NAFTA negotiation process and in the work by unions on this and related issues. Patricia Fernández, head of the gender and the economy program at Fronteras Comunes in Mexico said in an interview that this meeting was very useful and that some women expressed a desire to continue to "work together to build a common platform which respects the differences in the national contexts from which we come."[47] Furthermore, she suggested that one of the most difficult parts of nurturing transnational organizing efforts was ensuring respect for difference(s). This would prove to be particularly important in attempts to establish connections between groups in the United States and Mexico since anti-Mexico and anti-immigrant sentiment permeated the NAFTA debate in the United States in particular.

The collaboration between Mujer a Mujer in Mexico and the Global Strategies Committee of NAC in Canada continued after the conference in Mexico. By 1991 the Canadian branch of Mujer a Mujer was producing the group's tri-annual publication *Correspondencia* and was centrally involved in feminist transnational advocacy work in response to NAFTA. In June 1992, as part of the NAC's twentieth anniversary "Strategies for Change" conference and annual general meeting, the Global Strategies Committee, in collaboration with Mujer a Mujer, hosted an international consultation in Ottawa. The Global Strategies Committee brought together women from seven countries to this meeting: Nicaragua, the Philippines, South Africa, Chile, Mexico, the United States, and the host, Canada. The international guests participated in the NAC annual general assembly bringing issues of international solidarity to the fore. This was important because it increased Canadian feminist grass-roots participation in the NAFTA debate by educating NAC member organizations about the importance of transnational coordination. In addition, a working group that included the international guests and key contacts from NAC's Global Strategies Committee and NAC's Future of Women's Work Campaign met in a number of formal and informal sessions to identify the common interests and issues affecting women in different regions of the world. The goal of these meetings was to explore possible areas for future collaboration.[48]

In addition to NAC's work in facilitating transnational advocacy among women, smaller NAC affiliated groups—particularly Woman to Woman Global Strategies in Vancouver, British Columbia—were also instrumental. Established after the debate over the FTA in Canada, Women to Women Global Strategies began making connections with women in Mexico just as NAFTA was proposed. They were involved in a number of efforts to bring Mexican women activists to Canada and to send Canadian activists to Mexico. The goal of these exchanges was to build international solidarity and to enhance education and advocacy work on free trade and global economic issues.[49] For instance, Women to Women Global Strategies developed a cross-sectoral training program for women organizers focused on global restructuring and the future of women's work. The program was adapted from a training by Mujer a Mujer in Mexico City called Promotoras Internacionales. It brought women together on a weekly basis from diverse sectors of society to examine the gendered impact of globalization of the economy and to develop coordinated strategies for minimizing the negative, and maximizing the positive aspects of these changes. Both the program in Mexico and the one in Vancouver challenged participants to explore the consequences of global economic restructuring. Both training programs were designed to counteract women's traditional absence from political economic policy debates. Training women organizers was expected to have a multiplier effect where women would go back to their organizations and apply the skills and the international perspective that they gained to their work.[50] As Denise Nadeau, an organizer with Woman to Woman Global Strategies in Vancouver stated in her interview, the goal of the organization was to empower politically and economically marginal communities to engage in policy debates.[51]

The strength of the links between organizations in Canada and in Mexico can, in part, be attributed to the fact that Canadian nationalist sentiment, which framed their anti–free trade position, was directed at the United States and not at Mexico. The U.S.-Canadian Free Trade Agreement had generated an enormous amount of concern in Canada because social movements saw it as yet another indication of the "Americanization" (read U.S. hegemony) of Canada.[52] By and large, Canadians believed that Mexico stood to lose from the agreement in ways that were similar to the impact that the FTA had had in Canada. Thus, they believed that it was possible to find common ground with Mexican organizers in order to defeat the agreement. They believed that women as women had an interest in defeating NAFTA.

Nationalist sentiment also framed opposition to NAFTA in the United States, but it was very clearly focused on Mexico. The primary argument against NAFTA in the United States was that U.S. jobs were going to flood over the border into Mexico. This is what Ross Perot dubbed the "giant sucking sound." Nationalism pervaded the rhetoric of both the anti- and pro-NAFTA forces. The most prominent example of U.S. nationalism was the way that NAFTA proponents argued that, in addition to creating economic growth in the United States, NAFTA would slow the flow of illegal immigrants into the United States by giving "those people" jobs in "their own country."

Questions about the Mexican economy, democracy, labor relations, child labor, treatment of women workers, human rights, health and safety standards, and the environment moved to the center of popular discourse during the U.S. debate over NAFTA. This attention represented a victory for NGOs working to frame the policy debate as a series of political, rather than strictly technical, economic concerns. In the past, debates over free trade, including bilateral trade deals between the United States and Mexico, had been routine.[53] In the United States, they had attracted little attention and were supported by Republicans and by most Democrats, especially those whose districts included economic sectors that appeared to benefit from free trade. The debate over NAFTA radically altered this political terrain. Yet, the attention directed toward trade with Mexico was often sensationalized. Political activists and the media focused blame on Mexico for many regional problems, particularly environmental degradation, the exploitation of labor, and deindustrialization in the United States. Economic integration was framed as a zero-sum game. Everything that the Mexicans stood to gain from NAFTA was presented as coming directly from the pockets of U.S. citizens. This rhetoric employed stereotypes, racism, and nationalism to create Mexicans as "others" who were to be feared and who were less deserving than the "hard-working" U.S. labor force. In essence, this strategy legitimated fear and prejudice.

Constructing Mexicans as "others" was, and continues to be, an important part of the discussion of economic integration. This construction of others both inside and outside of U.S. national borders is important since it exploits fears of economic instability and uncertainty among U.S. workers. In this case, blaming either immigrants in the United States for taking the jobs of Americans or arguing that NAFTA's passage would send U.S. jobs to Mexico serves the same purpose. It helps to justify discriminatory treatment of those who are constructed as different. In an interview with a manager of a maquila plant, Claire Sjolander encountered this sentiment toward Mexican workers: "'Mexicans,'" he said, "'are not like us. If they ate like us— if they liked meat, vegetables, fruit—the peso devaluation would be a problem. But they are not like us. All they eat is rice, beans, tortillas, and Coca-Cola.'"[54] Although the value of the peso had fallen precipitously and inflation was running rampant, this attitude allowed the plant manager to downplay the significance of the situation for Mexican maquila workers. Indeed, he absolved himself of any responsibility for the well-being of the workers he managed. He had no reason to worry about paying the workers in his plant higher wages. They simply didn't need the additional money. They were not like him.[55]

Even if the vast majority of feminist organizers resisted or challenged the racist and nationalist rhetoric, like that of the maquila manager, they still grappled with the way that this discourse affects transnational political cooperation. Indeed, racist nationalism played a major role in constituting the political discourse around NAFTA and it influenced the desirability and efficacy of cross-border advocacy.

While many organizers on the ideological left recognized the problems of framing opposition to free trade in purely nationalist terms, they often worked collaboratively with individuals and organizations who promulgated these views. Indeed, conflict around issues of difference was an important aspect of feminist transnational advocacy in response to NAFTA.

Feminists grappled with questions of difference and identity in a number of different ways during their work on gender and NAFTA. In an article discussing a tri-national organizing meeting held in Berkeley, California, Canadian Lynn Bueckert expressed concerns about issues of difference. She wrote: "We parted knowing that our challenge continues to be to develop common strategies that are relevant locally, nationally, and internationally and that do not homogenize us, but rather, reflect and interweave our diversities and our commonalities."[56] In other words, organizers came together as women across borders to challenge NAFTA. However, various conflicts made it clear that questions of difference—race, class, and nation—complicated the notion of a globalized (or regional) women's agenda. There was a need to recognize that NAFTA brought with it both the homogenizing and fragmenting impulses of globalization.

Mujer a Mujer, for instance, grappled with these issues as the first women's organization in Mexico to address gender and NAFTA. The role of Mujer a Mujer is interesting, in part, because the organization was started by white women from the United States who were living in Mexico in the mid-1980s. While the organization commenced by connecting feminists in Mexico and the United States, their work around free trade was ultimately much more closely linked to feminists in Canada, as it was difficult to get women's organizations in the United States to pay attention to international issues on the one hand and regional economic issues on the other. Issues of identity were particularly complicated in Mujer a Mujer because of who constituted the group. After a few years of operating, the organization began to integrate nonwhite women into the organization, but that proved to be difficult. Both Mexican and Chicana women began participating, but this was not an easy process. The first thing that Mujer a Mujer did, was to open the organization to Chicana student interns from the United States as a way to bridge the gap.[57] In my interview with Mujer a Mujer activist Mary McGinn, she noted that it "was a very hard experience. It was very good, but very hard.

The Chicana women came [up] against a lot of racism." For instance, the white women in Mujer a Mujer worked as translators and were constantly being praised for their Spanish language abilities. But, the "Latina who [who grew up in the United States and] was scolded by her parents not to speak Spanish and . . . had taught herself the language . . . was constantly being accused of being a traitor to her nation."[58] In other words, the U.S. born women of Latin American descent who came to Mexico to participate in the work of Mujer a Mujer were expected to speak Spanish, and when they could not do so perfectly, they were sometimes treated with suspicion and/or contempt by the Mexicans with whom they interacted. This experience was in direct contrast to the way that the white women in Mujer a Mujer were treated. In addition, the group had to confront difference, particularly issues of class and race, when they tried to recruit Mexican women to participate. The white women who started the organization made enough money working part time as translators to devote a substantial amount of time to the organization without pay. However, by and large, the Mexican women could not afford to donate a substantial portion of their time to Mujer a Mujer's activities. This meant that the entire volunteer basis of the organization was called into question. Raising money and setting up a more formal office did not prove to be a strong point of Mujer a Mujer and this ultimately contributed to the organization's demise.

SUMMARY

The women's organizing efforts I have examined shared a common commitment to addressing issues of gender and macroeconomics, and faced similar challenges in addressing the significance of difference(s) within their groups. At the same time, they also were quite varied in organizational structure, institutional strength, and the domestic political context from which they originated. These variations put each group in a different position to deal with the challenge of identity and difference in the larger context of gender, free trade, and globalization.

While women's organizations and movements are fundamentally diverse, thinking about organizing based on women's rights or women's interests necessarily illuminates the tensions that exist surrounding questions of identity, sameness, and difference. The very basis of women's organizing is a common identity that ostensibly serves to cohere these efforts—rhetorically, analytically, and practically. In this case, globalization in the form of NAFTA highlighted common gender interests at the same time that it brought differences into sharp relief.

More than two decades of second-wave organizing and feminist scholarship have illustrated clearly that attention to differences among women must be a central focus. Feminist organizing efforts which neglect differences among women invariably flounder and fracture along these lines and become rife with the consequences of often unintentional exclusionary practices. Issue-focused transnational advocacy networking, like women's organizing around NAFTA, represents a strategy for organizing across differences. It attempts to do this by articulating common interests in reference to the issue at hand. Indeed, such organizing strategies draw on a multiplicity of perspectives by relying upon the input of those in different national contexts. Furthermore, the impact of this work is by definition strengthened via the coordination of different organizations in a variety of sociopolitical and national locations. As such, this strategy has a great deal of promise to grapple with both the polarization and convergence engendered by the trend it seeks to resist—globalization. However, this is an effective strategy only if attention to difference is a fundamental part of working conversations and strategy building. Alternative forms of political organizing cannot be substituted for attention to the power differences that social location or identity (gender, race, class, nation) create.

The story of feminist transnational networking around NAFTA demonstrates that "[A]n inclusive movement cannot emerge from the search for a common good, however, but only from careful attention by each vulnerable social segment to the specific experience and vulnerabilities of others."[59] The notion of a shared identity, or a perception of commonalities among the experiences of women, brought feminists together across borders to challenge NAFTA's version of economic restructuring. Their articulation of women's interests served to create a shared movement across national borders. Yet, as I have argued in this chapter, questions of difference and identity also fragmented these efforts. Addressing differences among women of race and class and the intersections of race and class with gender identity is crucial to network building. Gender and race structure economic

opportunities and therefore the experience and definitions of globalization in concrete terms.

NOTES

1. I use the word feminist to describe the activities of those involved in raising gender issues during the NAFTA debate for two reasons. First, the work of these women was designed to improve the conditions of women's lives and to provide women greater access to decision-making arenas. In other words, their work had what many would term feminist goals. Second, while not all of the women whom I interviewed for this project self-define as feminist, the overwhelming majority do.

2. Philip G. Cerny, "Globalization and the Changing Logic of Collective Action," *International Organization* 49:4 (autumn 1995): 595–625. See also Mancur Olson, *The Logic of Collective Action* (Cambridge: Harvard University Press, 1971). Furthermore, Arturo Escobar suggests that social movements emerge largely because of economic inequality and the failure of development. Arturo Escobar, "Culture, Economics, and Politics in Latin American Social Movements Theory and Research," in *The Making of Social Movements in Latin America: Identity, Strategy, and Democracy,* ed. Arturo Escobar and Sonia E. Alvarez (Boulder, Colo.: Westview Press, 1992).

3. The November 1997 defeat of "fast-track" trade negotiating authority in the U.S. House of Representatives exemplifies this change.

4. Information for this paper comes from research and interviews done in Mexico, Canada, and the United States between 1995 and 1997. I conducted interviews with political organizers, researchers, and policy makers in two trips to Mexico: December 1995–January 1996 and September–December 1996. Many interviews were conducted in Spanish and I am also responsible for the translations herein. Interviews with Canadian activists were done in March 1997 in Toronto and the rest were conducted by telephone in 1996 and 1997. Interviews in the United States have been spread throughout the period 1995–1997. In particular, my interviews with women members of Congress and U.S. congressional staff were conducted as part of a large-scale research project at the Center for the American Woman and Politics at Rutgers University. This portion of the research was funded by the Charles H. Revson Foundation.

5. On globalization see, for instance, Arjun Appadurai, *Modernity at Large: Cultural Dimensions of Globalization* (Minneapolis: University of Minnesota Press, 1996); Philip G. Cerny, "Globalization and Other Stories: The Search for a New Paradigm for International Relations," *International Journal* 51:4 (autumn 1996): 617–637; Eleonore Kofman and Gillian Youngs, "Introduction: Globalization—the Second Wave," in *Globalization: Theory and Practice,* ed. Eleonore Kofman and Gillian Youngs (New York: Pinter, 1996), 1–8; Malcolm Waters, *Globalization* (London: Routledge, 1995).

6. See Roland Robertson, *Globalization: Social Theory and Global Culture* (London: Sage, 1992); Sidney Tarrow, "Fishnets, Internets and Catnets: Globalization and Transnational Collective Action" (Paper presented at Rutgers University Emerging Trends Seminar, November 1996).

7. For examples of those who talk about the contradictory impulses of globalization, see Richard J. Barnet and John Cavanagh, *Global Dreams: Imperial Corporations and the New World Order* (New York: Simon and Schuster, 1994); Janet Abu Lughod, "Going beyond Global Babble," in *Culture, Globalization and the World-System: Contemporary Conditions for the Representation of Identity,* ed. Anthony D. King (London: Macmillan Education Ltd., 1991), 131–138; James H. Mittelman, "How Does Globalization Really Work?" in *Globalization: Critical Reflections,* ed. James H. Mittelman (Boulder, Colo.: Lynne Rienner Publishers, 1996), 229–242; Claire Turenne Sjolander, "The Rhetoric of Globalization: What's in a Wor(l)d?" *International Journal* 51:4 (autumn 1996): 603–616.

8. Keck and Sikkink define a transnational advocacy network to "include those relevant actors working internationally on an issue, who are bound together by shared values, a common discourse, and dense exchanges of information and services" (1). Margaret E. Keck and Kathryn Sikkink, "Transnational Advocacy Networks in a Movement Society" (Paper presented at the American Political Science Association Annual Meeting, Washington, D.C., August 28–31, 1997).

9. For a detailed account of the importance that "communicative structures" play in the constitution of the public sphere, see Jürgen Habermas, *The Structural Transformation of the Public Sphere,* 1st English Edition, trans. Thomas Burger (Cambridge, Mass.: MIT Press, 1989 [1962]).

10. Keck and Sikkink, "Transnational Advocacy Networks in a Movement Society." For an analysis and description of a variety of networks of activists, see Keck and Sikkink, ibid.

11. The proliferation of new forms of communication technology like the fax and the internet have helped to facilitate this process. For an exposition on the possibilities for electronic networking written by the primary international women's organization involved in the NAFTA debate, see Mujer a Mujer Collective, "Communicating Electronically: Computer Networking and Feminist Organizing," *Resources for Feminist Research* 20:1–2 (1991): 10. See also Erika Smith, "Electrifying Women: Women's Networking On-Line," *Correspondencia* 17 (May 1995): 29–31.

12. In the United States there were two and in Canada there were three primary anti–NAFTA coordinating bodies. In both cases one of the groups concentrated on international networking. The Action Canada Network and the Citizens' Trade Campaign focused on domestic political work while their counterparts, Common Frontiers and the Alliance for Responsible Trade, concentrated on cross-border networking. However, this division of labor was not absolute in either case. The coordinating body in Quebec, *Réseau Canadien d'Action,* was involved in both national and cross-border organizing.

13. Teresa Healy and Laura Macdonald, "Continental Divide? Competing Approaches to Understanding Social Movement Organizing across North America" (Paper presented at the International Studies Association Meeting, Toronto, Ontario, March 18–22, 1997), 1–21.

14. These critiques were articulated from the beginning of the second-wave feminism in books, including those by Toni Cade, *The Black Woman: An Anthology* (New York: Signet, 1970); bell hooks, *Ain't I a Woman: Black Women and Feminism* (Boston: South End Press, 1981); and Gerda Lerner, ed., *Black Women in White America: A Documentary History* (New York: Vintage, 1972). Similar critiques were also articulated by lesbians, see Nancy Myron and Charlotte Bunch, *Lesbianism and the Women's Movement* (Baltimore: Diana Press, 1975).

15. bell hooks, "Postmodern Blackness," in *Yearning: Race, Gender, and Cultural Politics* (Boston: South End Press, 1990), 27. Page 27 quoted in Inderpal Grewal and Caren Kaplan, "Introduction: Transnational Feminist Practices and Questions of Postmodernity," in *Scattered Hegemonies: Postmodernity and Transnational Feminist Practices,* ed. Inderpal Grewal and Caren Kaplan (Minneapolis: University of Minnesota Press, 1994), 1–33.

16. Chandra Talpade Mohanty, "Women Workers and Capitalist Scripts: Ideologies of Domination, Common Interests, and the Politics of Solidarity," in *Feminist Genealogies, Colonial Legacies, Democratic Futures,* ed. M. Jacqui Alexander and Chandra Talpade Mohanty (London: Routledge, 1997), 3–29.

17. Mohanty, "Women Workers and Capitalist Scripts: Ideologies of Domination, Common Interests, and the Politics of Solidarity." For a detailed discussion about the relevance of a "common context of struggle," see Chandra Talpade Mohanty, "Cartographies of Struggle: Third World Women and the Politics of Feminism," in *Third World Women and the Politics of Feminism,* ed. Chandra Talpade Mohanty, Ann Russo, and Lourdes Torres (Bloomington: Indiana University Press, 1991), 1–47.

18. Marjorie Griffin Cohen, "Feminism's Effect on Economic Policy," in *Canadian Women's Issues: Volume II, Bold Visions,* ed. Ruth Roach Pierson and Marjorie Griffin Cohen (Toronto: James Lorimer, 1995), 263–298, 277.

19. Amy Gottlieb, ed., "A Discussion Facilitated by Maureen FitzGerald and Alice de Wolff: What about Us? Organizing Inclusively in the National Action Committee on the Status of Women," in *And Still We Rise: Feminist Political Mobilizing in Contemporary Canada,* ed. Linda Carty (Toronto: Women's Press, 1993), 371–385.

20. This description of these first meetings comes from my interview with Marjorie Griffin Cohen. She was also on the NAC executive board at the time and, as an economist, did one of the first alternative analyses of the Macdonald Commission's report. This alternative analysis was published for the NAC and titled "Weakest to the Wall," *Policy Options* (December 1985). See also Cohen, "Feminism's Effect on Economic Policy."

21. This effort was largely successful and public opinion surveys at the time showed a significant gender gap where women in Canada were between 12 and 20 percent less likely to

support free trade than men. Sylvia B. Bashevkin, *True Patriot Love: The Politics of Canadian Nationalism* (New York: Oxford University Press, 1991), 145.

22. See NAC, *What Every Woman Needs to Know about Free Trade* (Toronto: National Action Committee on the Status of Women, 1988); Marjorie Griffin Cohen, *Free Trade and the Future of Women's Work: Manufacturing and Service Industries* (Toronto: Garamond Press and the Canadian Centre for Policy Alternatives, 1987).

23. From my telephone interview with Marjorie Griffin Cohen, Simon Fraser University, Department of Women's Studies, April 24, 1997.

24. From my interview with Lynda Yanz, Mujer a Mujer, Canada and Maquila Solidarity Network (Toronto, October 9, 1996).

25. Lynda Yanz and Global Strategies Committee, "Confronting Global Restructuring with Women's Global Solidarity" (Final Report of the NAC Global Strategies Consultation, June 4–7, 1992, held in Ottawa and in Toronto, July 1992).

26. Cohen, "Feminism's Effect on Economic Policy," 283.

27. From a statement by Mujer a Mujer called the "Women's Plan of Action." The statement was signed by women from Mexico, Canada, the United States, and Central America at the First Tri-national Conference of Women Workers on Economic Integration and Free Trade *(Primer Encuentro Trinacional de Trabajadoras ante la Integración Económica y el Tratado de Libre Comercio)*, February 1992.

28. For additional information about the connections between gender- and class-based organizing in Mexican politics, see Teresa Carrillo, "Women and Independent Unionism in the Garment Industry," in *Popular Movements and Political Change in Mexico*, ed. Joe Foweraker and Ann L. Craig (Boulder, Colo.: Lynne Rienner Publishers, 1990), 213–233; Carmen Ramos Escandón, "Women's Movements, Feminism, and Mexican Politics," in *The Women's Movement in Latin America: Participation and Democracy*, ed. Jane S. Jaquette (Boulder, Colo.: Westview Press, 1994), 199–222; Marta Lamas, "El Movimiento Feminista en la Década de los Ochenta," in *Crisis y Sujetos Sociales en México*, ed. Enrique de la Garza (Mexico City: UNAM-Porrúa, 1992); Kathleen Logan, "Women's Participation in Urban Protest," in *Popular Movements and Political Change in Mexico*, ed. Joe Foweraker and Ann L. Craig (Boulder, Colo.: Lynne Rienner Publishers, 1990), 150–159.

29. Joe Foweraker, "Popular Movements and Political Change in Mexico," in *Popular Movements and Political Change in Mexico*, ed. Joe Foweraker and Ann L. Craig (Boulder, Colo.: Lynne Rienner Publishers, 1990), 3–20.

30. For more information, see Nikki Craske, "Women's Political Participation in Colonias Populares in Guadalajara, Mexico," in *"Viva": Women and Popular Protest in Latin America*, ed. Sarah A. Radcliffe and Sallie Westwood (London: Routledge, 1993), 112–135.

31. For more information about CONAMUP, see Ingo Bultmann, "Movimiento Populares Vecinales y Transformaciones del Sistema Político en México y Chile," in *Democracia Sin Movimiento Social? Sindicatos, Organizaciones Vecinales y Movimientos de Mujeres en Chile y México*, ed. Ingo Bultmann et al. (Caracas, Venezuela: Nueva Sociedad, 1995), 131–209.

32. From my interview with Elaine Burns, Mujer a Mujer-Mexico, Mexico City, January 10, 1996.

33. From my interview with Burns, Mujer a Mujer-Mexico.

34. From my telephone interview with Mary McGinn, Mujer a Mujer-Mexico, February 19, 1997. For more information, see the December 1990 issue of *Correspondencia*, the tri-annual publication of Mujer a Mujer.

35. From my interview with Burns, Mujer a Mujer-Mexico.

36. The connections between Canadian groups that organized around the Canada-U.S. Free Trade Agreement and anti-NAFTA activism in Mexico are quite extensive. For instance, Canadian groups like the Action Canada Network and Common Borders were instrumental in the founding of the broad-based anti-NAFTA coalition in Mexico, La Red Mexican de Acción Frente al Libre Comercio (The Mexican Action Network on Free Trade).

37. Canadian Centre for Policy Alternatives, *Which Way for the Americas: Analysis of NAFTA Proposals and the Impact on Canada* (Ottawa, Ontario: Canadian Centre for Policy Alternatives, November 1992).

38. From my interview with Yanz, Mujer a Mujer, Canada and Maquila Solidarity Network.

39. For additional discussions of this conference, see Christina Gabriel and Laura Macdonald, "NAFTA, Women and Organising in Canada and Mexico: Forging a 'Feminist Internation-

ality,'" *Millennium: Journal of International Politics* 23:3 (1994): 535–562; Anne Sisson Runyan, "The Places of Women in Trading Places: Gendered Global/Regional Regimes and Inter-Nationalized Feminist Resistance," in *Globalization: Theory and Practice*, ed. Eleonore Kofman and Gillian Youngs (New York: Pinter, 1996), 238–252.

40. Interview with Burns, Mujer a Mujer-Mexico.

41. Mujer a Mujer, "Changes in the Workplace, Changes in Labor Relations," *Correspondencia* 13 (summer 1992): 5–9.

42. Mujer a Mujer, "Impact on Culture and the Community," *Correspondencia* 13 (summer 1992): 10–13.

43. Mujer a Mujer, *Correspondencia* 9 (December 1990).

44. Mujer a Mujer, "Economic Integration: Structural Readjustment, Free Trade," *Correspondencia* 13 (summer 1992): 4.

45. Mujer a Mujer, "Changes in the Workplace, Changes in Labor Relations."

46. In 1965 the governments of Mexico and the United States launched a border-area industrialization program which legalized the establishment of off-shore plants for U.S. corporations. The term *maquiladora* is a derivative of the old Spanish word *maquilar* which refers to the work performed in an oat or corn grinding mill. Maquila originally meant "the unit of grain a mill held back as payment for grinding the farmer's grain, hence its association with the assembly plants, whose foreign owners pay duty only on the value added to the product on the Mexican side." Carnegie Corporation, "Promoting Binational Cooperation to Improve Health Along the U.S.-Mexico Border," *Carnegie Quarterly* 36:1–4 (1991): 1–8. Mujer a Mujer, "Impact on Culture and the Community."

47. Interview with Patricia Fernández, Fronteras Comunes, Directora de la Programa de Genero, Mexico City, November 11, 1996.

48. Yanz and Global Strategies Committee, "Confronting Global Restructuring with Women's Global Solidarity."

49. Woman to Woman Global Strategies was also involved in a number of projects that were coordinated with the Canadian labor movement. For instance, in 1991 they cosponsored an exchange with the British Columbia Federation of Labour Women's Committee on free trade and the global economy. For more information, see Gabriel and Macdonald, "NAFTA, Women and Organising in Canada and Mexico: Forging a 'Feminist Internationality.'" Woman to Woman Global Strategies also coordinated efforts with Oxfam Canada's *Women in the Americas* program, Mujer a Mujer, Mujeres en Acción Sindical, and Fronteras Comunes in Mexico. This information also comes from my telephone interviews with Denise Nadeau, Woman to Woman Global Strategies, Vancouver, B.C., February 27, 1997; and with Miriam Palacios, Director, Women in the Americas Program in Oxfam, Canada, Vancouver, B.C., April 16, 1997.

50. Mujer a Mujer, "Training Project for Women Organizers," *Correspondencia* 16 (May 1994): 24; Denise Nadeau, "Training of Women Organizers: Project Update," *Correspondencia* 17 (May 1995): 21–22.

51. From my interview with Nadeau, Woman to Woman Global Strategies.

52. Interestingly, Canadians did not see themselves as part of the "Americas" identifying only with their "first world" counterparts. This denial, symbolized by Canada's empty seat in the Organization of American States until after NAFTA was signed, was called into question by the prospect of North American economic integration.

53. As I've discussed above, this was not the case in the debate over the 1989 Canada-U.S. Free Trade Agreement, as the discussion was particularly contentious in Canada.

54. Sjolander, "The Rhetoric of Globalization: What's in a Wor(l)d?"

55. It was such rhetoric like Mujer a Mujer pointed to when arguing that women's organizations needed to pay attention to international economic issues. See, for instance, Mujer a Mujer, "Come to Mexico! Or, You $ Me 4-Ever, Amigo," *Correspondencia* (December 1990): 10–13.

56. Lynn Bueckert, "So Where Do We Go from Here?" *Correspondencia* 16 (May 1994): 25.

57. From my interviews with Vicki Villanueva, Mujer a Mujer-Mexico and CONAMUP, Toronto, March 21, 1997; and Burns, Mujer a Mujer-Mexico.

58. From my interview with McGinn, Mujer a Mujer-Mexico.

59. Iris Young, "The Complexities of Coalition," *Dissent* (winter 1997): 64–69.

CYNTHIA SALTZMAN

THE MANY FACES
OF ACTIVISM

The struggle of clerical and technical workers to form a union at Yale University, a school with one of the stormiest labor histories of any institution in the United States, was long and difficult.[1] After decades of failed drives, white-collar employees won an election victory on May 18, 1983, and formed Local 34 of the Hotel and Restaurant Employees International Union (HERE). Then in 1984, Local 34, with the support of service and maintenance workers, staged one of the first strikes in the private sector over the issues of comparable worth in order to obtain a first union contract. The organizing drive culminating in the 1984–1985 strike—the one for which Yale has become famous—succeeded for many reasons.[2] To some extent, the conditions of work and the social and economic position of workers had changed. To some extent, national trends were making themselves felt in the institutional politics of Yale. But also to some extent, the last drive succeeded because that union was finally able to tap the diversity in the Yale landscape while uniting at least the majority of Yale clerical and technical workers in opposition to management.

This chapter posits that the "class" position of clerical and technical workers (C & T's) at Yale was not only tied to their labor market situation and their gender, but was further complicated by their disparate socioeconomic backgrounds and varying exposure to unions, and partly as a result, by their widely divergent views about unionization. In particular, women and men with different educational backgrounds had, in Weber's terms, different life chances. For some, Yale was a step up the ladder, an improvement over a factory job or a low-level service job like waitressing or sales work. For others, particularly technical workers, Yale was a way station to obtain valuable experience and credentials before going on to graduate or medical school, or a more lucrative job at a pharmaceutical firm. Yet a third group was downwardly mobile, their professional ambitions thwarted, their college or graduate degrees devalued, their work unchallenging, their pay low. Marshall and his colleagues have studied white-collar unionization and class consciousness in Britain and note that, "since women clerical workers include women from middle-class origins who have been downwardly mobile and women from working-class origins who have been upwardly mobile, it is not surprising to find equally high levels of middle-class and working-class identification."[3] This diversity in class identification was also evident among C & T's at Yale. It meant that unions had the complex task of fostering mutual identification and a sense of a collective mission out of workers' heterogeneity.

Employees' reasons for supporting a union were not straightforward nor reducible to a simple calculus of economic need. I found that whether or not individuals were prone to support a union was partly determined by their structural position in the work force and their experience on the job: their pay, their relationship to their particular boss, the nature of the work they performed, their sense of job efficacy and upward mobility. But it also had at least initially to do with their familial and social-class backgrounds and their level of education. For some women, as I will show, unionization became a way to protest their declining mobility, their sense of disjunction between their middle-class social backgrounds and expectations and their low-economic and status positioning at Yale. A woman's marital status, familial obligations, and stage of life also played a role in shaping employees' varied views toward unions.[4] Although women did not simply assume the class position and status of their husbands, their attitudes toward unionization were nonetheless influenced by their husband's occupation and outlook.[5] Moreover, race acted as a cultural marker, shaping women's expressions of union identity and collectivity.

CULTURES OF ACTIVISM

The successive union organizing efforts at Yale were expressions of what I will call local cultures of activism. I use the term *cultures of activism* in part to stake out a certain theoretical stance—a stance that tries to make sense of my data while also situating myself in a set of ongoing scholarly debates about class identity, collective resistance, and individual agency.

The notion of cultures of activism is meant to echo, but also bounce against, Rick Fantasia's concept of cultures of solidarity. Fantasia defines *cultures of solidarity* as:

> more or less bounded groupings that may or may not develop a clear organizational identity and structure, but represent the active expression of worker solidarity within an industrial system and a society hostile to it. They are neither ideas of solidarity in the abstract nor bureaucratic trade union activity, but cultural formations that arise in conflict, creating and sustaining solidarity in opposition to the dominant structure.[6]

Fantasia focuses on how cultures of solidarity are formed in the course of struggle and become defined by particular "tactical activities, organizational forms, and institutional arrangements."[7] Central to Fantasia's thesis is the idea that "militant activity creates the context in which class consciousness emerges."[8] For Fantasia, classes have no independent being except as they function in relationship to other classes within the context of collective activity and mobilization in a conflictual setting: "As such class consciousness essentially represents the cultural expression of the lived experience of class, an experience shaped by the process of interaction of these collectivities in opposition to one another."[9] Fantasia views oppositional cultures of solidarity—which may take myriad forms depending on tactical activities and institutional forms—as emerging in opposition to the individualism of American culture.

Unlike Fantasia my approach focuses on workers' cultures of activism and how they achieve political solidarity, and I do not come into the inquiry with an a priori assumption about how class consciousness is formed during the process of organizing. I do not see Yale organizing as an instance in which individuals shed their individualism but as a process in which workers come to see collective representation as the best way to fulfill both their individual and collective aspirations. In fact, it is this very tension between the individual, or groups of individuals, and the collective that may paradoxically represent both the strength and volatility of movement cultures. Moreover, a group dynamic may be an expression of class solidarity even as individuals hold onto core identities that partially contest the group's definition of an oppositional class dynamic.

For Fantasia, a culture of solidarity creates a group that, in its collective identity, seems to function as a "homogenous political actor." My own theoretical leanings and ethnographic observations, however, lead me to emphasize the polyvocal diverse expressions of workers' activism.[10] Fantasia acknowledges only in passing the internal divisions that have limited workers mobilization historically. He is less concerned with deciphering the plurality of levels in collective action than with showing how oppositional cultures can erupt. But as Melucci notes, "Contemporary movements, in particular, weave together multiple meanings, legacies from the past, the effects of modernization, resistances to change."[11]

Cultures of activism, as I define them, are collective expressions of oppositional behavior, thought, symbols, and action that arise as groups of individuals seek societal or institutional change in specific settings. These political groupings may be marked by internal pluralism and incorporate people from broad social backgrounds even as individuals unite against the status quo or engage in confrontational tactics. Cultures of activism may be linked to larger social movements (i.e., the labor movement) and may entail a class consciousness (an awareness of being in an economically inegalitarian relation), but they are often characterized by views and goals that remain particular to a local domain. Thus, cultures of activism may be connected to larger social struggles but are not synonymous with them.

Union politics, that may at first glance appear to define for workers a totalizing class-based identity, upon closer consideration, may reveal a dynamic, shifting coalition that is fragile in its transcendence of pluralistic, identity-based, individual differences. Labor coalitions may be as much about an assertion of individuality as they are about the formation of a collective identity.[12] These two tendencies are in tension—what Melucci has termed *integralism,* the yearning for a totalizing identity—and a preoccupation with individualism.

Even among the singly defined Yale clerical and technical work unit, there were cultural and racial divisions that threatened to undermine the activists' quests for solidarity. These differences cannot be overlooked just because they pose a threat to the common denominator category of class or feminist unity.[13] I detach the word solidarity from any association of sameness of identity. Women's fate at Yale was linked by their institutional connections and the unfolding process of unionization. Although women were commonly united in that they worked at Yale, they were differently located subjects from varying social backgrounds.[14]

I find the notion of "social location" helpful to contextualize women's experience and to understand the complex and problematic construction of difference—how class, gender, ethnicity, and marital status came together to shape women's lives. Studying factory workers in Albuquerque, Louise Lamphere and her coauthors use this concept to study how women of different backgrounds interact with similar structural constraints in varied work settings in order to understand how women's behaviors and ideologies converge and diverge.[15] Looking at woman's identities and collective action in the Yale 1985 strike itself, Nina Gregg, in a similar vein, builds on the ideas of Adrienne Rich and talks about a "politics of location."[16] Gregg emphasizes how women interpret their experience and make meaning in the context of everyday experience, and she focuses on women's responses to union organizing at Yale and their overlapping and sometimes conflicting identities. She argues, "Work is not the only (or even the primary) self-defining activity for many people." Thus, she concludes, "We should not be surprised when appeals to U.S. workers based on homogeneity, solidarity or class fail or are only marginally successful. A multitude of identities, nurtured by the ideology of individualism, compete for allegiance with those put forward by labor."[17] Although I do not agree with all of Gregg's specific findings, her emphasis on diversity and the individual is helpful in understanding the complexities involved in constructing cultures of activism. But in focusing on a politics of location, Gregg emphasizes questions of meaning, identity, and subjectivity to a degree that the narrative of social life and the cultural process of collective action is put to one side.

It is important to strike a balance between Fantasia's emphasis on the dynamics of collective action and Gregg's emphasis on the formation of individual and collective identities. Both perspectives— one emphasizing the shared experience of cultures of solidarity and the other emphasizing the differential social location of women in the workplace and the politics of difference—are important in understanding the processes of unionization at Yale.

WOMEN'S SOCIAL LOCATION AND POLITICAL RESPONSE

In the remainder of this chapter, I discuss representative case studies of women who, occupying different social locations, traveled different routes of understanding and decision making as they came to favor a union. At first, women's social differentiation through their level of education and social backgrounds divided women into different status groupings at Yale. But during the course of organizing, women's recognition of their low pay and their growing sense that they were exploited because they worked in pink-collar jobs, served to unite them. In other words, women's burgeoning union consciousness resulted in women developing a sense of their exploitation in real economic terms. Their status-focused sense of class gave way during the course of organizing to a definition of class based on women's low economic capital.

Women's identity began to take the form of a gender solidarity that cut across employees' diverse social and class backgrounds and became based instead on a mutual identification of women's shared discrimination in the workplace. At Yale, women's conceptions of class began to be transformed during the course of organizing, and women began to place more emphasis on their class position in terms of low job pay. I am not arguing that women's growing solidarity meant that they came to recognize their true or natural class interests. Indeed, Yale women's new economic understanding of their class identity was just as socially constructed as their old status-based understanding. Local 34, through its emphasis on grass-roots organizing, issues of voice, improvisational tactics, and the rhetoric of comparable worth, were able to effect that new socially constructed understanding.

Rena Lerner, for example, worked in a close intimate office not in a large factory-like typing pool that researchers have described as characteristic of the proletarianization of office work. But Rena's work situation epitomized how the "office-wife" relationship was breaking down at Yale. Rena protested against working in a gender subservient role to her boss where she had to perform wifely chores of office housekeeping that mirrored patriarchal relations in the home. She identified how her office situation demeaned her credentials and confirmed her downward mobility.

Rena, who worked briefly at Yale as a clerical worker in the medical area, said that she resented her boss's large ego and prima donna antics. She was particularly miffed by the social injustice of having her educational credentials overlooked and even dismissed in both the hiring process and in her workplace setting. She recalled her frustration when first the personnel department and then her boss disregarded her academic credentials. Rena told me, "Well, I think that they [personnel] didn't care at all that I had gone to Bryn Mawr, because maybe a lot of secretaries at Yale have graduated from seven sisters or ivy league schools. Nobody ever brought it up. They acted like it was nothing, including [my boss], you know, asking me if my grammar were good after I pointed out to him what my academic credentials were."

Rena's personal capital—educational training and intelligence—were key to her self-identity and finding these credentials dismissed was a negation of her selfhood and personal status. Her situation represented how in a hierarchical meritocracy where the emphasis was on the Ph.D., M.D. or M.B.A., women who were overeducated for their jobs found that their academic credentials were disregarded. Moreover, Rena held Yale to a higher standard. Being highly educated herself and valuing academia, she had placed higher expectations on the university as an employer than she did on other business establishments. She said, "I don't care what bank presidents think about me, anyhow, or bank managers, but I guess I do care what academicians think because I'm used to having them judge my work which I was serious about academically. So to be treated badly at a job interview made me feel pretty destroyed. And so because they're educated, I expect them to be enlightened and liberal and they seem to be absolute jerks about working women."

Despite Rena's educational credentials and identification with the middle class, she sought unionization as a protest against her devaluation in the workplace. Crompton draws our attention to education as "a central element in the creation and reproduction of cultural capital, among the new middle classes."[18] Better education, though, as Inglehart notes, can lead to a postmodern materialist perspective that clashes with individual, entrepreneurial, money power strategies that rule out possibilities for social consciousness and collective action.[19] Women concentrated in service-related professional work especially in the state sector have become radicalized and have supported unionization. Moreover, women in female-dominated occupations who support comparable-worth legislation have shared in the increase in women's collective action. Many women working in clerical jobs that social stratification theorists label "working class" also wield a measure of cultural capital by virtue of their social background, educational level, and position in the work force. But their experience of marginalization and deprivation on the job results in a sense of exploitation that radicalizes them. Women in clerical or low-level technical jobs like Rena often experienced their low pay and devaluation of their labor as a form of gender debasement that eroded their personal cultural capital.

Gregg in her study of Local 34's organizing during the mid-1980s noted that many women who rejected the union often did so in order to keep alive the promise of middle-class status. They felt that if they accepted the union's oppositional worldview, they "could no longer assume that the privileges, possibilities, and acceptance connoted by middle-class status were theirs."[20] I also found evidence that some employees opposed Local 34 because they saw it as antithetical to middle-class status. But probably just as many employees held onto their middle-class identification and voted against Yale as a protest against their downward mobility and also in political solidarity with those whom they believed to be less fortunate. In particular, many divorced and widowed women at Yale suddenly confronted harsh economic realities when they became single heads of households and had to adjust to a single Yale salary.[21] But the definition of female downward mobility as characterizing the plight of the newly single woman needs to be broadened to encompass the dilemma of those women who with undergraduate or even graduate degrees confronted severely limited job opportunities in a gender-segregated job market. In New Haven such women often became pigeonholed in low-paid "female" jobs at Yale, the largest employer in the city. A vote for the union was a vote against downward mobility.[22]

Among the spectrum of C & T's from those most financially insecure (by virtue of either their employment in the lowest rungs of the clerical ladder and/or their status as single heads of households supporting children) to those who were relatively financially well-off (by virtue of either their marital status and/or employment in one of the higher-paying technical jobs) it was the middle range of employees, not at either extreme of the spectrum, who were initially the most likely to support clerical and technical unionization on campus. (Under this middle-range rubric, I include male technical employees who were self-identified as politically liberal or who had prior exposure to unions.)

On one end of the financial spectrum, women who regarded themselves as particularly vulnerable to job loss and at great risk in the event of a strike or the suspension of employee benefits were not as likely as others to support one of the unions during the initial stages of organizing on campus. Women who were single heads of household and who relied upon their wages to support themselves and dependent children were among the least likely initially to support the union drive. Older women close to retirement, particularly those widowed and divorced, who did not want to jeopardize their pensions and were concerned about their ability to find alternative employment in the event of job loss, were also unlikely to be among the first promoters of the drive on campus; initially, they were not prone to distinguish themselves as activists. Because of their fear and vulnerability, they supported the status quo.

It was striking to me though how women who had withheld their support of a union began to alter their views of unionization as the Local 34 organizing campaign gained momentum and attracted a critical mass in different work settings. As co-workers expressed their visible support for one of the unions, women in vulnerable household and workplace positions—older women who were close to retirement and fearful of losing their pension or single heads of households with children—began to outwardly express their support for Local 34. By the time of the first Local 34 contract strike, it was quite common to speak with women who were single mothers with children who strongly supported the union and who later made the decision to walk off their jobs in support of the strike. Local 34 reached out to women who stood at different ends of the economic spectrum—those who were self-supporting and could barely make ends meet on a Yale salary, and those who were married and by virtue of their dual income status were cushioned against extreme financial hardship, but who needed to work in order to maintain their standard of living. Moreover, even women who saw themselves as relatively financially well-off and as earning a supplemental income began to recognize the importance of a union for the sake of their co-workers. By convincing women that the union could be sensitive to their special needs and affirm their status as single heads of household, wives, and mothers, it won their support and devotion.

Victoria O'Toole, a single head of household, sought a broad-based union that would allow her to have a voice in the workplace. She acknowledged that some people were fearful of going out on strike. One woman's husband had gone on strike at the Olin plant in New Haven, and was fearful that now she too would have to strike. She also noted, that for the most part, "People are scared, but not of losing their jobs. They are afraid of offending their boss." But what was essential to Victoria was that Local 34 become a broad-based union, not dominated by only four or five people at the top. The strength of the union movement in her view would help mitigate women's fears and for her it was a way to achieve pragmatic goals.

She had worked at Yale for six years and first sought employment at the university when she became widowed. She and her husband had lived in New Haven years earlier when her husband was a psychiatrist at Yale, but they then moved to St. Louis where Victoria worked for a publishing company. Bypassing personnel, she found her job at Yale through the chairman of the department whom she knew. Working in the business office in the department of psychiatry and administered grants, Victoria kept records of appointments and promotions and of affirmative action. She described working conditions as "good" and her office atmosphere as "pleasant," but she had begun to look for a better job, stating that six years at a "dead-end" job was enough, and that "psychiatry was really my husband's field."

Victoria had received a mailing from Local 34, but said, "I did not find it very impressive." It did not speak enough about the specific advantages of a union for Yale employees, but talked instead about a New York local. But when a young Local 34 organizer stopped by her house for a home visit and Victoria was able to engage in a process of one-on-one questions and answers, she began to comprehend how a union could not only lead to the institution of regular cost-of-living increases but also could fulfill her personal vision of fulfilling some of the goals and visions of the women's movement. She agreed to become active, but not to become the floor organizer, a role she felt would make her vulnerable while she was searching for a new job. The union, by allowing her to limit her involvement, helped her to maintain her sense of autonomy and individual mobility. This was significant, because others with whom I spoke, as I will discuss, complained that the union had a cult-like intensity and demanded too much commitment too soon. Moreover, even as Victoria was pursuing her career plans for a promotion at Yale and desired individual mobility, she sought a lateral peer-based tie with co-workers. Victoria said that she saw the union as a symbol of strength and a solution to her low pay and concern about receiving a poor pension.

Victoria's experience at Yale also shows how Local 34 was able to build on feminist currents of thought and feeling already in motion at Yale.[23] Victoria said that she believed that the women's movement was a major factor in women's burgeoning union consciousness. She explained that she had six children and that years earlier had gone back to school to get a master's degree in Greek for her own pleasure, but noted with regret, "I never had a profession. I feel shafted. Women of my generation were raised according to such rigid stereotypes." She explained that now she had to live on her "paltry" salary. The "women's movement," she said, had led her and other women "to question the value of their work." "In general, women at Yale feel they are worth more than they're getting. They feel that their job is important. Moreover, everyone is hurting because of inflation. I don't think that Yale is an ogre, [but] if a union doesn't win, I will be disappointed." The union spoke to her feminist concerns. Her union involvement became an opportunity for her to rewrite her life's script and recapture a lost vision of herself.

Rose Cordo, a Latino woman, hedged her involvement in Local 34. She was the only Latino woman in the circulation department of Sterling Library, and was very conscious of being an ethnic minority at Yale. She had arrived in the United States from Colombia, South America, without a good command of English and when she first began working at Yale in a low-level cataloguing position she was content just to have a job. She called filing books "pointless" work, but at the time her salary helped bolster her husband's income and was adequate for them to raise their seven-year-old daughter. But then Rose's life's circumstances changed. Rose's husband left her, and she became seriously ill, hospitalized for a time with a paralyzed leg. When Rose returned to work, it was as a single head of household who needed to support a daughter. She not only found her pay insufficient to meet her new financial responsibilities but felt that over the course of time, conditions of work had begun to deteriorate. Yale no longer hired temporary or part-time workers to compensate for lost staff when someone called in sick. When someone permanently left a job at the library, no one was hired as a replacement and the job was phased out. Shift-work assignments during vacations added to Rose's overall workload. When Rose became trained to use the library computer system she was hopeful that she would receive a pay raise, but her pay scale was never adjusted to reflect her new skills. Rose began to find herself overworked and under stress.

Indicative of her racial consciousness, Rose gauged her position in the workplace in comparison to the three black women with whom she worked. Rose observed that they were all unhappy with their jobs, overburdened and underpaid, but too intimidated to renegotiate their workload or ask for raises. She said, "The atmosphere is very unfriendly. There is an oppressive atmosphere. The supervisors have risen to their positions from lower levels and then oppress you. Everyone is unhappy where I work, but they are afraid to do anything about it. . . . I am afraid to speak out, but I would not let anyone discriminate against me as a minority." The fear of loss of autonomy in decision making, that a union would destroy employee independence and initiative and impose a new bureaucracy, acted as a major deterrent to joining a union. Yet despite Rose's fears of strikes and her feeling of vulnerability she began to network and meet other employees at the library who were exploring unionization.

By the time of the Local 34 union election, most of the black women working in Sterling Memorial Library had thrown their support behind Local 34. Organizers met with minority employees one-on-one and peers exerted enormous pressure on co-workers, minority and nonminority, to join the union. This was particularly true in large offices where peer contact was more intensive than relationships with higher-ups. The sense that Rose had of being on display and at risk, of being hypervisible as a Latino woman who was pro-union, was less of an issue for black women in her midst who once they became part of a critical mass of Local 34 supporters no longer felt isolated. As library employees strategized, meeting in the dining halls during lunch to talk union, they became bolder in greeting students and faculty at the circulation desk and wore a smile and a union button.

How to incorporate into the union black and other minority clerical and technical workers who were clearly in the numerical minority at Yale posed a tactical problem for Local 34. To build a multiracial union, Local 34 ultimately crafted a discourse concerned with racial discrimination and argued that Yale discriminated against both women and minorities, and they also invited nationally renowned civil rights activists to campus. Many minority women became active in the union, but some doubted the union's sincerity and urged Local 34 to more fully articulate issues of racial discrimination at Yale.

Women of color at Yale often spoke about societal prejudice or forms of discrimination that they had experienced on the job and how this had hindered their mobility. In this regard, they shared the common experience of societally imposed racial stigmatization. As Howard Winant acknowledges, in the United States "racial minority status still serves as a negative marker, a stigma, in the class formation process."[24] Gregg observes that one unifying feature of African American women's union experience at Yale was that they were more acutely conscious of the intersection of class and race than white women employees.[25] Black women understood union dynamics from a race-conscious perspective, whereas most white women did not include race as a factor influencing their experiences of union events at Yale. But Gregg argues that nevertheless race did figure into white women's subjective experience of identity. The omission of talk about race, she adds, was "evidence of these women's unconsciousness, or a less immediate awareness, about the relationship between race, subjective experience, and possibilities."[26]

Minority women's racially aware subjective experience of their union identity was consistent with their past experiences of racial subordination and, thus, not altogether surprising. A group of black employees concerned that Local 34 had failed to adequately address minority issues formed a black caucus. Its purpose was to pressure the union to incorporate minority concerns directly into the language of the contract and to foster black leadership within the union movement. Furthermore, a small group of minority women concerned about how comparable worth would affect them, formed an affirmative action group to analyze the comparable-worth issue. This group gave women a place in the union to make minority concerns a priority, but the feeling remained that the union focused on winnable issues and that they didn't see race as a winnable issue. Although the group felt they acted as a consciousness-raising group for nonminority members, they criticized the union for failing to address the issue of minority discrimination in the workplace and for failing to consider how the drive could be extended to "take a place in the global struggle for workers' rights."[27]

Refusing to link race and class in a way that reduced race to class, black caucus women became what Winant calls "radical democratic challengers" of the labor movement. They raised "the question of discrimination as a racial process with class consequences."[28] Winant himself argues that a race-conscious challenge to U.S. political and cultural life, one that thinks about "class, inequality, and redistribution in ways that take racial divisions and conflicts into primary account" are necessary to overcome racism and racial poverty.[29] Women in the black caucus, in this same vein, advocated that the union adopt a broad critique of how race functions in society to subjugate blacks. But not all black women at Yale highlighted racial identity over class issues.[30]

Many minority women decided to support unionization despite their suspicion of bureaucracies and, in some cases, despite their misgivings that Local 34 was not sensitive enough to issues of race and gender. Also noteworthy was how union organizing and the strike provided a context for interethnic and interracial alliances. Black-white alliances that formed as co-workers mobilized to form a union are important in light of the way in which racial representations have mediated labor struggles and confrontations in the past. Anthropologist Leith Mullings makes the general point, "In the United States racial representation is crucial to constructing a history that encourages working-class whites to identify with white power holders, facilitating labour control of both blacks and whites."[31] Buck demonstrates "a racialized version of history—which underplays and distorts the role of African Americans," denies their activism, presents race and racism "as part of nature rather than a reflection of a specific historical moment, and cuts people off from a history that could empower them, presenting protest as pointless."[32] At Yale, black women not only became union activists but they became role models for white co-workers.

Cecily Morgan, for instance, adopted what Winant would call a more pragmatic, liberal approach to her union activism. Rather than align herself with other black employees as a power bloc to reform the union, she sought coalitions with both black and white women in the central area of campus where she worked. She talked about the forces in her life that seemed to fuel her activism and organizing style and that gave her strength: her earlier experience in Catholic schools, her home in an integrated neighborhood, and her personal network and support system. Cecily was raising four children by herself, and although she was quite concerned about her low pay, she knew that she could share child-care and financial resources with her mother and sister, who had reciprocally helped one another in the past. Cecily's boyfriend, whom she later married, although "not political" believed that she needed a union.

Cecily described the road that she had traveled to become a union activist at Yale. Earlier in life, she had wanted to become a nurse, but unable to afford nursing school, she became a nurse's aid without a certificate and worked in a private home. She then took a night job at New Haven's Olin gun factory, but when the factory closed, she accepted employment at Yale for less pay. "Conditions," she said, "are bad for everyone. Yale is not receptive if you ask for a raise—now especially. It seems like they keep women down."

Cecily had earlier worked to form a union affiliated with the Office and Professional Employees International Union (OPEIU) making phone calls, passing out leaflets, and withstanding confrontations with her boss, who swore, "Hell with unions!" Still she persisted in her activism and when OPEIU lost by two hundred votes, Cecily said, "Everyone was depressed." She believed that OPEIU lost because employees who had worked at Yale for twenty or thirty years remained loyal to Yale. Married women seemed more concerned about losing their five weeks of vacation time than in fighting for higher pay, and some women were intimidated by "very strict bosses." In short, she was convinced that union sentiment in the workplace differed more by age and marital status than by racial identity.

After the drive, she continued to be deeply concerned about low wages and how Yale treated its office workers, but she did not interpret her own low-salaried job in the accounting office in dining halls as a sign of racial discrimination but believed that everyone was hurting. Cecily agreed reluctantly to "start again" when two white co-workers, with whom she had an easy camaraderie, urged her to become involved with the United Auto Workers, which had also tried to form a union at Yale. But that drive, she said, never amassed more than "a small committee of about ten people to attend meetings." Despite its defeat, Cecily never lost her desire to "have a say" in her job, to "gain respect and recognition," to "get higher wages, and to gain ease in obtaining transfers." She saw these as core issues to be fought for by all women, whom she believed were equally oppressed in their jobs at Yale. She ultimately became a visible activist and strong supporter of Local 34. Her approach to union activism was gender and class based, representing a pragmatist's approach to building coalitions that minimized racial differences.

One sociological study evaluating the class situation of United States clerical workers according to their level of education and father's and husband's social backgrounds concluded that married clerical workers are almost evenly divided in terms of their husband's jobs: about half have white-collar husbands and 41 percent have blue-collar husbands.[33] Women's diverse educational backgrounds and lack of a shared familial class position hindered the development of a sense of common identity on the job and the potential for collective action. This kind of diversity and fragmentation among workers was particularly true at Yale and helps to explain why so many Yale employees opposed labor organizing. But ultimately the process of unionization created a momentum that helped employees overcome differences in racial identity and status affiliation. Despite women's diverse backgrounds and differing expectations, many shared similar grievances about low pay and working conditions at Yale. Local 34 ultimately sought and gained the support of employees whom past union officials viewed as resolutely antiunion and outside their reach. The union also helped to build bridges among workers who did not feel that they shared a similar work culture or socioeconomic background.

Local 34's "culture of activism" focused on grass-roots organizing, a coalition with the blue-collar workers on campus who were already members of the Hotel and Restaurant Workers Union, the advocacy of comparable-worth issues, the use of media-catching tactics, and the creation of local faculty and students' support groups and wider women's and labor movement backing. This kind of attention to both individual needs and broad-based coalition building created the possibility for workers' shared perspective and political solidarity where no former all-embracing, campus-wide work culture existed at Yale. Hank Johnston notes that how successful a social movement is, how well it can articulate grievances and hopes, how well its discourse resonates with its constituency, has often to do with individuals as actors diversely situated with plural and sometimes contradictory perceptions of events. Social movement theorists have moved us in the direction of understanding collective and organizational processes of mobilization, but Johnston directs our attention to cognitive processes and individual needs.[34] I would argue that individuals' self-formulations and adherence to multiple identities sometimes exist in an uneasy balance correspondence with collective definitions of social movements and that this very tension tells us something about how individuals preserve their autonomy from the group and how social movements stop short of becoming cults. The diversity in individuals' self-identification and the tensions that characterized the relationship between the individual and the collective defined the complexity of a politics of location and ultimately represented both the union's volatility and its greatest strength.

NOTES

My special thanks to Marianne DeKoven for her inspiration as a seminar leader and her commitment to this book. My warmest thanks to Perry Dane for his perceptive comments and his loving encouragement. Thanks also to the National Institute of Mental Health and the National Science Foundation for awarding me predissertation grants. And I want to express my gratitude to the Institute for Social and Policy Research at Yale, which allowed me to be a postdoctoral fellow, and to the Institute for Research on Women at Rutgers University, which provided me with a faculty fellowship. In keeping with government guidelines attached to grants that I received in conducting this research, I have used pseudonyms to protect the privacy of those employees whom I interviewed directly. Quotations and references from secondary sources are not pseudonymous.

1. Most recently Yale employees (including both the clerical and technical workers as well as the service and maintenance staff) struck in 1996. One of the hotly debated issues of that strike was Yale's right to hire subcontractors. In its confrontation with the Yale administration, Yale union members formed a coalition with community groups. The model of labor/community alliance in New Haven has become the centerpiece of further local activism. See Warren T. Dorian and Cathy J. Cohen, "Organizing at the Intersection of Labor and Civil Rights: A Case Study of New Haven," *University of Pennsylvania Journal of Labor and Employment Law* 2:4 (spring 2000): 629–655.

   A new dimension of union politics at Yale since the 1984–1985 strike has also been the organization of Yale's graduate students. In 1990, a small group of students organized into the Graduate Employees and Students Organization (GESO) to help them lobby for better fellowships, medical and dental benefits, and a stronger voice in university policies. In April 1994, graduate students in humanities and social sciences voted for the GESO to become their collective bargaining agent. Yale has consistently opposed the unionization of graduate students, whereas Locals 34 and 35 have expressed their ongoing support for the graduate students. Between April 2 and 7, 1995, graduate student teaching assistants staged a brief walkout, resulting in several canceled classes. Their withholding of student grades became the subject of a court hearing.

2. There are already several interesting and informative accounts of the Yale organizing drive and the strike of 1984–1985. See, for example, Crocker Coulson, "Labor Unrest in the Ivy League," *The Arbitration Journal* 40:3 (1985): 53–62; Aldo Cupo, Molly Ladd-Taylor, Beverly Lett, and David Montgomery, "Beep, Beep, Yale's Cheap: Looking at the Yale Strike," *Radical America* 18:5 (1984): 7–19; Tony Gilpin, Gary Isaac, Dan Letwin,

and Jack McKivigan, *On Strike for Respect: The Yale Strike of 1984–5* (Chicago: Charles H. Kerr, 1988); Nina Gregg, "Telling Stories about Reality: Women's Responses to a Workplace Organizing Campaign," in *Women Making Meaning: New Feminist Directions in Communication,* ed. Lana R. Rakow (London: Routledge, 1992), 263–288; Kathleen Kautzer, "'We Can't Eat Prestige': The Yale University Workers' Campaign for Comparable Worth," *Equal Value/Comparable Worth in the UK and the USA,* ed. Pegg Kahn and Elizabeth Meehan (New York: St. Martin's Press, 1992), 137–165; Molly Ladd-Taylor, "Women Workers and the Yale Strike," *Feminist Studies* 11:3 (1985): 465–490; Cynthia Saltzman, "Unseen Women at the Academy," in *The Negotiation of Gender in American Culture,* ed. Faye Ginzberg and Anna Tsing (Boston: Beacon Press, 1990), 152–168; Cynthia Saltzman, "The New Wave of Union Organizing: Shifting Paradigms, Changing Myths," in *Locating Capitalism in Time and Space: Papers on the Influence of Joan Vincent,* ed. David Nugent (Stanford, Calif.: Stanford University Press, forthcoming); Ruth Sidel, *Women and Children Last* (New York: Penguin Books, 1986). On the history of organizing at Yale, see Herbert Janick, "Yale Blue: Unionization at Yale University, 1931–1985," *Labor History* 28:3 (1987): 349–369.

3. Fiona Devine, *Social Class in America and Britain* (Edinburgh, Great Britain: Edinburgh University Press, 1997), 183; G. Marshall et al., *Social Class in Modern Britain* (London: Hutchinson, 1988), 130.

4. Rosabeth Moss Kanter, *Work and Family in the United States: A Critical Review and Agenda for Research and Policy* (New York: Russell Sage Foundation, 1977); Phyllis M. Palmer and Sharon Lee Grant, *The Status of Clerical Workers: A Summary Analysis of Research Findings and Trends* (Women's Studies Program, George Washington University, Business and Professional Women's Foundation, 1979); Rosemary Pringle, *Secretaries Talk: Sexuality, Power, and Work* (London and New York: Verso, 1988).

5. Pringle, *Secretaries Talk,* 207.

6. Rick Fantasia, *Cultures of Solidarity: Consciousness, Action, and Contemporary American Workers* (Berkeley and Los Angeles: University of California Press, 1988), 19–20.

7. Fantasia, *Cultures of Solidarity,* 23.

8. Fantasia, *Cultures of Solidarity,* 22.

9. Fantasia, *Cultures of Solidarity,* 14.

10. Alberto Melucci, "The Process of Collective Identity," in *Social Movements and Culture,* vol. 4, *Social Movements, Protest, and Contention,* ed. Hank Johnston and Bert Klandermans (Minneapolis: University of Minnesota Press, 1995), 54.

11. Melucci, "The Process of Collective Identity," 54.

12. Arlene Stein, "Sisters and Queers: The Decentering of Lesbian Feminism," in *Cultural Politics and Social Movements,* ed. Marcy Darnovsky, Barbara Epstein, and Richard Flacks (Philadelphia: Temple University Press, 1995), 144.

13. Norma Alarcón, "The Theoretical Subject(s) of This Bridge Called My Back and Anglo-American Feminism," in *Making Face, Making Soul: Hacienco Caras,* ed. Gloria Anzaldúa (San Francisco: Aunt Lute Foundations Books, 1990), 359.

14. Nina Gregg, "Politics of Identity/Politics of Location: Women Workers Organizing in a Postmodern World," *Women's Studies in Communication* 16:1 (spring 1993): 1–33, 7–8.

15. Louise Lamphere, Patricia Zavella, Felipe Gonzales, and Peter B. Evans, *Sunbelt Mothers: Reconciling Family and Factory* (Ithaca, N.Y.: Cornell University Press, 1993).

16. Gregg, "Politics of Identity/Politics of Location," 1.

17. Gregg, "Politics of Identity/Politics of Location," 3.

18. Rosemary Crompton, *Class and Stratification: An Introduction to Current Debates* (Cambridge, Mass.: Polity Press, 1993).

19. R. Inglehart, "Post-Materialism in an Age of Insecurity," *American Political Science Review* 75:4 (1981): 880–900; Crompton, *Class and Stratification,* 206.

20. Gregg, "Politics of Identity/Politics of Location," 14.

21. Katherine Newman, *Falling from Grace: The Experience of Downward Mobility in the American Middle Class* (New York: Free Press, 1988).

22. Another reason that educated employees became discontented and sought unionization was that they had few opportunities at Yale to further their education, to work and support themselves while attending classes. Unlike universities of similar stature such as Harvard and Columbia, Yale then offered adults very limited opportunities to attend school on a part-time basis; the problem became well publicized. One newspaper reporter wrote:

Since 1977, Yale has allowed the public to attend the majority of its regularly scheduled classes, only after they pass a selection process, pay $880 per course (there is no financial aid) and find a way to fit daytime classes around other responsibilities, such as full-time jobs. Auditing a class is not allowed. Eight years ago, even this limited access did not exist.

"It seems to me that Yale has been remiss in serving the needs of the community," says Michael Shinagel, the dean of Harvard's continuing education and extension program. "They could be doing a lot more." (Barbara Stevens, *New Haven Register*, September 17, 1984)

For employees who had aspirations to pursue their education at Yale while they worked, Yale became a site of stalled mobility.

23. Gregg (1992) writes that few of the women whom she interviewed described union organizing at Yale as gender focused, but that the dynamics of gender subjectivity nonetheless help contribute to an understanding of women's responses to the union. My findings, in contrast, indicate that many women's views of the union changed as Local 34 began to champion the cause of comparable worth, and its discourse specifically championed women's rights on the job.

24. Howard Winant, "Race: Theory, Culture, and Politics in the United States Today," in *Cultural Politics and Social Movements*, ed. Marcy Darnovsky, Barbara Epstein, and Richard Flacks (Philadelphia: Temple University Press, 1995), 181.

25. Gregg, "Telling Stories about Reality: Women's Responses to a Workplace Organizing Campaign," 279.

26. Gregg, "Telling Stories about Reality: Women's Responses to a Workplace Organizing Campaign," 271; bell hooks, "Sisters of the Yam: Overcoming White Supremacy," *Zeta* 1:1 (1988): 24–27; Marsha Houston Stanback, "What Makes Scholarship about Black Women and Communication Feminist Scholarship?" *Women's Studies in Communication* 11:1 (1988): 28–31.

27. Gregg, "Politics of Identity/Politics of Location," 8.

28. Winant, "Race: Theory, Culture, and Politics in the United States Today," 185.

29. Winant, "Race: Theory, Culture, and Politics in the United States Today," 185.

30. My thinking has been influenced by others who look at how African Americans may define their personal identities as racially and/or class based and may place varying degrees of emphasis on aspects of class and race. Judith Goode and Jo Anne Schneider, for example, build upon the work of Elijah Anderson, who in *Streetwise* generalizes about two types of middle-class African Americans: "those who think that maintaining racial identity is primary and always suspect that whites are racist, and those who consider class more important and, while maintaining mostly African American close friends, move comfortably in mixed-race, middle-class circles." (223) The identity of black clerical and technical employees at Yale who considered the question of unionization also characterized by complex considerations of the interplay of class and racial issues.

31. Leith Mullings, "Ethnicity and Representation," in *Social Construction of the Past: Representation as Power*, ed. George C. Bond and Angela Gilliam (London: Routledge, 1994), 26.

32. Pem Davidson Buck, "Racial Representations and Power in the Dependent Development of the United States South," in *Social Construction of the Past: Representation as Power*, ed. George C. Bond and Angela Gilliam (London: Routledge, 1994), 29–43; Mullings, "Ethnicity and Representation."

33. Evelyn Nakano Glenn and Roslyn L. Feldberg, "Clerical Work: The Female Occupation," in *Women: A Feminist Perspective*, 4th edition, ed. Jo Freeman (Palo Alto, Calif.: Mayfield, 1989), 287–311.

34. Hank Johnston, "A Methodology for Frame Analysis: From Discourse to Cognitive Schemata," in *Social Movements and Culture* [*Social Movements, Protest, and Contention*, Vol. 4], ed. Hank Johnston and Bert Klandermans (Minneapolis: University of Minnesota Press, 1995), 217–246.

REFERENCES

Alarcón, Norma. "The Theoretical Subject(s) of This Bridge Called My Back and Anglo-American Feminism." In *Making Face, Making Soul: Hacienco Caras*, edited by Gloria Anzaldúa, 356–369. San Francisco: Aunt Lute Foundations Books, 1990.

Anderson, Elijah. *Streetwise: Race, Class, and Change in an Urban Community.* Chicago: University of Chicago Press, 1990.

Buck, Pem Davidson. "Racial Representations and Power in the Dependent Development of the United States South." In *Social Construction of the Past: Representation as Power,* edited by George C. Bond and Angela Gilliam, 29–43. London: Routledge, 1994.

Coulson, Crocker. "Labor Unrest in the Ivy League." *Arbitration Journal* 40:3 (1985): 53–62.

Crompton, Rosemary. *Class and Stratification: An Introduction to Current Debates.* London: Polity Press, 1993.

Cupo, Aldo, Molly Ladd-Taylor, Beverly Lett, and David Montgomery. "Beep, Beep, Yale's Cheap. Looking at the Yale Strike." *Radical America* 18:5 (1984): 7–19.

Devine, Fiona. *Social Class in America and Britain.* Edinburgh, Great Britain: Edinburgh University Press, 1997.

Fantasia, Rick. *Cultures of Solidarity: Consciousness, Action, and Contemporary American Workers.* Berkeley and Los Angeles: University of California Press, 1988.

Feldberg, Roslyn, and Evelyn Nakano Glenn. "Clerical Work: The Female Occupation." In *Women: A Feminist Perspective,* edited by Jo Freeman, 313–339. Palo Alto, Calif.: Mayfield, 1979.

Gilpin, Tony, Gary Isaac, Dan Letwin, and Jack McKivigan. *On Strike for Respect: The Yale Strike of 1984–1985.* Chicago: Charles H. Kerr, 1988.

Goode, Judith, and Jo Anne Schneider. *Reshaping Ethnic and Racial Relations in Philadelphia: Immigrants in a Divided City.* Philadelphia: Temple University Press, 1994.

Gregg, Nina. "Women Telling Stories About Reality: Subjectivity, the Generation of Meaning, and the Organizing of a Union at Yale." Ph.D. Dissertation, McGill University, 1991.

———. "Politics of Identity/Politics of Location: Women Workers Organizing in a Postmodern World." *Women's Studies in Communication* 16:1 (spring 1993): 1–33.

———. "Telling Stories about Reality: Women's Responses to a Workplace Organizing Campaign." In *Women Making Meaning: New Feminist Directions in Communication,* edited by Lana F. Rakow, 263–288. London: Routledge, 1992.

hooks, bell. "Sisters of the Yam: Overcoming White Supremacy." *Zeta* 1:1 (1988): 24–27.

Inglehart, R. "Post-materialism in an age of insecurity." *American Political Science Review* 75:4 (1981): 880–900.

Janick, Herbert. "Yale Blue: Unionization at Yale University, 1931–1985." *Labor History* 28:3 (1987): 349–369.

Johnston, Hank. "A Methodology for Frame Analysis: From Discourse to Cognitive Schemata." In *Social Movements and Culture,* (*Social Movements, Protest, and Contention,* Vol. 4), edited by Hank Johnston and Bert Klandermans, 217–246. Minneapolis: University of Minnesota Press, 1995.

Kanter, Rosabeth Moss. *Work and Family in the United States: A Critical Review and Agenda for Research and Policy.* New York: Russell Sage Foundation, 1977.

Kautzer, Kathleen. "'We Can't Eat Prestige': The Yale University Workers' Campaign for Comparable Worth." In *Equal Value/Comparable Worth in the UK and the USA,* edited by Peggy Kahn and Elizabeth Meehan, 137–165. New York: St. Martin's Press, 1992.

Ladd-Taylor, Molly. "Women Workers and the Yale Strike." *Feminist Studies* (fall 1985).

Lamphere, Louise, Patricia Zavella, Felipe Gonzales, and Peter B. Evans. *Sunbelt Working Mothers: Reconciling Family and Factory.* Ithaca, N.Y.: Cornell University Press, 1993.

Marshall, G. et al. *Social Class in Modern Britain.* London: Hutchinson, 1988.

Melucci, Alberto. "The Process of Collective Identity." In *Social Movements and Culture,* edited by Hank Johnston and Bert Klandermans, 41–64. Minneapolis: University of Minnesota Press, 1995.

Mullings, Leith. "Ethnicity and Representation." In *Social Construction of the Past: Representation as Power,* edited by George C. Bond and Angela Gilliam, 25–28. London: Routledge, 1994.

Newman, Katherine. *Falling from Grace: The Experience of Downward Mobility in the American Middle Class.* New York: Free Press, 1988.

Palmer, Phyllis M., and Sharon Lee Grant. *The Status of Clerical Workers. A Summary Analysis of Research Findings and Trends.* Women's Studies Program, George Washington University. Business and Professional Women's Foundation, 1979.

Pringle, Rosemary. *Secretaries Talk: Sexuality, Power, and Work.* London and New York: Verso, 1988.

Rich, Adrienne. "Notes toward a Politics of Location." In *Women, Feminist Identity, and Society in the 1980's, Selected Papers,* edited by Myriam Diaz-Diocaretz and Iris M. Zavala, 7–22. Philadelphia: Johns Benjamin, 1995.

Saltzman, Cynthia. "You Can't Eat Prestige: Women and Unions at Yale." Ph.D. Dissertation, Columbia University, 1988.

———. "The New Wave of Union Organizing: Shifting Paradigms, Changing Myths." In *Locating Capitalism in Time and Space: Papers on the Influence of Joan Vincent,* edited by David Nugent. Stanford, Calif.: Stanford University Press, forthcoming.

———. "Unseen Women at the Academy." In *The Negotiation of Gender in American Culture,* edited by Faye Ginzberg and Anna Tsing, 152–168. Boston: Beacon Press, 1990.

Sidel, Ruth. *Women and Children Last.* New York: Penguin Books, 1986.

Stanback, Marsha Houston. "What Makes Scholarship about Black Women and Communication Feminist Scholarship?" *Women's Studies in Communication* 11:1 (1988): 28–31.

Stein, Arlene. "Sisters and Queers: The Decentering of Lesbian Feminism." In *Cultural Politics and Social Movements,* edited by Marcy Darnovsky, Barbara Epstein, and Richard Flacks, 133–153. Philadelphia: Temple University Press, 1995.

Stevens, Barbara. *New Haven Register,* September 17, 1984.

Winant, Howard. "Race: Theory, Culture, and Politics in the United States Today." In *Cultural Politics and Social Movements,* edited by Marcy Darnovsky, Barbara Epstein, and Richard Flacks, 174–188. Philadelphia: Temple University Press, 1995.

RAJESWARI SUNDER RAJAN

FEMINISM AND THE POLITICS OF THE HINDU GODDESS

Disinterested scholarship and academic discussion by Indologists and South Asia studies experts in the Western academy from different fields, religion, anthropology, philosophy, psychology, language, culture, and history is given a political edge when the question of the *feminism* of the Hindu goddess is posed.[1] For a different constituency, made up of Hindu worshipers, Hindu "nationalists," feminists of varying hues, left secularists, and others who are located within contemporary social movements and politics in India, the goddess is, as we might expect, primarily a symbolic resource. Thus the implications of the *is* in the question "Is the Hindu Goddess a feminist?" would differ in these different contexts: from the universal present tense indicating a perpetual condition or an indication of abstract potentiality (as it were, *can* the Hindu goddess be feminist?) in the former instance, to a historical present tense, our contemporary context, local and global, within which the question would resonate with the deployment and role of a majority religion's idiom in a postcolonial "secular democracy," India, in the latter.

Despite the different locations of these voices, they may be allied in and through their common perception of the goddess's feminism. One section would agree that the goddess is, indeed, a feminist, that being a feminist is a good thing to be for a goddess, and that this position is enabling, that is, it is in the interests of women, India,

Hinduism, and Indian women. From the other side, for reasons that
I shall be rehearsing shortly, the conclusion will be called into question. I shall focus on the disagreement centering on the claim that
the goddess's feminism is enabling. But I shall assume consensus on
the following views: one, that "feminist" here will mean "pro-
woman," "empowering women"; two, that the Hindu goddess is
unique in that Hinduism is the only contemporary world religion that
has a tradition and continuing practice of goddess worship; three, that
Hindu goddess worship is radical in so far as the goddess is not inscribed in the mainstream of deities and her devotees are drawn
largely from lower castes, women and even non-Hindus, thus clear-
ing certain spaces of alternative belief and practice in the monolith
of Brahminical Hinduism; and finally, that it is not only the existence and worship of the goddess, but also her representations in feminist ways—as complementary female principle, as autonomous female
agent, or as powerful cosmic force—that are under discussion here
as aspects of her feminist recuperation.

To talk of *the* Hindu goddess as if she were a single or composite
figure is, of course, already problematic. The debate over the meaning of the goddess would have to take into account the range and
diversity of her representation, the sheer numbers of goddesses, major and minor, mainstream and local, that are to be found in the pantheon. David Kinsley's *Hindu Goddesses* provides a useful list and also
a chronological history of the evolution of various goddess-figures,
and John Grimes's essay on Hindu goddesses constructs a taxonomy
based on their different functions, provenance, and attributes.[2] One
direction for the discussion to take would be to examine the distinctive attributes of different goddesses, or the anthropological aspects
of their cults and worship, in order to decide upon their greater or
smaller potential for feminist appropriation. It would be generally
agreed that despite the great symbolic value and veneration bestowed
on the consorts of the trinity, the goddesses Lakshmi, Saraswathi, and
Parvathi, it is the autonomous constructions of female divinity such
as Kali, Durga, and their numerous spinoffs who are representative
of *stri shakti* (woman power) and are therefore of relevance in this
discussion. I shall sidestep the more nuanced and elaborate discrimi-
nations that this discussion would call for. As I clarified earlier, even
if one does not dispute the claim that these goddesses belong to the
radical rather than mainstream—hence more patriarchal—tradition

of Hindu social and religious practice, the implications of such radicalism are open to contestation.

In my view the recuperation of the/an Hindu goddess as feminist is problematic at the present historical juncture both for its assumption of an undifferentiated "woman power," as well as for its promotion of a certain radicalized Hinduism. Some Indian feminists, among whom I count myself, would be cautious of buying into the constituency of women by extending the scope and politics of contemporary Hinduism. I shall, however, first rehearse, briefly, both sides of the debate over the question, though the arguments are likely to be familiar ones. I shall push them further by interrogating their politics: who is saying this? who is opposing it? what is at stake here? what investments can we discern in the investment in the goddess? what are the grounds of skepticism? These will lead to the elucidation of my argument in the concluding section of the essay.

Those who assert that the Hindu goddess is feminist celebrate, first, the Hindu religion's richness and plurality of traditions. In contrast to the singular patriarchal god of the Judeo-Christian tradition, Vedic Hinduism had female deities and (arguably) a "matriarchal world view." Joanna Liddle and Rama Joshi are quoted frequently in this context:

> The worship of the mother goddess does not constitute a matriarchy, but it does constitute a matriarchal *culture*, in the sense that it preserves the value of women as life-givers and sources of activating energy, and it represents the acknowledgment of women's power by women and men in the culture.[3]

When a community's object of worship and veneration is female, it is logical to expect that women in general benefit by sharing that elevated status. The widespread acceptance, even valorization of positive constructions of femininity in goddess figures must serve as enabling models for women that would supplement, contest, or displace the more prevalent models of female meekness, subordination, and obedience, in the form and in the service of *pativrata* (husband worship), derived from the mythological Sita-Savithri-Anasuya paradigm. Their dissemination via popular cultural forms such as folk theater, mythology, song-and-dance performances, oral storytelling, and cinema has assisted the rise and dominance of women political leaders like Indira Gandhi and folk heroines like Phoolan Devi; or, at least, such women have been accommodated and accepted within the cognitive frame provided by goddesses or the allied historical/mythological figures of the *viranganas*.[4] In Hinduism, gender stereotypes are broken down in the attribution of power, whether negative—unruly, destructive, sexually unbridled—or positive—maternal, protective, asexual—to female divinity. The phenomenon of "possession" (by the spirit of the goddess) may also be used by some women to effectively resist oppression or devaluation in the family by laying claim to spiritual prowess. And even where the goddess is not a resource she is a solace to women.

The connections suggestively drawn here, between goddesses and women in Indian society, may be questioned, however. We must distinguish the feminization of certain attributes like righteousness, justice, wealth, learning, or more accurately their embodiment in the female figure, from the elevation of strong or aberrant women with these attributes to divinity. The goddess is, correctly, a product of the first process, not the second. The implication of this distinction lies in this: that the symbolic valuation of forms is not a reflection of the actual material and historical conditions in which they take shape. If we locate the indices of the status of women in the latter, that is, in female sex-ratios, life expectancy, literacy, income, subjection to violence, equality of opportunity, legal equality, then the evidence shows that societies that have goddesses (or even women leaders) score poorly on these counts.[5] That the ideological promotion of powerful female models does not contribute to ordinary women's well-being may be logically contrary to certain feminist expectations, but it appears to be an empirically valid finding. Tracy Pintchman resolves her puzzlement over this contradiction by describing women's status in India as ambiguous.[6] But the divide between goddesses and women as social beings can be maintained by patriarchy without any sense of contradiction. Furthermore, though unconventional women may find sanction for their behavior through reference to them, goddesses, unlike Sita or Savithri, are rarely invoked as explicit role models in the socialization of girls.

Women's empowerment as goddesses may also meet with rational and modern skepticism of the kind made memorable in Satyajit Ray's film, *Devi*.[7] Ray highlights as well the patriarchal investments in this transformative process and poignantly evokes the cost to the young girl—the sacrifice of "normal" conjugal life, sanity and finally life itself—as a result of the pressures of the role she is obliged to play as the devi of her father-in-law's fantasies. Beyond these arguments lies the more substantial issue of power of certain kinds, individualistic, absolute, aggressive, or anarchic, and in certain contexts, those of authoritarian politics or fascistic social movements, in relation to women, specifically to women's putative *agency*, that I shall return to.

These arguments can be taken further, on both sides; but I want to move here into questions of identity, location, and their politics: who speaks? from where? to what ends or purposes?

The feminist Hindu goddess, or more accurately the claim for the progressive potential of the goddess for women's liberation, is to be found chiefly in the following sites of discourse: some South Asia studies scholarship in the Western academy; Hindu nationalism; radical Indian feminism of a certain kind and, allied with it, Gandhian secularism. These are widely separated locations, and each operates with a distinctive voice and politics that cannot be collapsed into the other; nevertheless, the connections and overlaps among their arguments draw them into a single discursive field. I shall try to briefly identify the different sites in what follows.

I begin with the Hindu goddess-scholars from various fields engaged, as Alf Hiltebeitel put it, in "scholarly reflexivity," the "attempt to think about one's relation to what one studies."[8] This relationship he frankly admits to be one of "complicity." Apart from the generalized complicity—the identification with the objects of one's study that is an aspect of such studies—the scholars are also responsive to recent calls to "think difference" relativistically in ethnographic fieldwork, to refuse to see solely through ethnocentric lenses. The main consequence of this is a displacement of the earlier view of women in Indian society as universally exploited and submissive—which is now regarded as an unacceptable inferiorization of Hindu culture—through attempts to instead recover the spaces of their autonomy and the resources of their positive self-images, and to identify their agency. The goddess and her worship are a means to establishing these. Some of this results in what Bernard Williams has called "vulgar relativism," an uncritical, naive, and patronizing acceptance of other cultures' viewpoints that are unacceptable to one's own. The obverse of this, the temptation to idealize non-Western societies as a "resource" to meet the inadequacies of Western philosophies and lifestyles, is also visible in some of the interpretations: the goddess clearly meets one such lack, especially among feminist theologians.[9] But relativism is a complex position, and it is treated complexly for the most part in judging the question of the Hindu goddess's feminism. There is the bold deployment of the deliberate anachronism of the term itself, and the attempt to achieve commensurability between the non-Western feminine principle that the goddess represents and contemporary Western feminism: both moves that push beyond the relativizing exercise. Apart from the ethnographic evidence of studies of the worshipers themselves (in many cases women) in specific regions of India which supports a favorable interpretation of the impact of the goddess, these scholars also, interestingly, draw support from Hindu nationalist rhetoric, from the work of Indian feminists, and from aspects of the Indian women's movement in more visibly ideological ways.[10] This locates their interest in their "subject" within the frames of feminist inquiry and contemporary subcontinental politics.

Hindu Indian nationalists in the nineteenth century and in the subsequent decades of the Indian freedom movement had promoted the image of the militant goddess/heroic woman toward several ends: as propagandistic and reformist measure for elevating both Hindu women's and Hinduism's self-image and status, as in the Arya Samaj's programs; to mobilize women to participate in the struggle; and above all to provide an inspirational symbolic focus—as in the evolution of the *Bharat-mata* figure—for national and communal identity.[11] By and large South Asia scholars have been sympathetic to and have endorsed these ends. In contrast to their acceptance, Gayatri Spivak has alerted us to the possibility that, in their resistance to the imperialist effacement of "the image of the luminous fighting Mother Durga," nationalist (male) elites were simultaneously perpetuating a "reverse ethnocentrism."[12] Feminist historians in India have identified the development of the myth of the "advanced" Aryan (upper-caste) woman in nationalist historiography in the second half of the nineteenth century as belonging to the same ideological configuration.[13] Present-day Hindu nationalist parties have produced aggressive women leaders and set up strong organizational structures for women volunteers for similar purposes and based on similar arguments, al-

though in the quite different context of electoral politics and organized religious revivalism in the postcolonial nation-state. The actual
modalities of the formation of women leaders in the organized
Hindutva movement, centered around the shakthi/goddess ideology,
has been investigated in detail by Paola Bacchetta.[14] I shall be returning to Hindutva feminism in the last section of this essay; before I
do so, I shall attend to feminist "uses" of the goddess in other fields.

The Indian women's movement of the mid-seventies, initiated
by urban middle-class professional women (for the most part), invoked "traditional Indian" (read: Hindu) symbols in some cases as a
means of diluting if not countering the Western bias of "feminism."[15]
The goddess-figure, or in a more diffusive way the concepts of stri
shakthi and the feminine principle, were resorted to in order to mobilize women around women's issues: thus the logo and name of
India's first feminist press, Kali for Women. Soon this was to be placed
consciously on the agenda of some feminists. Madhu Kishwar, for instance, editor of *Manushi* (a journal of "women and society"), declared
her nonallegiance to "feminism" as a sign of her refusal of all-ism
ideologies, and began instead to explore "our cultural traditions" to
"identify their points of strength and use them creatively to combat
reactionary and anti-woman ideas."[16] As part of this trend *Manushi*
has carried articles on women Bhakthin poets, on Gandhi's relevance
for women, on women's negotiations with religious worship and practices like austerity, goddess cults, bhakthi, and spirit possession.

Gail Omvedt links this to a radical rethinking of theory and practice in the Indian women's movement in the eighties, which had earlier been tied mainly to a left tradition which rejected religion outright
as patriarchal. The new perspective, she argues, had some profound
implications:

> On one hand, the idea of the "feminine principle" challenged tradi-
> tional Marxism by posing the nature-maintaining, subsistence-based
> rural peasant woman against the male industrial worker who em-
> bodied the "proletarian vanguard"; on the other, it questioned the
> feminist tendencies to locate violence in the family, in the relations
> of women against men, by stressing the "feminine principle" as some-
> thing that men and women both could unite around. The notion of
> *stri shakthi* similarly implied not so much a separate women's move-
> ment as the leading role of women in various popular movements,
> helping these movements to transcend some of their own limita-

tions. As with the slogan "the liberation of women and men through the awakening of women's power," it was a significant departure from the tendency of both urban feminists and party women to depict women as primarily victims.[17]

Omvedt expresses the confidence that within this redefined attitude to religion/ethnicity/culture, traditional gender resources could be drawn upon by women without subscribing to, indeed while actively opposing, Hindu communalism.

Omvedt draws mainly upon the examples of the struggles of rural women in the Shetkari Sanghatana in Maharashtra for property rights and political representation, and of hill women in the Chipko movement in Uttar Pradesh for forestry rights and preservation of natural resources.[18] In the influential work of Vandana Shiva on the Chipko and similar struggles against the widespread depredations of the environment in the name of development (which include anti-dam struggles), nature is celebrated as Prakriti, the feminine principle, women as its representatives, and their power in collective struggle as *stri shakthi*.[19]

This position on women and religion is closely related to those working from within what we may call a Gandhian secular tradition, which recuperates or freely recasts the symbols and idiom of "Sanatan dharma" in progressive, universal noncommunal ways, and exploits their affective potential for communal coexistence and harmony. Gandhi's use of Sita as a symbol for women in the nationalist movement has been discussed by Madhu Kishwar.[20] More recently Ramachandra Gandhi's *Sita's Kitchen,* a philosophical and historical treatise written in the thick of the Ayodhya dispute, expounds the overlooked Sita tradition in Hindu, Jain, and Buddhist folklore and philosophy as an argument to counter the militant masculinity of the new Hindutva movements and their streamlining of a canonical Hinduism.[21] Here too women are associated with their tribal origins, with nature, nurture, and hence motherhood, preservation, and pacifism.

The question about the Hindu goddess's feminism is embedded, as we can see, within the larger question about the instrumentality of religion in the postcolonial nation—both for a secular politics and for women's struggles in mass movements—and thus moves far afield of a de-contextualized if more focused consideration of an answer. In the following section I shall problematize some of the connections between the Hindu goddess and feminism, between religion and women that have been made here, and the locations, theoretical and political, from where disagreement is articulated.

There are unresolved theoretical issues for feminism, among which the question of power—women's access to it, especially in political life, their modes of exercising it, the ethics of domination versus democracy—is increasingly recognized as a major one. I have rehearsed in more detail elsewhere the feminist debates over the meaning of power for women. Radical feminists repudiate male values and spheres of power, and valorize in their place women's traditional qualities of care, sacrifice, and sustenance in family and community; while other feminists argue that women's equality calls for struggle and requires participation in and control of the existing structures of political power.[22] The arguments in support of the feminism of the goddess deploy both arguments, the former in the celebration of Prakriti, nature as feminine principle, and the latter of shakti, the autonomous force of the destructive goddess principle. The problem with women's embrace of alterity is that it is based on an essentialized concept of female-ness, which is also an idealized one; with the argument for power is that it is often conceptualized as anarchic rather than as embedded in political process.[23]

Power is in both cases an instrument of agency. Agency (autonomous action by the individual or collective subject) tends to be regarded as an inherently radical force or attribute of women and other subordinated groups, and therefore the recovery of their agency in the study of society, culture, and history has been uncritically pursued as a politically correct objective. But women's agency (like their empowerment) can neither be viewed as an abstraction, nor celebrated as an unqualified good. Agency is never to be found in some pure state of volition or action, but is complexly imbricated in the contradictory structures of patriarchy. In her extended reflections on the questions of women's "consent, agency and the rhetorics of incitement," formulated in the context of contemporary Hindutva feminism, more specifically in light of the phenomenon of its aggressive women leaders and ideologues, Kumkum Sangari observes that patriarchal sanction for women's participation in political life in India is at present to be found most readily forthcoming in "conservative, indigenist or right wing formations."[24] We must therefore be alert to the implications of "who or what is women's agency on behalf of," and ask whether "all modes of empowerment for women are equally desirable."[25] We need to also recognize that the celebration of a certain kind of feminism as one that is always-already available in our tradition serves the function of preempting Western feminist demands, even as it simultaneously aggrandizes the scope and politics of that tradition and co-opts women's agency for its own ends.[26]

Omvedt anticipates some of the objections to locating women's struggles in India within the framework of stri shakthi from a left feminist secular orientation:

> Didn't the concept of *stri-shakti*, with its reference to sometimes bloody mother goddess traditions, imply too much of an endorsement of power and violence? Wasn't it too readily being picked up by conservatives who could twist it to see women's ability to endure all kinds of oppression as a symbol of magnificent power? Didn't Hindu nationalists have a tradition of appealing to mother goddesses? Wasn't it a Rajput defender of the sati-murder of Roop Kanwar who said, "Sati is shakti, the power that upholds the universe"? And wasn't the related theme of *virangana*, the historical tradition of heroic women queens who had taken arms against one or other invader or oppressor, simply an endorsement of feudalism as well as warfare? Could the question of empowerment be separated from that of violence?[27]

If in Omvedt's opinion, "by 1988–89, the need to do so was compelling," then in the following years the issue was once again open to urgent reconsideration following the BJP-instigated destruction of the Babri Masjid and the riots that followed.[28]

The membership of women in large numbers in the Sangh *parivar,* the promotion of feminist as well as traditional roles for women by the Rashtriya Swayamsevak Sangh (RSS) organization, the xenophobic rhetoric of Hindutva propagated by Sadhvi Rithambra and Uma Bharati, women sanyasin (ascetic) leaders in the Vishwa Hindu Parishad (VHP) and BJP, respectively, and women's active participation in the Bombay and Surat riots, are related phenomena that have been examined with care and detail in several essays in the recent volume, *Women and the Hindu Right,* edited by Tanika Sarkar and Urvashi Butalia.[29] In another post-Ayodhya collection of feminist essays, *Against All Odds,* Gabriele Dietrich marks this as a transitional moment in feminist politics in India.[30] The subjectivity and agency of a Hindu feminist (Kamalabehn) as shaped within the ideological and organizational structures of the Rashtra Sevika Samiti, is undertaken by Paola Bacchetta in the same volume, and reveals in particular the instrumentality of the goddess in her self-fashioning.[31] Kamalabehn rationalizes her paramilitary training and activity as follows: "Did Kali fight the rakshasas with her hands? All our goddesses are armed. Why should I not be armed?"[32] As a militant Hindu woman committed to ridding the Hindu nation of the Muslim enemy, she finds her model in "Kali's ridding of the world of evil in the form of demons in the Devi Mahatmya."[33]

Goddess-inspired Hindu feminism is problematic not only for reasons having to do with recent majoritarian communalism in India. Flavia Agnes has pointed out that Hindu religious symbols and practices treated as an unquestioned secular "norm," have a tendency to alienate women in the movement who belong to minority communities.[34] More recently, Kancha Ilaiah, launching a "sudra critique" of "Hindutva philosophy, culture and political economy" has called for a disassociation of the dalitbahujan caste and community from allegiance to Hinduism.[35] The question of the feminism of the Hindu goddess is subject to a different orientation in light of this disavowal. Though Ilaiah's argument may be (merely) polemical in this regard, his representation of the non-Hindu dalit goddess is politically more in consonance with the goals of a secular and democratic feminism:

> What is their [dalits'] notion of Pochamma? [a popular dalitbahujan goddess in Andhra Pradesh, typical of local village deities all over India] She is the person who protects people from all kinds of diseases; she is a person who cures the diseases. Unlike Sita, her gender role is not specified. Nobody knows about Pochamma's husband. Nobody considers her inferior or useless because she does not have a husband. The contrast [with] Lakshmi and Saraswathi . . . is striking. Pochamma is independent. She does not pretend to serve any man. Her relationship to human beings is gender-neutral, caste-neutral and class-neutral. . . . She herself relates to nature, production and procreation. . . . The people can speak with her in their own tongues.[36]

Ilaiah regards the influence of Hindu goddesses upon upper-caste women in Indian society as pernicious, particularly as this emerged in their aggressive opposition to the Mandal reforms in 1990.[37] This antagonism jeopardizes the possibility of alliances between dalit and women's movements.[38]

These then, broadly, the left, left feminist, and dalit movements, are the sites from where caution about the recuperation of the Hindu goddess, and of Hinduism in general, as a radical, progressive force for social change, is articulated. This essentially rational and skeptical attitude reflects a belief in what D. R. Nagaraj calls the "emancipatory potential of the project of modernity," a belief which is mainly a result of the "qualitative change in the lives of the dalits" (and, we may add, of women) brought about by the "modern institutions of polity and social engineering."[39] But the pristine days of that uncomplicated belief may now be over. Both religious tradition and secular modernity have become fraught, contradictory, and complex realities, and their identities as separate and oppositional are difficult to maintain. Critiques of enlightenment reason and of projects based upon its premises, including secular modernity, reason, science, and postcolonial nation-statehood, are growing in influence. The struggle for meaning (of the goddess, in this instance) has been joined on religious terrain, as I have pointed out, and folk myths, bhakti, syncretic faiths, goddess worship, and other "little" traditions have been resurrected and recast for their rich possibilities of contesting and subverting the hegemonic Hindutva ideology in the making. Strategically, radical and now left secular movements feel the need to wrest religion from the sole domination of the right and to exploit the spaces within a plural and living tradition of Hinduism for progressive purposes.[40]

But the contemporary politics of Hindutva is, as seems increasingly clear, expansionist and adaptable, and shows itself to be (selectively) incorporative of various progressive elements in the political interests of enlarging its appeal to women, lower castes, and other minority communities. Feminist activists/intellectuals, as I have indicated, have been particularly alert to these moves. In a modernizing postcolonial nation, the authority of majoritarian religious discourse and practice can only be countered, it seems to me, by a clear-cut and visible secular alternative. And to privilege religion as the sole available idiom of the social would be to surrender the hardwon gains of democratic and secular struggles in postindependence India. Above all, for "elite" intellectuals to recommend the use of religious symbols in social movements for change, in the absence of personal religious conviction—whether as a capitulation to its perceived appeal to the "masses," or as a show of identification with them—is, quite literally, bad faith.

NOTES

1. As at the Religion in South Asia panel on "Is the Goddess a Feminist?" at the American Academy of Religion Annual Meeting, Chicago, November 1994. This essay was originally written as a response to this panel, and I thank Alf Hiltebeitel for inviting me to do so.
2. The figure of Mahadevi, or the Great Goddess, is discussed by David Kinsley. Grimes, however, stresses the diversity of goddesses. See David Kinsley, *Hindu Goddesses: Visions of the Divine Feminine in the Hindu Religious Tradition* (Berkeley and Los Angeles: University of California Press, 1986), 132–150; John Grimes, "Feminism and the Indian Goddess: Different Models," in *Ethical and Political Dilemmas of Modern India*, ed. Ninian Smart and Shivesh Thakur (London: Macmillan, 1993), 126–143.
3. Joanna Liddle and Rama Joshi, *Daughters of Independence: Gender, Caste and Class in India* (London: Zed Books, 1986), 55.
4. Hansen undertakes an extensive investigation of the *virangana* or heroic woman in "history, myth and popular culture." See Kathryn Hansen, "The *Virangana* in North Indian History, Myth and Popular Culture," *Economic and Political Weekly*, April 30, 1988, WS25–WS33.
5. Grimes points out that "there is no stronghold of goddess-worship found in Kerala," which has the highest literacy rate, the highest ratio of women to men, and the second highest age of marriage for women in India. Grimes, "Feminism and the Indian Goddess: Different Models," 136.
6. The title of Pintchman's essay indicates this: "The Ambiguous Female." See Tracy Pintchman, "The Ambiguous Female: The Conception of Female Gender in the Brahmanical Tradition and the Roles of Women in India," in Smart and Thakur, *Ethical and Political Dilemmas of Modern India*, 144–159.
7. Satyajit Ray, dir *Devi* (Bengali, 1960).
8. Alf Hiltebeitel, Opening Remarks at Religion in South Asia Panel, "Is the Goddess a Feminist?" American Academy of Religion Annual Meeting, Chicago, November 1994.
9. See, for example, Rita Gross, "Hindu Female Deities as a Resource for the Contemporary Rediscovery of the Goddess," *Journal of the American Academy of Religion* 46:3 (September 1978): 269–292.
10. Erndl's *Victory to the Mother* is one such study. Katherine Erndl, *Victory to the Mother: The Hindu Goddess of Northwest India in Myth, Ritual and Symbol* (New York: Oxford University Press, 1993). Hansen's article (note 4) and some of the papers presented at the panel on the Hindu Goddess (note 1) are examples.
11. The Arya Samaj is a Hindu reformist movement/organization founded by Dayanand Saraswati. *Bharat-mata* literally means "Mother India."
12. Gayatri C. Spivak, "Can the Subaltern Speak? Speculations on Widow-Sacrifice," *Wedge* 7/8 (winter/spring 1985): 129.
13. See Uma Chakravarti, "Whatever Happened to the Vedic Dasi? Orientalism, Nationalism and a Script for the Past," in *Recasting Women: Essays in Colonial History*, ed. Kumkum Sangari and Sudesh Vaid (New Delhi: Kali for Women), 27–87.
14. Paola Bacchetta, "All Our Goddesses Are Armed: Religion, Resistance and Revenge in the Life of a Militant Hindu Nationalist Woman," in *Against All Odds: Essays on Women, Religion and Development from India and Pakistan*, ed. Kamla Bhasin et al. (New Delhi: Kali for Women, 1994).
15. Flavia Agnes has advanced this explanation. See Flavia Agnes, "Redefining the Agenda of the Women's Movement within a Secular Framework," in *Women and the Hindu Right: A Collection of Essays*, ed. Tanika Sarkar and Urvashi Butalia (New Delhi: Kali for Women, 1995), 136.
16. Madhu Kishwar and Ruth Vanita, eds., *In Search of Answers: Indian Women's Voices from Manushi* (London: Zed Books, 1984), 47.
17. Gail Omvedt, *Reinventing Revolution: New Social Movements and the Socialist Tradition in India* (New York and London: M. E. Sharpe, 1993), 226.
18. The Shetkari Sanghatana is a major peasant movement that has its locus in the western state of Maharashtra. It is led by Sharad Joshi, an extremely erudite peasant leader who has, unlike some of the other major peasant leaders of the last ten or fifteen years, consistently advocated industrialized development policies. Joshi has been outspoken on issues of women's participation in rural politics, and the Shetkari Sangathana has an

active women's wing. The Chipko movement is an environmental movement founded by Sunderlal Bahuguna in the foothills of the Himalayas in Northern India.

19. Vandana Shiva, *Staying Alive: Women, Ecology and Development* (New Delhi: Kali for Women, 1989).

20. Madhu Kishwar, *Gandhi and Women* (Delhi: Manushi Prakashan, 1986).

21. Ramachandra Gandhi, *Sita's Kitchen: A Testimony of Faith and Inquiry* (New Delhi: Penguin Books, 1992).

22. See my chapter on "Indira Gandhi," in *Real and Imagined Women: Gender, Culture, Postcolonialism*, ed. Rajeswari Sunder Rajan (London: Routledge, 1993).

23. For a discussion of popular Hindi cinema whose protagonists are avenging women, see my chapter, "Name of the Husband," in Sunder Rajan, *Real and Imagined Women*. Their prototype is the figure of Kali.

24. Kumkum Sangari, "Consent, Agency and the Rhetorics of Incitement," *Economic and Political Weekly*, May 1, 1993, 868.

25. Ibid., 870–871.

26. For a more extended discussion, see Sunder Rajan, *Real and Imagined Women*, 129–146.

27. Omvedt, *Reinventing Revolution*, 216.

28. Omvedt gives the following reasons for the urgently felt need to redefine women's empowerment at the decade's end: political representation for women in legislatures and local boards was being talked about; women themselves were seeking entry into these areas; "conventional left politics" was dead-ended; and revolutionary violence was being questioned. Omvedt, *Reinventing Revolution*, 216–217.

29. *Parivar* literally means family. The Sangh *parivar* refers to the Rashtriya Swayamsevak Sangh (RSS), which is the grass-roots ideological wing of the ruling Hindu nationalist party BJP (Bharatiya Janata Party). The BJP presently heads the ruling coalition in power in India. The VHP is the Vishwa Hindu Parishad (World Hindu Organization), not formally associated with the BJP or RSS, but allied to both of these organizations in significant ways. It is at some level difficult to clearly demarcate organizational boundaries of the BJP, the RSS, and the VHP, but some broad generalizations can be made. The RSS is an ideological, cadre-based grassroots organization that trains young volunteers (*swayamsevaks*) in schools (*shakhas*) around the country. While they officially claim distance from electoral politics, most of the leading BJP politicians are closely affiliated with the RSS, and it is understood that RSS sanction is generally required for many political activities/decisions of the BJP. The overlap between the VHP and the BJP/RSS is less clear-cut: the VHP largely rose to prominence as an activist Hindu organization in the controversy over the demolition of the Babri mosque and its replacement by a Ram temple in Ayodhya, and a large part of its agenda has been to collect money for the construction of the temple. Reflecting the global character that is self-posited in its nomenclature, the VHP is actively involved in fund-raising amongst nonresident Indians (NRIs), especially in the United States. This is, again, reflective of a broad caste division between the three organizations: while the VHP is largely an organization of the trading communities (which have historically been the most loyal supporters of the BJP in its various incarnations without actually being in the top echelons of the party leadership), the RSS is a substantially Brahminical organization. See, in particular, the essays by Basu, Sarkar, Banerjee, and Setalvad.

30. "Post-Ayodhya" here refers to events after the demolition of the Babri mosque in Ayodhya on December 6, 1992, by Hindu nationalists. Gabriele Dietrich, "Women and religious identities in India after Ayodhya," in Bhasin et al., *Against all Odds*, 35–50.

31. Literally meaning National (Female) Helpers' Committee, the women's wing of the RSS.

32. Bachetta, "All Our Goddesses Are Armed," 144.

33. Ibid., 153.

34. Agnes, "Redefining the Agenda of the Women's Movement within a Secular Framework," 139.

35. Kancha Ilaiah, *Why I Am Not a Hindu: A Sudra Critique of Hindutva Philosophy, Culture and Political Economy* (Calcutta: Samya, 1996). "Dalit" is the present politically accepted term for the "sudra" caste, earlier referred to as Untouchables. Gandhi's subsequent nomenclature, *harijans* (or children of god), has been rejected by the Dalits as too condescending and paternalistic. Dalitbahujan implies the Dalit community, a term that has the valence of a Dalit political identity attached to it.

36. In his review of Ilaiah's book, D. R. Nagaraj questions the model of "binary opposition" that Ilaiah creates between Hindu and dalitbahujan deities. See D. R. Nagaraj, "The Pathology of Sickle Swallowing," (review of Kancha Ilaiah, *Why I Am Not a Hindu*), *Book Review* 20:10 (October 1996): 8. On the contrary, he argues, sudra goddesses may be praised in Sanskrit *slokas* and Brahmin deities appear in shudra temples, and refers to the "competent" anthropological work that is available on this "double phenomenon." He reads this as a sign of "the radical energies of the *dalits* to transform the experience of intimate enmity" (7). Kinsley's book does indeed carry a chapter on "village goddesses" (197–211). Ilaiah, *Why I Am Not a Hindu*, 92.

37. The Mandal Commission was a governmental commission set up in the 1950s to look into the question of affirmative action for backward castes in central government jobs. The recommendations of the commission, which suggested a substantial increase in quotas for a greater proportion of castes than hitherto provided for under affirmative action programs, were left unacted upon August 1990, when the then V. P. Singh government implemented them. This led to a huge outcry amongst upper castes, especially in North India. The immediate consequence was the fall of the Singh government. In the longer term, Mandal has led to a serious reconfiguration of Indian electoral politics, with considerable implications for the sociopolitical mobility of many backward castes.

38. Ilaiah, *Why I Am Not a Hindu*, 78.

39. Nagaraj, "The Pathology of Sickle Swallowing," 8.

40. The activities of the leftist theater group Sahmat have been particularly noticeable in this sphere.

PART THREE

GLOBAL LOCATIONS
Body Politics

ANNE C. BELLOWS

THE PRAXIS OF FOOD
WORK IN POLAND

This chapter considers the social processes that work toward, and at the same time make vulnerable, food security at the local and household levels. Definitions for food security are highly political and much debated.[1] For the purposes of this essay, food security can be understood as grounded in human rights doctrine and broadly as "all persons obtaining, at all times, a culturally acceptable, nutritionally adequate diet through . . . non-emergency sources."[2] Food praxis integrates demands for economic rights to food security and political rights to articulate those needs. It operates throughout diverse and connected spaces of a food system: markets, farms, research facilities, kitchens, families, communities, political economies, and the like.[3] The work of food praxis strives to produce spaces that are safe from the violence of hunger, malnutrition, and poisoning caused by unsafe foods. The way food security is defined locally and the work undertaken to achieve it correspond to the physical and social environments at the local and nonlocal scale. Food praxis and security are deliberated in this essay within the context of postcommunist Poland where recent structural transformation highlights the consistent work of food praxis across diverse and changing political economies.

I address the political capability of mobile networks of under-recognized social actors who operate in diverse spatial settings.[4] To ground the dynamic work of local and household food security and its concurrent social invisibility, I employ Penny Van Esterik's theory of feminist food praxis and Joanna Regulska's call, with specific reference to the local scale and to women in Poland, to redefine "the political."[5] I emphasize Henri Lefebvre's attention to physical spaces and the dynamic movement of groups and individuals through them, passages that change the conditions of space and its inhabitants en route.[6] I argue that these theoretical premises contribute to a model of food praxis that acknowledges the political outside of the more limited activities, spaces, and memberships recognized in public space theory (as introduced by Jürgen Habermas) and that challenges the disconnect between the labor engaged in diverse community participations and formal government representation in legislative and policy development.[7]

Political activity can be understood as concurrently rooted, migratory, and fundamentally shifting in space. Mapping food praxis recovers a continuum of *located* activisms, knowledges, and power. These activities include household-based food work, the range of possible community participations, and ventures to influence social policy through participation in formal political institutions. Locating political activity helps to explain how it can be as constant as it is erased from recognition, as potentially volatile as seemingly passive, and even as collusive as it is resistant to its own structured marginalization.

Before continuing, it is necessary to discuss my use of the words household and family. I generally use household to refer to physical space; and families, to the people inside. To some extent, however, I introduce them interchangeably. I recognize that this is troublesome from a number of different discipline-based and activist-oriented perspectives. I will present three issues that problematize a singular or static usage of the terms *household* and *family*. First, in the Polish context, the family, and not the household, locates a site of social resistance. A household still infers the experience of the pre-1989 centralized state's attempt to erase individuality and difference through the semantics and practice of creating a populace aggregate. In particular, this occurred through census taking and government-sponsored surveys, which served as a form of monitoring as well as data collection for an inaccessible state ideological policy. The family represented and still represents a form of personalized opposition to the state. One identified oneself, one's family, and one's political affiliates in direct contrast to the anonymous and monolithic state.[8]

A second problem arises from the predicament of configuring women and families together as one and the same identity in analyses of activism. Recognizing that the family is the identity of resistance, and women as progenitors of resistance inside household (space)-based opposition, invokes a slippery slope toward essentializing women's social roles of nurturing at the same time that I am framing an argument for the political role of women's labor in families and at the family scale. My theoretical conundrum parallels a Polish reality. After 1989, the new Solidarity political leadership eliminated the government's Plenipotentiary for Women's Affairs and established a Ministry of Women, Youth, and Family. Polish feminists viewed this as the inability or unwillingness of the government to distinguish women from mothers.[9] The choices I make in using "family" or "household" reflects a balancing act of identifying political work, social life, and physical space with historically loaded words whose meanings overlap.

The third problem relates to different disciplinary interpretations of household. In economics and sociology, for example, households indicate standard, stable, and distinct units of analysis. The field of geography provides conceptual tools to place households in a vector-like spatial construction that maps the physical home as a point on a continuum of human transit through social and tangible environments.[10] This offers a more fluid landscape with which to think about who (e.g., gender, race, class) occupies which space and when and why. Despite structural social barriers, marginalized people can and do move through physical space, especially when en masse or through networks of collaborators. Geographical theory of scale and power facilitates the consideration of how multiple spaces can be influenced by linked actors who cooperate across close, medium, and longer distances (e.g., the local-global arguments) as well as across private, neighborhood, civic, and formal economic and political spaces and spheres.[11] The value of this different conceptualization of the household rests in its potential to be concurrently maintained and recast while interrogating social constructions like the public-private divide. Additionally, it provides a spatial schema to leverage the potential of agency and political participation in households instead of limiting a household-based location to a destiny of either victimization or escape.

THE POLITICAL PRACTICE OF FOOD PRAXIS

The term *praxis* was used by Marx to separate practice for social change from other actions. Praxis is informed by critical theory, an intellectual position of social critique. The Frankfurt School of Horkheimer, Adorno, Fromm, Habermas, and others (1967–1972) revived Marx's use of praxis to critique the position of assumed neutrality and objectivity in the academy. In other words, there can be no disinterested perspective and academics should consciously take a position and make public their politics. In this respect, praxis for the Frankfurt school was the pursuit of intellectual (i.e., academic) engagement with society.[12]

The integration of theory and praxis has been central to the emancipatory objectives of feminist inquiry. Feminists critique the Frankfurt school for not taking political identity beyond the privileged university walls. Mies recasts the relationship between praxis and theory in her discussion of feminist methodology. She pushes the idea of subjective knowledge toward a recognition of the plurality of knowledges and the multiple locations of their construction, for example, both within and without the academy. Likewise, praxis as politicized action happens inside and outside of the academy. Practice and theory inform each other through a dialogue of communication and action. Similarly the interaction between *located persons* and *located knowledges*, that is, the movement of experienced and "experience-able" persons through spatially situated knowledges enhances interpretations of the "real."[13] In political terms, this increases the representation of voices that can define social needs and participate in the development of just policy.

In her discussion of feminist food praxis, Van Esterik relocates praxis even further from the academy. She focuses on the knowledge and the practices of those ultimately responsible for protecting food security: mostly, but not only women. I argue that feminist food praxis is critically different from Marx and from the Frankfurt school, and that it is controversial within feminist theory, because it is not only delineated as revolutionary. It includes as *politicized action* those labors conducted in cooperation with, as well as in opposition to, society. Van Esterik explains the labor of food praxis as that which spans the "practical 'mastery'" of the daily needs of households and the *negotiative practices* that mediate household needs within society.[14] Food praxis, then, works for change and for continuity, as necessary, to meet the immediate and long-term needs of food security. This is the strength and the weakness of such political practice. It is a source of its problematic reception as part of the political, and its invisibility and the suspicion it garners, perhaps especially among feminists. Indeed, there is grave risk that in the pivot between collusion and opposition lies the potential to grow apathetic to social change needs and to accept and internalize social marginalization by working within its constraints.

Negotiating food security engages a spatial mobility between where food needs are *defined,* in the household, and where they are *claimed,* in the formal private sector and government as well as in households and communities. This continuum of labors and spaces of practice is specific to place, culture, and historical context. It is more often the work of informal networks, groups, and extended families than of individuals. It is the labor of women and men, but there is a common predominance of women's leading role in food work, especially in unpaid conditions and in household spaces. Recognizing women as the main, though not the only, "gate-keepers of the food system and mediators between food produced and consumed" also exposes the paradox of a largely male and paid presence in public decision-making practices that impacts food security as maintained largely by women.[15]

THE POLITICAL PRACTICE OF FOOD PRAXIS IN POLAND

In Eastern Europe, as elsewhere, women undertake the majority of food labors. I introduce here a discussion of food praxis in Poland as a case study of food labor that is concurrently expected and ignored in society. Polish women's participation in food work is not unique, per se. However, the specific adaptation of a roughly constant set of basic food labors to changing political economies brings the dynamics of gendered food politics into unusually high relief. Under the closed military state of the communist regime of the 1980s, for example, Poland experienced severe food shortages. Long lines of anxious, disgruntled, and tired customers waited outside shops for hours, sometimes overnight, queuing for rumored shipments of the minimal stocks of butter, meat, or eggs. Family meals were prepared according to what could be waited for and found and with supplements from the ubiquitous urban allotment gardens and from relatives on farms in the country. These food labors of shopping (frustrated by inconsistent market supply); gardening (structured by land access, season of the year, available time and help, weather, etc.); and food storage, preservation, and preparation (impacted by market and self-produced supply, and to a lesser extent cost) engaged massive amounts of community labor, especially by women.[16] After the political upheaval of 1989, a Western liberal market economy was quickly introduced in Poland. Suddenly the communist right to work was lost and unemployment and underemployment rose dramatically, particularly affecting women and persons over age thirty-five as two overlapping groups, the effect on middle-aged and older women being most dramatic. At the same time, the decentralized economy and Western trade filled, multiplied, and diversified the post-1989 stores and shopping options. The changes, however, secured food and other commodity supplies inside stores at the same time the ability to buy was becoming an unevenly distributed social capacity. The labors of shopping, gardening, food storage, preservation, and preparation continued, but the transformation of the political economy changed aspects of those labors. Although still undertaken mostly by women, time and attention to food tasks has become re-weighted according to whether and what kind of work is available, whether one can afford to travel to lower-priced large-volume stores, and how one balances the need and the recreation of gardening for household consumption against the uneven ability to buy.

Many have argued that the processes of democratic transition in Central and Eastern Europe are gendered. Since 1989 in the region, women have been excluded from formal paid workplaces and sites of government. Regulska has argued that in fact women have been active, but the tools have not been employed that might recognize their participation. The reason recognition is critical is to make visible women's political and civic participation and therefore their rights to political access. However, recognition requires a redefinition of *where* and *what* constitutes "the political."

The new definition of political rights needs, then, to encompass both the right to de jure equal representation and to de facto women's participatory experiences. It should include women's local experiences and by doing so give women's political culture needed legitimacy. Women's diverse experiences of participation in NGOs, in informal networks, neighborhood organizations, and administrative and economic spheres need to be part of the new definition along with their participation in formal structures.[17]

Representation means not only a right, for example, to vote, but also a right to services, participation in public policy decision making, and rights to lobby.[18] It has also been argued that political rights should guarantee group access to political office.[19]

The political potential of activist groups and neighborhood networks can be threatening. Capitalist states try to decollectivize behavior by defining the political in the individual. The socialist state tries to control the collectivity by giving it an homogenized and individually anonymous character.[20] Political economies generally (i.e., capitalist states, including the market, and communist states) rely on specific groups to conduct specific social tasks. The political economies then erase those connections or "naturalize" them to underplay the power relations that link particular work and particular groups. In the case of women as the majority of food workers, their activist potential is harnessed by depoliticizing the collective efforts of food praxis; marginalizing the collectivity by not paying the labor; atomizing food laborers' collectivities inside household spaces; and denying household workers their political rights.

Unpaid and paid work combine to develop resources to protect household food security. Access to living wage work, to well-stocked stores, to urban garden allotment land, and to health care are examples of social and food security variables that fluctuate with changing political economies. The unpaid labor that produces food and care on behalf of family health facilitates household-scale adjustments to lost social resources in periods of transition. Polish women, as women everywhere, perform the majority of this labor. Unpaid work effectively plays the role of alternative social functions in alternative sites of participatory activity. This work reflects social functions that cannot easily be separated into political or economic activities, according to traditional definitions. In particular, I emphasize the economy of use value labors. In use economies, community wealth and human resources are traded without monetary exchange. The economic goods are services and products. Their exchange represents the administration and distribution of public welfare outside of the formal institutions and mechanisms of political economies. Women are particularly active in this economy, in part, because they are marginalized in the formal paid-work and monied-exchange economy.[21]

Paid work also sustains successful food praxis. However, in Poland, women form a decreasing proportion of those in formal working spaces where wages can be earned. They also form the minority in formal political life where public food policy is legislated and administered. This exacerbates the paradox between women's paramount contributions to food praxis and their relative invisibility in formal public life. In other words, women's food praxis labors might change public food policy, but their contributions are neither regarded as political in public discourse, nor stabilized in public life in terms of women's access to work or public appointment. Further, I argue that higher-scale economies, like national states, expect and depend upon labor interstitial to food praxis in the use economy to make up for their limitations. The omission of praxis experience in policy development is not practical in terms of having adequate information with which to develop policy. The unique capacity of praxis to integrate food practice in multiple spaces is made vulnerable through food labor's devaluation. This vulnerability threatens food security and community public health.[22]

If food praxis has this eclipsed value, how can it be formally recognized, supported, and stabilized? One way is to employ a theory of feminist food praxis that examines women's work, power, and agency relative to social structures (cf. Van Esterik 1999). Another way is to align redefinitions of political space, political practice, and political individuals (cf. Regulska 1998) closer to interpretations of feminist food praxis. This forces an engagement with the apparent contradictions in food praxis; that is, praxis for food security incorporates strategies of both colluding with, and contesting, social systems. Specifically, women's food labors operate within the gendered role constraints on their lives. In other words, to varying degrees women take on the role of politically underrepresented and unpaid household workers. At the same time, women contest the system as necessary to maintain their moral rights to achieve food security for their families. Within this contradiction lies the potential to render women's food praxis labor either as ancillary and invisible or as empowering and contestatory. Assuredly, this analysis has important implications for men who regularly or occasionally contribute food labor. However, the inquiry has immediate and specific relevance to women who conduct most food work and whose praxis labor is specifically constructed as politically invisible.

THE MOBILE PRACTICE AND POLITICAL MIGRATIONS OF FOOD PRAXIS

Political practice is informed in formal (government, paid work, the academy) and informal (household, community) spaces and it is enacted in all of those multiple spaces. Conducted in one location, political practice can also impact political economies at various scales. In the case of food praxis discussed above, practices like urban domestic food production accommodates the state when the state cannot or will not successfully distribute food stocks or guarantee jobs and living wages. At the same time, allotment gardening protects household needs in the face of the state's ineptitude or detachment.

Much of the delineation of what composes the political originates in a literature built on the idea of a public sphere. Habermas defined the public sphere as a field of discursive opposition by a citizenry in critical dialogue with the state.[23] The terminology of *sphere* is thus built on the conception of containment and exclusion. The related problem is that it can as easily serve political hegemony as it would resistance.[24] Some of the limitations of Habermas's influential study reside in the assumption that the public sphere of political life and opposition is separate from the private sphere.[25] The effort to amend Habermas's relatively static construction into a public sphere with greater transformative power and labile form has evolved into a degree of significant confusion. In the use of public sphere theory to analyze household activisms, for example, Maurizio Passerin d'Entrèves proposes that wherever people converge, that demarcates a public sphere. By his definition, a household certainly constitutes a public sphere.[26] Given its alternative politics, a household should also represent a subaltern public, or one of a potential multiplicity of publics and subaltern counterpublics or an ersatz public sphere and so on.[27] However, these public spheres are defined in constrained space that is always ersatz, always second best. Paraphrasing Wahneema Lubiano, the interpolation of household-based politics into a form of the public sphere immediately imposes relations of domination and of strong and weak publics, that in turn "preempts opposition by already inhabiting the vectors where we would resist."[28]

The idea of strong and weak publics originates with Benajmin Barber's strong and weak models of democratic activity.[29] Nancy Fraser refines this in terms of weak publics that only form opinions and strong publics that make or influence public decisions.[30] However, Michael Dawson points out (with reference to the North American black public sphere), that if a weak public sphere cannot transform politics, then it really is no public sphere.[31] Comparing and extrapolating from Lani Guinere, a democracy is not a democracy if the tyrannical and static majority (the bigger and stronger team) always wins.[32] Using the available theories on public sphere, the household begins to look like less and less of a public sphere in terms of public participatory and political efficiency, integrity, or capacity.

For the purposes of this study, I refer to more public and more private space. The former includes formal political and economic institutions of government and paid work enterprises. "More private" refers to more informal locations where participation is not so specifically counted and therefore, to some extent, less visible. These would include households and community spaces where labor is unpaid or unofficially paid. I argue that in this purposely approximated division of spaces, what is commonly understood as civic participation—for example, nongovernmental organization (NGO) activities, city commissions, and the like—could be counted as extensions of either "more formal public" or "more informal private" depending on who controls the activities, where (if any) funding originates, and to what extent participation is publicly documented.

In place of the language of public spheres, I advance a discussion of public and private physical spaces wherein political life concurrently lodges and migrates. Even more important than delineating spaces as either public or private, is recognizing mobility through them. While public and private spaces can and will be differentiated in this discussion, concentration on their boundaries diverts attention from the importance of corporeal movement through them to build political agency and effect food praxis. This is especially relevant when trying to determine the physical locations of not-for-profit and NGO activities. NGOs are, by space and purpose, dedicated neither to private households nor public institutions. In spatial terms, grass-roots and NGO activities emerge fluidly between and from home to paid workplace, kitchen garden to food market, sickbed to hospital and laboratory. This practice merges participants' resources of time, experience, meeting spaces, influence, and money.

The potential for, and reality of, political engagement exists in all human identities, in all of the physical spaces of habitation, work, and passage, and through the diverse knowledges that develop from experience in space. Fluidity between these multiple locations of political engagement accentuates agency. Agency becomes a product of physical migration, mobility, and action. It builds from transmutations of learned localized and political knowledges into ideas for change or "social imaginaries."[33] Lefebvre contributes the idea of spatialized "thoughtful experience" which he describes as the potential of politicized reflection on personal experience as mediated by and upon the physical space through which we pass and in which we live and work. This passage of conscientization can transform individuals, their activities, and the space itself into an empowered environment or community capable of autonomous collectivity.[34] The concept of mobile politics in physical space—homes, clubhouses, grange halls—differs fundamentally from Habermas's thesis of recognizing the political through a public sphere of written and spoken discourse. The relevance of mobility also reveals the consequence of its dissipation. The disappearance of multiple spatial referentials that inform dynamic social knowledge parallels the collapse of difference and diversity within a population. Homogenized intelligence controls because nothing contradicts it. According to Lefebvre, this enables unemployment, poverty, and violence to be labeled individual, and not social, problems.[35] Giving greater exposure to tangible places in geographic space allows us to foreground the web of actors and their networks of people and locations as functions of political activity and agency.

Spatialized, thoughtful experience that grows from diverse labors, networks of help, and multiple knowledges describes well what Van Esterik called feminist food praxis. The practical mastery of everyday acts on behalf of household food security and the negotiative practices that mediate household needs within society require spatial mobility throughout communities, across political scale, and among a diversity of more private and more public spaces. Food praxis, especially for groups constrained by income or commodity availability, does not unfold successfully in the isolation of an individual or in a static household unit. Food praxis entails mobility in and across socially weaker (e.g., the household) and stronger (e.g., the market or government) places corresponding respectively to where food security needs are largely defined and where they are claimed. It requires access in many locations for funds (e.g., through a job in the formal exchange economy) and for help (e.g., in the informal use economy garnering gardening assistance or knowledge of where to find food during scarcity). In the diversity of colleagues and family and community spaces, food praxis can build an "unhomogenized intelligence" that has the capacity to resist an identity of victimized individual and to develop a cooperative strategy to define and claim food security.

And yet, food praxis always faces short-term and practical as well as long-term and strategic challenges.[36] Practical mastery produces the daily dinner on the table. It grounds the social imaginary in tasks and compromises as necessary to protect immediate family needs. This grounding and the time and repetitive tasks it commandeers can either (or both) inform and fuel impassioned engagement with more public settings or (and) annihilate the potential for empowerment. Regardless, the labor remains political, I argue, even as a consciousness about its character and potential might be impaired. To return to Regulska, the "where" and the "what" of "political" need redefinition. These new definitions of politicized food praxis work are needed by practitioners, academics, and policy makers. Yet even with the mystification of food labor power, food praxis does not stop its mobile labors or lose its peopled networks of support because daily dinners require these activities as much as does social negotiation. Further, women will demand their right to deliver these dinners— regardless of successive political economies' inability to stock stores or their incapacity or unwillingness to produce living wage jobs—even as they might have few social choices beyond the gendered duty to serve those dinners.[37] The praxis work in this pivot between collusion and enacted defiance is, I claim, always political, largely erased, rarely claimed by food workers, and consistently underrepresented in academia and public policy.

MOBILE FOOD PRAXIS IN POLAND

Mobile food praxis operates under constraints and advantages that differ according to place, history, and geographies of people and land. Obviously, mobile food praxis is not unique to Poland; however, its specific manifestations help to illuminate some basic theoretical ideas. Food praxis for households and communities is enhanced by networks of cooperating family, friends, and other social partners who are spread across places of both problem definition and problem resolve, informal and formal economies, and more private and more public spaces. Food praxis is challenged when mobility by individuals or groups is restricted or threatened. In the context of political and economic transition, I foreground the subject of networks and constraints of political mobility against three historical aspects of food praxis in Poland. The first addresses mobility between largely home-based unpaid and use economy labor and the formal sector, paid job places. The second considers location and mobility of resistance to the different political economies that have dominated Poland before and after 1989. The third describes mobility across landscapes of food production, access, and purchase power, followed by a discussion of the implications of household-based food praxis under contradictory conditions of safety and violence.

Under the East European forms of communism, most countries experienced chronic problems with commodity supply due largely to centralized and inefficient distribution systems. In these economies of shortage, acquaintances with persons who had formal access to goods, services, and jobs (often, but not only, through unequal political power relations) could result in informal, "under the table" distributions of those resources. Transactions in formal monied and informal economies alike relied on reserved favors and loyalties and sometimes on simple corruption.[38] *Connections were more important than money.* For example, if you knew the store clerk, perhaps she would put aside several bottles of oil or a choicer cut of meat for you, saving you a multitude of hours of standing in line. Of course, it was not only who you knew, but how many people were indebted to favors you had bestowed. Such favors would be accumulated and traded as equivalent or more valuable assets than money in the bank. The relevance of such informal economies persists in post–Soviet era Eastern countries where economic transformation has left many uncertainties for labor and even for supply. In lieu of money or strictly legal production and supply of goods, connections continue to provide households with everything from emergency medical services to the sparkling wine necessary to substantiate a traditional wedding.[39]

The underground or use economies of connections and favors were engaged in by women and men alike, although their use on behalf of food security was mostly undertaken by women. Before 1989, networks that were organized in more formal assemblages like private nonprofit groups (nongovernmental organizations) were largely forbidden or closely monitored in Poland and across the Soviet Bloc region. After 1989, privatization and political liberalization decentered the government's attempt to monopolize all sectors of society. The economy began to form individualist market conditions at the same time that "civil society" legitimated the right of groups to work openly and formally on almost every issue.[40] However, the new economy also exhibited the Western market outcomes of uneven wealth and access to resources. Gender differences in access to paid work figured strongly into the polarizing post-1989 experiences of economic vulnerability and security. In terms of labor and the new post-1989 social sectors, women were moved out of the newly privatized economy and formal government policy-making centers. Women in Poland and Eastern Europe today figure strongly in the development of grass-roots and NGOs. Not surprisingly, the civil society sector is endowed with three consistent characteristics of women's labor: the labor depends upon networks and networking; it addresses social reproduction and protected communities issues; and, of course, it operates with, relatively speaking, minimal monetary resources.[41] Additionally, that individualistic market economies develop institutionalized civil society largely maintained by women and other nonelite groups (by race, class, age) indicates the un/der/paid services that are both socially expected and critically ignored.

Food praxis in use and formal economies transects spaces arranged by different economic advantages. For example, urban and built-up environments in more rural areas often have more jobs; rural and open spaces in urban areas encompass more food-producing possibilities. Jobs that produce wages fuel the exchange economy. Domestic food production stimulates the use economy through gifts, help, and trade. Participation in both use and exchange economies—

through multiple and shared labors and travel to areas with different relative advantage—increases overall economic security, especially under unstable or unjust political economies.

The centralized communist economy of Poland developed planning and land use schemes that organized spatially separated, instead of integrated, economic advantage. Theoretically, the state served as the equitable and efficient distributor of production. In reality, the results were not ideal. In the case of an inelastic commodity like food, inconsistency in supply (e.g., dinner often, but not always, on the table) cannot be tolerated. Thus the government expected, and the people (mostly women) complied, with their own production and distribution systems of inelastic commodity requirements like food. Food production landscapes, especially in rural areas, were considered more economically secure by the populace. They became meccas for food-securing pilgrimages. Travel between more rural-based and more urban-based extended families stabilized household-level food security across urban and rural advantages. Under the post-1989 economy that has provided well-stocked stores, the populace has come to consider urban areas more economically secure than rural areas.[42] Money and paying jobs have become the key commodity and waged-labor landscapes, mostly but not only in urban areas, have experienced inflows of rural populations, especially of young women.[43] Nevertheless, while post-1989 consumption opportunities might have made paid jobs a more important commodity than food production opportunities, per se, national Polish surveys show that overall, participation in the use economy has become even more important in the postcommunist era. This includes domestic food production along with various forms of help and traded favors designed to reduce household expenditures and maintain community supportive networks as bulwarks against inept and neglectful governments.[44]

Even as political household-based work seeks to address social and physical violences, the location of the labor faces challenges of underrepresentation and violence inside the household. The way constraints on political activity operate also change over place and time. Household-based, family-oriented work, might not be public, but it is political.[45] The political capacity of household-based work is magnified in totalitarian states that suppress public forms of free expression. Before 1989 in communist-era Poland, parks, cafes, and streets were all closed to group meetings and open discourse, especially under

martial law in the 1980s. East European communist states were threatened by household political capacity and tried to subdue it through
the delivery of services and universal wage labor access.[46] The populace temporarily recognized that households do locate political life.
That is because other, more public spaces were exempt, and even more
so, because men shifted their political work into household space.
Yet under the state that severely restricted civil rights, women were
continuing an ongoing tradition of organizing both inside household
spaces, as well as, in those paid labor and government positions that
the communist system extended to them.

Households accommodate a pivot of veneration and violence;
political autonomy and institutionalized patriarchal control; social
recognition and public erasure. The household political "hideout" for
social negotiation by sympathizers of the Solidarity (Solidarnosc) labor union, and social movement did not correspond with a spirit of
participation by women and men in daily tasks food work.[47] While
men were hiding out, women were already being urged into exclusive domesticity in the 1980s both by a government attempt to
deconcentrate women's presence in the troubled economy and to reduce its social welfare burden to households and by the Solidarity
underground that wanted the movement dominated by men.[48] Finally, it can be argued that the real threat of state-inspired physical
and psychic violence in public life was not countered by consistent
safety for women in the household.[49] Polish households do not differ
from others in their historical and contemporary capacity to literally
house, as well as hide, physical and psychic violences against women.[50]

I am thus addressing two sets of violences that can reside in
household space. One is the physical and psychic violences of food
insecurity—hunger, malnutrition, and poisoning from environmen-
tally contaminated products. Even as it is designed to protect, the
household veils incidences of food insecurity from the public. The
second set concerns the household as a site of statistical vulnerability to violence for women. Experience with a single or diverse violences can chill overt forms of political expression. It terrorizes the
function of independent mobility. Real or threatened violence will
encourage strategies that interweave contradictory postures of compliance and resistance. These multiple violences are also most often
located in the household, spaces that traditionally separate women's
activities from those in public. What then are the implications of

gendered household roles and the politicized mobility of food praxis? Women form the majority of those engaged in food praxis. Successful praxis requires an active spatial mobility. Thus, women form the population most engaged with the outcomes of food violences at the same time that they experience a statistical vulnerability to household-based physical and psychic violences. In the end, if and when the potential for successful food praxis is damaged, it affects not only the food laborers, but the entire community that depends upon them even as their labors are ignored in the formal economy. The implications, then, for the gendered character of household roles and the politicized mobility of food praxis are that women require greater physical security inside the household and more institutionalized integration into the formal political economy. There must be respect for the political nature of more private and more public locations of food praxis work. This acknowledgment must be extended to political rights in public that include access to, and participation in, the public decision-making bodies that administer public policy by those whose "thoughtful experience" grows from defining and claiming food security on behalf of the broad population.

SUMMARY

Unpaid food work, most typically undertaken by women, is expected and extracted by state political economies, at the same time that it is enacted in resistance to the state and as a political freedom and economic right. Thus, the household-based resistance of food labor takes place in a contradiction. On the one hand, the home is the safe, even mythical retreat from the psychic and sometimes physical oppression of the public world, especially under a totalitarian state. On the other hand, it is in the household space where enactments of the physical and psychic violences of hunger and battery unfold. Violences hide from a shamed exposure to the public. Making their existence visible, however, is also frustrated by a public unwillingness to guarantee political rights and needs within private spaces. Food praxis, like most political work to protect bodily integrity, is located in significant part in those household spaces where its efforts are discouraged from access to, or reception in, public decision making.

Bodies carry signatures of difference—gender and safety, health, age, job status, race, and ethnicity—labels that signal restriction or mobility. The physical body will display many signs of political and economic want; for example, malnutrition, disease, disfigurement, inertia. A safe and healthy body works most effectively, although, less safe and less healthy bodies are often those most politically engaged because they have the fewest alternatives for survival.[51] The conditions of a mobile food praxis are directly influenced by the safety and access that food workers have being in, and moving in and out of, the multiple spaces that support food security. The body needs mobility between multiple spaces and respect for its "thoughtful experience" in order to kindle a social imagination that can fashion change.

Functions of public access and reception frustrate or facilitate mobile praxis. Cooperation between friends, families, colleagues, and acquaintances reflect praxis as much as, or more than, the efforts of individuals. Human activity networks resist barriers faced by individuals who face prejudice on the basis of group membership (e.g., to women, or to ethnic, religious, age-specific, or other group identity) by responding with group strategies. Networks are enlivened by use economies that promote the trade of help, favors, gifts, and information, and that operate in relationship with formal exchange economies. Food security relies on the resources available in both formal exchange and informal use economies. The networking and mobility of food workers through spaces and labors of food praxis is neither an idealized reflection of a communist collectivity nor a market-generated household division of labor where men work for pay and women manage families. Mobile networking, as a function of food praxis, is the work of political lives and knowledges that defend communities against the vagaries of communist and capitalist systems alike. It incorporates both resistance to political economy abuses and colludes with them by invisibly protecting community survival. This work deserves respect, critical attention, and formal participation in public policy development.

NOTES

1. At one end of the spectrum, international agreements like the General Agreement on Tariffs and Trade (1994) interpret food security as, roughly, the availability of food in stores as a product of efficient free trade (T. Lang, "Food Security: Does It Conflict with Globalization?" *Development* 4 [1996]: 45–50). In contrast, a local and household definition of food security is interpreted according to diverse local needs and conditions and should fulfill three criteria: availability (e.g., adequate and appropriate food in the markets); stability (e.g., food reserves across all seasons); and access (e.g., affordability in

the market, a right of welfare, living wage work, use of arable land). Food and Agriculture Organization, "Food and International Trade," WFS 96/TECH/8, provisional, (April 1996), 5, para. 3.1; in Lang, "Food Security," 46.

2. See United Nations documents: International Declaration of Human Rights, 1948, Article 25 (A/RES/217 A [III]) and the International Convention on Economic, Social, and Cultural Rights, 1966, Article 11 (A/RES/2200 A (XXI)). A. Fisher and R. Gottlieb, "Community Food Security: Policies for a More Sustainable Food System in the Context of the 1995 Farm Bill and Beyond," Working Paper no. 11 (Los Angeles: Lewis Center for Regional Policy Studies, School of Public Policy and Social Research. University of California, 1995), 2. Note, I deleted the word "local" from the statement (i.e., "through l ocal, non-emergency sources"). Local food sourcing is relevant, but not intrinsic, to the essay.

3. Penny Van Esterik, "Gender and Sustainable Food Systems: A Feminist Critique," in For Hunger-Proof Cities: Sustainable Urban Food Systems, ed. M. Koc, R. MacRae, L.J.A. Mougeot, and J. Welsh (Ottawa: International Development Research Centre and Toronto: Ryerson Polytechnic University, 1999), 157–161. See also, K. Dahlberg, "Regenerative Food Systems: Broadening the Scope and Agenda of Sustainability," in Food for the Future, ed. P. Allen (New York: John Wiley & Sons, 1993), 75–102.

4. A. Sen, Resources, Values, and Development (Cambridge: Harvard University Press, 1984); and Commodities and Capabilities (Amsterdam: Elsevier Science Publishers, 1985).

5. Penny Van Esterik, "Gender and Sustainable Food Systems," and Joanna Regulska, "The 'Political' and Its Meaning for Women: Transitional Politics in Poland," in Theorising Transition: The Political Economy of Post-Communist Transformations, ed. J. Pickles and A. Smith (London: Routledge, 1998), 309–329.

6. Henri Lefebvre, The Production of Space, trans. D. Nicholson-Smith (First Published in 1974, Editions Anthropos) (Oxford: Blackwell Publishers, 1991).

7. Jürgen Habermas, The Structural Transformation of the Public Sphere: An Inquiry into a Category of Bourgeois Society, trans T. Burger with the assistance of F. Lawrence (Cambridge, Mass.: MIT Press, 1989).

8. With thanks to Joanna Regulska for this point.

9. The government's Plenipotentiary for Women's Affairs was originally established in 1986 by the Ministry of Labor and Social Policy. See E. Pakszys and D. Mazurczak, "From Totalitarianism to Democracy in Poland: Women's Issues in the Sociopolitical Transition of 1989–1993," Journal of Women's History 5:3 (1994): 144–150, 147; private conversation with Elzbieta Pakszys (1991].

10. See, for example, the following collections: N. Duncan, ed., BodySpace (London: Routledge, 1996), especially, N. Duncan, "Renegotiating Gender and Sexuality in Public and Private Spaces," 127–145; T. Fenster, Gender, Planning and Human Rights (London: Routledge, 1999]; and J. P. Jones III, H. J. Nast, and S. M. Roberts, eds., Thresholds in Feminist Geography: Difference, Methodology, Representation (Lanham, Md.: Rowman and Littlefield, 1997).

11. See, for example, N. Smith, "Homeless/Global: Scaling Places," in Local Culture, Global Change, ed. J. Bird et al. (London: Routledge, 1993), 87–119; L. A. Staeheli and A. Thompson, "Citizenship, Community, and Struggles for Public Space," Professional Geographer 49 (February 1997): 28–38; Melissa R. Gilbert, "From the 'Walk for Adequate Welfare' to the 'March for Our Lives': Welfare Rights Organizing in the 1960s and 1990s," Urban Geography (forthcoming).

12. J. M. Nielsen, ed., "Introduction," Feminist Research Methods: Exemplary Readings in the Social Sciences (Boulder, Colo.: Westview Press, 1990), 1–37, 9, 34; and M. Mies, "Towards a Methodology for Feminist Research," in Theories of Women's Studies, ed. G. Bowles and R. D. Klein (London: Routledge and Kegan Paul, 1983), 117–139, 119.

13. Mies, "Towards a Methodology for Feminist Research," 122.

14. Van Esterik, "Gender and Sustainable Food Systems," 160.

15. Ibid.

16. See, for example, M. Fuszara, "Market Economy and Consumer Rights: The Impact on Women's Everyday Lives and Employment," Economic and Industrial Democracy 15 (1994): 75–87; A. Titkow, "Polish Women in Politics: An Introduction to the Status of Women in Poland," in Women in the Politics of Postcommunist Eastern Europe, ed. M. Rueschmeyer (Armonk, N.Y.: M. E. Sharpe, 1994), 29–34; A. Titkow and H. Domanskiego, eds., Co to

Znaczy Byc Kobieta w Polsce [What it means to be a woman in Poland]. (Warsaw: The Polish Academy of Science, Institute of Philosophy and Sociology, 1995).

17. Regulska, "The 'Political' and Its Meaning for Women," 318–319.
18. Ibid., 319.
19. Ibid., 320. Note Regulska's discussion of the Parliamentary Women's Group in Poland and the model Equal Status legislation that has been passed in various forms in, i.a., Norway, Denmark, Sweden, and Great Britain.
20. N. Smelser Jr., *Theory of Collective Behavior* (New York: Free Press of Glencoe, 1963).
21. K. R. Cox and R. J. Johnston, "Conflict, Politics and the Urban Scene: A Conceptual Framework," in *Conflict, Politics and the Urban Scene*, ed. K. R. Cox and R. J. Johnston (New York: St. Martin's Press, 1982), 1–19; and K. R. Cox and A. Mair, "Locality and Community in the Politics of Local Economic Development," *Annals, Association of American Geographers* 47:2 (1988): 307–325. These articles revive Marx's theory of use economies to discuss political and economic dynamics of the local state, and specifically, what nonmonetarized use values the corporate world will not or cannot guarantee. A major limitation of these North American-based discussions is, however, their assumption that an unhappy populace has unlimited mobility and can move at will; K. R. Cox and J. J. McCarthy, "Neighborhood Activism in the American City: Behavioral Relationships and Evaluation," *Urban Geography* 1:1 (1980): 22–38.
22. A. C. Bellows, "Where Kitchen and Laboratory Meet: The 'Tested Food for Silesia' Program," in *Feminist Political Ecology: Global Perspectives and Local Insights*, ed. D. Rocheleau, B. Thomas-Slater, and E. Wangari (London: Routledge, 1996); "Urban Food Security in Poland," *Ecology and Agriculture* 16 (September 1997): 24–25; "The Invisible Food and Agriculture Revolution," *Ecology and Agriculture* 16 (September 1997): 19–20.
23. Habermas, *The Structural Transformation of the Public Sphere*.
24. For this insight, I am indebted to the ferment of a discussion on September 25, 1997, at the Rutgers University, Institute for Research on Women and Institute for Women's Leadership co-sponsored seminar, "Women in the Public Sphere: Power, Practice, Agency."
25. Habermas (1989) included paid work and the family in the private sphere. "The sphere of the market we call 'private'; the sphere of the family, as the core of the private sphere, we call the 'intimate sphere'" (55). Fraser further refines the distinctions of the private sphere in terms of social forms of reproduction, including "symbolic reproduction" or the activities and practices of nonpaid work, especially child raising, and "material reproduction" or social labor that includes the activities and practices of paid work; N. Fraser, *Unruly Practices: Power, Discourse and Gender in Contemporary Social Theory* (Oxford: Polity Press, 1989), 114–115. These interpretations of a private-public divide are bounded by an analysis of capitalist and bourgeois societies. N. Fraser, *Justice Interruptus: Critical Reflections on the "Post-socialist" Condition* (London: Routledge, 1997). For example, because the paid work space was an extension of central state power in recent history in Soviet socialist states, Habermas's definition is deficient here.
26. M. P. d'Entrèves, "Hannah Arendt and the Idea of Citizenship," in *Dimensions of Radical Democracy: Pluralism, Citizenship, Community*, ed. Chantal Mouffe (London: Verso, 1992).
27. See respectively, G. C. Spivak, "Subaltern Studies: Deconstructing Historiography," in *Subaltern Studies IV*, ed. R. Guha (New York: Oxford University Press, 1985), 330–363; N. Fraser, "Rethinking the Public Sphere: A Contribution to the Critique of Actually Existing Democracy," *Social Text* 25/26 (1990): 56–80, 65–70; S. Gal, "Feminism and Civil Society," in *Transitions, Environments, Translations: Feminisms in International Politics*, ed. J. W. Scott, C. Kaplan, and D. Keates (London: Routledge, 1997), 30–45, 37; N. Funk, "Feminism East and West" in *Gender Politics and Post-Communism: Reflections from Eastern Europe and the Former Soviet Union*, ed. N. Funk and M. Mueller (London: Routledge, 1993). In her dissertation (Princeton University, 1997), "Reproducing Russia: Women's Health and Moral Education in the Construction of a Post-Soviet Society," M. Rivkin-Fish proposes an alternative to public and private spheres, namely personal and bureaucratic spheres where people use private and personal networks to achieve what recalcitrant and/or inept contemporary bureaucracies cannot or will not. This ongoing people-versus-the-state divide in the post-Soviet era is relevant here. However, it maintains the same static fuzziness of which I despair with regard to public and private spheres.
28. W. Lubiano, "Like Being Mugged with a Metaphor: Multiculturalism and State Narra-

tives," in *Mapping Multiculturalism*, ed. A. F. Gordon and C. Newfield (Minneapolis: University of Minnesota Press, 1996), 64–75, 66.

29. Benjamin Barber, *Strong Democracy: Participatory Politics for a New Age* (Berkeley and Los Angeles: University of California Press, 1984).

30. Fraser, "Rethinking the Public Sphere: A Contribution to the Critique of Actually Existing Democracy," 76.

31. M. C. Dawson, 1995. "A Black Counterpublic? Economic Earthquakes, Racial Agenda(s), and Black Politics," in *The Black Public Sphere*, ed. the Black Public Sphere Collective (Chicago: University of Chicago Press, 1995), 199–227.

32. L. Guinier, *The Tyranny of the Majority: Fundamental Fairness in Representative Democracy* (New York: Free Press, 1994).

33. The term social *imaginaries* is borrowed from authors who use it in discussions of nationalism. A. Appadurai, "Disjuncture and Difference in the Global Cultural Economy," in *The Phantom Public Sphere*, ed. B. Robbins (Minneapolis: University of Minnesota Press, 1993), 269–295, 272–274; and B. Anderson, *Imagined Communities: Reflections on the Origin and Spread of Nationalism* (London: Verso, 1983). Appadurai (1993) connects "the old idea of images, especially mechanically produced images (in the Frankfurt School sense); the idea of the imagined community (in Anderson's sense); and the French idea of the imaginary (*imaginaire*), as a constructed landscape of collective aspirations . . . the imagination has become an organized field of social practices, a form of work . . . and a form of negotiation between sites of agency ('individuals') and globally defined fields of possibility. . . . The imagination is now central to all forms of agency, is itself a social fact, and is the key component of a new global order" (273–274). Rival knowledges, their vitality, and the relative power of their communities reflect maps of contrasting social imaginaries.

34. Paolo Freire, *The Pedagogy of the Oppressed* (New York: Seabury Press, 1970).

35. Henri Lefebvre, *The Survival of Capitalism: Reproduction of Relations of Production*, trans. Frank Bryant (New York: St. Martin's Press, 1976), 21.

36. M. Molyneaux, 1984. "Mobilisation without Emancipation? Women's Interests, State, and Revolution in Nicaragua," *Critical Social Policy* 4 (summer 1984): 59–75; and C. Moser, "Gender Planning in the Third World: Meeting Practical and Strategic Gender Needs," *World Development* 17:11 (1989): 1799–1825.

37. T. Kaplan, "Female Consciousness and Collective Action: The Case of Barcelona, 1910–1918," *Signs* 7:3 (1982): 545–566; J. Walton and D. Seddon, *Free Markets and Food Riots: The Politics of Global Adjustment* (Oxford: Blackwell Publishers, 1994).

38. J. Kurczewski, *The Resurrection of Rights in Poland* (New York: Oxford University Press, 1993), 177.

39. Cf. for post-1989 use economy: in Poland, E. Dunn, "Privatization and Personhood: Transforming Work in Postsocialist Poland," Ph.D. Dissertation, Johns Hopkins University, 1998; in Russia, M Rivkin-Fish, "Reproducing Russia: Women's Health and Moral Education in the Construction of a Post-Soviet Society," 28.

40. J. Regulska, "Local Government Reform," in *Transition to Democracy in Poland*, ed. R. F. Starr (New York: St. Martin's Press, 1998), 113–132.

41. A. Graham and J. Regulska, "Expanding Political Space for Women in Poland," *Communist and Postcommunist Studies* 30:1 (1997): 65–82; A. Graham and J. Regulska, "Where Political Meets Women: Creating Local Space in Poland," *Anthropology of East Europe Review* 15:1 (1997): 4–12; J. Regulska, "Local Government Reform," 6.

42. In 1981, 72 percent of the population claimed that life in the country was easier than in the city, as opposed to 35.7 percent in 1990. L. Beskid et al., *Warunki Zycia i Kondyczja Polakow na Poczatku Amian Systemowych* [Living standards and conditions of Poles at the beginning of system change] (Warsaw: Polish Academy of Science, Institute of Philosophy and Sociology, 1992).

43. Personal interviews with John Ragland, 1991, 1992, 1993, USDA senior extension specialist, Ministry of Agriculture, Warsaw; Elzbieta Dec, 1992, 1994, program manager, Foundation for the Development of Polish Agriculture.

44. Beskid et al., *Warunki Zycia i Kondyczja Polakow na Poczatku Amian Systemowych*, 176–181; L. Beskid, R. Milic-Czerniak, and Z. Sufin, *Polacy a Nowa Rzeczywistosc Ekonomiczna* [The Poles and the new economic reality] (Warsaw: Polish Academy of Science, Institute of Philosophy and Sociology, 1995), 175–187; Z. Sufin, "Households at the Beginning of Economic and Social Transformation," *Polish Sociological Review* 1:105 (1994): 69ff.

Note, in the early 1990s, 30 to 40 percent of the Polish population lived at subsistence levels; Beskid et al., *Warunki Zycia i Kondyczja Polakow na Poczatku Amian Systemowych*, 244–245; W. Michna, *Poland's Food Security and Agricultural Policy at the Turn of the 20th and 21st Centuries* (Warsaw: Friedrich Ebert Foundation, 1992), 50. Real income, post-1989, dropped below the 1980s food crisis era level. Because of inflation, an adjustment to underemployment, and the loss of many food subsidies, retail food demand dropped at that moment when the supply in shops finally stabilized; Sufin, "Households at the Beginning of Economic and Social Transformation"; Michna, *Poland's Food Security and Agricultural Policy at the Turn of the 20th and 21st Centuries*, 47; M. Kabaj and T. Kowalik, "Who Is Responsible for Postcommunist Successes in Eastern Europe?" *The Newsletter about Reforming Economies. The World Bank* 6 (July–August 1995): 7–8, 8. By 1995, a little more than one-third of the population had difficulty paying for food; 62 percent had no trouble; Centrum Badania Opinii Spolecznej (CBOS), *Kto Stracil na Transformacji? Slask na Tyle Innych Regionow Kraju* [Who lost out during transformation? Silesia in comparison to the rest of the country] (Warsaw: CBOS, 1995), 20. Kabaj et al. reported the per capita percentage change of consumption in thirteen staple food items between 1989 and 1994. The most dramatic drop was all in the formally heavily subsidized dairy group: butter (-54.8 percent), milk (in liters, -23.8 percent), cheese (-21.7 percent). Vegetables show the smallest drop (-1.2), suggesting that these prices remained fairly constant; there was little import competition; vegetable production remained locally controlled and involved few intermediary handlers (middlemen, wholesalers, post-farm processors, etc.); and consumers had secure home production that had protected them during the communist era food crises and that continued to do so in the post-1989 period.

45. S. Drakulic, *How We Survived Communism and Even Laughed* (New York: Harper Perennial, 1991).
46. S. Gal, "Feminism and Civil Society," in *Transitions, Environments, Translations: Feminisms in International Politics*, ed. J. W. Scott, C. Kaplan, and D. Keates (London: Routledge, 1997), 30–45, 30. Cf. G. Stokes, *And the Walls Came Tumbling Down: The Collapse of Communism in Eastern Europe* (New York: Oxford University Press, 1993).
47. S. Gal, "Feminism and Civil Society," 47, 37.
48. K. Verdery, *What Was Socialism, and What Comes Next?* (Princeton, N.J.: Princeton University Press, 1996), 67; S. Gal, "Gender in the Post-Socialist Transition: The Abortion Debate in Hungary," *East European Politics and Societies* 8 (1994): 266–267. Sufin, "Households at the Beginning of Economic and Social Transformation," 45; D. Smith, *Geography and Social Justice* (Oxford: Basil Blackwell, 1994), who points out that emphasis on women's "natural" role does not lead to an improvement in their [public] political power (20); Goven (referenced in Verdery, *What Was Socialism, and What Comes Next?*, 80) demonstrates that in Hungary, the socialist promise of a universal right to work was compromised in the 1980s as women were reconstructed into reserve and flexible labor resources. In 1980, Solidarity graffiti in Gdansk urged, "Women, return to your homes! We are fighting for a free Poland." [*"Kobiety wracajcie do domu! My walczmy o wolna Polske"*]. Private conversations with Magdalena Sroda (Philosophy Faculty, University of Warsaw) and Julita Agnieszka Rybczynska (Law Faculty, Catholic University of Lublin).
49. The government of Poland violently suppressed riots several times including in 1955, 1968, 1971, 1976, and with the beginning of martial law in 1981. It has watched and even participated, under the accords of the Brezhnev Doctrine, as Soviet troops squelched uprisings in Hungary in 1956 and in Czechoslovakia in 1968. See also, A. Snitow, "Response," in *Transitions, Environments, Translations: Feminisms in International Politics*, ed. Joan W. Scott, Cora Kaplan, Debra Keates (London: Routledge, 1997), 176–184.
50. Fuszara, "Market Economy and Consumer Rights: The Impact on Women's Everyday Lives and Employment," 84. Cf. S. Benet, *Song, Dance, and Customs of Peasant Poland* (New York: Roy Publishers, 1951), 174–176, on Polish peasant life and violence against women; C. Corrin, *Women in a Violent World: Feminist Analyses and Resistance across "Europe"* (Edinburgh: Edinburgh University Press, 1996), for a regional review of gender and violence.
51. With thanks to Karen Zivi for stressing this point.

REFERENCES

Anderson, Benedict. *Imagined Communities: Reflections on the Origin and Spread of National-ism.* London: Verso, 1983.

Appadurai, Arjun. "Disjuncture and Difference in the Global Cultural Economy." In *The Phantom Public Sphere,* edited by Bruce Robbins, 269–295. Minneapolis: University of Minnesota Press, 1993.

Arato, Andrew, and Jean Cohen. "Civil Society and Social Theory." *Thesis Eleven* 21 (1988): 40–64.

———. *From Neo-Marxism to Democratic Theory: Essays on the Critical Theory of Soviet-type Societies.* Armonk, N.Y.: M. E. Sharpe, 1993.

Ash, Timothy Garton. *The Polish Revolution: Solidarity.* New York: Charles Scribner's Sons, 1984.

Attwood, Lynne. "The Post-Soviet Woman in the Move to the Market: A Return to Domesticity and Dependence?" In *Women in Russia and the Ukraine,* 255–266. Cambridge: Cambridge University Press, 1996.

Bajan, Konrad. "Dzialki pracownicze—zjowisko speleczne o duzej perspektywie." [Workers' gardens—a social phenomenon that has a big perspective]. *Biuletyn, Polski Zwiazek Dzialkowcow, Krajowa Rada w Warszawie.* Nr. 2:26 (1988): 25ff.

Baker, Houston A., Jr. "Critical Memory and the Black Public Sphere." In *The Black Public Sphere,* edited by the Black Public Collective Sphere, 7–37. Chicago: University of Chicago Press, 1995.

Barber, Benjamin. *Strong Democracy: Participatory Politics for a New Age.* Berkeley and Los Angeles: University of California Press, 1984.

Bell, David, and Gill Valentine. *Consuming Geographies: We Are Where We Eat.* London: Routledge, 1997.

Bellows, Anne C., and Joanna Regulska. "'Setting the Agenda': Environmental Management and Leadership Training for Women in Silesia." New Brunswick, N.J.: Center for Russian, Central and East European Studies, Rutgers, the State University of New Jersey, 1994.

———. "Where Kitchen and Laboratory Meet: The 'Tested Food for Silesia' Program." *Feminist Political Ecology: Global Perspectives and Local Insights,* edited by Dianne Rocheleau, Barbara Thomas-Slater, and Esther Wangari. London: Routledge, 1996.

Benet, Sula. *Song, Dance, and Customs of Peasant Poland.* New York: Roy Publishers, 1951.

Benhabib, Seyla. *Situating the Self: Gender, Community and Postmodernism in Contemporary Ethics.* London: Routledge, 1992.

Beskid, Lidia, et al. *Warunki Zycia i Kondyczja Polakow na Poczatku Amian Systemowych.* [Living standards and conditions of Poles at the beginning of system change]. Warsaw: Polish Academy of Science, Institute of Philosophy and Sociology, 1992.

Beskid, Lidia, Roza Milic-Czerniak, and Zbigniew Sufin. *Polacy a Nowa Rzeczywistosc Ekonomiczna.* [The Poles and the new economic reality]. Warsaw: Polish Academy of Science, Institute of Philosophy and Sociology, 1995.

Bilski, Zdzislaw. "Zlekcewazenie nie mieszkancow, Sejmu i Prezydenta." ["Negligence of the inhabitants by the Sejm and President"]. *Biuletyn, Polski Zwiazek Dzialkowcow, Krajowa Rada w Warszawie* 7:59 (1995): 8–9.

Boserup, E. *Women's Role in Economic Development.* London: Allen and Unwin, 1970.

Brown, Elsa Barkly. "Negotiating and Transforming the Public Sphere: African American Political Life in the Transition from Slavery to Freedom." In *The Black Public Sphere,* edited by the Black Public Sphere Collective, 111–150. Chicago: University of Chicago Press, 1995.

Centrum Badania Opinii Spolecznej (CBOS). *Kto Stracil na Transformacji? Slask na Tyle Innych Regionow Kraju.* Warsaw: CBOS. July 1995 [Who lost out during transformation? Silesia in comparison to the rest of the country].

———. *Materialny Poziom Zycia Gospodarstw Domowych.* Warsaw: CBOS. January 1996. [Households' material level of life].

Cornell, Drucilla. "Gender, Sex, and Equivalent Rights." In *Feminists Theorize the Political,* edited by Judith Butler and Joan W. Scott, 280–296. London: Routledge, 1992.

Corrin, Chris, ed. *Superwomen and the Double Burden: Women's Experience of Change in Central and Eastern Europe and the former Soviet Union.* London: Scarlet Press, 1992.

———, ed. *Women in a Violent World: Feminist Analyses and Resistance across "Europe."* Edinburgh: Edinburgh University Press, 1996.

Cox, Kevin R. "Capitalism and Conflict around the Communal Living Space." In *Urbanization and Urban Planning in Capitalist Society*, edited by M. Dear and A. Scott, 431–456. New York: Methuen, 1981.

———, and Jeffery J. McCarthy. "Neighborhood Activism in the American City: Behavioral Relationships and Evaluation." *Urban Geography* 1:1 (1980): 22–38.

———, and R. J. Johnston. "Conflict, Politics and the Urban Scene: A Conceptual Framework." In *Conflict, Politics and the Urban Scene*, edited by K. R. Cox and R. J. Johnston, 1–19. New York: St. Martin's Press, 1982.

———, and A. Mair. "Locality and Community in the Politics of Local Economic Development." *Annals, Association of American Geographers* 47:2 (1988): 307–325.

Croll, Elisabeth J. "Rural Production and Reproduction: Socialist Development Experiences." In *Women's Work: Development and the Division of Labor by Gender*, edited by Eleanor Leacock and Helen Safa and Contributors, 224–252. South Hadley, Mass.: Bergin and Garvey, 1986.

Crosby, Christina. "Dealing with Difference." In *Feminists Theorize the Political*, edited by Judith Butler and Joan W. Scott. London: Routledge, 1992.

Dawson, Michael C. "A Black Counterpublic? Economic Earthquakes, Racial Agenda(s), and Black Politics." In *The Black Public Sphere*, edited by the Black Public Sphere Collective, 199–227. Chicago: University of Chicago Press, 1995.

d'Entrèves, Maurizio Passerin. "Hannah Arendt and the Idea of Citizenship." In *Dimensions of Radical Democracy: Pluralism, Citizenship, Community*, edited by Chantal Mouffe. London: Verso, 1992.

Dietz, Mary. "Context Is All: Feminism and Theories of Citizenship." *Daedalus* 4 (1987): 1–24.

Drakulic, S. *How We Survived Communism and Even Laughed*. New York: Harper Perennial, 1991.

Dunn, Elizabeth. "The Good Mother: Ideas of Kin and Home on the Shop Floor" (Chapter Title). Dissertation forthcoming. Department of Anthropology, Johns Hopkins University.

Einhorn, Barbara. "Where Have All the Women Gone? Women and the Women's Movement in East Central Europe." *Feminist Review* 39 (winter 1991): 16–36.

Ekiert, Grzegorz, and Jan Kubik. *Rebellious Civil Society: Popular Protest and Democratic Consolidation in Poland, 1989–1993*. Ann Arbor: University of Michigan Press, 1999.

Enloe, C. *Sexual Politics at the End of the Cold War: The Morning After*. Berkeley and Los Angeles: University of California Press, 1993.

Feldman, Shelley, and Rick Welsh. "Feminist Knowledge Claims, Local Knowledge, and Gender Divisions of Agricultural Labor: Constructing a Successor Science." *Rural Sociology* 60:1 (1995): 23–43.

Ferree, Myra Marx. "Nationalism in Eastern Europe and the Former Soviet Union." Paper presented at the "Transitions, Environments, Translations: The Meanings of Feminism in Contemporary Politics" Conference of the Institute for Research on Women, Rutgers University, New Brunswick, N.J., April 28–30, 1995.

Firestone, David. "Agriculture Department to Settle Lawsuit by Black Farmers." *New York Times*, January 5, 1999, A1+.

Fraser, Nancy. *Unruly Practices: Power, Discourse and Gender in Contemporary Social Theory*. Oxford: Polity Press, 1989.

———. *Justice Interruptus: Critical Reflections on the "Post-socialist" Condition*. London: Routledge, 1997.

Friedman, Marilyn. "The Practice of Partiality." *Ethics* 101 (1991): 818–835.

Freire, Paolo. *The Pedagogy of the Oppressed*. New York: Seabury Press, 1970.

Funk, Nanette. "Feminism East and West." In *Gender Politics and Post-Communism: Reflections from Eastern Europe and the Former Soviet Union*, edited by Nanette Funk and Magda Mueller. London: Routledge, 1993.

Fuszara, Malgorzata. "Gender Equality in the Process of Transformation." Unpublished paper. September 1991.

———. "Abortion and the Formation of the Public Sphere in Poland." In *Gender Politics and Post-Communism: Reflections from Eastern Europe and the Former Soviet Union*, edited by Nanette Funk and Magda Mueller, 241–252. London: Routledge, 1993.

———. "Market Economy and Consumer Rights: The Impact on Women's Everyday Lives and Employment." *Economic and Industrial Democracy* 15 (1994): 75–87.

———. "Women's Movements in Poland." In *Transitions, Environments, Translations: Femi-*

nisms in International Politics, edited by Joan W. Scott, Cora Kaplan, and Debra Keates, 128–142. London: Routledge, 1997.

Gal, Susan. "Gender in the Post-Socialist Transition: The Abortion Debate in Hungary." *East European Politics and Societies* 8 (1994): 266–267.

———. "Feminism and Civil Society." In *Transitions, Environments, Translations: Feminisms in International Politics,* edited by Joan W. Scott, Cora Kaplan, and Debra Keates, 30–45. London: Routledge, 1997.

Gibson-Graham, J. K. *The End of Capitalism (As We Knew It): A Feminist Critique of Political Economy.* Oxford: Blackwell Publishers, 1996.

Graham, Ann, and Joanna Regulska. "Expanding Political Space for Women in Poland." *Communist and Post-Communist Studies* 30:1 (1997): 65–82.

———. "Where Political Meets Women: Creating Local Space in Poland." *Anthropology of East Europe Review* 15:1 (1997): 4–12.

Guinier, Lani. *The Tyranny of the Majority: Fundamental Fairness in Representative Democracy.* New York: Free Press, 1994.

Habermas, Jürgen. *The Structural Transformation of the Public Sphere: An Inquiry into a Category of Bourgeois Society.* Translated by Thomas Burger with the assistance of Federick Lawrence. Cambridge, Mass.: MIT Press, 1989.

Harding, Sandra. *The Science Question in Feminism.* Ithaca, N.Y.: Cornell University Press, 1986.

Havelkova, Hana. "Transitory and Persistent Differences: Feminism East and West." In *Transitions, Environments, Translations: Feminisms in International Politics,* edited by Joan W. Scott, Cora Kaplan, and Debra Keates, 56–62. London: Routledge, 1997.

Kabaj, Mieczyslaw, and Tadeusz Kowalik. "Who Is Responsible for Postcommunist Successes in Eastern Europe?" *The Newsletter about Reforming Economies* 6 (1995): 7–8.

Kaplan, Temma. "Female Consciousness and Collective Action: The Case of Barcelona, 1910–1918." *Signs* 7:3 (1982): 545–566.

———. *Red City, Blue Period: Social Movements in Picasso's Barcelona.* Berkeley and Los Angeles: University of California Press, 1992.

Kurczewski, Jacek. *The Resurrection of Rights in Poland.* New York: Oxford University Press, 1993.

Lake, Robert W., and Joanna Regulska. "Political Decentralization and Capital Mobility in Planned and Market Societies: Local Autonomy in Poland and the United States." *Policy Studies Journal* 18:3 (1990): 702–720.

Lefebvre, Henri. *The Survival of Capitalism: Reproduction of Relations of Production.* Translated by Frank Bryant. New York: St. Martin's Press, 1976.

———. *The Production of Space.* Translated by Donald Nicholson-Smith. First published in 1974, Editions Anthropos. Oxford: Blackwell Publishers, 1991.

Logan, John R., and Gordana Rabrenovic. "Neighborhood Associations: Their Issues, Their Allies, and Their Opponents." *Urban Affairs Quarterly* 26:1 (1990): 68–94.

Lubiano, Wahneema. "Like Being Mugged with a Metaphor: Multiculturalism and State Narratives." In *Mapping Multiculturalism,* edited by Avery F. Gordon and Christopher Newfield, 64–75. Minneapolis: University of Minnesota Press, 1996.

Luxemburg, Rosa. *Die Industrielle Entwicklung Polens.* Leipzig, 1898. Translated from the German by Tessa DeCarlo. *The Industrial Development of Poland.* New York: Campaigner Publications, 1977.

Mann, S. A. *Agrarian Capitalism in Theory and Practice.* Chapel Hill: University of North Carolina Press, 1990.

Mansbridge, Jane. "Feminism and Democracy." *American Prospect* 1 (spring 1990): 126–139.

Maslarova, Liliana. "Political Action and Environment in East and Central Europe." Unpublished paper delivered at the Association of Women in Development biennial conference. Washington, D.C., October 21–24, 1993.

Lepak, Keith John. *Prelude to Solidarity: Poland and the Politics of the Gierek Regime.* New York: Columbia University Press, 1988.

Michna, Waldemar. *Poland's Food Security and Agricultural Policy at the Turn of the 20th and 21st Centuries.* Warsaw: Friedrich Ebert Foundation, 1992.

MilieuKontakt Oost-Europa. "Women and Environment in Central and Eastern Europe: Stories and Ways of Working for Change." 10th East-West Consultation of the MilieuKontakt

Oost-Europa "East-West Project." Lipnik nad Becvou, Czech Republic. October 28–30, 1993.

Mirovitskaya. "Women and Environment in Russia: Two Variables of Reforms." Unpublished paper presented at the International Studies Association. Acapulco, Mexico. March 22–28, 1993.

Molyneaux, Maxine. "Mobilisation without Emancipation? Women's Interests, State, and Revolution in Nicaragua." *Critical Social Policy* 4 (summer 1984): 59–75.

———. "Women's Rights and the International Context: Some Reflections on the Post-Communist States." *Journal of International Studies* 23:2 (1994): 287–313.

Moser, Caroline. "Gender Planning in the Third World: Meeting Practical and Strategic Gender Needs." *World Development* 17:11 (1989): 1799–1825.

Mouffe, Chantal. "Feminism, Citizenship and Radical Democratic Politics." In *Feminists Theorize the Political*, edited by Judith Butler and Joan W. Scott, 369–384. London: Routledge, 1992.

Nielsen, Joyce McCarl. "Introduction." In *Feminist Research Methods: Exemplary Readings in the Social Sciences*, edited by J. M. Nielsen, 1–37. Boulder, Colo.: Westview Press, 1990.

Nowicka, Wanda. "Two Steps Back: Poland's New Abortion Law." *Journal of Women's History* 5:3 (winter 1994): 151–155.

Orloff, Ann Shola. "Gender and the Social Rights of Citizenship: The Comparative Analysis of Gender Relations and Welfare States." *American Sociological Review* 50 (June 1993): 303–328.

Pakszys, Elzbieta, and Dorota Mazurczak. "From Totalitarianism to Democracy in Poland: Women's Issues in the Sociopolitical Transition of 1989–1993." *Journal of Women's History* 5:3 (1994): 144–150.

Papanek, Hanna. "False Specialization and the Purdah of Scholarship: A Review Article." *Journal of Asian Studies* 44:1 (1984): 127–148.

———. "To Each Less than She Needs, from Each More than She Can Do: Allocations, Entitlements, and Value." In *Persistent Inequalities: Women and World Development*, edited by Irene Tinker, 162–181. New York: Oxford University Press, 1990.

Pateman, Carol. *The Sexual Contract*. Stanford, Calif.: Stanford University Press, 1988.

Penn, S. "The National Secret." *Journal of Women's History* 5:3 (1994): 55–69.

———. "Political Action and Environment in East and Central Europe." Unpublished paper delivered at the biennial conference of the Association of Women in Development, Washington, D.C., October 21–24, 1993.

Peto, Andrea. "Hungarian Women in Politics." In *Transitions, Environments, Translations: Feminisms in International Politics*, edited by Joan W. Scott, Cora Kaplan, and Debra Keates, 153–161. London: Routledge, 1997.

Pimbert, Michael P., and Jules N. Pretty. "Participation, People and the Management of National Parks and Protected Areas: Past Failures and Future Promise." United Nations Research Institute for Social Development, International Institute for Environment and Development, and World Wildlife Fund, mimeo, 1994.

Poborski, Piotr S. *Air Pollution in Upper Silesia. Katowice.* Polish Ecological Club: Information Center for Air Protection, 1993.

Polish Committee of NGOs. *The Situation of Women in Poland*. Warsaw, 1995.

Purcell, Kate. "Research Value-Loaded Issues: The Management of Food in Households." In *Gender Relations in Public and Private*, edited by Lydia Morris and E. Stina Lyon, 176–202. New York: Macmillan, 1996.

Raynolds, Laura. "Women and Agriculture in the Third World: A Review and Critique." In *Toward a New Political Economy of Agriculture*, edited by William H. Friedland, Lawrence Busch, Frederick H. Buttel, and Alan P. Rudy, 339–363. Westview Special Studies in Agriculture Science and Policy. Boulder, Colo.: Westview Press, 1991.

Regulska, Joanna. "Urban Development under Socialism: The Polish Experience." *Urban Geography* 8 (1987): 321–339.

———. "Transition to Local Democracy: Do Polish Women Have a Chance?" In *Women in the Politics of Postcommunist Eastern Europe*, edited by M. Rueschmeyer, 35–62. Armonk, N.Y.: M. E. Sharpe, 1994.

———. "Women and Power in Poland." In *Women Transforming Politics, Worldwide Strategies for Empowerment*, edited by Jill M. Bystydzienski. Bloomington: Indiana University Press, 1992.

————. "Local Government Reform in Central and Eastern Europe." In *Local Government in the New Europe*, edited by R. J. Bennett, 183–196. London and New York: Belhaven Press, 1993.

————. "Self-Governance or Central Control? Rewriting the Constitutions in Central and Eastern Europe." In *Constitution Making in Eastern Europe*, edited by A.E.D. Howard, 133–161. Washington, D.C.: Woodrow Wilson Center Press, 1993.

————. "The 'Political' and Its Meaning for Women: Transitional Politics in Poland." In *Theorising Transition: The Political Economy of Post-Communist Transformations*, edited by John Pickles and Adrian Smith, 309–329. London: Routledge, 1998.

————. "Local Government Reform." In *Transition to Democracy in Poland*, edited by Richard F. Starr, 113–132. New York: St. Martin's Press, 1998.

Regulski, Jerzy. "From Centralism to Local Democracy." In *Proceedings of the International Workshop on Local Government Reforms in Central and Eastern Europe*, edited by Ann Graham, 7–13. Krakow, Poland, 1992.

Rivkin-Fish, Michele R. *Reproducing Russia: Women's Health and Moral Education in the Construction of a Post-Soviet Society.* Princeton, N.J.: Princeton University Press, 1997.

Rocheleau, Dianne, Barbara Thomas-Slater, and Esther Wangari, eds. *Feminist Political Ecology: Global Perspectives and Local Insights.* London: Routledge, 1996.

Rogers, Barbara. "Women's Control of Resources." In *The Domestication of Women: Discrimination in Developing Societies*, 122–151. Tavistock, 1980.

Ryan, Mary P. "Gender and Public Access: Women's Politics in Nineteenth-Century America." In *Habermas and the Public Sphere*, edited by Craig Calhoun, 259–288. Cambridge, Mass.: MIT Press, 1992.

Rybicki, Zygmunt. "The Territorial Structure of the Polish People's Republic." In *Regional Studies in Poland. Bulletin: Special Issue*, edited by Antoni Kuklinski, 7–37. Warsaw: Polish Academy of Science, Committee for Space Economy and Regional Planning, 1977.

Sadowski, Christine. "Citizen, Voluntary Associations, and the Policy Process." In *Background to Crisis: Policy and Politics in Gierek's Poland*, edited by Marice D. Simon and Roger E. Kanet, 199–219. Boulder, Colo.: Westview Press, 1981.

Schuler, Margaret. *Freedom from Violence: Women's Strategies from Around the World.* New York: UNIFEM, 1992.

Sen, Gita, and Caren Grown. *Development, Crises, and Alternative Visions: Third World Women's Perspectives.* New York: Monthly Review Press, 1987.

Shiva, Vandana. *Staying Alive: Women, Ecology and Development.* London and New Jersey: Zed Books, 1989.

————, ed. *Monocultures of the Mind: Perspectives on Biodiversity and Biotechnology.* London and New Jersey: Zed Books; Penang: Third World Network, 1993.

Siemienska, Renate. "Women in the Period of Systemic Changes in Poland." *Journal of Women's History* 5:3 (1994): 70–90.

Slodczyk, Krystyna. "Environmental Degradation and Mortality in Poland." Unpublished paper presented at the panel on "Women and Environmental Health in Silesia" at the Women, Politics, and Environmental Action conference, Moscow, June 1–4, 1994.

Smelser, N., Jr. *Theory of Collective Behavior.* New York: Free Press of Glencoe, 1963.

Smith, David. *Geography and Social Justice.* Oxford: Basil Blackwell, 1994.

Snitow, Ann. "Feminist Futures in the Former East Bloc." *Peace and Democracy News* 7:1 (summer 1993).

————. "Response." In *Transitions, Environments, Translations: Feminisms in International Politics*, edited by Joan W. Scott, Cora Kaplan, and Debra Keates, 176–184. London: Routledge, 1997.

Soper, Kate. "Eco-Feminism and Eco-Socialism: Dilemmas of Essentialism and Materialism." *Capitalism, Nature, Socialism* (September 1992): 111–114.

Spivak, G. C. "Subaltern Studies: Deconstructing Historiography." In *Subaltern Studies IV*, edited by R. Guha, 330–363. New York: Oxford University Press, 1985.

Stokes, Gayle. *And the Walls Came Tumbling Down: The Collapse of Communism in Eastern Europe.* New York: Oxford University Press, 1993.

Sufin, Zbigniew. "Households at the Beginning of Economic and Social Transformation." *Polish Sociological Review* 1:105 (1994): 69–76.

Szabo, Mate. Unpublished paper. "Social Protest in a Post-Communist Democracy: The Taxi Drivers' Demonstration in Hungary."

Szczypiorski, Andrzej. *The Polish Ordeal: The View from within.* Translated from the Polish by Celina Wieniewska. London: Croom Helm, 1981.

Szelenyi, I. *Urban Inequalities under Socialism.* New York: Oxford University Press, 1983.

———. "Housing Inequalities and Occupational Segregation in State Socialist Cities: Commentary on the Special Issue of IJURR on East European Cities." *International Journal of Urban and Regional Research* 11 (1987): 1–8.

Szymanski, Leszek. *Candle for Poland: 469 Days of Solidarity.* San Bernardino, Calif.: Borgo Press, 1982.

Thompson, E. P. *The Making of the English Working Class.* New York: Vintage Books, 1966.

———. "The Moral Economy of the English Crowd in the 18th Century." *Past and Present* 50 (February 1971): 76–136.

Tinker, Irene, ed. *Persistent Inequalities: Women and World Development.* New York: Oxford University Press, 1990.

Titkow, Anna. "Status Evolution of Polish Women: The Paradox and Chances." In *The Transformation of Europe: Social Conditions and Consequences,* edited by Matti Alestalo, Erik Allardt, Andrzej Rychard, Wlodzimierz Wesolowsi, 316–336. Warsaw: Institute of Philosophy and Sociology, Polish Academy of Science, 1994.

———. "Polish Women in Politics: An Introduction to the Status of Women in Poland." In *Women in the Politics of Postcommunist Eastern Europe,* edited by M. Rueschmeyer, 29–34. Armonk, N.Y.: M. E. Sharpe, 1994.

———, and H. Domanskiego, eds. *Co to Znaczy Byc Kobieta w Polsce.* Warsaw: The Polish Academy of Science, Institute of Philosophy and Sociology, 1995.

Touraine, Alain, Françoise Dubet, Michel Wieviorka, and Jan Stzelecki. *Solidarity: The Analysis of a Social Movement: Poland 1980–1981.* Cambridge, U.K.: Cambridge University Press, 1983. Written in collaboration with Grazyna Gesicka et al. Translated by David Denby. Originally published, Paris: Librairie Arthème Fayard, 1982.

Townsend, Janet G., with Jenny Bain De Corcuera. "Feminists in the Rainforest in Mexico." *Geoforum* 24:1 (1993): 45–54.

Turshen, Meredeth. *The Politics of Public Health.* New Brunswick, N.J.: Rutgers University Press, 1989.

United States National Research Council. *The Problem of Changing Food Habits: Report of the Committee on Food Habits, 1941–1943.* Bulletin of the National Research Council, No. 108. Washington, D.C.: National Research Council, National Academy of Sciences. October 1943.

Van Esterik, Penny. "Women and Nurture in Industrial Societies." *Proceedings of the Nutrition Society* 56 (1997): 335–343.

Verdery, Katherine. *What Was Socialism, and What Comes Next?* Princeton, N.J.: Princeton University Press, 1996.

Wallerstein, Immanuel. "Household Structures and Labor-Force Formation in the Capitalist World-Economy." In *Households and the World Economy,* edited by J. Smith, I. Wallerstein, and H. Evers, 17–22. Beverly Hills, Calif.: Sage Publications, 1984.

Walton, John, and David Seddon. *Free Markets and Food Riots: The Politics of Global Adjustment.* Oxford: Blackwell, 1994.

Waring, Marilyn. *If Women Counted: A New Feminist Economics.* San Francisco: Harper and Row, 1988.

Watson, Peggy. "The Rise of Masculinism in Eastern Europe." *New Left Review* 198 (1993).

———. "Civil Society and the Politics of Difference in Eastern Europe." In *Transitions, Environments, Translations: Feminisms in International Politics,* edited by Joan W. Scott, Cora Kaplan, and Debra Keates, 21–29. London: Routledge, 1997.

Women's Environment and Development Organization (WEDO). *World Women's Congress for a Healthy Planet: Official Report.* Includes "Women's Action Agenda 21" and "Findings of the Tribunal." Miami, November 8–12, 1991.

World Women's Congress for a Healthy Planet (WWCHP). *Official Report.* Convened by the WWCHP's Women's International Policy Action Committee. Miami, November 8–12, 1991.

Young, Iris M. *Justice and the Politics of Difference.* Princeton, N.J.: Princeton University Press, 1990.

Youssef, Nadia H. "Women's Access to Productive Resources: The Need for Legal Instruments to Protect Women's Development Rights." In *Women's Rights Human Rights: International Feminist Perspectives,* edited by Julie Peters and Andrea Wolper, 279–288. London: Routledge, 1995.

COCO FUSCO AND NAO BUSTAMANTE

"STUFF"

In 1996, we decided to create a performance that dealt with Latin women, food, and sex. We started with our own stories. Nao is from an immigrant farmworker family that was involved in the Chicano political struggles of the 1960s and 1970s. She grew up in the San Joaquin Valley of California, a region that at one time produced more fruit and vegetables than any other in the world. Coco's family is from Cuba, a country that gained a reputation in the 1950s as an international whorehouse and, in response to its present economic crisis, has reverted to sex tourism as a strategy of survival. In the course of writing "Stuff," Coco traveled to Cuba to interview women in this burgeoning industry. Then we both went to Chiapas, the center of indigenous-culture tourism in Mexico and the site of the 1994 Zapatista insurrection. We spent several weeks in conversation with women and children whose livelihoods are linked to their daily contact with foreigners.

"Stuff" premiered at the National Review of Live Art in Glasgow in November 1996. Among other places, it has been performed at London's ICA, Highways in Santa Monica, PICA in Portland, the Brady Street Theatre in San Francisco, Stockholm's Backstege, Artspace in Auckland, Otego Polytechnic in Dunedin (New Zealand), ASU West in Phoenix, and the Ex-centrics Festival in Vordinborg, Denmark.

"Stuff" is our look at the cultural myths that link Latin women

FIGURE 1. Nao Bustamante and Coco Fusco entertain a "sex tourist" in their performance of "Stuff" at London's ICA, November 1996. *(Photo by Hugo Glendinning)*

and food to the erotic in the Western popular imagination. We weave our way through multilingual sex guides, fast food menus, bawdy border humor, and much more. In the course of the performance, we mingle with audience members, treating them to a meal, a host of rituals and exotic legends, an occasional rhumba, and at least one Spanish lesson as part of our satirical look at relations between North and South. Our spoof, however, is not without a serious side. Latin American literature is full of references to cannibalism—as the European colonial's fear of the indigenous Other as a cannibal, as a trope for Europe and America's ravaging of Latin America's resources, and, finally, as the symbolic revenge of the colonized who feed off the colonial. If food here serves as a metaphor for sex, then eating represents consumption in its crudest form. We are dealing with how cultural consumption in our current moment involves the trafficking of that which is most dear to us all: our identities, our myths, and our bodies. "Stuff" is our commentary on how globalization and its accompanying versions of "cultural tourism" are actually affecting women of color both in the third world and in Europe and North America, where hundreds of thousands of Latin women are currently migrating to satisfy consumer desires for "a bit of the Other."

CAST

BLANCA	Coco Fusco
ROSA	Nao Bustamante
EEE JONES (ON VIDEO)	Adam Bresnick
TRAVEL TASTERS	variable

[*The audience has received with their tickets a colored slip of paper. There are four colors—red, blue, yellow, and green—and an equal number of audience members have received stubs of each color.*]

Preshow

[*Top-of-show lights and music fade out. COCO and NAO take their places onstage at the small dressing tables, stage left and right. Lights up over the two tables. COCO and NAO are sitting at the table in their street clothes, writing postcards.*]

COCO: (*Picks one up and reads from it*) March 15, New York—Dear Liz, I finally had that meeting about my piece on Cuban hookers. First, the editor was disappointed that I didn't want to say that Cuban women turned tricks because of the U.S. blockade. Then the editor says to me, "You know, if I go to a bar here to pick up a guy, it's for my enjoyment, but if a girl there does it, she has to give the guy what he wants." Imagine a bunch of overeducated women sitting in an office on Madison Avenue, saying things to me like, "I mean, if a guy says put my cock in your mouth, those girls just have to do it. How could that possibly be pleasurable?"

NAO: (*Reading from a postcard*) April 4, Copenhagen—Dearest D.L., Last night I was walking home at 3:00 A.M. when a young guy started following me. He asked me to go home with him and said he just wanted to make me feel good. At one point he noticed that I had dark hair sticking out from under my cap, and that made him very excited. He wanted to know if I was Mexican. When we got to the house where I was staying and I started to go inside, he made one last attempt to win my affections. And then he said, with a smile on his face as if it were some big turn-on, "I have chips and salsa at my place and you can have some if you come home with me." That asshole thought I was some little chihuahua or something, desperate for mama's home cooking.

COCO: (*Picks up another postcard*) November 20, Toronto—Dear Kim, I really ticked off some people at the film festival when I joked about how the documentary on Zapatista women looked like a rerun of films about Sandinistas, Salvadoran guerrilleras, and Cuban milicianas. It's not that I don't agree with the Zapatistas. I mean, come on, those women are saying they want to marry the men they choose, and they're enjoying getting free condoms when they're in combat. Who wouldn't sympathize with someone who says they'd rather wash clothes in a machine than on a riverbank? It's just that I'm not that crazy about seeing yet another movie about women getting off on guns.

NAO: [*Picks up another postcard*] May 10, Hamburg—Hello my sweet Suzy, I just can't seem to get away from sex! I'm staying in St. Pauli, the bizarre sex district of this city. The working girls here dress like aerobics instructors. I guess it's more practical than the usual puta-wear. Well, the locals and the tourists are eating it up. They are really crazy about the Brazilian girls. Ooh la la, the Brazilenias are beautiful, and I guess it's cheaper for the men to have them here than to go to Brazil. Dark-skinned women drive the Germans wild! Everywhere I go there is a lingerie ad staring me in the face that features a gorgeous black girl with huge breasts. I see the ad all over the place, but I can't seem to remember which company I'm supposed to buy from. The girl is oh oh oh-so-distracting.

COCO: [*Picks up another postcard*] July 14, San Cristobal de las Casas, Chiapas—Dear Consuelo, Last night we had dinner with Marieta. She told us about how the fighting between the mestizos and indians here goes way way back. The indians don't really believe that anyone else has the right to live on this land, and the mestizos are afraid of the prophecies that say they'll have to leave one day. Marieta said that one thing people don't talk much about is that the mestizos in San Cristobal rape indian women from the countryside all the time. She told us about one indian woman from the market who was raped and got pregnant. When the baby was born the guy went and took it away from her. That woman went mad. From then on, she would only go out with her face covered with mud so that no one would ever go near her again.

[*Lights fade out on stage-left table. NAO exits. Jorge Reyes music plays, starting at a high level and lowering as speaking begins. A large video screen—or TV set—is lowered in front of a platform with dim lights, and, if possible, drawn curtains. Weird, New Age music tunes in and then out, slowly. A man's face fills the screen. He is wearing a conservative dark-colored suit. His hair is slicked back, and he has a moustache. He smiles in a geekish way and holds his smile a little too long.*)

Scene One

EEE JONES: Good evening and welcome. I am your host, Elizardo Eduardo Encarnación Jones (also known as Triple E). I am the director of the Institute for Southern Hemispheric Wholeness. Please allow me to ask you this: Have you thought about what are you going to do on your next vacation? Would you like to try something . . . different?

Most of my clients have endured the pain of waiting all year long for their holiday trip to someplace warm and inviting. They long to bask in the sensual beauty and ancient wonders that my part of the world offers up so willingly. Then, much to their chagrin, they come back irritated by all the tropical storms, masked bandits, parasites, and poverty. They find themselves saying, "Why not stay home, get some of that spicy take-out food, and fondle some crystals instead?"

To them, and to you, I say, objects are not enough. You need complete nutrition for the spirit, and only people can provide that. Why not have the best without suffering the worst? I have devised a service that will bring you heat without sweat, ritual without revolution, and delicacies without dysentery. And you don't have to go anywhere—we deliver it to you. In just a few moments you'll begin to sample the delights of post-spacial travel as we approach the third millennium. (*Music fades out.*)

For our first session, we will need four members of our audience. (*House lights up. He anticipates BLANCA's entrance.*)

My agency representative, Blanca (*pause; she stops abruptly and poses like a stewardess*), will escort each post-spacial traveler into our studio. (*Lights up on dining table and entire stage.*)

Would all those with red tickets please raise your hand? (*Pause*)

Blanquita, please escort a male with a red ticket onstage. (*Video pauses. BLANCA picks male and escorts him onstage. Video plays.*) For this evening's first event, you are going to be an economist in search of authentic precolombian food and music. Your name is François. (*Male sits down at table.*) Good.

Now would all those with yellow tickets please raise your hand? (*Pause*) Blanquita, please escort a woman with a yellow ticket onstage. (*Video pauses. BLANCA picks woman and escorts her onstage. Video plays.*) You were orphaned at birth and you just found out that you're Cher's cousin. You want to train as a medicine woman. Your name is Wanda Desert Flower. (*Woman sits at table.*) Wonderful.

Now would all those with blue tickets please raise your hand? (*Pause*) Blanquita, be a dear and find a man with a blue ticket, please. (*Video pauses. BLANCA picks male and escorts him onstage. Video plays.*) You've been wanting to quit smoking for ages and are ready to try anything. Your name is . . . um, Bert. (*Man sits at table.*) Marvelous. Only one more.

This time, those with green tickets please raise your hand. (*Pause*) You know what to do, Blanca darling. Female again. (*Video pauses. BLANCA picks woman and escorts her onstage. Video plays.*) You're a creative consultant for The Body Shop and you're eavesdropping on my seminar. Your name is Tippy O'Toole. (*Woman sits at table.*)

I'm sure you're all comfortable. Please notice that you each have a spiritual guidebook in front of you, which you will be asked to read from occasionally. You have entered a new realm and will be known from now on as Travel Tasters. Are you ready?

BLANCA: All Travel Tasters nod your heads.

EEE JONES: Marvelous, marvelous. Let the program begin. Course number 1.

(*EEE strikes a pose, then video fades to black. Lights reveal a large book being lowered from the ceiling. It stops at chest level. A different Jorge Reyes song plays. All the while, BLANCA is playing the rainstick and praying to the heavens.*)

BLANCA: (*Going off at moments and not remembering she's onstage reading*) A long, long time ago, before the times of our mothers, our grandmothers, and our great-grandmothers, before credit-card debt, toxic waste, and computer viruses, life was good. The sun shone, the rain was light, and it was never cold. No one had to make decisions about anything because the gods decided everything. Adults and children alike frolicked all day long, since the land bore fruit without any need of human effort. Corn, yucca, potatoes, papaya, tomatoes, Chile, and cacao sprang forth from the soil in abundance. (*Pause*) Recognizing their extreme good fortune, the people occasionally ceased their playing to give thanks. Travel Tasters, you give thanks too. (*Music fades out.*)

TASTERS: (*In unison*) We give thanks and praise that the dead once ate.

BLANCA: At the end of each lunar cycle, the people prepared an homage to their most revered goddess, Cuxtamali, keeper of the earth, the mother of all things; Travel Tasters, repeat—

TRAVEL TASTERS: The keeper of the earth, the mother of all things.

[*BLANCA moves rainstick as a downstage-left floor light comes up on ROSA. ROSA appears with a small food cart on wheels from stage right. She starts to dance toward downstage center, pounding her feet in a rhythm complementary to BLANCA's reading. ROSA faces the audience, standing behind her cart. Front light comes up on ROSA, as the floor light fades out.*]

BLANCA: Cuxtamali not only provided for the world, but she was wise enough to provide for herself. Being somewhat insatiable, she kept three lovers. One of them was water (*ROSA spits to the side*), the second one was the wind (*ROSA yawns*), and the last one was fire (*ROSA lights her cigarette and takes a drag*). Cuxtamali needed all three of them to fulfill her needs. When she took up with the wind, together they spread seeds (*from her apron pocket ROSA throws seeds at audience*), when she embraced water, they increased the land's bounty (*ROSA serves drinks to TASTERS*), and when she fought with fire, the world shook and spat forth its insides (*ROSA looks at BLANCA and shrugs*). To satisfy herself, she rotated her sessions with her three lovers on a regular basis. Tasters—

TRAVEL TASTERS: The goddess is wise.

ROSA: You betcha she's wise.

BLANCA: In honor of this wise and lustful goddess, the people would make a feast at the end of each lunar cycle and would eat and eat and eat and eat . . .

ROSA: (*Getting corn from cart*) I've been serving up this corn mush for three thousand years, and boy, am I fed up. (*ROSA moves around table, spooning corn mush [or tamales] onto each TASTER's plate.*)

BLANCA: Oh, priestess, please tell the Tasters what you are about to serve them.

ROSA: (*Serving, speaking very casually*) Oh . . . yeah. The feast would begin and end with corn, because corn is the beginning and end of all things.

BLANCA: Yes, this is true. Most of the people would be given corn to eat.

Filling themelves with the wealth of the earth, they celebrated the generosity of their great goddess. When they had filled themselves with corn, they would begin to eat potatoes. And when there were no more potatoes, the people would eat papaya. Then tomatoes, and then avocados, and then chiles, which were, of course, seeded and finely chopped in advance. (*Meanwhile, ROSA takes each food off of cart and puts it on the table.*)

ROSA: Don't look at me! I ain't no prep cook, and I'm not doing the dishes either! Tasters repeat after me: The goddess does not do dishes!

TASTERS: The goddess does not do dishes!

BLANCA: Let us continue. Between each course the people would commemorate the rise and fall of the great goddess's love affairs with the wind, water, and fire. They sprinkled water on their food, burned incense, and blew sanctified melodies with horns made of giant shells. Tasters, raise your horns and blow!

TASTERS: With this, we honor the goddess. (*They blow on paper horns.*)

BLANCA: Then, the priestesses of the people would take corn, the potatoes, the papaya and tomatoes, the cacao and the avocado, and they would begin to make an offering to the great sensual goddess Cuxtamali with them. (*ROSA scrambles to pick up each fruit as it is being named.*)

ROSA: Actually, the priestesses had the feeling at one point that the goddess was getting a little sick of her three boyfriends . . .

BLANCA: Excuse me?

ROSA: Yeah, over it. Cuxtamali had had enough. One day, she decided that she was going to make the perfect mate for herself and dump those machos.

BLANCA: Uh, well yes, let us praise the goddess for being an independent spirit! Tasters! Raise your cups! Que puta madre!

TASTERS: (*They raise their cups.*) ¡Que puta madre!

ROSA: She decided to make her mate out of the stuff she loved the most—food!

BLANCA: You must have gotten a revised version of the legend . . .

ROSA: She started with corn, figuring that, since corn is the beginning and the end of all things, why not make it the middle too?

BLANCA: And so with that, she made the torso.

ROSA: (*Piecing together the figure*) Then she took the yucca and fashioned it into delectable arms and legs. The potato became the head. And from the tomato she created her lover's soft and tender heart. When that was done, she took a nice, big banana and—

BLANCA: Uh yes, well, and then the dancing to the goddess, mother of all things and keeper of the earth, would begin.

ROSA: The dance?

BLANCA: Yes, the dance of the blade. For on the occasion of the twelfth lunar cycle, the ceremonies included a knife dance that would be led by the priestesses. (*She pulls out a knife.*)

ROSA: Could I have some ritual blade-dance music with drums, flutes, and horns please?

(*Tribu music starts high and fades down quickly. ROSA starts "The Dance."*)

BLANCA: The dance was a particularly sacred element of the celebration of the great goddess. All the people would sway back and forth while the priestesses surrounded them. Tasters, please sway! (*The sculpture lies on the table. ROSA is circling the table sensually with the knife.*) And then, the priestesses would reach the climax of their dance. At that point there would have to be a blood sacrifice—

ROSA: (*Turns the knife on herself, then stops abruptly.*) Are you kidding or something?

BLANCA: No. No. Not at all. Blood sacrifice was needed to satisfy the great, lustful, and all-powerful goddess. By order of the goddess, the priestess must self-sacrifice.

ROSA: Oh for Christ's sake! (*Music fades out.*)

BLANCA: I beg your pardon, priestess, there was no Christ in those times. Tasters, repeat after me: self-sacrifice!

TASTERS: Self-sacrifice! Self-sacrifice!

ROSA: (*Staring at the knife*) OK, OK, listen to this. The priestess did sacrifice a part of herself—

BLANCA: Oh really?

ROSA: Yes. The fruits they had used for their offerings were born of the earth, of the goddess herself. Hence it was flesh of her flesh.

BLANCA: Oh. I hadn't thought of that.

ROSA: (*Turning her knife on her food sculpture*) Die, Mr. Potato Head, die!

BLANCA: Tasters, please move back and give the priestess enough space for her to carry out her blood-letting ritual. And so, they would first baptize their creations and then begin to draw and quarter them, crying tears of blood as they completed their sacrifice.

BLANCA: (*ROSA is tearing away at the food in a frenzy.*) Rosa, you'd better get a hold of yourself!

ROSA: (*Ranting*) The priestess cried tears of blood! Tears of blood!

BLANCA: Tasters, please don't worry, I'm sure the priestess will be finished shortly. And so, according to the legend left to us by our mothers, our grandmothers, and our great-grandmothers, the priestesses would reach a state of ecstasy in the course of their sacrifice, while the people stood witness. Their wild state was said to symbolize the goddess's happiness at having a new lover who was more pleasing to her than those she had had before. And then, as night fell on them, and the people grew weary, they would begin their return to their cute little grass-roofed huts. (*ROSA is still pounding away at the sculpture.*)

Tasters, please rise and return to your seats in the audience. I'm sure this has been an enriching experience for you. I thank you for your participation.

[*TASTERS rise and file offstage with BLANCA assisting them. House lights are brought on until audience participants are seated. Book is lifted out. Colored lights shine on the screen. ROSA keeps on cutting up the sculpture and is now groaning. The video comes on with EEE's face on it, smiling.*]

BLANCA: Rosa, the session is over. You can stop now. (*ROSA ignores her.*)

EEE JONES: Well, my friends, wasn't this wonderful? The energy circulating in this room is so powerful it makes my soul jump for joy. I am so glad to see how well our first session with you has gone and how satiated and spiritually satisfied you all look.

BLANCA: OK, Rosa. Do you realize that you've wrecked everything? First, you wrecked the ritual, then you go nuts on me and scare everyone at the table—what is your problem? (*ROSA ignores her.*)

EEE JONES: Do you feel as cleansed and fortified as I feel that you are?

BLANCA: Rosa, are you listening to me? I can find somebody else to do this with, you know—

EEE JONES: Isn't it simply marvelous to move in and out of a distant time and place at the flick of a switch?

BLANCA: All right, let's stop things right here. (*BLANCA points remote control toward screen. Video pauses.*)

ROSA: What do you mean, I blew it? That was a great finale!

BLANCA: Come on, Rosa, you're not supposed to make a mess of everything and groan like some weird extraterrestrial.

ROSA: I thought our ancestors were extraterrestrials, and, besides, whose idea was this blood-spilling business?

[*ROSA takes remote control and turns on video.*]

BLANCA: Gimmie that control!

(BLANCA and ROSA start a catfight for the control. ROSA wrestles it away and points it at screen; video resumes. BLANCA pulls off ROSA's wig. ROSA turns to BLANCA and pulls off her wig. They fight throughout TRIPLE E's speech.)

EEE JONES: It is at this stage of our sessions that our guests feel so spiritually renewed that they are ready to embrace the world anew. But first they must embrace one another. So, now, turn and hold out your arms to your neighbor. Share with one another the richness you carry inside yourselves!

Thank you. And thank you, my beloved initiates, for being part of this occasion. You have received a taste, only a taste, of what we'll be offering to you via satellite in the very near future. So keep tuned in and turned on.

[*TRIPLE E poses in a smile, video fades to black. Stagehand gives ROSA her clipboard and begins to clean up mess.*]

ROSA: (*Breathing and approaching downstage*) Hi, I'm Nao. I need to get some information about your experience of our Travel Taster service this evening. Some of the questions may be a bit embarrassing, but I'm not afraid to ask them. You see in my other life I also service people's desires. I work as a mail-order sex educator and sales associate for a women-owned sex-toy cooperative. I help men and women decide which dildos and vibrators work best for them.

As you can imagine, the most common question I get is, "What size is right for me?" Not for me, I mean, for them. Although a part of my mission is to truly help people, I can't tell what sort of a dildo a person needs just by looking at them. So I tell customers to take a trip to the supermarket, and check out some vegetables. Long, thin vegetables. Then they've gotta take them home, and let them reach room temperature. Then put condoms on them and try them out. Once they've figured out which ones satisfy them the most, I tell them to measure them and come back to me with this information, and then I can help them out.

Now talking to you about this has made me a little curious, so before I get to our questionnaire, let me ask you this: Let's say you're in the supermarket, and you're in the cucumber section. There are the smooth, short, waxy, fat ones, and then there are the English kind, long with ridges. Or those yellow summer squash with the curved tip—great for G-spot stimulation . . . Which ones would you prefer? Can I see a show of hands for the regular cucumbers? OK, I understand that this is a delicate question, and you may not want to reveal the information to your neighbors . . . So everyone close your eyes. Come on, close your eyes. Now you're with me and we are walking hand in hand at the supermarket. You feel safe. You feel the cooling mist from the lettuce . . . You breathe in the refreshing scent of the citrus . . . and there we stand in front of the cucumbers and the squash. You reach to pick one out. Which one is it? Can I see a show of hands for the English cucumber? Now we go to the dairy section for a canister of whipped cream. You don't wait until you get home, you begin to spray cream all over your body, and your fellow shoppers begin to lick and lick . . . and you feel moist and creamy and sticky . . .

[*Lights dim out slowly as NAO walks backward offstage, leaving a spotlight on COCO's dressing table. COCO stands by her small table with the spotlight on her. She puts on nerd glasses.*]

COCO: (*Reads a postcard*) [Date and place of performance]—Dear Audience,

I think it's time to explain why we are so interested in Latin women and food. Actually, this piece is about consumption—of our bodies and our myths—and food. Let's start with Anthropophagias. That's what the Brazilians used to call it in the 1920s. An-thro-po-pha-gi-a. That was supposed to be our great, creative, cannibalistic revenge. Absorb our sacred enemies and transform them into totems, they said. Take everything that is thrown our way and have our way with it. That's how we were supposed to live up to our ancestors. So when you come charging in our direction, running from whatever it is you're running from, you may not think that we who serve you could be eating as well. But we do. Gently but efficiently, we devour you. The more visceral your desires, the more physical our labor.

(*Lights out*)

Scene Two

(*Stage is dark. When NAO [CUSTOMER #1] is downstage center, a spotlight comes up on her. Her hair pulled back, she wears a ripped "Bahamas" T-shirt. She does yoga poses.*)

VOICE-OVER: (*Airy voice*) I hadn't really grasped why I felt so . . . empty. I just couldn't satisfy myself. Then, a true friend referred me to Triple E. I didn't know what to expect when I called. But everything was as promised, no surprises and no problems. I can tell I've made contact with the deepest parts of myself. My spiritual practice has grown, and I feel desirable again. I'm eternally grateful to the Institute and, of course, to the goddess.

(*Voice pauses. Light out. CUSTOMER #1 leaves the stage. Table light comes up on COCO, wearing a black bathrobe, resetting the table.*)

VOICE-OVER: The first lesson I learned about gringos when I was little was that their food tastes gross. I thought I was supposed to learn how to cook decent food as a matter of cultural survival. I ended up as the only one in my crowd who doesn't live on take-out. I'm the one who makes the big dinners for everybody. I got so into it that I never even complained when guys never did shit to help. I even told one guy I wanted to cook for all his friends, no matter how many stopped by unannounced. I said I wanted to cook for his family, even though I was terrified they wouldn't

like my food. Once, one of them showed up with a ham-and-cheese crois-
sant that was oozing with mayonnaise, and I took it as a personal affront.
When another one asked for a beer while I was cutting up the lasagna,
and I knew there were no more in the fridge, I dropped the knife and
ran out to the store and let my own food get cold. Every once in a while
I would fall asleep at dinner while the guests were still around because I
was so tired. And they say we use food to trap them.

[*Voice pauses. Light out. COCO exits. Meanwhile, CUSTOMER #2
[NAO] stands at stage left, in the book position. Lights up on her,
in a baseball cap, with dreadlocks and a "human race" T-shirt.*]

VOICE-OVER: (*Whiny voice*) Well, it's not exactly what I expected. Kind of a
hodgepodge of stories, or, what do ya' call 'em, ancient tales or something like that. I think it had to do with women and their sexual appe-
tites, and well . . . I dunno. The corn was OK, nothing to write home about.
The bit with the knife was cool. Did I say enough?

[*Voice pauses. Light out. CUSTOMER #2 exits. Meanwhile JUDY
[COCO] is downstage-center, wearing a black bathrobe and wild wig,
as she begins to style her hair and primp "herself." Light comes up
on her. An English translation slide is projected on the screen.*]

VOICE-OVER: (*Spanish-speaking transvestite*) Me puedes llamar Judy. ¿Me
preguntas si me deprimo? Por supuesto que me deprimo. Pero esto es un
trabajo, vieja. ¿Qué puedo hacer? Nadie escogió vivir en medio de esta
mierda. Trato de no pensar mucho en estas cosas. Cuando me siento mal,
pienso en un peinado nuevo. A los italianos les fascina el pelo rizado, asi
que me hize este permanente para estar más morena. ¿Qué te parece? Es
que chica, ¿hay que comer, no? ¿Mi familia? Ya estan acostumbrados.
Cuando traigo un gallego a la casa, mi familia no lo ve a él—ven un pollo,
arroz, frijoles, y platanos, ven un refri lleno. Les digo a los pepes que estoy
haciendo esto para comprarme una libra de picadillo, y asi se sienten más
culpables de mi situación y entonces me dan más plata. No digo que me
gusta estar en un lugar con aire acondicionado. Yo pudiera estar en una
oficina todo el día, como hacia cuando trabajaba en el banco. ¿Pero que
saqué de eso? Ay mi cielo, absolutamente nada.

(*Translation slide reads.*) You can call me Judy. Depressed? Sure I get
depressed. But it's a job, honey. What can I do? Nobody chooses to be
born in the middle of a mess like this one. I try not to think about things
too much. When I feel down, I start thinking about a new way to fix my

hair. The Italians like wild hair, so I permed mine to look more *morena,* what do you think? We have to eat, right?

My family? Oh, they're used to it. When I bring a *gallego* home, my family doesn't see him, they just see a chicken, rice, beans, and *platanos*—a full fridge. When I tell the guys that I'm doing it to buy a pound of ground beef, they feel better about giving me money, and they leave me more. I don't say I like to be in a nice room with air conditioning for a change. I could sit in an office all day—I did that when I was working in a bank. What did I get then? Oh darling, absolutely nothing.

(*Voice pauses. Slide and light out. JUDY exits. Meanwhile, NAO enters and sits at table. Light up over dining table. She begins to pick her teeth with a toothpick.*)

VOICE-OVER: I once asked an astronaut what he missed most about Earth, and he replied, "food and sex." I can relate to that.

I am eating her and she tastes so tangy, a bit like a rusty papaya, unlike any other person I've tasted. Women taste strong, not like men. Men don't taste like anything if they are properly washed. Women always have a taste even if they are freshly bathed. When you consume a woman there is a taste and a smell left in your mouth and in your nose, which are connected by the way, as are your asshole and your mouth. But a woman's flavor changes depending on what she has eaten, how aroused she is, where she is in her cycle, and who is in her vicinity. They say it's the same for men, with semen, but whatever, to me the taste of semen is repulsive. I think those who enjoy eating women must enjoy the flavor and scent and juice of seriously potent fruit . . . I've eaten both, and it takes more raw talent . . . to eat a woman.

(*Voice pauses. Light out. NAO exits. Meanwhile MARTA [COCO] enters wearing a braided wig and a rebozo. Lights up downstage center. Translation slide is projected on MARTA as voice tape continues.*)

VOICE-OVER: (*In Spanish. MARTA lays out several dolls on top of a rebozo.*) Yo he trabajado aquí en el zócalo desde los siete años. Así que conozco bien como son los turistas que vienen a este lugar. Primero les ofresco mis muñecos. Mi mama hace muy bonitos muñecos zapatistas, muy hermosos con pasamontañas de terciopelo. Nunca he visto a Marcos, pero tengo muñecos de Marcos, Ramona y Trini, Moisés y David. Yo digo siempre que el dinero es para mi tortilla. Algunos compran al tiro. Si eso no funciona les muestro mis pulseras. La gente que ya conozco a veces no quieren comprar, entonces les pido una coca. A veces hay otros que me llevan a cenar. Siempre trato de ver si mis amigos y mi mamá pueden venir también. Asi nos sentamos en los restaurantes donde a veces nos echan, y los meseros no pueden decir nada. Mi amigo Alex de Alemania me regaló este traje. Lo uso para trabajar. El también me retrató y me pagó 20 pesos por haberme tomado la foto. Ahora les cobro 30 pesos a los gringos por cada foto.

(*Translation slide reads:*) I've been working here since I was seven, and I guess I've gotten to know what the tourists who come here are like. First, I offer them my dolls. My mother makes good Zapatista dolls, nice ones with velvet ski caps. I've never seen the real Marcos, but I have dolls of Marcos, Ramona, Trini, Moisés, and David. I tell people that the money is for my tortillas. Some people buy them right away. If that doesn't work I show them my bracelets. People I already know, though, sometimes they don't want to buy dolls or bracelets, so I ask them for a soda. Then sometimes there are people who will even buy me a meal, and then I always ask for chicken. I always try to see if my friends and my mother can come too. Then we can sit in the restaurants where we usually get thrown out and the waiters can't say anything. My friend Alex from Germany bought me my dress. This is what I work in. Alex also took my picture and paid me 20 pesos. Now I charge the gringos 30 pesos for one shot.

[*Voice pauses; slide and light out. She picks up her dolls and puts the bundle on her back. MARTA exits. Meanwhile CUSTOMER #3 [NAO] enters. Book light comes up, stage left, on her. She wears sunglasses and a slick jacket.*]

VOICE-OVER: If you really wanna know, I think Triple E is a crackpot. I can't believe what I paid for this. I didn't feel a thing. They said the camote was an aphrodisiac, so I ate five and all they gave me was the runs. I was hoping to get a little more—you know what I mean. And those girls weren't exactly spring chickens. I thought it would be more like those kinds of places—it's like the way everybody moves, the way they let you know things with their hands.

You don't need to speak the language even—you can just get into the music. The girls there, the way they . . . it's so . . . smooth, so . . . well, I'd to see a little more of that.

[*Voice-over ends. Light out. CUSTOMER #3 exits. Video of Triple E comes on. Lights come on over two dressing tables, where COCO and NAO are changing into new costumes throughout sequence.*]

EEE JONES: (*Video*) I gather from your comments that our next intensive program will be more to your liking. Our aim is to please all sorts of tastes, and we recognize that serving you a meal is only one of the ways of heightening your experience of the senses and your connection to the spiritual. Many of you out there are demanding more of an immersion in another way of living—in, of course, the safest setting possible. In fact, our current research suggests that intercultural growth areas are the ones that offer the highest degree of, shall we say, intimate personal contact. (*Esquivel music starts.*) Therefore, in order to attend to our increasingly diversified client base, and, to satisfy your hunger for transformative physical encounters, we are upgrading our services to provide the most extensive and sophisticated multilingual intercourse you could imagine. Blanca, Rosa, would you like to give our studio audience tonight a preview?

BLANCA: Estoy lista, Triple E.

ROSA: Orale, jefito.

EEE JONES: Fine. Now, if a Travel Taster says, "je veux t'offrir un verre," that means—

BLANCA: I would like to buy you a drink.

EEE JONES: And you say—

BLANCA: Je voudrais de l'eau minérale.

ROSA: No, je veux un martini.

EEE JONES: If a Travel Taster says, "Come ti chiami?" you say—

ROSA: Mi chiamo Lola.

EEE JONES: Now if a Travel Taster says, "Ist das dein Freund?" he means—

ROSA: Is that guy your boyfriend?

EEE JONES: And you say—

BLANCA: Das ist mein Bruder.

EEE JONES: Which means?

BLANCA: He's my brother.

EEE JONES: When a Travel Taster says, "¿De qué signo eres?" what does that mean?

BLANCA: What's your sign? So we say—

ROSA: Soy virgo, soy virgen.

EEE JONES: Good. So if he says, "I'm married," you say—

BLANCA: Oh, do you have an open relationship? (*Music out.*)

EEE JONES. Yes, and if he says, "Was magst du?" meaning—

BLANCA: What are you into?

EEE JONES: You'll answer—

ROSA: How do you want it? or, Wie willst du es? Right?

EEE JONES: Very good, ladies. I think you're ready. Can we have the lights up on our audience please?

> [*Video off. Audience lights up, general front, flashing colors from back. Music comes on—Herb Alpert and the Tijuana Brass. BLANCA and ROSA go to get their microphones and then go out into the audience.*]

BLANCA: Bienvenidos mis amigos, bienvenus mes amis, willkommen meine Freunde, ahora queremos haceles algunas preguntas, so let's see who's the most ready to participate in our new program. Dale Rosa! (*Lights stop flashing, colored lights stay on.*)

ROSA: (*Standing in one of the aisles*) Who knows how to say, "Bring me another margarita" in another language?

ROSA: (*If an audience member answers*) Let's have a round of applause for this gentleman.

> [Or . . .]

ROSA: (*If no one answers, ROSA goes to one audience member.*) Try saying: Traeme otra margarita, por favor.

BLANCA: That was great! Does anyone know what this means: No puedo comer fritangas?

BLANCA: (*If an audience member answers*) Let's have a round of applause for our friend!

> [Or . . .]

BLANCA: [*If no one answers*] It means: I can't eat fried food.

ROSA: [*Standing next to a male audience member*] OK, I have a feeling about you. Fuiste maestro de conga en tu vida anterior, ¿no es verdad? Know what that means?

ROSA: [*If the audience member answers*] Well, I can't wait to get up and dance with you, baby!

    [Or . . .]

ROSA: [*If he doesn't answer*] You may not know it but I can tell you were a bongo player in your past life.

BLANCA: [*To a woman, doing a moño*] ¿Quiéres mover tu cintura como una mulata buena? Do you know what I said?

BLANCA: [*If the woman answers yes; if not, continue saying the phrase to other women until one says yes*] Well, I think all of you have done marvelously! Rosa, could I see you onstage for a moment? (*BLANCA and ROSA go back onstage. They whisper to each other briefly.*)

ROSA: (*Pointing to those in the audience who spoke*) Would you please stand? Would you please stand? Would you, and you? Thank you! Congratulations, all of you have proven your multilingual potential. Please now join us onstage for an Afro-Frenetic extravaganza.

(Lights begin flashing! Four audience members go onstage. Lights stop flashing. Music fades out.)

BLANCA: (*Pointing to guy marked as CONGERO*) Ven aca Señor Congero. Música por favor.

("Afro-Frenetic" music plays. ROSA grabs the guy and sits him down, hangs mini bongos on him, a white cap, and a cigar. She begins to show him the rhythm, and he starts drumming. ROSA signals for the audience to applaud. Meanwhile, BLANCA puts the other three audience members on their marks. BLANCA and ROSA take their positions in front of dancers. They begin to step and clap to the music.)

BLANCA: Soy Blanca—

ROSA: Soy Rosa—

TOGETHER:—and we're going to teach you to rhumba!

BLANCA: Are you ready for an Afro-Frenetic dance extravaganza?

ROSA: Yeah, let's do it!

TOGETHER: Vamonos!

ROSA: This is the basic step you'll need. (*BLANCA and ROSA start moving their feet only.*) We'll add the shoulders later. (*BLANCA goes around behind the dancers and starts correcting their positions.*)

ROSA: Fantastico! OK, let's add the shoulders!

BLANCA: Everybody!

ROSA: OK! Try to keep control of your upper body!

BLANCA: Yeah, no window washing!

ROSA: (*Demonstrating*) And no funky chicken either!

BLANCA: Gimme a minute, I'm gonna check Maestro Bongo. (*BLANCA goes over to CONGERO.*) OK, OK. That was great. Now you're ready to learn how to moño.

ROSA and BLANCA: Moño! (*Quick music change to Eddie Palmieri. They start gyrating.*) Do it! (*Dancers do moños. ROSA and BLANCA motion for audience to applaud dancers.*)

ROSA: And now, it's time for the frenetic part. Let's go freestyle!

[*Music cranks up. Lights begin to flash, chaotic scene. BLANCA, ROSA, and dancers go bananas. After 30 seconds or so of unbridled dance, music fades out. Lights go back to general wash. ROSA and BLANCA pull out fans and take dancers over to table.*]

BLANCA: You guys deserve a rest. (*ROSA fans dancers.*)

ROSA: And a drink! (*ROSA serves drinks.*)

BLANCA: Well, that was just great. Now Travel Tasters, Rosa and I are just beginning to develop this part of our repertoire and would like to ask for your help. Would one of you be willing to volunteer for a test dialogue to get us going?

[*A TRAVEL TASTER volunteers. BLANCA, ROSA, and TRAVEL*

TASTER move to downstage center. She and ROSA set up two chairs. A downstage center spot comes up from the front.]

BLANCA: OK, you're going to have a conversation with me, and Rosa will show you what you need to say. Now, let's take our little game down here, so the two of us can get to know each other better. (*BLANCA and TRAVEL TASTERS sit downstage center.*)

ROSA: We've been working on our conversational abilities with our fantastic *Hot International* guide, which comes with translations for love and sex in seven different languages. Tonight though, we're going to work on our Spanish. Ready? Or should I say, listo? Now you've just come off the dance floor with Blanca, and you're going to ask her if she liked the dance. Say, "¿Te gustó el baile?"

TRAVEL TASTER: ¿Te gustó el baile?

BLANCA: ¡Sí! ¡Eres buenísimo!

ROSA: She's saying that you're really great—so you ask her if she wants to go to your place. Say, "¿Quiéres ir a mi casa?"

TRAVEL TASTER: ¿Quiéres ir a mi casa?

BLANCA: ¿Vamos a esperar a conocernos mejor, no?

ROSA: Oh, oh, she's says you have to get to know each other better. So make small talk. Ask her what her name is—"¿Cómo te llamas?"

TRAVEL TASTER: ¿Cómo te llamas?

BLANCA: Me llamo Lola. ¿Y tú de donde eres?

ROSA: She wants to know where you're from. Tell her you're Nigel from England. "Soy Nigel de Inglaterra."

TRAVEL TASTER: Soy Nigel de Inglaterra.

BLANCA: Ya es tarde. Debo ir a mi casa.

ROSA: Oh, oh, she wants to go home. You better offer to take her. Say, "¿Te llevo?"

TRAVEL TASTER: ¿Te llevo?

BLANCA: Bueno, vamonos.

ROSA: Lucky guy. She said yes! OK, now you're home together, and you've gotten through the initial formalities. You've got to tell her to get on the bed. Say, "¡Echate en la cama!"

TRAVEL TASTER: ¡Echate en la cama!

BLANCA: OK.

ROSA: That was easy! Now, get her on her knees. "Ponte en rodilla."

TRAVEL TASTER: ¡Ponte en rodilla!

BLANCA: ¡Ya voy! Esperate, ¡eres muy grande!

ROSA: She thinks you're a little big. You tell her to try another way. "Vamos a probar otra cosa."

TRAVEL TASTER: Vamos a probar otra cosa.

BLANCA: ¡Que rico es asi!

ROSA: Great—she likes it.

BLANCA: ¡Me estas volviendo loca!

ROSA: You're driving her wild. Now you can tell her to get some rope. "Busca la cuerda."

TRAVEL TASTER: Busca la cuerda.

BLANCA: ¡No me ates, por favor!

ROSA: Oops, she doesn't want to be tied up. Tell her she's gotta be punished. "¡Hay que castigarte!"

TRAVEL TASTER: ¡Hay que castigarte!

BLANCA: ¡Eres un animal!

ROSA: You better tell her to calm down. Say, "¡Cálmate!"

TRAVEL TASTER: ¡Cálmate!

BLANCA: ¡Vete al carrajo!

ROSA: She's very angry. Tell her you lost control and that you're sorry. "Perdóname, perdí el control."

TRAVEL TASTER: Perdóname, perdí el control.

BLANCA: ¡Me estas usando!

ROSA: She thinks you're using her. Say it isn't true, that you're looking for love. " ¡No es cierto, busco amor!"

TRAVEL TASTER: ¡No es cierto—busco amor!

BLANCA: Y yo estoy buscando apoyo financiero.

ROSA: And she's looking for financial support. Travel Taster, why don't you suggest that you could live together in your country? "Podemos ir a vivir en mi país."

TRAVEL TASTER: Podemos ir a vivir en mi país.

BLANCA: Vamos a conocernos un poquito mejor.

ROSA: She still wants to get to know you better. But I think it's going very well. The next morning, you offer to take her out for breakfast. Say, "¿Quieres ir a desayunar?"

TRAVEL TASTER: ¿Quieres ir a desayunar?

BLANCA: ¡Ay sí!

ROSA: She's game. Now, just to be sure, ask her for her name again. "¿Como era que te llamabas?"

TRAVEL TASTER: ¿Como era que te llamabas?

BLANCA: Me llamo Lola.

ROSA: Tell her you'll never forget her. "Nunca me olvidaré de tí."

TRAVEL TASTER: Nunca me olvidaré de tí.

BLANCA and ROSA: Gracias guapo.

ROSA: (*To the audience*) Aren't they fantastic? Let's give them a hand.

(*Applause. BLANCA and ROSA lead TRAVEL TASTERS back to audience. House lights remain up until audience participants are seated.*)

MALE VOICE: Un momento compañera. I saw you with that foreigner. (*Lights change to flashlight at BLANCA*) ¿Como te llamas?

BLANCA: (*Walking back into the spotlight*) Me llamo Lola.

MALE VOICE: Sure. Where do you live?

BLANCA: En Centro Habana.

MALE VOICE: Where do you work?

BLANCA: Wherever I can. (*She clasps her hands in prayer.*) Todos seguimos al Señor. You know, the man in charge here? (*She makes a gesture to show a beard on a chin.*) He's bending every which way to keep things going. And we're following him.

MALE VOICE: What did you say your name was again?

BLANCA: (*Taking off her wig*) Coco.

MALE VOICE: You know, that guy you talked to didn't seem like the kind of man who would take advantage of a third-world woman.

BLANCA: Not all the guys who come here are pigs you know.

MALE VOICE: Aren't you making light of a very serious situation?

BLANCA: What else can I do? Haven't you ever had sex with someone who had more than you?

MALE VOICE: More?

BLANCA: More. More power. More money. More food. More youth. More. (*Lights out. ROSA comes onstage with two microphones.*)

ROSA: Did I hear more? It's time for our grand finale. But first I would like to introduce my wonderful partner in crime, the divine, the marvelous, Miss Blanca de la Blanquita!

BLANCA: Thanks, Rosa. You know, when we first wrote the song we're about to present to you, we thought we would sing it ourselves. But since then, we've decided it would be much better to turn it into a karaoke number so we can all share in the fun! (*Cabaret-style spotlight comes up on ROSA and BLANCA, off to the side of back screen, where karaoke video is projected.*)

ROSA and BLANCA:

> Señor John is a Malibu swinger
> Who decided to take a trip south.
> His friends said he should first learn some Spanish
> But that John insists that he's learned enough.
> I learned from my be-lov-ed maid
> When I was a little muchacho
> And then from the gardener, the butler,
> The driver, the waiter and cook.

(*Yell:*) And John started singin':

Yo quiero Bananas and nuts
Tu quieres mi Concha-Biscocha
It's your pinche salchica I lust.

And with that he took off with his backpack.
Some days later he lands on our isle
And he stumbles right into our hangout,
A hip bar called the Crocodile's Smile.

There we two girls work hard for our money
Putting up with a whole lot of schmucks.
We dance and sing, and grind our hips nightly
To be sure we take home lots of bucks.

(*Yell:*) And he says:

May I squeeze tu melon y papaya?
You can pinch my panocha if you want.
How I relish the zest of your chile.
That chamoya 'n' chorizo is enough.

Our poor John, he has never been sober.
But on holiday he gets much worse.
Married ladies must tolerate spouses
But drunk gringos are the island girls' curse.

(*This last line is repeated over and over while curtained platform is wheeled off. Spot fades into general light that can catch the exit of the platform. Applause. Jorge Reyes music resumes. The video comes on.*)

EEE JONES: Ladies and gentlemen, I am sure that you will agree with me that this has been an absolutely exceptional evening. I have no doubt that each and every one of you will go home transformed. Thank you for choosing our first-class Travel Tasters' service, brought to you by the Institute for Southern Hemispheric Wholeness. For complete tour information, please pick up one of our brochures located in the lobby of the theatre. We also offer a frequent travelers' card that will allow you to accumulate a host of exotic and lustful benefits. Adios and bon appetit.

(*TRIPLE E smiles, as the video fades to black. All lights fade out with the video. Music fades out.*)

(*End of play*)

RADHA S. HEGDE

SONS AND M(OTHERS)
Framing the Maternal Body and the Politics of Reproduction in a South Indian Context

The female body has been regarded as a site for ideological appropriation both historically and cross culturally. Discursive definitions of femininity permeate the materiality of women's bodies and have serious repercussions on everyday experiences and the constitution of women's identities. Cultural assumptions about womanhood are reproduced through stipulations regarding the appropriate embodiment and practice of femininity. Both discursively and materially, women serve as instruments for the perpetuation of the patriarchal thematics of culture.[1] The female body becomes, as Susan Bordo notes, both a text of culture and a site of social control.[2] In India, the naturalization of femininity is epitomized in the discursive definitions of motherhood and the appropriate maternal body.

Motherhood has historically been exalted and eulogized in Indian texts and rituals, but it is only the "right" kind of mother who is socially validated in most parts of Indian society—the mother who can bear sons. Traditional images of motherhood and the ideal woman continue to shape and circumscribe women's roles in contemporary Indian society. Individual lives are constructed within ideological frameworks that devalue women and reify the maternal body as a receptacle to bear sons. With this widespread preference for sons in India, comes the dire neglect of daughters, multiple pregnancies, high mortality rates for women, sex-selective abortions, female infanticide, and a male-biased population ratio.[3]

Reproductive practices provide a space to examine the processes that make the female body serviceable to the circulation of patriarchal power. Therefore, as Faye Ginsburg and Rayna Rapp argue, meanings about reproduction have to be situated within the broader ideological context and content of a culture.[4] In India, the intense yearning for sons, the attendant religious rituals, and the increasing popularity of the fetal sex determination test are all elements of a discursive field that interpellates Indian women into positions of subordination.[5] Unpacking cultural constructions of motherhood and its emblematic status reveals the complex social machinery that is involved in disciplining the female body. The examination of reproductive politics as it is played out in everyday life leads to a complex interplay of gendered meaning, social hierarchies, economic mobility, property rights, and, above all, the personal experiences of women dealing with the appropriation of their bodies as reproductive instruments. How does this appropriation affect the lives of women, reproductive experiences, and the constitution of their identities?

This chapter examines the narratives of three women from a rural area in south India. The women spoke of how only certain types of reproductive experiences are privileged and receive social confirmation while others are stigmatized. In the shame and suffering of being the "unproductive" maternal body, we see how dominant discourses intersect with the everyday practices of women. Hegemonic visions of reproductive futures merge normative definitions of womanhood and a particular type of motherhood. Regimes of representation, as Stuart Hall writes, play a constitutive and not merely a reflexive, after-the-event role in the understanding of identities.[6] The fact that the birth of a son is celebrated while the birth of a daughter is an occasion for sorrow and the fact that a woman who has not conceived a son is seen as one who has failed her duty are expressions of a systematic rearticulation of patriarchal ideologies that ensure the dependence and vulnerability of women.

Reproduction is not just about the population problem, but it involves also the personal worlds of women, their bodies, interactions, and their locations within a nexus of power forces. The number of women who abort their female fetuses illegally is staggering.[7] Who are these women whose corporeality is denied even as the counting goes on? Each devalued reproductive experience entails a woman's story of struggle. Reproductive labor and motherhood provide a terrain to observe how individual subjectivity is constituted within the dialectic tension between representation and material practices. My objective here is to focus on the embodied presence of marginalized women in order to understand how individual struggles over reproductive meaning are constituted.

The location of women at the nexus of discursive fields suggests the complete overdetermination of individuality and evokes the common stereotypical representation of the poor rural Indian woman as a passive victim. In the course of my fieldwork in the south Indian state of Tamil Nadu, I saw women living and enduring a system that worked relentlessly to devalue them. As I traveled in this rural community, women spoke of the oppressive social structure and of their hopes and dreams of an alternative future. My presence as an ethnographer was perceived in multiple ways. The stories told to me were constructed around my location and conditioned by the politics of the research encounter. The narratives primarily provide a point of departure to think about the meaning of resistance in a context where oppression seems woven into the fabric of daily life.

A web of crisscrossing discourses fix the subject positions available to women in India and give meaning to women's place and conduct. To be part of a community is to be defined as a particular kind of subject and positioned within a grid of expectations.[8] Paying attention to the ways in which women affirm or resist these subject positions within the structures of inequality provides an opportunity to examine how individual identities are negotiated. It also allows us to observe and interpret the productive tension and balance between subalternity as discursive effect and the subaltern as social agent.[9]

What is the meaning of agency in light of a patriarchal ideology that works by discrediting/marginalizing experience that might question and/or redefine hegemonic norms? More specifically, how are gendered subjectivities formed in the contestation of reproductive meaning? How does gender politics permeate the "everydayness" of women's lives in this rural environment? Which leads me to the thrust of my ethnographic quest—how do women deal with the birth of a daughter?

THE STORY OF SONS AND DAUGHTERS

I traveled deep into the rural heartland of southern India to a cluster of small villages where "it" had taken place. In hushed tones, I was told of the practice of female infanticide by social workers who were helping me network with women in the area. The desire and longing for sons runs high among women in the Kallar community. The Kallars are historically a warrior community, the men renowned for their deeds of bravery and machismo.[10] Now engaged in low-paying agricultural occupations, the Kallars are a tightly knit group who maintain a very strong male agenda.

"Raising a daughter is like watering a neighbor's plant," a Kallar saying proclaims. My interviews revealed that the preference for sons runs deep for a variety of reasons which are very similar to the ones Barbara Miller found among groups in parts of north India.[11] Sons alone ensure the perpetuation of this warrior race. A son is considered the rightful heir to the family name and property.[12] Only a son can light the funeral pyre and perform for his parents the final death rites that assure them safe passage to the afterlife according to Hindu beliefs. A son also spells upward mobility in terms of his future earning and potential to bring in a substantial dowry from the bride he marries.

On the other side, the disfavor of daughters hinges on the question of dowry. Girls are a liability, and dowry requirements are progressively escalating. From birth, girls are seen as a drain on the family resources—the ear-piercing ceremony, the coming-of-age ceremony, the jewels to beautify and keep up with the neighbors, and finally the wedding. A daughter's wedding can financially ruin a Kallar family, since the dowry alone includes cash, land, household amenities, furniture, gold, and other things. Expenses continue past the wedding, from festive occasions when the son-in-law is honored and thanked for accepting the daughter, to the birth of the grandchild and other events.

I heard from both the women and the men in the community about how easy it was to set women free even as soon as they were born.[13] The methods were simple, they told me with candor. A little spoon of steaming hot curry down the infant's throat. A drop of milk from a poisonous plant that grows wild in the area, mixed with a little sugar so the baby does not spit it up. A few grains of rice, a pinch of snuff—this is usually done within the first week of birth. These responses were often accompanied by a bashful laughter. The infant is not named but is referred to as the Kuzhipapa or the baby of the burial pit.

Of Victims, Murderers, and Liberators

Female infanticide is viewed by the press and public opinion as a barbaric practice of a backward people. Infanticide has been documented in the northern state of Rajasthan and in the southern state of Tamil Nadu. There are no definitive statistics, because the family usually identifies it as a natural death. Besides, being a remote rural area, there is very little police intervention in this problem.[14] Only social workers from social service organizations maintain contact with pregnant women and identify high-risk cases in order to counsel them about the injustice of discriminating against girls.[15] The counselors and the counseling seem to be received indifferently and regarded as an interference from outsiders who could effect little change in the overall system. The words high risk have nothing to do with the health and progress of the pregnancy, but rather the women's potential to commit female infanticide. Those considered high risk are usually women who have had two or more daughters, who have only one son. It was clear that all women were considered "at risk" of committing infanticide.

The women I met individually and in groups attested to this. Having only one son was a problem—what if he were to die? No son at all was an even more serious problem. And so, in order to maintain their status and fulfill their maternal duty, women work their bodies for the birth of the male child. The thought engages them continually—in their conversations, their banter, their insults, and in short their whole existence. To cite Drucilla Cornell's comments from another context: "Her womb and body are no longer hers to imagine. They have been turned over to the imagination of others, and those imaginings are then allowed to reign over her body as law."[16]

The demonization of mothers who reject their female children makes good journalistic copy and is a recurrent theme both in the Indian and international media. The tone was set by the British, who, while in India, documented the practice of infanticide as expressions of heathenism and the ultimate degradation of parental love.[17] The mother in Indian tradition is the giver of life and is personified in popular and mythological representations as the ultimate fountain-head of love and self-effacement. The women in the Kallar community who could "dispose" of their children symbolize the complete antithesis.

I followed two social workers on their beat to catch up with high-risk pregnant women. There are informal networks of women in the village who help each other in their work and child care. The social workers identify a woman from this community network who is usually older, perhaps widowed, or who has survived abandonment by her husband. This woman is handpicked and trained to reach and counsel high-risk mothers. Often these mediators, as they are called, are ostracized as troublemakers, especially by the men. Their role clearly was to raise consciousness at a grassroots level. It was through the mediators that I met women in the village. I wanted to meet the women behind these representations of ruthless and demonic cruelty. I sat amidst groups of women and talked about the costs and pain of raising a daughter, about how they saw the ideological devaluation of women affecting their own lives, choices, and identities. I met with individual mothers who talked of their anxieties and fears. I now introduce three women, Jaya, Kumari, and Pandi, and their narratives.

All three women shared the experience of living in dire poverty and the stigma of being mothers who had only daughters and no sons. Their reproductive experiences seem to represent three versions of responses to the disciplining of the maternal body. The stories revolve around fear, anger, and above all the instinct to survive and live within the suffocating structures of patriarchy. I present these case studies, particularly Kumari's, in depth, in order to capture the sensory nuances of my interaction with these women.

Jaya. Under a large spreading banyan tree, a group of men were gambling in the afternoon sun. They looked at me suspiciously but did not talk to me directly. One, however, muttered even as he rearranged his cards: "Must be another journalist talking to the women about the death of girl babies." I walked to the home of Muniamma, an older woman, a widow with no children, and the head of the women's group that had been started with the help of local social workers.

We talked about the men in the community, marriage, the customs, the practice of dowry, which was becoming a quick route to affluence. Then Muniamma blurted: "*It* happened a few days back, right here." She stepped out for a few minutes and brought back with her a young woman, Jaya, about twenty years old who had a little two-year-old girl in her arms. Jaya stood almost motionless in her obvious sorrow. She looked at Muniamma and whispered, "You tell her my story."

It had happened in the early hours of the morning, just a few weeks ago. Muniamma, the women's group leader, recalled that Jaya had come to her screaming, "He did it, he did it."[18] Muniamma went to Jaya's house and not finding the week-old baby ran out to the paddy fields. Jaya's husband told the villagers that the child had started coughing, could not breathe, and had died. "But he killed it," said Muniamma emphatically, as she continued in a slow and leisurely manner. The night before, Jaya had apparently protested vehemently when her husband had suggested infanticide. But her pleading had no effect. In a very wise and guileless manner, Muniamma added, "Now whether this girl helped him kill the child, I don't know. But she is suffering and I know that."

Jaya now clutched her first daughter tightly and looked away in shame. She tried to talk to me but shook her head and was unable to. Her silence was telling, her despair real, her shame visible.

Taking her role as mediator, Muniamma interjected in a serious tone: "Now, Jaya, will you get pregnant again, or what?" Jaya looked up and nodded almost to say, "I will give him his male child." I saw her twist the ends of her sari in her hand almost to the point of tearing it. She seemed the archetypal Foucaldian docile body, disempowered, shame ridden, filled with guilt, standing in what seemed to me to be a complete condemnation of self.

There was little she told me orally. But the encounter with Jaya lasted over an hour filled with silences. I wondered if this constituted an interview. Toward the end Jaya was anxious for me to meet her daughter: "This is my daughter," she said softly. Then again her voice faded off as she whispered to no one in particular: "She saw the baby soon after it was born." Speech and silence seemed to have lost their distinction and meaning in Jaya's life.

Kumari. I met Kumari on the last day of my visit to this area. It was an unexpected, serendipitous meeting. The social worker who was with me had an errand to run. Kumari, who had just given birth to a daughter a few days earlier, had angrily sent back a gift for the baby from the social service agency. The social worker wanted to see if Kumari would reconsider accepting the gift. So we went to a one-room tenement on the outskirts of a village surrounded by green rice fields. Seated on a bench outside the home was Kumari's husband, smoking a cigarette and relaxing. Inside was Kumari with her five-day-old daughter asleep in a makeshift cradle made out of a sari hanging from the ceiling.

The social worker introduced me as a writer who had come from out of town and was accompanying her. Kumari paid no heed to the introductions and shouted at us: "What do you think? I am going to raise this child on your stupid ten rupees gift of baby powder and wash clothes? Hey, look here. I have given birth to five girls, this is my third living daughter. I am a totally useless, uneducated woman, but I am angry. I have just given birth to this thing, but I will produce a son, and I will keep on having babies till I get my son."

Kumari motioned me to sit by her. All the time she was alternately muttering or shouting. Two other women, hearing the noise, peered through the door. Her husband continued to smoke and gaze into the distance. I asked her if her mother had come to help her with the birth of her daughter as is the customary practice. Kumari snapped: "That bitch, my mother, stopped me from killing this girl, so I threw my mother out. Get out, go, I told her and chased her out of my house. What shall I do? Will you keep five daughters?"

Kumari could not control her outburst: "If I kill, then they say she has no conscience, she's not a mother. If I don't, they ridicule me that I have all girls, good for nothing girls. You want to put me in jail, go ahead. But no, you tell me, you will give me a present for ten rupees. Or you tell me that you will give me a goat to milk. What do you people take me for?"[19] And then focusing on her baby: "Because of this girl, I am humiliated every day. And when she gets married, they'll taunt and harass her because she has no brothers."

Kumari turned to me and said, "Listen, I don't care a damn about my health, I will have another and another till I have a son. I will kill them all, till I get a son." As she spoke, Kumari, who was seated on her bed, pushed the makeshift cradle with her legs to calm the crying infant. Instinctively, I held the cradle as it violently rocked from side to side. Kumari started laughing. "What, you are afraid I'll kill it with my legs, what are you thinking, Amma?"[20]

Then, in an unexpected move, she imitated my accent and said, "You will hold your child like this . . . " She cradled her hands near her chest and rocked the imaginary baby gently. "But I am an uneducated woman and I do this." With that she pushed the cradle with a violent kick. I restrained myself from holding it again. "A woman has no guarantee." Kumari meant that women's lives come with no promise of quality. Not expecting an English word, I was taken aback by her usage of the word *guarantee*. It was an unexpected intrusion of a global term that resonated with market implications in a world so steeped in poverty. Once again, the commodity in question, perceived as so flawed that it came without a warranty, was the female body.

The social worker rose and reprimanded Kumari for being so rough with a newborn child. After all, it was not the child's fault. Would she consider giving up the child for adoption? "No way, not as long as I live." Her child was not to suffer the indignity of being an orphan put up for adoption. At this time I asked Kumari what happened to her other children. She had said that she had given birth to five and now she had but three daughters. I was wondering why and how she had decided to raise her daughters. Kumari burst into laughter: "I know what Amma wants to know." Again laughter. "She wants to know *how* and *what* I will use to kill my child. Where did you do it, what sleeping pills did you use?" She sighed, rocked her child some more, and after a few minutes, she said, "What do you know of my suffering?" Within seconds, she regained her sarcastic vehemence and talked about the killing: "It is not difficult at all. Five minutes. That is all it takes."

Kumari was full of startling surprises as she blended her emotions and rage with jokes about killing methods: "What, Amma?" She pointed to her stomach, "Does God put it there? No, no, no, we do. What do you think? Let me see how smart you are." She looked at the social worker and asked where I was from: "Ceemay, right?"[21] It was her guess that I came from overseas.[22] She snapped at me: "So, Amma, how many children do you have?" I replied that I had one. "Oh," she exclaimed sarcastically. "Then what did you do? Did he or you?" Then as if I were not even present, Kumari added: "She probably got operated after one. See her handbag. I know her type." (My pocketbook from the United States assumed emblematic proportions, standing in for elitism and liberation in Kumari's mind.)

I don't know what type she thought I was. I also don't know whether she had in fact killed her other daughters. The social worker (and I) had a fairly good guess that she had. Kumari, by now, had had enough of our visit. "That's it. I'll see you later," she said. "I have a murder to take care of," she quipped again in her own macabre style.

Kumari's husband interjected for the first time from outside the room, "She is a nut. There is no changing her." His words captured his total disregard and rejection of her feelings and anxieties. In his eyes, Kumari was nothing more than a ranting, unproductive maternal body. Kumari's husband was not interested in talking about 'women's things' with me. The subject of children, of girls versus boys, was not a topic he cared to talk about, particularly with another woman!

Kumari, however, was taking on the system. Her body would be overworked and will beget the right product. Her determination was fierce. She saw herself not as a criminal plotting a murder but rather as a liberator. The daughters were not to suffer as she had. If they had to die, that has to be borne with resignation. Motherhood became for Kumari a matter of defiance and laborious endurance.

Pandi

"A barren wife may be superseded in the eighth year, she whose children (all) die in the tenth, she who bears only daughters in the eleventh but she who is quarrelsome without delay."
—Ancient laws of Manu IX, 81[23]

I met Pandi in an adoption center run by the social service agency that was helping me. She had come to give up her sixth daughter, three months old, for adoption. Her story was bitter but brief—she was harassed by her mother-in-law, her husband, and other members of her husband's family. Every day, Pandi woke up to "Who will take care of you in your old age?" "Who will light your husband's pyre?" Or on worse days, her mother-in-law would get abusive: "I give you a prince and you bear girls for outsiders to marry. Who are you producing these girls for?"

To Pandi, the suffering and humiliation was unbearable. In an unthinkable turn of events, she was resorting to the ultimate humiliation of giving up her child. To her, this was proclaiming to the world that she was incapable of taking care of her own child. But poverty and distress prohibited her from keeping the child. Her husband was already preparing to divorce Pandi and remarry. To him, Pandi's body and its labor had no value. He was in fact anxious that the child be given up for adoption. The biological fact that it is the male who determines the sex of the child was completely ignored. It is common and easy for Kallar men to leave their wives under such conditions. There is a saying that a Kallar husband can divorce his wife with a settlement of a single blade of grass.

With her six daughters, Pandi was wrecked emotionally. She had resisted the idea of infanticide every time it was broached by her mother-in-law. As the baby was taken away, Pandi murmured, "Never, never be born a woman."

She went about planning how to get a loan to set up a small produce stand where she can fend for herself and her (now) five daughters. She was worried about what this would mean to her daughters' future. Pandi was nervous but determined to make it on her own. Pandi was on her way to a temple to pray for divine intervention. For the first time, it was not for a male child, but for strength to make it by herself. She had decided to take control.

THE LABOR OF TRANSFORMATION

> For if the subject is constituted in power, that power does not cease at the moment the subject is constituted, for that subject is never fully constituted, but is subjected and produced time and again.
>
> —Judith Butler[24]

The traumatic struggles over reproduction and motherhood reveal the complex ways in which the discursive structures of gender inequality permeate the material realities of everyday practices. The lives of the women appear to be enveloped within the interpellative force of the ideology. As they struggle with the material conditions of being stigmatized for not bearing sons, women contest and at the same time reproduce the ideological representation. How do we explain both the support and resistance of patriarchy that is so prevalent in their responses? Or, to draw on Dorothy Smith's argument, how do women survive the exclusions and erasure imposed by the ideological apparatus that maintains the relations of ruling?[25]

Resistance and oppositional practices play a very important role in the understanding of marginalized experiences. There has been considerable research attention paid to the role of resistance and the constitution of the subaltern subjectivity.[26] For feminist scholars, the motivation to focus on resistance and agency has been to restore a voice to the oppressed female subject who has stereotypically been portrayed as the passive victim of false consciousness. To postcolonial feminists, the attention on oppositional agency allows a recuperation of third-world women from what Chandra Mohanty calls "the debilitating generality of their 'object' status."[27] According to Donna Haraway, the only way to avoid gross error and false knowledge is to come to terms with the agency of the "objects" studied.[28] A central challenge for feminist inquiry has been to locate the female subject through discourses of exclusion and account for the political processes that undercut women's agency.

It is the liberatory impulse that drives feminist scholars to present the female subject as an actor who has the capacity to challenge and refuse the dominant ideology. This has led to the romanticization of resistance, the reconfiguring of the subaltern as a self-constituting subject of liberal humanism and/or the belief that subject can move freely to a noninterpellative space.[29] A recurring theme in this recent research on resistance has been to identify unconventional forms of opposition as a way of theorizing subaltern agency. This attention on everyday forms of resistance is based on the assumption, following Michel Foucault, that change does not happen by a transformation of the whole system but rather through localized and strategic tactics of resistance.[30]

Everyday forms of resistance are in fact a continuous struggle and might not involve any direct symbolic confrontation with authority. It is not just about reading resistance but also about uncovering the complex circuitry of domination. Domination and resistance are so entangled that it becomes difficult to analyze one without analyzing the other.[31] In the case of the Kallar women, examining the simultaneity of resistance and compliance throws light on how women manage the pervasive power of dominant representations. The consumption of the dominant discourse not only reproduces it but also contributes to its critique and thereby to the slow deflection of power.[32] When the women talk about the birth of daughters, there is a tone of fatalistic resignation. As they retort that they will not see change in their lifetime, there is despair and a sense of pragmatic acceptance of the risks involved in defiance. There is at the same time a clear recognition of the suffocating oppression of patriarchy. It was revealing that the women wanted to share stories of the oppression that they could barely escape except through death via infanticide. Resignation to forces that seem inevitable is not the same as according it legitimacy.[33]

In the case of the Kallar women, one sees how various types of oppression—economic, class, and gender—weave together and coalesce to create the crises of subordination. The female subaltern subject is clearly not the free, normative (male) actor of Western liberalism.[34] Theirs is not a life of free autonomy and their structural location significantly limits their potential for action. The concept of agent conceptualized in autonomous, voluntaristic terms just does not apply to the lives of women whose realities are shaped and constrained by organizing ideological structures.[35] The acquiescence to the gender ideology is not about passive compliance but rather evidence of the fact that agency, as Judith Butler writes, "is always and only a political prerogative."[36] In the prosaic dailiness of their experience, women wrestle with the oppressive politics of gender relations.

The women in this study provide a classic example of the problematic dichotomy of representing women as either victims or agents. Theoretically, this binary vision runs counter to feminist goals of doing emancipatory research. Arguing the point, Rajeswari Sunder Rajan writes that if "'victim' and 'agent' are adopted as exclusive and excluding labels for the female subject, and if, further, victimhood is equated with helplessness and agency with self-sufficiency, all feminist politics will be rendered either inauthentic or unnecessary."[37] This translates into methodological questions of whether to focus exclusively on individual agency or structure. Either choice leads to an impasse—a focus on structure reduces women to being victims and a focus on agency often winds up blaming women for conditions over which they have little control.[38]

Pandi's speaking out her misery and opting out of it, Jaya's protest through silence about the death of her infant, and Kumari's defiant stance as the anti-mother are individual struggles to assert a sense of identity and personal space. Muniamma, the women's group leader, stood out as a symbol of female oppositional power who spoke out vociferously about the injustice of the social system. As women gathered to talk to one another about the injustices, an alternative space is created, a space that is exclusively theirs, although momentarily. The discussion of patriarchy is initiated at the level of their personal lives even as they suffer its oppression. In the routines of every day, women confront the tensions and contradictions of living between resistance and submission, of hegemonic control and autonomy.

The act of infanticide itself is seen by the public and the popular press as either a premeditated barbaric crime or as an act of ignorance or false consciousness. But returning to Kumari, to her, the act of murder was a demonstration of strength and by her logic a way to fracture the oppressive system of patriarchy.

> What do you think this girl will face? She can't run around with a pair of shorts like a boy can, she has to cover herself. I have to protect her. I have to manufacture her dowry from God knows where. And when she dies, her brother needs to pour the water before her funeral pyre is lit. And she does not have a brother. She has nothing but suffering ahead of her. With these Kallar men, it's not going to change. So tell me, am I mad or what is wrong with my killing this child?

While Kumari ranted, raved, and blamed others for stopping her from infanticide, the poignant fact was that she had not killed the infant. She was the anti-mother, the mythological Kali, who could create and destroy, care, nurture, and devastate at the same time.[39]

There were two other mothers I met who insisted that their two- and three-day-old infant daughters had developed strange symptoms like difficulty in breathing and epileptic fits. I was told that the babies had died natural deaths. I was told by the social workers that this was not true and they were indeed cases of infanticide. The women are routinely accused of lying and plotting with each other and their menfolk in killing the children. On one level, we have women carrying out the hegemonic rituals of female oppression, participating in the socially sanctioned violence against women, infants in this case. But a closer examination of individual lives belies this easy image of the ruthless murderer. There is a poignant and wrenching struggle of despair and turmoil over the tyranny that surrounds them.

Douglas Haynes and Gyan Prakash argue that the notion of resistance should take into account the ways in which "the subjectivity of the dominated is constrained, modified and conditioned by power relations."[40] What we see here is how disciplinary micropractices constitute subjectivity through negation, through violent erasure and silences. Their bodies objectified as social reproductive machines, the women labor and hope for transformation. Their resilience is reflected in the very tenacity with which they endure the harshness of everyday life.

TELLING THE OTHER STORY

The experience of talking to Kallar women unleashed questions about my role as a researcher and the meaning of the enterprise that I was engaged in. Or, following Stuart Hall, what was my position of enunciation?[41] How was I to present the outpour of self that I had heard? What were my blind spots? For, after all, as Donna Haraway points out, our struggles with what will count as rational accounts of the world are in fact struggles over how to see.[42]

Feminist scholars have problematized the issue of location to challenge the implicit hierarchy in the social scientific research transaction, and many have been vocal about the inherent inequalities embedded in the production of academic research on third-world women.[43] Much as I tried to establish common ground, it was obvious that our positions were separated by vast spaces. My purse, my accent, my coming from Ceemay (the land beyond our borders where the colonizers came from) were setting me apart, not to mention my pad, my pen, and my cautious use of the tape recorder. There is a heavy traffic of journalists from the West with their cameras and equipment to capture the natives murdering their babies. The Kallars were weary of spectators and the curiosity about their infant killing notoriety. In their eyes, perhaps, there was no difference between my role and the journalists. What was I doing—celebrating, sensationalizing, or mystifying female infanticide? I was continually reminded that, after all, it is murder. One young girl in the village asked me, "How come you don't have big, big cameras?" I was being constructed in multiple ways: the one who speaks differently; the one who carried a strange purse; and of course, my reproductive choices were a source of wonder. I was the other, and my coordinates were completely unknown to them.

I elaborate on this process and of my own experience as it was very much a part of my understanding of these women. These stories were experiential capital and I was very aware that my retelling of these stories would wind up eventually in the North American academic trail. How do I represent oppression and subordination without essentializing? How do readers/audiences make sense of the stories of suffering in faraway places? If we begin with the assumption that research is informed by our historical coordinates, then we need to problematize representation as both a political and an epistemological problem.[44]

Everyday experiences of women in rural communities border on some aspect of reproduction or reproductive labor whether it be the desire or inability to conceive, birthing, or child care. A whole social network of action develops around the social circumstances of reproduction. Yet the representation of lived experience and a feminist engagement with issues of reproduction in third world contexts are only recent research developments.[45] When representing oppression, it is quite easy to paint images of gloom and misery which deny women the rightful recognition of their presence and potential for action. As Chandra Mohanty writes, monolithic representations of third-world women barely capture the diverse realities of women's lives constituted within multiple hierarchies of oppression.[46] It certainly does not read experiences of Kallar motherhood and female infanticide in terms of agency, resistance and identity narratives.

In reading speech and silence in the subaltern experience, Rajeswari Sunder Rajan states, "Our caution must be neither to pronounce definitionally that 'the subaltern cannot speak' nor to romanticize silence as the subaltern's refusal to speak."[47] The endeavor to make voices of oppression heard may seem a gratuitous venture of new "Orientalists" vindicating the subalterns, as Rey Chow reminds us.[48] Finding the appropriate intellectual space and location to represent the politics of exclusion in women's lives is a challenge for a feminist scholar. The three episodes presented are a few bracketed moments from my many meetings with Jaya, Kumari, and Pandi. These moments encapsulated how their everyday interactions and reality collapse into the ideologically driven definition of the maternal body.

To theorize from the perspective of those on the margins allows feminist scholarship to examine not only the processes by which women are subjugated but also their potential, strength, and resilience for action. In a very fundamental way, the lives of Jaya, Pandi, and Kumari reveal the complex configurations of power that constitute the subject. Motherhood, in their experience, symbolizes the ultimate co-optation of agency.

NOTES

I wish to thank my colleagues at Rutgers University for the vibrant exchange of ideas which helped shape this essay during fellowships held at the Institute for Research on Women and also at the Center for Critical Analysis of Contemporary Culture, Rutgers University. Above all, I wish to express my gratitude to the women in India who shared difficult experiences with me.

1. For further discussion on these themes, see Sandra Lee Bartky, *Femininity and Domination: Studies in Phenomenology of Oppression* (London: Routledge, 1990); Judith Butler, "Performative Acts and Gender Constitution: An Essay in Phenomenology and Feminist Theory," in *Writing the Body: Feminist Embodiment and Feminist Theory*, ed. Katie Conboy, Nadia Medina, and Sarah Stanbury (New York: Columbia University Press, 1997), 401; Elizabeth Grosz, *Volatile Bodies: Towards a Corporeal Feminism* (Bloomington: Indiana University Press, 1994); Alison Jaggar and Susan Bordo, eds., *Gender/Body/Knowledge: Feminist Reconstruction of Being and Knowing* (New Brunswick, N.J.: Rutgers University Press, 1989); Lois McNay, *Foucault and Feminism* (Boston: Northeastern University Press, 1992).

2. Susan R. Bordo, "The Body and the Reproduction of Femininity: A Feminist Appropriation of Foucault," in Jaggar and Bordo, *Gender/Body/Knowledge*, 13.

3. Almost throughout the twentieth century there has been a continuing decline in the number of women accounting for the male-biased population ratio of India. The high male/female ratio is concentrated in the northern and western states. For an analysis of demographic patterns and female mortality, see Kirstey McNay, "Fertility and Frailty: Demographic Change, Health and Status of Indian Women," *Economic and Political Weekly,* October 28, 1995, WS81–WS86. The 1991 Census of India recorded 32 million more men than women in India, about an 8 percent male advantage; see Leela Visaria and Pravin Visaria, "India's Population in Transition," *Population Bulletin* 50:3 (1995): 2–50. For further discussion on this subject, see Barbara Miller, *The Endangered Sex* (Ithaca, N.Y.: Cornell University Press, 1981); Vibhuti Patel, "Sex Determination and Sex-Preselection Tests in India: Modern Techniques for Femicide," *Bulletin for Concerned Asian Scholars* 2:1 (1989): 2–10; Madhu Kishwar, "The Continuing Deficit of Women in India and the Impact of Amniocentesis," in *Man-made Women*, ed. Gena Corea et al. (Bloomington: Indiana University Press, 1987).

4. Faye D. Ginsburg and Rayna Rapp, eds., *Conceiving the New World Order* (Berkeley and Los Angeles: University of California Press, 1995).

5. Rural women in India resort to ultrasound procedures to ascertain the sex of the fetus. The test costs about Rs.500 (around $12). Women mainly use the results of the test to decide on sex-selective abortions. Feminists in India have been very vocal in protesting the use of this test for discriminatory practices; for example, see Rashmi Luthra, "Toward a Reconceptualization of Choice: Challenges by Women at the Margins," *Feminist Issues* (spring 1993): 41–54; and Viola Roggencamp, "Abortion of a Special Kind: Male Sex Selection in India," in *Test-Tube Women*, ed. Rita Arditti, Renata Duvelli Klein, and Shelley Minden (London: Pandora Press, 1984), 266.

6. Stuart Hall, "New Ethnicities," in *Race, Culture, Difference*, ed. J. Donald and A. Rattansi (London: Sage), 252.

7. There is a great deal of anecdotal evidence about the number of women in India seeking abortions based on discovering a female fetus. Popular magazines and activist groups project numbers; see Manju Parikh, "Sex-Selective Abortions in India: Parental Choice or Sexist Discrimination," *Feminist Issues* 10:2 (1990): 19–32. However, according to Sripati Chandrasekhar: "Adequate statistics on the incidence of such abortions based on sex discrimination are understandably not available either with the government or any private agency, and perhaps in the nature of things reliable figures may not be available at all." See Sripati Chandrasekhar, *India's Abortion Experience* (Denton: University of North Texas Press, 1994), 127.

8. For a discussion on the themes of identity, place, and resistance, see Akhil Gupta and James Ferguson, eds., *Culture, Power, Place: Explorations in Critical Anthropology* (Durham, N.C.: Duke University Press).

9. For further discussion on these issues, see Ranajit Guha and Gayatri Spivak, eds., *Selected Subaltern Studies* (New York: Oxford University Press, 1988); Rosalind O'Hanlon, "Recovering the Subject: Subaltern Studies and Histories of Resistance in Colonial South Asia," *Modern Asia Studies* 22:1 (1988): 189–224; Lisa Rofel, "Rethinking Modernity: Space, and Factory Discipline in China," in Gupta and Ferguson, *Culture, Power, Place*, 155.

10. S. Krishnaswamy, "Female Infanticide in India," in *Women in Indian Society*, ed. Rehana Ghadially (New Delhi: Sage, 1988), 186; Sabu George, Rajaratnam Abel, and Barbara Miller, "Female Infanticide in Rural South India," *Economic and Political Weekly*, May 30, 1992, 1153–1156.

11. Barbara Miller, *The Endangered Sex* (Ithaca, N.Y.: Cornell University Press, 1981).

12. One of the frequently cited reasons for sons being the preferred heirs is that daughters pass on their inheritance to their husbands and therefore deplete the material resources of their natal family.

13. A social worker told me that Kallar women don't find out fetal sex in advance because of the cost and unavailability of the procedure in the deep rural areas where they live.

14. For more details on this, see R. Venkatachalam and Viji Srinivasan, *Female Infanticide* (New Delhi: Har-Anand Publications, 1993); Radha S. Hegde, "Marking Bodies, Reproducing Violence: A Feminist Reading of Female Infanticide in South India," *Violence against Women* 5:5 (1999): 507–524.

15. The social service organizations in the area are mainly NGOs which are funded by the private sector and international agencies, with minimal assistance from the Indian government.

16. Drucilla Cornell, *Imaginary Domain: Abortion, Pornography and Sexual Harassment* (London: Routledge, 1995), 47.

17. The media has been responsible for recent attention paid to infanticide in this particular area. *India Today* (1986) did a piece on infanticide which has since been followed by many other Indian magazines and journals. See S. H. Venkatramani, "Born to Die," *India Today*, June 15, 1986, 10–17. The most extensive international coverage was done by the British Broadcasting Corporation in a 1993 television documentary entitled "Let Her Die."

   The colonial documentation of female infanticide is typically a representation of native barbarism which needed Western intervention; see John Cave Browne, *Indian Infanticide* (London: W. H. Allen, 1857).

18. Facts often blurred as women recalled these gruesome events. On another occasion during my fieldwork, Muniamma told me the neighbors and not Jaya had come running to her on that fateful night.

19. Kumari was referring to a scheme where women in financial hardship are given a goat or poultry to start making some money independently. Kumari was highly contemptuous of the meagerness of this incentive scheme.

20. Amma means mother in Tamil, the language of the southern state of Tamil Nadu. It is also a word of respect used for women to mark their age and/or status.

21. Ceemay in Tamil vernacular refers to England. The word comes from the Sanskrit word for border and clearly gained currency in colonial India.

22. I introduced myself to my respondents as a writer/researcher working on women's issues. For the most part, the women were eager to talk to me and were quite disinterested in knowing my academic background. The majority of these women had very little or no reading or writing skills.

23. George Buhler, trans., *The Laws of Manu* (New Delhi: Banarasidas, 1964).

24. Judith Butler, "Contingent Foundations: Feminism and the Question of Postmodernism," in *Feminists Theorize the Political*, ed. Judith Butler and Joan Scott (London: Routledge, 1992), 13.

25. Dorothy Smith, *The Everyday World as Problematic: A Feminist Sociology* (Boston: Northeastern University Press, 1987), 40.

26. There has been recent interest in understanding subaltern identities, resistance, and contestation of authority among feminist and postcolonial scholars and more generally in the field of cultural studies. For example, see Aihwa Ong, *Spirits of Resistance and Capitalist Discipline: Factory Women in Malaysia* (Albany: State University of New York, 1988); Sherry B. Ortner, "Resistance and the Problem of Ethnographic Refusal," *Comparative Studies in Society and History* 2 (1995): 173–193; Rajeswari Sunder Rajan, *Real and Imagined Women: Gender, Culture and Postcolonialism* (London: Routledge,

1992); James Scott, *Domination and the Arts of Resistance: Hidden Transcripts* (New Haven, Conn.: Yale University Press, 1990).

27. Chandra Mohanty, "Under Western Eyes: Feminist Scholarship and Colonial Discourse," in *Third World Women and the Politics of Feminism,* ed. Chandra Mohanty, Ann Russo, and Lourdes Torres (Bloomington: Indiana University Press, 1991), 71.

28. Donna Haraway, "Situated Knowledge: The Science Question in Feminism and Privilege," *Feminist Studies* 14:3 (1988): 574–599.

29. For a discussion of these themes, see Lila Abu-Lughod, "The Romance of Resistance: Tracing Transformations of Power through Bedouin Women," *American Ethnologist* 17:1 (1990): 41–55; Rosalind O'Hanlon, "Recovering the Subject: Subaltern Studies of Resistance in Colonial South Asia," *Modern Asian Studies* 22:1 (1988): 189–224; Paul Smith, *Discerning the Subject* (Minneapolis: University of Minnesota Press, 1988).

30. Michel Foucault, *Power/Knowledge: Selected Interviews and Other Writings,* trans. Colin Gordon (New York: Pantheon Books, 1980).

31. Douglas Haynes and Gyan Prakash, *Contesting Power: Resistance and Everyday Social Relations in South Asia* (Berkeley and Los Angeles: University of California Press, 1991). Also see James Scott, *Weapons of the Weak: Everyday Forms of Peasant Resistance* (New Haven, Conn.: Yale University Press, 1985).

32. For a discussion of the subversive patterns of consumption, see Michel de Certeau, *The Practices of Everyday Life,* trans. Steven Rendall (Berkeley and Los Angeles: University of California Press, 1984).

33. See James Scott, *Weapons of the Weak.*

34. See Zakhia Pathak and Rajeswari Sunder Rajan, "Shahbano," in *Feminists Theorize the Political,* ed. Judith Butler and Joan Scott (London: Routledge, 1992) for a compelling discussion of subaltern subjectivities.

35. See also Radha S. Hegde, "Narratives of Silence: Rethinking Gender, Agency and Power from the Communication Experiences of Battered Women in South India," *Communication Studies* 47:4 (1996): 303–317.

36. Butler, "Contingent Foundations: Feminism and the Question of Postmodernism."

37. Sunder Rajan, *Real and Imagined Women.*

38. Kathy Davis and Sue Fisher, "Power and the Female Subject," in *Negotiating at the Margins: The Gendered Discourse of Power and Resistance,* ed. Sue Fisher and Kathy Davis (New Brunswick, N.J.: Rutgers University Press, 1993), 3.

39. Kali is the name of the Hindu goddess who wields complete control of her sexuality. She is represented as a wild and fearful mother who creates and annihilates at the same time. See David Kinsley, *Hindu Goddesses* (Berkeley and Los Angeles: University of California Press, 1988).

40. Haynes and Prakash, *Contesting Power.*

41. Stuart Hall, "Cultural Identity and Diaspora," in *Identity, Community, Culture,* ed. Jonathan Rutherford (London: Lawrence and Wishart, 1990).

42. Haraway, "Situated Knowledge: The Science Question Feminism and Privilege."

43. See Annie Opie, "Qualitative Appropriation of the 'Other' and Empowerment," *Feminist Review* 40 (1992): 52–69; Angela McRobbie, "The Politics of Feminist Research: Between Talk, Text, and Action," *Feminist Review* 12 (1982): 46–57; Bette J. Kaufman, "Feminist Facts: Interview Strategies and Political Subjects in Ethnography," *Communication Theory* 2:3 (1992): 187–206; Gayatri Spivak, "Can the Subaltern Speak?" in *Marxism and the Interpretation of Cultures,* ed. Carey Nelson and Lawrence Grossberg (Urbana: University of Illinois Press, 1988), 271; Lata Mani, "Multiple Mediation: Feminist Scholarship in the Age of Multinational Reception," *Inscriptions* 5 (1989): 49–73; Mary John, *Discrepant Dislocations: Feminist Theory and Postcolonial Histories* (Berkeley and Los Angeles: University of California Press, 1996); Daphne Patai, "U.S. Academics and Third World Women: Is Ethical Research Possible?" in *Women's Words: The Feminist Practice of Oral History,* ed. Sherna Burger Gluck and Daphne Patai (London: Routledge, 1991), 137.

44. Keya Ganguly, "Accounting for Others: Feminism and Representation," in *Women Making Meaning,* ed. Lana Rakow (London: Routledge, 1992); Gayatri Spivak, *In Other Worlds* (London: Routledge, 1988).

45. See M. Jacqui Alexander and Chandra Talpade Mohanty, *Feminist Genealogies, Colonial Legacies, Democratic Futures* (London: Routledge, 1997); Marianne Marchand and Jane Parpart, *Feminism, Postmodernism, Development* (London: Routledge, 1995).

46. Mohanty, "Cartographies of Struggle: Third World Women and the Politics of Feminism," in Mohanty et al., *Third World Women and the Politics of Feminism*.
47. Sunder Rajan, *Real and Imagined Women*.
48. Rey Chow, *Writing Diaspora: Tactics of Intervention in Contemporary Cultural Studies* (Bloomington: Indiana University Press, 1993).

REFERENCES

Abu-Lughod, L. "The Romance of Resistance: Tracing Transformations of Power through Bedouin Women." *American Ethnologist* 17:1 (1990): 41–55.
Alexander, M. J., and C. T. Mohanty, eds. *Feminist Genealogies, Colonial Legacies, Democratic Futures*. London: Routledge, 1997.
Bordo, S. R. "The Body and the Reproduction of Femininity: A Feminist Appropriation of Foucault." In *Gender/Body/Knowledge: Feminist Reconstructions of Being and Knowing*, edited by A. M. Jaggar and S. R. Bordo, 3–33. New Brunswick, N.J.: Rutgers University Press, 1989.
Browne, J. C. *Indian Infanticide: Its Origins, Progress and Suppression*. London: W. H. Allen, 1857.
Buhler, G., trans. *The Laws of Manu*. New Delhi: Banarasidas, 1964.
Butler, J. "Contingent Foundations: Feminism and the Question of Postmodernism." In *Feminists Theorize the Political*, edited by J. Butler and J. Scott, 3–21. London: Routledge, 1992.
———. "Performative Acts and Gender Constitution: An Essay in Phenomenology and Feminist Theory." In *Writing on the Body: Feminist Embodiment and Feminist Theory*, edited by K. Conboy et al., 401–417. New York: Columbia University Press, 1997.
Chandrasekhar, S. *India's Abortion Experience*. Denton: University of North Texas Press, 1994.
Chow, R. *Writing Diaspora: Tactics of Intervention in Contemporary Cultural Studies*. Bloomington: Indiana University Press, 1993.
Cornell, D. *Imaginary Domain: Abortion, Pornography and Sexual Harassment*. London: Routledge, 1995.
Davis, K., and S. Fisher. "Power and the Female Subject." In *Negotiating at the Margins: The Gendered Discourse of Power and Resistance*, edited by S. Fisher and K. Davis, 3–20. New Brunswick, N.J.: Rutgers University Press, 1993.
De Certeau, M. *The Practices of Everyday Life*. Translated by S. Rendall. Berkeley and Los Angeles: University of California Press, 1984.
Foucault, M. *Power/Knowledge: Selected Interviews and Other Writings*. Translated by C. Gordon. New York: Pantheon Books, 1980.
Ganguly, K. "Accounting for Others: Feminism and Representation." In *Women Making Meaning: Feminist Directions in Communication*, edited by L. Rakow, 60–79. London: Routledge, 1992.
George, S., R. Abel, and B. Miller. "Female Infanticide in Rural South India." *Economic and Political Weekly*, May 30, 1992, 1153–1156.
Ginsburg, F., and R. Rapp, eds. *Conceiving the New World Order: The Global Politics of Reproduction*. Berkeley and Los Angeles: University of California Press, 1995.
Grosz, E. *Volatile Bodies: Toward a Corporeal Feminism*. Bloomington: Indiana University Press, 1994.
Guha, R., and G. Spivak, eds. *Selected Subaltern Studies*. New York: Oxford University Press, 1988.
Gupta, A., and J. Ferguson, eds. *Culture, Power, Place: Explorations in Critical Anthropology*. Durham, N.C.: Duke University Press, 1997.
Hall, S. "Cultural Identity and Diaspora." In *Identity, Community, Culture, Difference*, edited by J. Rutherford. London: Lawrence and Wishart, 1990.
———. "New Ethnicities." In *Race, Culture, Difference*, edited by J. Donald and A. Rattansi, 252–259. London: Sage, 1992.
Haraway, D. "Situated Knowledge: The Science Question in Feminism and Privilege." *Feminist Studies* 14:3 (1988): 575–599.
Hartsock, N. "Foucault on Power: A Theory for Women? In *Feminism/Postmodernism*, edited by L. J. Nicholson, 157–175. London: Routledge, 1990.
Haynes, D., and G. Prakash. *Contesting Power: Resistance and Everyday Social Relations in South Asia*. Berkeley and Los Angeles: University of California Press, 1991.

Hegde, R. S. "Marking Bodies, Reproducing Violence: A Feminist Reading of Female Infanticide in South India." *Violence against Women* 5 (1999): 507–524.
———. "Narratives of Silence: Rethinking Gender, Agency and Power from the Communication Experiences of Battered Women in South India." *Communication Studies* 47:4 (1996): 303–317.
Jaggar, A. M., and S. R. Bordo, eds. *Gender/Body/Knowledge: Feminist Reconstructions of Being and Knowing.* New Brunswick, N.J.: Rutgers University Press, 1992.
John, M. *Discrepant Dislocations: Feminist Theory and Postcolonial Histories.* Berkeley and Los Angeles: University of California Press, 1996.
Kakar, S. "Feminine Identity in India." In *Women in Indian Society*, edited by R. Ghadially, 44–68. New Delhi: Sage, 1998.
Kaufman, B. J. "Feminist Facts: Interview Strategies and Political Subjects in Ethnography." *Communication Theory* 2:3 (1992): 187–206.
Kinsley, D. *Hindu Goddesses.* Berkeley and Los Angeles: University of California Press, 1988.
Krishnaswamy, S. "Female Infanticide in India." In *Women in Indian Society*, edited by R. Ghadially, 186–195. New Delhi: Sage, 1988.
Mani, L. "Multiple Mediation: Feminist Scholarship in the Age of Multinational Reception." *Inscriptions* 5 (1989): 49–73.
Marchand, M. H., and J. L. Parpart. *Feminism, Postmodernism, Development.* London: Routledge, 1995.
McNay, K. "Fertility and Frailty: Demographic Change and Health and Status of Indian Women." *Economic and Political Weekly*, October 28, 1995, WS81–WS86.
McNay, L. *Foucault and Feminism.* Boston: Northeastern University Press, 1992.
McRobbie, A. "The Politics of Feminist Research: Between Talk, Text and Action." *Feminist Review* 12 (1982): 46–57.
Mohanty, C. T., A. Russo, and L. Torres. *Third World Women and the Politics of Feminism.* Bloomington: Indiana University Press, 1991.
Mohanty, C. T. "Cartographies of Struggle: Third World Women and the Politics of Feminism." In *Third World Women and the Politics of Feminism*, edited by C. T. Mohanty, A. Russo, and L. Torres, 1–47. Bloomington: Indiana University Press, 1991.
———. "Under Western Eyes: Feminist Scholarship and Colonial Discourse." In *Third World Women and the Politics of Feminism*, edited by C. T. Mohanty, A. Russo, and L. Torres, 51–80. Bloomington: Indiana University Press, 1991.
Nandy, A. "Woman vs. Womanliness in India: An Essay in Social and Political Psychology." In *Women in Indian Society*, edited by R. Ghadially, 69–80. New Delhi: Sage, 1988.
O'Hanlon, R. "Recovering the Subject: Subaltern Studies and Histories of Resistance in Colonial South Asia." *Modern Asian Studies* 22:1 (1988): 189–224.
Ong, A. *Spirits of Resistance and Capitalist Discipline: Factory Women in Malaysia.* Albany: State University of New York Press, 1988.
Opie, A. "Qualitative Appropriation of the 'Other' and Empowerment." *Feminist Review* 40 (1992): 52–69.
Ortner, S. "Resistance and the Problem of Ethnographic Refusal." *Comparative Studies in Society and History* 2 (1995): 173–193.
Parikh, M. "Sex-Selective Abortions in India: Parental Choice or Sexist Discrimination." *Feminist Issues* 10:2 (1990): 19–32.
Patai, D. "U.S. Academics and Third World Women: Is Ethical Research Possible?" In *Women Words: The Feminist Practice of Oral History*, edited by B. Gluck and D. Patai, 137–153. London: Routledge, 1991
Pathak, Z., R. Sunder Rajan, and R. Shabano. In *Feminists Theorize the Political*, edited by J. Butler and J. W. Scott, 257–279. London: Routledge, 1992.
Rofel, L. "Rethinking Modernity: Space, and Factory Discipline in China." In *Culture, Power, Place: Explorations in Critical Anthropology*, edited by A. Gupta and J. Ferguson, 155–178. Durham, N.C.: Duke University Press, 1997.
Roggencamp, V. "Abortion of a Special Kind: Male Sex Selection in India." In *Test-Tube Women*, edited by R. Arditti, R. D. Klein, and S. Minden, 266–277. London: Pandora Press, 1984.
Scott, J. *Weapons of the Weak: Everyday Forms of Peasant Resistance.* New Haven, Conn.: Yale University Press, 1985.
———. *Domination and the Arts of Resistance: Hidden Transcripts.* New Haven, Conn.: Yale University Press, 1990.

Smith, D. *The Everyday World as Problematic: A Feminist Sociology.* Boston: Northeastern University Press, 1987.

Smith, P. *Discerning the Subject.* Minneapolis: University of Minnesota Press, 1988.

Spivak, G. C. "Can the Subaltern Speak?" In *Marxism and the Interpretation of Cultures,* edited by C. Nelson and L. Grossberg, 271–313. Urbana: University of Illinois Press, 1988.

Sunder Rajan, R. *Real and Imagined Women: Gender, Culture and Postcolonialism.* London: Routledge, 1992.

Venkatachalam, R., and V. Srinivasan. *Female Infanticide.* New Delhi: Har-Anand Publications, 1993.

Visaria, L., and P. Visaria. "India's Population in Transition." *Population Bulletin* 50:3 (1995): 2–50.

Weedon, C. *Feminist Practice and Poststructuralist Theory.* London: Blackwell, 1987.

E. ANN KAPLAN

TRAUMA, AGING, AND MELODRAMA
(With reference to Tracey Moffatt's Night Cries)

A Crumbling scaffold riddled with osteoporosis probably is not an ideal one to go through nine months of pregnancy.
—Dr. Healey, *New York Times*, 1995

The difficult problem for public education and practice would be to reorient both emotion and value in the direction of victims who are indeed deserving objects of mourning. In this sense, any attempt to facilitate processes of mourning and to further the emergence of viable public rituals would require an effective critique of anti-Semitism and related forms of scapegoating and victimization.
—Dominick LaCapra, *Representing the Holocaust*, 1994

Suicide is disproportionately common among the elderly, as people face loneliness, infirmity, and the prospect of a mental slide into oblivion.
—*New York Times*, September 22, 1996

MELODRAMA AND TRAUMA

This chapter develops a theoretical model of the intersections of trauma and melodrama within modernism (sketched in briefly below) to use for a project about women and aging in postmodern times. While many kinds of trauma could be usefully explored with the model, I use it to contribute new thoughts about women and aging. I will argue first that, at least for Western women, aging has been, and may yet be, experienced as a kind of trauma; second, that in the tradition of Hollywood melodrama, contemporary advertising constructs mini melodramas that both reveal contemporary constructions of aging and constitute aging as a category. Ads solicit consumption, passively, from the newly enlarged 60plus generation—focusing, significantly, on women—a group which culture is in the process of constructing in specific ways. Finally, I will discuss a powerful short film by Australian aboriginal Tracey Moffatt which arguably performs the trauma of aging for a traumatized middle-aged, aboriginal daughter of an old, infirm white mother. Spectators become active "witnesses" of these traumas.

But first, the theoretical model: Literary and film scholars do not necessarily agree on definitions of melodrama nor on the causes or dates for its emergence.[1] The debate hinges on whether to ascribe melodrama's emergence mainly to loss of Medieval and even Renaissance constructions of a sacred world (as Peter Brooks argues), or to the political upheaval of the industrial revolution in which the bourgeoisie, emerging out of the working and entrepreneurial classes, replaces the old aristocracy, whose decadence inflicted traumas on the aspiring class (as Geoffrey-Nowell Smith and Thomas Elsaesser argue).[2] In arguing here that melodrama functions in culture in the way a traumatic symptom does for individuals, I find both theses useful, especially since the two in some way depend on each other.

Melodrama, then, evolving in eighteenth-century Europe, proliferates and develops into a genre in modernist nineteenth-century Europe and America as the newly formed bourgeois family seeks to represent itself to itself. This need for images is part of the effort by the bourgeoisie to shape an identity other than that of either the aristocratic classes it is displacing or the working and lower classes it emerged from.[3] As an aesthetic form, I argue, melodrama (on the stage and in popular fiction) is produced from the traumas of class struggle and in the context of a search for identity, social order, and clear moral rules by which to live. Stories and images, giving shape to fictional lives, were needed especially as a disruptive modernism got underway to bolster other modes creating a new stable society.[4] Personal and social traumas were displaced into fictional melodrama forms where they could be more safely approached. By the twentieth century, as Miriam Hansen has argued, the cinema also "attracted and made visible to itself and society an emerging, heterogeneous mass public," and "engaged the contradiction of modernity at the level of the senses, the level at which the impact of modern technology on human experience was most palpable and irreversible."[5]

Trauma, as a psychological category, emerged with the nineteenth-century modernist development of psychoanalysis. The bourgeois family that nineteenth-century melodrama was to image back to the middle classes in Europe and America became the site for female hysteria (caused partly by that family's patriarchal and puritanical codes); and industrialization (that required the bourgeois class and was, circularly, produced by that class) provided the social conditions for the train and machine accidents and large-scale wars, that in turn prompted attention to the traumatic symptoms such accidents and wars produced in men.[6] Interestingly, as Judith Herman explains, because the political context was favorable, female hysteria was prominently studied by Charcot in the 1880s, attracting the attention of Pierre Janet, and then Freud and Breuer.[7] However, as the climate changed, so male scientists turned to study war neuroses focusing on soldiers in developing theories about trauma within modernism. Women's hysteria was then pushed aside and, until recently, regarded as resulting from mere fantasy.[8]

The links between melodrama and psychoanalysis are evident in Freud's own understanding of the functions fiction fulfills: In his essay "Thoughts on War and Death," Freud notes: "In the realm of fiction we discover that plurality of lives for which we crave. We die in the person of the hero, yet we survive him, and are ready to die again for the next hero just as safely."[9] Hollywood melodramas from the 1920s to at least the 1960s endlessly repeat family and war traumas and recoveries, bringing audiences back time and again by ensuring closure and cure at the film's end.[10] As Lauren Berlant argues in a project somewhat related to mine, "The politics of rage and pain and powerlessness that motors so much of the sentimental complaint and protest industry [in America, ed.] has been accompanied by a desire for amelioration at any cost."[11]

The notion of melodrama repeating in fictional form a suppressed cultural trauma to do with the overthrow of prior authority parallels Freud's theory developed toward the end of his life in *Moses and Monotheism.* Freud theorizes that the trauma of the Jews in the killing of Moses repeated an earlier crime of the primal horde's murder of the powerful father leader.[12] Traces of the crime continue throughout history. Extending Freud's theory, it is reasonable to argue that at certain historical moments aesthetic forms emerge to accommodate fears and fantasies related to suppressed historical events. In repeating the trauma of class struggle, melodrama, in its very generic formation, may evidence a traumatic cultural symptom.[13]

WOMEN, TRAUMA, AND AGING

Before I link this brief argument about trauma and melodrama to the matter of women, trauma, and melodramas of aging that I take up in what follows, some general caveats and definitions: Scholars tend to use the term *aging* as an abstract developmental concept, and as if it connoted experiences common to all. Yet the specific contexts within which one ages make a difference outside of the possibly general existential human predicament. I have in mind not only gender and race, but one's culture, nationality, religion, and even geography—all of which also matter, as will be clear in discussing Moffatt's film.[14] In addition, scholars need to distinguish aging without severe health problems from aging with readily visible problems. Another difference is the historical moment in which one is aging, since discourses about aging even within the same culture change with other historical and social changes. Like most human experiences, aging needs to be situated, and linked to gendered, raced, and cultural specificities.[15]

Further, I need to clarify my use of the term *trauma* for aging, since it is mainly found in the context of holocaust victims or the trauma of nonwhite skin, and most often the implied victims are male. In relation to aging, I use the concept to refer to ideologically and historically produced trauma—that is, trauma caused by cultural beliefs, domestic customs, and interpersonal practices in a particular location and time, rather than trauma produced through the practices of political regimes like fascism or through natural disasters or accidents. I understand the danger of distinguishing men and women in regard to aging. But I am encouraged in regard to both dangers by Judith Herman's research (1992–1997) and the psychotherapist Laura S. Brown's 1995 essay. Herman shows how "the late nineteenth-century studies of hysteria foundered on the question of sexual trauma," and how at that time "there was no awareness that violence is a routine part of women's sexual and domestic lives" (28). Herman sees the women's movements of the 1970s as making visible, finally, female traumas of sexual abuse.[16] Laurie Brown, meanwhile, rehearses the Psychiatric Association's (1987) DSM III-R definition, which states, "The person has experienced an event that is outside the range of human experience" (250). She argues that "human" here really means "male" and that the kinds of abuse many women endure at the hands of men they depend upon within the private, interpersonal realm represents a sufficient kind of damage to be named "trauma." It is a kind not often recognized in studies, and it may bear a similar *structure* to more dramatic and vast *public* damage usually focused on.[17]

Awareness of aging (even if only unconscious), with its increasing series of losses—of bodily functions and smooth, unwrinkled skin, of mental agility, of ideologies and values one grew up with, of friends and family—is arguably traumatic for people in Western culture.[18] And yet, I want also to argue for the social construction of aging—a construction that may partly produce the trauma I'm describing.[19] What may appear as an existential human dilemma in Sartre's terms may itself be a product of how aging and death are imagined in the West, as will be discussed in relation to melodramas of aging in ads.

Regardless of type of trauma, it has been argued that in trauma the event has affect only, not meaning.[20] It produces emotions—terror, fear, shock—but perhaps above all disruption of the normal feeling of comfort. Only the sensation sector of the brain is active in trauma; neuroscience has now shown that the meaning-making one shuts down because the affect is too much to be registered cognitively—something Pierre Janet and Sigmund Freud grasped intuitively but could not prove without tools of postmodern science.[21] Just because the experience has not been given meaning, the subject is continually haunted by it in dreams, flashbacks, and hallucinations. But, as we saw above in discussing bourgeois melodrama—whose modalities Hollywood took up—and Freud's theories about Moses, cultures too can be traumatized by events not cognitively processed and which intrude persistently. As I will show below in analyzing select ads addressed to the aging, melodrama is one form in which trauma intrudes: Cultures repeat and repeat traumas too problematic to confront directly. The traces of the event or anticipated fears (in relation to aging) remain culturally active but not remembered or taken in as such: If national public traumas, they are displaced into dramas about the domestic sphere, where traumas could be shown as caused by individual error, not by nations or people responsible for government. If in fact domestic traumas, every effort is made to shift focus away from such traumas and their implications.

While, then, melodrama and trauma are closely linked, their structures and ends are different. Each is produced by a specific historical formation, addresses largely one class (the white middle class), and is intended to serve specific ends, but these ends are widely divergent.[22] The one end is for aesthetic closure and ultimately relief from pain; the other aims to produce new structures in relation to a specific trauma, and to refuse the hunger for solutions, cures, resolutions. It aims to keep the wound open, while authors hope that the new structures, that I call performative because they may elicit action, will start the crucial process of working through on both the individual and cultural levels.[23] Let me now turn to specific case studies in which the differences in the structures and ends of melodrama and trauma will become clear.

MELODRAMAS OF AGING

Because melodrama seeks at once to reveal and to conceal the cultural traumas that gave rise to it, it represents traumas but seeks closure, cure, and satisfying completion of a narrative conflict. Melodrama seeks to repeat loss and disruption and crisis, only to have such catastrophes narratively resolved.[24] To put it succinctly, then, and as I develop below: Melodrama is an aesthetic modality, while trauma is a performative one: Melodrama is passive, involving a one-way text/ spectator structure; trauma is interactive, involving a triadic structure.[25]

I have elsewhere discussed how remarkable it is that cultural concepts about aging women have remained problematic despite the changes that feminisms have managed to produce in relation to other female stereotypes.[26] Hollywood has only recently begun to find roles for aging women—and at that they remain heavily stereotyped. Like minorities, aging women have traditionally been relegated to the fringes of classical narratives or, if central, then imaged as witches or "phallic" mothers. Popular culture has no category for women between sexy youth or young motherhood, on the one hand, and old-aged women, represented as tired, bitter, evil, or jealous on the other.[27] The main conflict figured in film melodramas of aging women usually (and interestingly) focuses on mother/daughter issues.

This in itself displaces troubles about aging onto women (leaving men out of the picture except as loving support figures or impediments of some kind); and ensures that narratives will mainly deal with the domestic sphere, not the workplace or public spaces. Aging is shown as trauma for women, but not for men. (Indeed, the opposite is shown for men: In films like *Grumpy Old Men* [so successful that they made a sequel, *Grumpier Old Men*], the men are shown miraculously revitalized by the love of a younger woman.)[28] In general a male discourse of aging as "decline" for women prevails. All the films end with narrative conflicts being resolved (the older woman learns to cede terrain to the younger, to move on to the role of observer not actor in life; the older woman is no longer dependent on the daughter). These films do touch upon genuine issues about aging as trauma for women in the United States; however, cultural constructs already in place are not challenged. Nor is there any awareness that the shape of the trauma is so heavily produced by U.S. culture itself.

Numerous articles in popular magazines and newspapers provide evidence of how aging trauma is being sensationalized. Typical sentiments are those in an article on "New Wrinkles for an Aging World," one of many on this topic.[29] Worries about the graying of the world population as births decline and as older people are living longer are on the increase. The economic concern that these older people will weigh down the young—especially in regard to social security savings—feeds the growing battle of the generations that could, at some future point, turn ugly.[30] Anecdotally, let me note generational conflicts in so-called adult communities in southern California. People in the lower age ranges resent having to pay for services they do not need (at the moment, at any rate). There is no ability to think of their own future needs. But this pertains to future parts of my research. While there is some justice for attention to a globally growing group of older people, clearly both ageism and racism are at work here— racism, because it is white births that are in steep decline; ageism, because it is the largely white baby-boomers who are beginning to complain about having to support their parents and who are worrying about increasing medical costs and whether there will be social security sufficient for their needs. A *Newsweek* image of a barely middle-aged white man staggering beneath the burden of his aging, helpless mother in a heavy wheelchair, again collapses normal aging

Since Mom Moved To *May 13 NYT*

Prospect Park Residence

We All Sleep Better At Night.

Mom is an amazing woman. She's always making new friends, learning new things. But I worried that it was getting harder for her to take care of herself. What if she needed help and couldn't reach me? At Prospect Park Residence, she enjoys her own private apartment with plenty of room for visits from her grandchildren. And she can choose from a full schedule of stimulating daily activities. Most importantly, we have the peace of mind of knowing assistance is available to her 24 hours a day, which helps us all rest a lot easier. Visit Prospect Park Residence today, and discover supportive living with a personal touch.

PROSPECT PARK
RESIDENCE
RETIREMENT COMMUNITY

One Prospect Park West
Brooklyn, New York 11215-1613

Just 12 Minutes from Manhattan

(718) 622-8400
For other locations, call 1-888-TO CASTLE

Name
Address
City
State _____ Zip
Phone ( )

Mail to: Prospect Park Residence
One Prospect Park West
Brooklyn, New York 11215-1613

A Castle Senior Living Residence

Now Open! *THE LIVING ROOM –*
**Providing Quality of Life to Seniors
with Memory Loss and Alzheimer's**

EQUAL HOUSING
OPPORTUNITY

FIGURE 1

with ill-health among some aged, and plays on the fears and fantasies of vulnerable readers worried about the future.[31]

What about contemporary ads? How is aging trauma turned into
a mini-melodrama in these? I will take the example of select ads addressed increasingly, as noted, to women over sixty years. But it
should be noted that ads fall into many different categories of address.[32] I focus here on those which rely on conventional constructs
of the family and the heterosexual domestic sphere, and which imply a mini-narrative, suggesting a conflict. Not surprisingly, ads for
assisted living and insurance are ones that readily use traditional family constructs to sell their services to the elderly.[33]

The first ad I want to discuss is for a Castle Senior Living Residence (see figure 1). The heading reads: Since Mom Moved to *Prospect Park Residence* We All Sleep Better At Night, and the image shows
an older woman hugging a cute young girl with ponytails. Both are
smiling. The text begins on an upbeat note, with a comment that
"Mom is an amazing woman. She's always making new friends, learning new things," but this is followed with a qualification about the
speaker's worries. Although there are no quote marks around the
heading, this appears to be the voice of a middle-aged married daughter, with her husband and children implied. The text refers to anxieties—worries about something happening to the grandmother, but
it is tactful: it states that daughter is worried because "it is getting
harder for her to take care of herself." Yet below the image we are
told that this LIVING ROOM residence provides quality of life "to
Seniors with Memory Loss and Alzheimer's." But more is at stake: The
fear is that some disaster will happen to the grandmother because
the family is not taking proper care of her. "What if she needed help
and couldn't reach me?" This suggests the guilt that the daughter
would feel if something happened because she could not be reached.
So a tragedy is conjured up, only to be put at rest because there is
this senior residence: Mom has her own space and choice of activities. The possibility of tragedy is averted and the ad ends with the
statement, "We have the peace of mind of knowing assistance is available to her 24 hours a day." The result is that this "helps us all rest a
lot easier." The story ends with an invitation to visit Prospect Park
Residence today in Brooklyn, "just 12 minutes from Manhattan."

The next two ads I consider are for life and health insurance (see
figures 2 and 3). The first has white words on a completely black page,

IT'S 1999.

YOU'RE DEAD.

WHAT DO YOU DO NOW?

Just for a minute, think the unthinkable. What would happen to your family if suddenly you weren't there? Where would the money come from for the mortgage? For the kids' education? To live on?

People with life insurance have the answer. Life insurance provides for the people you care about if you're not there.

Whether you're a breadwinner or a homemaker, you're indispensable. So when you make financial plans for the future, an agent can show you how life insurance will ensure your family's financial security if anything should happen to you.

Life insurance isn't for the people who die, it's for the people who live.

For a free consumer's guide to insurance, call 888-LIFE-777 or visit us on the Internet at http://www.LIFE-Line.org.

LIFE
LIFE AND HEALTH INSURANCE FOUNDATION FOR EDUCATION

FIGURE 2

LIFE INSURANCE ISN'T
FOR THE PEOPLE WHO DIE.
IT'S FOR THE PEOPLE
WHO LIVE.

"My husband Ron was everything — president, salesman,
manager, buyer, and warehouse
worker. The only thing he wasn't
was immortal."

Mary Vandenbroek's husband
Ron had a highly successful wine
brokerage business. But at age 49,
he discovered he had something
else — terminal cancer.
   Fortunately, he also had foresight.
Though he knew his business could
be sold if he died, his life insurance
provided Mary with the money to
keep the business and run it. Today,
employees still have their jobs; customers still have their fine wines; and
Mary is keeping Ron's dream alive.
   Are you prepared? Without insurance, your financial plan may be
just a savings and investment program that dies when you do. An
insurance agent or other financial
professional can help you create a
plan that will continue to provide
for the ones you love.
   To learn more call 1 888-LIFE-
777, or visit www.life-line.org.

Mary Vandenbroek

LIFE

FIGURE 3

and these read: "It's 1999: You're Dead. What Do You Do Now?" Put
out by the Life and Health Insurance Foundation for Education, this
ad plays on the addressee "thinking the unthinkable," namely, imagining the trauma of death, put (tactfully) in terms of "What would
happen to your family if suddenly you weren't there?" Once again,

the heteronormative family is called up in the naming of the addressee being either a "breadwinner" or a "homemaker." The ad wants to reach both genders it implies fill these roles. Having located the trauma as death of one of the couple, the ad seeks to heal, to cure: "An agent can show you how life insurance will ensure your family's financial security if anything should happen to you." The punch line hones the message in: "Life insurance isn't for the people who die; it's for the people who live."

This slogan—now in large capital letters—becomes the title for a second ad by the same group. This time the image is of a middle-aged, sad-looking white woman, Mary Vandenbrock, whose name implies Protestant stock. The ad focuses on the excellent qualities of the husband as breadwinner—the example par excellence of the Protestant ethic (he was "president, salesman, manager, buyer, and warehouse worker"), and his only negative was that "he wasn't immortal." Focus is on his foresight in getting life insurance so that Mary would have the money to keep the business running—not for her own fulfillment but only to fill out Ron's dream. Once again, the trauma is inserted—the tragic early death of the husband—only to have it recuperated by the agent who "can help you create a plan that will continue to provide for the ones you love."

A final example is an ad for Windsor Jewelers (see figure 4). This time, the image is of a punk kid, with dark glasses, ring in his nose, and chunky necklace on his T-shirt. At first, it does not look like an ad addressed to the aging! But in fact it is cleverly just that. The opposite of the previous ones, the ad appeals to the older person herself and plays on fears about what one's grandchildren will do with one's money. Playing on stereotypes of youth, it dramatizes fears about one's money being wasted on drugs or being thrown away on meaningless pursuits. The fear has to do with what happens after one's death. Like the first life insurance ad, death haunts the text, which plays with fears of death. The solution to this melodrama is that Windsor Jewelers will cash in the addressee's jewelry: "The good news is that there's still time to cash it in for a round-the-world cruise." This last clause also appeals to the older person's desire still to enjoy herself, to have fun, to refuse to just sit in a chair and die. In this case, the ad conjures death only to say there is still time, carpe diem, spend your money on yourself, and this will make unnecessary worrying about what happens to it after your death.

FIGURE 4

It is important that all these ads end with resolution of a suggested trauma. In this sense, the mini melodrama is aesthetic. Things are nicely rounded off, shaped, placed, and closed, so that the implied trauma can be put away, once, of course, one has taken advantage of what is being offered. The reader is a passive recipient of the ad's address, and her basic fears and fantasies about death and aging are eased.

It is also important that the very repeated presence of these ads on television, in newspapers, magazines, and journals functions like an intrusive traumatic cultural symptom very much in the manner of the melodrama genre proper as I argued above. Fears and anxieties about our individual aging are constantly before us, prodding at our minds, and forcing their attentions on us, only of course to demand that if we want peace of mind, we must buy something, or sign up for something, or agree to move our loved ones somewhere— all at significant cost to the reader of the ad. But underlying this constant appeal to the aging is an anticipated cultural trauma, namely that society will not be able to manage this ever-growing older group, that this group will be a social burden, that it will overwhelm the young and the middle-aged adult. Adequate life insurance would prevent the elderly from being a social burden; and the wealthy aging can provide jobs for others by traveling and spending their money before they die.

TRAUMAS OF AGING

For images of aging as trauma rather than as melodrama, I turn to independent film making. In the analysis which follows, I will show how trauma theory opens up old questions about the relationship of art to life, society, and culture and challenges us to think about the effect on the viewer. It prompts interesting questions about where the line can be drawn between lived experiences and certain kinds of art. As Shoshana Felman asks in *Testimony:* "What is the relation between literature and testimony, between the writer and the witness? What is the relation between the act of witnessing and testifying, and the acts of writing and reading, particularly in our era?" Furthermore, Felman queries "the relation between narrative and history, between art and memory, between speech and survival."[34] Art that takes trauma as its topic while refusing easy closure (like melodrama) may pull the spectator into its sphere in ways other topics may not, raising important questions about how art may be trans-forming—socially and personally.

Tracey Moffatt's *Night Cries* (Australia, 1989) is a case in point: I can begin to address some of Felman's questions by focusing on the film/spectator relationship that Moffatt's cinematic strategies pro-duces. This film follows the structure and performative modality of trauma, while self-consciously pitting that trauma against the illu-sory comforts of melodrama in the form of aboriginal entertainer Jimmy Little. In addition, Moffatt's film portrays a complex view of trauma and refuses to hide implications of traumatic cultural con-flict and aging. I will argue that, in contrast to the aesthetic closure of melodrama, *Night Cries* keeps the wound open: At the same time, however, the film starts the process of working through (in Dominick LaCapra's sense), establishing a triadic, interactive structure for en-gaging the spectator in what has been referred to as "vicarious trau-matization," and which I take up below. I will show how the spectator has to manage a kind of double trauma: first, there is the perform-ing by the text of the middle-aged daughter's childhood trauma re-garding an episode by the sea, and possibly simply through her adoption, as an aboriginal, by a white mother.[35] The spectator par-ticipates vicariously in this trauma through the cinematic techniques of intrusive flashbacks that come unexpectedly, apparently unher-alded periodically during the daughter's time with her mother. But, second, the spectator is made to witness the infirmity of the very aged, helpless mother, dependent on her angry, frustrated, and un-happy daughter, evidently trapped with her mother in some outback location—clearly Australian while at the same time mythic. I will re-turn to the concepts of vicarious traumatization and witnessing in concluding.

The first four frames of the film establish its basic themes: First, there is a blank screen (but, as Laleen Jayamanne reminds us, it is significantly a black void "not just black leader, not just a bit of empty time"), accompanied by low-level cries and various animal night sounds; next onto the black screen appears a piece of dialogue from Joshua Logan's 1956 melodrama, *Picnic*, about a tragic love affair, as the sounds of human and animal cries and of a train come onto the sound track; the third frame contains a striking image of the film's title, while the cries become loud shrieks and screams that increasingly sound like terrified humans in a horror film.[36] Finally, another black screen appears, and sounds of horror and terror gradually recede as the comforting, easeful song of aboriginal entertainer Jimmy Little—that brought him national acclaim—is heard even before his image emerges against the continuing black background.[37] Little's song here involves themes about a stairway to heaven and free calls to God. "You may talk to Jesus on this royal telephone." But this cuts to the deliberately stylized studio setting, made to suggest a shack in the hot Australian outback. An implacable blue sky is broken by purple mountains, and hot sun beats down on the shack. As night comes on, the set turns to dark blue sky with full white moon, the mountains now standing out starkly as silhouettes. Inside, we find seated the frustrated middle-aged aboriginal daughter taking care of her aged white mother and reading travel magazines in her longing to get away. Scraping noise on the sound track reveals itself, as the camera pans leftward, to be the noise of a prosthesis on a hand knocking on a plate of food. It is the aged mother's meal time. As the daughter angrily comes over to help her mother, she glances at the photos on a shelf made from rock. We briefly see an attractive white woman with a black child, two males, and a group photo behind these.

The film beautifully moves between images of the trauma of aging and the traumatic structure of the middle-aged daughter's memories of her past. The film mimics the structure of trauma in the way the daughter's images intrude increasingly into the narrative, without, as in trauma, being given meaning. It seems that the daughter, taking care of her aged, ill mother, is victim of a childhood trauma whose images intrude without warning into her present reality. The first series of intrusive images happens early on in the film, as the daughter hoses herself down to combat the incredible heat. Almost imperceptibly, we see first a flashback of a party dress and a white ribbon; we have no idea what it is about. We cut back to the now anguished face of the woman, breathing with difficulty and apparently having a panic attack. The next flashback gives us a bit more of the scene being remembered, in a close-up shot of a child's black curly hair and hands closing the back of a party dress at the neck. Once again, we return to the middle-aged daughter, whose face is distressed still. This is followed soon by a flashback of an image of the side of the child's face; finally, we have a full shot and see an attractive white mother attending to an aboriginal child in a party dress, wiping her hands clean. The mother's face has a resigned look; the child seems angry. Did the little aboriginal girl hate being made over in the image of a pretty middle-class white child? We do not know. The image is purely visual and emotional, as in traumatic attacks. Nothing cognitive is assigned to these images and emotions.

However, it is the third and longest flashback that dramatizes the main trauma. It is anticipated again by an activity involving water, this time the daughter washing clothes in a steel tub. She seems angry again, and when she pauses, we see that her face is more anguished than angry. Immediately, a quick shot of a rocky sea coast appears and disappears. The next day, we have an image of the mother quietly listening to a lullaby on a musical box. She falls asleep. The daughter is pacing up and down outside, and seeing her mother asleep, grabs hold of a whip and begins lashing and lashing. This provokes the third long flashback that is the central trauma of the film and to which the others seem to lead up. To the loud, almost deafening sound of a raging sea that floods the sound track, a white mother and aboriginal little girl are enjoying the wind and waves of the sea. The mother wants time alone, it seems (motives are impossible to assess given that there is no dialogue at all in this film); she seems to ask two little boys to take care of the girl. However, we soon see the boys wrap the child in large pieces of sea weed. The flashback cuts to the mother with back turned gazing out to sea; the girl's distress increases, the sound of the sea is deafening her cries, and the boys laugh and mock the girl. Birds shrieking loudly combine with the loud noise of the waves crashing on the rocks. The mother remains oblivious and immersed in her own thoughts. The child's distress increases as we see her panic-stricken face with tears streaming down.

In the midst of shots of the child's panic, Moffatt inserts images of Jimmy Little, singing a song of love again, but soundlessly. His message of love cannot help the little girl, as she experiences profound abandonment and terror of being hurt, lost, drowned. It seems the aboriginal daughter cannot forgive her white mother's (benign) neglect, despite a later shot of the mother comforting and warming the little girl after her crisis.

At the same time, as spectators witnessing this trauma, we also witness the trauma of the mother's aging that the protagonist daughter seems oblivious to—in fact, as oblivious as her mother was of *her* childhood trauma by the sea. The first sounds of the old lady, as we saw, are those of her prosthetic hand, banging on her plate as she tries to eat her food. As the camera pans across to where the sound is coming from, we focus on the ungainly apparatus and on the food barely making it into the woman's mouth. Later on, we experience her total dependence for bodily care on her daughter who must push her by wheelchair to the outside toilet. There the daughter waits impatiently outside, while noise of metal scraping on metal fills the scene. And finally, we witness the mother's toothless mouth, as she breathes at night with difficulty. The mother has nightmares, and she flails about in her bed and shrieks out in the night. We have to pit this trauma of aging against the daughter's vivid anger, which brings its own harsh sounds, as she angrily bangs on a bucket, creating the sound of the train she yearns to take her far, far away. Meanwhile, as if to mark the pain rather than ease it, the film brings back the image of Jimmy Little, airing his illusions of safety with a direct line to God—illusions that the film has shown are empty fantasies.[38]

Let me end by suggesting how the film's perhaps painful impact might be socially beneficial in a more direct way than is possible through melodrama. Two main concepts are useful for my task. These are the phenomenon of "witnessing" (already briefly noted in referring to Felman and Laub's research) and the effects of "vicarious traumatization" now being theorized by psychologists, therapists, and clinicians of different kinds.[39]

First, vicarious traumatization, the clinical term: In trauma texts where the usually assumed clear demarcation between what we call "life" and what a "text" is blurred, problems for the viewer may arise precisely because of this blurring. In films that take the viewer into trauma, and leave the wound open, as it were, spectators may be left vicariously traumatized. That is, their inner experience "may be transformed through empathic engagement with . . . trauma material."[40] While this may in some cases result in a pro-social transformation, it might also overstimulate the spectator and have the negative effect of inciting the spectator to push the experience away, as psychologists, therapists, and clinicians of different kinds have shown vis-à-vis therapists working with trauma victims.

More socially useful might be the position of witness—a position I think Moffatt's film in fact solicits.[41] How might this work out vis-à-vis Moffatt's film? Through our participation in the film's traumas, our witnessing (in Felman's sense), we also share in a certain "working through." Even before the end of the film, and immediately after the whipping scene, we have a shot of the daughter tenderly washing her mother's gnarled, arthritic feet. By the film's end, the mother's death frees the daughter into mourning for her loss. Movingly, the film shows the daughter curled up in fetal position beside her mother's corpse. We first see the couple at eye level: While on the sound track we hear only a baby's soulful cry, we are moved to a high-angle shot so that the daughter appears in fetal position, returned to the position within the womb. Can we say that the daughter has integrated her trauma now into her experience? Moved through it to find her unexpressed love for her pathetically aged mother—a love that seemed impossible before? For the spectator, the pain of family trauma (and its links to hideous aspects of colonialism vis-à-vis treatment of aboriginal children) remains: Yet watching the film's struggle to find a visual language to express the protagonist's pain, we bear witness to that pain. The daughter provides the testimony and we, as witnesses, mark the suffering. In this, as Dori Laub puts it, we participate in "history in the making" while at the same time witness the transgenerational (thus ahistorical) aspects of trauma.[42] The film has produced a triadic rather than passive structure. It is this structure that has arguably helped the kind of performative working through to take place for us and the subjects in the film.

The film also produces LaCapra's notion of working through as linked to "the possibility of judgement that is not apodictic or ad hominem but argumentative, self-questioning, and related in mediated ways to action" (210). La Capra argues that working through is also "bound up with the role of distinctions that are not pure binary oppositions but marked by varying and contestable degrees of strength and weakness" (210). Here I find relevant Moffatt's complex mixture of dealing with aboriginal/white relations, specific to Australia, and including influences from American, Japanese, Spanish, and Italian drama and film (readily cited by Moffatt in the interview alluded to earlier).[43] If the latter lends a universalizing, existential aspect to the film's themes—there are no pure binary black/white oppositions here, lending support to Moffatt's desire "not to be written about as a minority"—nevertheless the specificity of the Australian landscape and racial relations remain powerfully evident. The ravages of white culture on aboriginal life are exposed through the painful, conflicted mother-daughter relationship, which the spectator cannot avoid.

LaCapra's call, quoted in one of my epigraphs to this chapter, to find ways in public education and practice to move emotion and value toward victims "who are indeed deserving objects of mourning" (214) is important. For cultures need to facilitate processes of mourning and of discovering viable rituals for such mourning. While LaCapra mainly has victims of anti-Semitism in mind, I believe the same holds true for victims of family trauma who are largely women. Meanwhile, just as Felman, Laub, Lifton, and others argue in regard to victims of catastrophes, we need to establish structures within which there can be witnesses for the testimony of aging women, whose subjectivities are being drastically revised in their processes of aging. We need to be alert to these new subjectivities—partly formed by radical economic, scientific, technological, and social changes of postmodern times—and to the ensuing experiences, which the mini melodramas discussed here refuse to confront and seek to push away. We need structures within which such often silently endured traumatic experiences can be spoken or imaged, as in Moffatt's powerful short film, and in the process begin the task of working through.

NOTES

1. In making this broad claim, I am deliberately condensing the detailed research that justifies the statements. See Peter Brooks, *The Melodramatic Imagination Balzac, Henry James, Melodrama and the Mode of Excess* (New Haven, Conn.: Yale University Press, 1976); and Christine Gledhill, ed., *Home Is Where the Heart Is: Studies in Melodrama and the Woman's Film* (London: British Film Institute, 1987). In the latter volume, for an overview and mapping of melodrama as genre, and the history of its formal, cultural, and social development, particularly as linked to women, see essays by Christine Gledhill, Thomas Elsaesser, Laura Mulvey, and Geoffrey Nowell-Smith. Both volumes have extensive and useful bibliographies on the history and aesthetics of melodrama. Some of these texts are referred to in the notes that follow.

2. For Brooks (1976), melodrama's origins are in the French Revolution—a moment "that symbolically and really, marks the final liquidation of the traditional Sacred and its representative institutions (Church and Monarch)" (15). For Brooks, melodrama "becomes the principal mode for uncovering, demonstrating, and making operative the essential moral universe in a post-sacred era": Brooks notes that resacrilization can only be conceived in personal terms—the sphere of melodrama. Thus melodrama is a "mode of conception and expression . . . a certain fictional system for making sense of experience . . . a semantic field of force" (xiii), which he sees coming into existence in the form vital to the modern imagination "near the start of the 19th century" (xi).

   In his "Minnelli and Melodrama," Geoffrey-Nowell Smith claims that melodrama, as genre, arises from "a set of social determinations, which have to do with the rise of the bourgeoisie, and a set of psychic determinations which take shape around the family" (Nowell-Smith, in Gledhill, *Home Is Where the Heart Is*, 70). For Nowell-Smith, what's new is the assumption of a "world of equals, a democracy within the bourgeois strata) . . . (and) a world without social power" (71). Thomas Elsaesser, meanwhile, in his article,

"Tales of Sound and Fury: Observations on the Family Melodrama," sees the continuation of the French Romantic dramas Brooks discusses in the plots of British eighteenth-century novels (themselves leading to Italian operas) such as Richardson's *Clarissa*. This novel images "the quasi-totalitarian violence perpetrated by (agents of) the 'system'" (such as Lovelace, who, as an aristocrat, tries all kinds of extreme behaviour to force the lower class Pamela to marry him, ending up with rape) (Elsaesser, in Gledhill, *Home Is Where the Heart Is*, 45). The ideological 'message' of novels like *Clarissa* is recording "the struggle of a morally and emotionally emancipated bourgeois consciousness against the remnants of feudalism" (45). In the era of a "bourgeoisie in its militant phase, protagonists come to grief in a maze of economic necessities, *realpolitik*, family loyalties, and through the abuse of aristocratic privilege from a still divinely ordained, and therefore doubly depraved absolutist authority" (45–46).

3. In situating modernist melodrama for an argument about cultural trauma, I cannot detail ambiguities and contradictions inherent in melodrama as an aesthetic genre. As Thomas Elsaesser points out, there was a "radical ambiguity attached to the melodrama," and this applies to the French prerevolutionary and Restoration forms Elsaesser discusses, as to the nineteenth-century British melodramas and finally to the Hollywood film. As he puts it: "melodrama would appear to function either subversively or as escapism—categories which are always relative to the given historical and social context" (Elsaesser 1972/1987, 47).

4. In her introduction to *Home Is Where the Heart Is*, Gledhill stresses Brooks's list of forces acting on the bourgeoisie, including "the refiguring of Good and Evil in human life, demonstration of conflicting, unconscious forces in the psyche, and confrontation with the limits of language and the decentred subject exposed by modernism" (31).

5. See Hansen's' "Introduction," to Siegfried Kracauer's *Theory of Film: The Redemption of Physical Reality* (Princeton, N.J.: Princeton University Press), xi.

6. Freud developed his theories of trauma from studying the impact of train accidents and wars, and also late in life hypothesizes that a violent historical act can remain in cultural consciousness and continue to have a traumatic impact, as I note below in support of my thesis about melodrama. For more discussion of the history and development of the concept of trauma by Freud especially, see Cathy Caruth, *Unclaimed Experience: Trauma, Narrative, and History* (Baltimore: Johns Hopkins University Press, 1986). See also essays in Cathy Caruth, ed., *Trauma and Experience: Explorations in Trauma and Memory* (Ithaca, N.Y.: Cornell University Press, 1995). In an upcoming essay, "Trauma, Cinema, Witnessing," I discuss Freud's *Moses and Monotheism* in detail as a traumatic text.

7. See Judith Herman, *Trauma and Recovery: The Aftermath of Violence—from Domestic Abuse to Political Terror* (New York: Basic Books, 1992).

8. Ibid., 29–32.

9. Sigmund Freud, "Thoughts on War and Death (1915)," in *Collected Papers, Vol. 5*, ed. Joan Riviere (London: Hogarth Press, 1949), 307.

10. In his *Representing the Holocaust: History, Theory, Trauma* (Ithaca, N.Y.: Cornell University Press, 1994), Dominick La Capra quotes Eric Santer in Saul Friedlander, ed., *Probing the Limits of Representation: Nazism and the "Final Solution"* (Cambridge: Harvard University Press, 1992), developing a point similar to mine: "By narrative fetishism I mean the construction and deployment of a narrative consciously or unconsciously designed to expunge the traces of the trauma or loss that called that narrative into being in the first place. . . . [It] is the way an inability or refusal to mourn employs traumatic events; it is a strategy of undoing, in fantasy, the need for mourning by simulating a condition of intactness, typically by situating the site and origin of loss elsewhere" (144).

11. See Lauren Berlant's "Poor Eliza" essay, in *American Literature* 70:3 (September 1998): 635–668. Berlant argues that "the ravenous yearning for social change has installed the pleasures of entertainment . . . where a political language about suffering might have been considered appropriate. In these ways, the very emphasis on feeling that radicalized the sentimental critique also muffles the solutions it often imagines or distorts and displaces them from the places toward which they ought to be directed" (654). While Berlant does not engage the issue of trauma explicitly at this point, what she says about uses of the "sentimental" is close to some of my ideas. However, my stress here is on the potential pro-social impact of what I define as "trauma" texts.

12. In addition, as Caruth emphasizes and as I discuss in "Trauma, Cinema, Witnessing" (noted above), Freud is obsessed with repeating the history of his work on Moses. Caruth situated the book itself as "a site of trauma, a trauma that in this case, moreover,

appears to be historically marked by the events (the Nazis' arrival in Austria; Freud's departure to England) that, Freud says, divide the book into two halves" (21). In related work, I too investigate the history of my discourse on trauma, aging and melodrama, and its relation to my own specific historical moment, my own memory/history/cultural trauma. See my "Performing Trauma: On the Border of Fiction and Autobiography," in *Women and Performance* (April 1999): 33–58.

13. Other theorists also argue for literary genres as repeated forms in which a society's past is remembered. For Mikhail Bakhtin, for instance, as Robert Burgoyne points out, "genre memory" meant the "complex dialogue between the sedimented memories of history and nation preserved in genre forms and the alternative narratives of historical experience they bring into relief" (Robert Burgoyne, *Film Nation: Hollywood Looks at U.S. History* [1997], 7). Kaja Silverman's concept of historical trauma is especially important, since, like Freud, she theorizes cultural trauma as against only being concerned with individual types: By "historical trauma," Silverman means "an historical ramification extending far beyond the individual psyche" (Silverman, *Masculinity at the Margins* [London: Routledge, 1992], 55). Such historical trauma depends for its impact on what Silverman (following Jacques Rancière, as Burgoyne points out), calls the "dominant fiction"; namely, "the mechanism by which society 'tries to institute itself as such on the basis of closure, of the fixation of meaning, of the non-recognition of the infinite play of differences" (54). Historical trauma is what "interrupt[s] or even deconstitute[s] what a society assumes to be its master narratives and immanent Necessity" (55).

14. Indeed, of all these religion may be the most important, and the one that complicates my argument about anticipatory aging trauma: Most religions provide, for believers, the comfort of an after life that at least psychologically reduces the trauma I am talking about. But my main focus is on the agnostic's and atheist's predicaments.

15. I am interested in exactly when, why and how the very category of aging gets constructed in Western culture, but that is beyond my task here.

16. I believe that in the 1990s, political and social conditions are ripe for showing aging as trauma. But this is to anticipate.

17. Elsewhere, I address how I can argue that aging is something outside the range of "human experience," and how I can prove that aging is a more severe trauma for women. I suggest that the trauma that many share may be best expressed through Sartre's existentialist drama *Huis Clos*—life itself as a kind of prison, a hell, from which one cannot escape. The trauma of aging, in this view, consists in being *in time* and unable to get out of it. One irrevocably must age; one must deal with the ravages of the aging body; and confront the fact that death is inevitable. All of this can be experienced as a trauma, which, though basic to human existence, is paradoxically also "outside human experience" in that no one returns from death. See my essay, "Trauma and Aging: Marlene Dietrich, Melanie Klein, and Marguerite Duras," in *Figuring Age*, ed. Kathleen Woodward (Bloomington: Indiana University Press, 1999), 171–194.

18. In his *The Human Elder in Nature, Culture and Society* (Boulder, Colo.: Westview Press, 1997), David Gutmann has argued that there are strengths that come from survival. It is possible that those who can work through the losses I mention here are indeed strengthened. I am arguing that a great deal depends on the discursive frameworks one brings to the aging process, and in that I am not that far apart from Gutmann. But denying that there are real losses would not help.

19. For women, arguably the common trauma, given social constructions of ideal femininity, with its ideal Beauty, is the loss of youthful looks, youthful body, skin, hair. Elsewhere, I discuss this phenomenon in detail using the example of Marlene Dietrich as a case study of an extreme example. See E. Ann Kaplan, "Trauma and Aging: Marlene Dietrich, Melanie Klein, and Marguerite Duras." Faced with this common trauma, women handle it differently depending on their careers, life situations, and physicality.

20. Humanists have been debating theories of trauma taken up in literary, media and cultural studies. See, for discussion, Michael Roth, "Trauma and Historical Consciousness," in *Commona Knowledge* 7 (1998): 99–110. See also in press essays by Michael Roth, "Why Trauma Now?" and Susannah Radstone, "Screening Trauma: *Forrest Gump*, Film and Memory." In related work, I review and contribute to these debates. See my forthcoming essay, "Trauma, Cinema, Witnessing" in a volume coedited by Rosanne Kennedy and Jill Bennett.

21. See Josef Breuer and Sigmund Freud, *Studies on Hysteria,* trans. James and Alix Strachey [London: Hogarth Press, 1956]; and Freud, "On the Psychical Mechanism of Hysterical

Phenomena" (In collaboration with Dr. Josef Breuer, 1893), in Sigmund Freud, *Collected Papers, Vol. 1,* ed. Ernst Jones and trans. Joan Riviere (London: Hogarth Press, 1949), 24–41.

22. However, this middle class is becoming increasingly multiethnic, and as this happens, so ads will begin to include more images of elderly minorities. The whole issue of minorities and aging is important, and I will address it in future research.

23. On this important point, see Herman, *Trauma and Recovery,* 1–4. Herman argues that it is only in specific political climates that certain traumas can get social attention. See also LaCapra, *Representing the Holocaust,* 206–233. What LaCapra has to say about "acting out" and "working through" is especially pertinent to my interests in the impact of films dealing with trauma on spectators, as I explain in my conclusion.

24. See Berlant, "Poor Eliza," 636. As Berlant argues, sentimental structures have been "deployed mainly by the culturally privileged to humanize those very subjects who are also, and at the same time, reduced to cliche within the reigning regimes of entitlement or value."

25. As Shoshana Felman puts it: "What testimony does not offer is, however, a completed statement, a totalizable account of those events. In the testimony, language is in process and in trial, it does not possess itself as a conclusion, as the constatation of a verdict or the self-transparency of knowledge. Testimony is . . . a discursive practice, as opposed to pure theory. To testify—to vow to tell, to promise and produce one's speech as material evidence for truth—is to accomplish a speech act, rather than to simply formulate a statement. As a performative speech act, testimony in effect addresses what in history is action that exceeds any substantialized significance, and what in happens is impact that dynamically explodes any conceptual reifications and any constative delimitations." See Shoshana Felman and Dori Laub, eds., *Testimony: Crises of Witnessing in Literature, Psychoanalysis, and History* (London: Routledge, 1992).

26. See E. Ann Kaplan, "Body Politics: Menopause, Mastectomy and Cosmetic Surgery in Films by Rainer, Tom and Onwurah," in Kaplan, *Looking for the Other: Feminism, Film and the Imperial Gaze* (London: Routledge, 1997), 256–276. See also Jean Kozlowski, "Women, Film and the Midlife Sophie's Choice: Sink or Sousatzka?" in *Menopause: A Midlife Passage,* ed. Joan C. Callahan (Bloomington: Indiana University Press, 1993), 3–22; and essays in Paul Komarasoff and Philippa Rothfield, eds. *Reconstructing the Menopause* (London: Routledge, 1997).

27. In my *Motherhood and Representation* (London: Routledge, 1992), I discuss films from the silent era to the present, showing in what I call the "phallic" mother paradigm, the abundance of such stereotypes, from Griffith's films to *Now Voyager, Marnie* and many contemporary films.

28. One familiar melodrama conflict shows an older woman (often the mother) refusing to cede her central role in life. In films like *Postcards from the Edge* (1990), the daughter's psychological problems are seen to arise from an overly narcissistic, controlling mother, who always seizes center stage and cannot leave space for her daughter to grow up. It is as if there is only room for either the mother or the daughter, so that the older woman must, ultimately, cede space to the younger one. A second melodrama conflict represents aging mothers as overly dependent on their daughters, as in *Terms of Endearment* (1983). The "empty nest" syndrome, in which older widowed women have nothing in their lives except their children and their families, is repeated. In this film, though, at least the older woman is granted sexual desire (Shirley MacLaine, again playing the mother, dates Jack Nicholson). And the trauma of the daughter's cancer allows the older woman to be of genuine service.

29. *New York Times,* September 22, 1996, 3, 5.

30. See, for example, the public attention already being focused on inter-generational conflict in articles like that in *Newsweek,* September 18, 1995, 38–44, titled "Mediscare: Young vs. Old: Who Will Carry the Burden?" referred to below.

31. In his essay in the *Newsweek* issue cited in note 29, Robert Samuelson describes the enormous public costs of supporting the older generation While not predicting generational war, he says one could happen, as the baby boom generation hits sixty-five in 2011.

32. In my research over the past ten years, I have found many different kinds of ads and articles addressed to this growing 60plus group, being constituted through these very materials. Ads for antiaging products perhaps predominate—antiwrinkle creams and many other cosmetic items to delay aging for women; claims for certain herbs and

chemicals said to delay aging; increasing ads for Viagra, addressed to males. But another large category has to do with ads by travel agencies and holiday companies and hotels soliciting the retired in their availability to play. The ads for residencies for the aging and for life and other kinds of insurance are frequent. In terms of articles about aging, these include prominently articles about aging actresses, which I compare to discussions of aging men (often without noting their aging, however). Other articles deal with the science of aging and projects to learn about what makes us age in order again to prolong life. But some as I note here show concern about "the greying of the world" and fears of middle-aged children re their being called upon to take care of their aging parents.

33. For other scenarios are conceivable: A traumatic aging scenario is not the only possible one. Why not assume that menopausal women have untold possibilities awaiting them? And that they will be in good health? Without going to the lengths of an article on "Longevity," in *Mondo 2000: A User's Guide to the New Edge,* ed. Rudy Rucker, R. U. Sirius, and Queen Mu (New York: Harper, 1992), do we not live in an era when the idea of the body has in fact changed? When the body is no longer reduced to a machine, or seen in architectural metaphors, but rather is imaged as plastic, open to change, even as "communal" in the sense of sharing organs through transplants? As one author put it: "The body is no longer 'given' (meaning, traditionally, a gift of God); it is plastic, to be molded and selected at need or whim. . . . The body is not only plastic but bionic, with cardiac valves." Bernard Christian, *The Body Machine* (New York: Crown, 1981), 34. But this topic lies beyond my range here.

34. See Shoshana Felman, "Foreword," and her "Education and Crisis," in *Testimony,* 1–57.

35. Moffatt was born in Brisbane, Australia, and was brought up by a white Australian woman. For more details see interview on her film *Bedevil* by John Conomos and Raffaele Caputo, in *Cinema Papers* 93 (1993). In a personal communication with me, Moffatt told me that she "couldn't bear to be written about as a 'minority.' . . . I see myself as an artist who happens to cast black people (and other races—for various reasons) in my movies. I think my films break rules." In other work, I link the daughter's trauma to the tragedy of the so-called stolen generations, studied in depth by Corell Edwards and Peter Read in their volume *The Lost Children: A Hundred Years' War* (Sydney: Doubleday, 1989). See Kaplan, "Trauma, Cinema, Witnessing," forthcoming; and also Peter Read, *A Rape of the Soul so Profound* (St. Leonards, NSW: Allen and Unwin, 1999). As Pat Mellencamp reminds readers in her essay, "Haunted History: Tracey Moffatt and Julie Dash," *Discourse* 16:2 (winter 1993–1994): 127–163, by the 1930s the original policy of extermination was changed to absorption, so that "aboriginal children were taken away from their parents and given to white foster parents," with horrifying results (137).

36. See Laleen Jayamanne, "'Love me tender, love me true, never let me go . . .': A Sri Lankan Reading of Tracey Moffatt's *Night Cries—A Rural Tragedy,*" in *Feminism and the Politics of Difference,* ed. Sneja Gunew and Anna Yeatman (London: Allen and Unwin, 1993), 73–84.

37. Jayamanne has an illuminating discussion of cinematic uses Moffatt makes of Little's image so as to signal mediating "of several cultural forces via his body/voice. With style and panache he embodies cultural assimilation." (78). But this aspect of the film lies beyond my immediate concerns here.

38. Jayamanne also discusses this scene. She notes that the song being sung silently by Jimmy Little here is Elvis Presley's "Love me tender, love me true." See note in Jayamanne, 82.

39. Meanwhile, in relation to those testifying about traumas inflicted in the name of a government, race or cause, as in the case of South Africa's Truth and Reconciliation Trials, what Felman has to say also pertains: "A life testimony is not simply testimony to a private life, but a point of conflation between text and life, a textual testimony which can *penetrate us like an actual life*" ("Education," 14).

40. For detailed discussion of this phenomenon in relation to clinical practice, see Laurie A. Pearlman and Karen Saakvitne, *Trauma and the Therapist* (New York: W. W. Norton, 1995). They stress the specifically negative aspects of the transformation in their concept of "vicarious traumatization," while I would want to think through the potential benefit to society of empathic engagement with trauma in film. That is, such engagement may produce action—something that C. R. Figley talks about in his edited book *Compassion Fatigue* (New York: Brunner/Maze, 1995). The extensive bibliography in Pearlman/ Saakvitne will refer readers to other research in this area. For discussion of a similar

phenomenon (although they do not so name it), see Shoshana Felman and Dori Laub, eds.

41. See my forthcoming essay, "Trauma, Cinema, Witnessing," in a volume coedited by Rosanne Kennedy and Jill Bennett.

42. Dori Laub articulated these themes in this particular form in a lecture at New York University on May 25, 2000.

43. Elsewhere, I argued for *Night Cries* as a reworking of the Australian classic, *Jedda*, which deals also with an aboriginal daughter raised by a white homesteading couple, the McManns. However, while that film subscribes to the dangerous racial theory that race is in-born (the aborigines cannot be "educated") and essentializes and stereotypes the aboriginese, Moffatt's film renders her black subject in terms of powerful emotions, common to many no matter of what race, class or creed. See my essay, "Aborigines, Film and Moffatt's *Night Cries: A Rural Tragedy:* An Outsider's Perspective," in *Bulletin of the Olive Pink Society* 1:2 (1989): 13–17. Reprinted in Julie Marcus, ed., *Picturing the 'Primitif: Images of Race in Daily Life* (Canada Bay, NSW: LhR Press, 2000), 61–72.

Moffatt's declared influences are often from Western literature and drama: She was influenced by writers like Garcia Lorca, Eugene O'Neill, and Tennessee Williams, but also Japanese films by Ozu and Kobayashi, Italian ones by Fellini, and, of course, American cinema too, as she notes in the interview. For these reasons, there is certainly a deliberate universalist cast to *Night Cries.* However, the specificity of aboriginal/white Australia, and the Australian landscape is also very evident in the film. Influences of postwar Australian landscape painting from Arthur Boyd and Russell Drysdale to Albert Namatjira, a highly successful and popular aboriginal painter, are very evident.

About the Contributors

KAREN BARAD teaches physics, philosophy, women's studies, and critical social thought at Mount Holyoke College. Her Ph.D. is in theoretical particle physics. Her research has been supported by the National Science Foundation and the National Endowment for the Humanities, among others. She is the author of numerous articles on physics, feminist epistemology, philosophy of science, cultural studies of science, and feminist theory, and is currently completing a book entitled Meeting the Universe Halfway.

ANNE C. BELLOWS is a food systems geographer working in the nutritional sciences department at Rutgers University. She writes on food security, economic and political rights to food, urban agriculture, and feminist political ecology.

CHARLOTTE BUNCH founder and executive director of the Center for Women's Global Leadership at Douglass College, Rutgers University, has been an activist, author, and organizer in the women's and civil rights movements for three decades. Previously, Bunch was a tenured fellow at the Institute for Policy Studies and a founder of the Washington, D.C., Women's Liberation and of *Quest: A Feminist Quarterly*. She has edited seven anthologies, and her latest books are *Passionate Politics: Feminist Theory in Action* and *Demanding Accountability:*

The Global Campaign and Vienna Tribunal for Women's Human Rights. Bunch's contributions to networking and organizing for women's human rights have been recognized by many and include her induction into the National Women's Hall of Fame in October 1996. Bunch is currently a professor in the Bloustein School of Planning and Public Policy at Rutgers University and serves on the Boards of the Ms. Foundation for Women and the Human Rights Watch Women's Rights Division.

NAO BUSTAMANTE is a performance artist pioneer who is originally from the San Joaquin Valley (central California). She has been living and developing her work for the past fourteen years out of San Francisco's Mission District. In addition to performance, Nao works with video and installation mediums. Her performance work has been seen in Mexico, Asia, Europe, Canada, Australia, New Zealand, Northern Africa, and the United States. Check out her websites: www.sfgate.com/offbeat/nao1.html and www.slowburn.com/rosa.html.

ELAINE K. CHANG began teaching in the School of Literatures and Performance Studies in English, University of Guelph, in the fall of 2000. She is currently writing a book on problems of "the middle" in contemporary historical representation and at conjunctures of feminist and postcolonial theory.

MARIANNE DEKOVEN is a professor of English at Rutgers University. She is the author of *Rich and Strange: Gender, History, Modernism* and *A Different Language: Gertrude Stein's Experimental Writing.* She has been a Guggenheim Fellow, and from 1995 to 1998 she was the director of the Institute for Research on Women at Rutgers University. She has published widely on feminist theory and criticism and twentieth-century literary and cultural studies. Her current book project concerns the 1960s and the emergence of postmodernism.

LEELA FERNANDES teaches political science and women's studies at Rutgers University. She is the author of *Producing Workers: The Politics of Gender, Class, and Culture in the Calcutta Jute Mills.* She is currently writing a book on the middle class and the politics of economic reform in India.

SUSAN STANFORD FRIEDMAN is the Virginia Woolf Professor of English and Women's Studies at the University of Wisconsin-Madison. She is the author of *Psyche Reborn: The Emergence of H.D.*, *Penelope's Web: Gender, Modernity, H.D.'s Fiction*, and *Mappings: Feminism and the Cultural Geographies of Encounter*. She is the coauthor of *A Woman's Guide to Therapy*, the coeditor of *Signets: Reading H.D.*, and the editor of *Joyce: The Return of the Repressed*. She has published many articles on feminist theory and pedagogy, narrative theory, women's poetry, modernism, psychoanalysis, multiculturalism and transnationalism, and academic feminisms. She is at work on a critical study on modernism and an edition of letters, H.D. and Freud: Diary of an Analysis, 1932–1935. She is the founder and coordinator of the Border and Transcultural Studies Research Circle at the University of Wisconsin-Madison.

COCO FUSCO is a New York-based interdisciplinary artist and writer and an associate professor at the Tyler School of Art of Temple University. She is the author of *English Is Broken Here: Notes on Cultural Fusion in the Americas* and the editor of *Corpus Delecti: Performance Art of the Americas*.

RADHA S. HEGDE teaches in the department of communication at Rutgers University. Her research has focused on global feminism, reproductive politics, and South Asian diasporic women. She is currently completing a book concerning motherhood and female infanticide. Her work has been published in *Communication Theory*, *Communication Studies*, *Women's Studies in Communication*, and *Violence against Women*.

CHERYL JOHNSON-ODIM is professor and chair of the liberal education department of Columbia College, Chicago, and serves on the board of directors of the American Council of Learned Societies. Her research centers on African women's history and particularly their grassroots anti-colonial struggles, as well as African American women's history and third-world feminist theory. Her publications include *Restoring Women to History* (coedited with Margaret Strobel), *For Women and the Nation: Funmilayo Ransome-Kuti of Nigeria* (with Nina Mba), and *Expanding the Boundaries of Women's History* (coedited with Margaret Strobel).

E. ANN KAPLAN is professor of English and comparative studies at SUNY, Stony Brook, where she also founded and directs the Humanities Institute. Kaplan has written many books and articles on topics in women's studies, literary and media studies, and cultural studies. Her perspectives include feminism, psychoanalysis, postmodernism, and postcolonialism. Noted books are *Women in Film: Both Sides of the Camera, Women in Film Noir, Rocking around the Clock, Motherhood and Representation,* and most recently *Looking for the Other: Feminism, Film, and the Imperial Gaze.* Recent coedited books include *Generations: Academic Feminists in Dialogue* and *Playing Dolly: Technocultural Fantasies and Fictions of Assisted Reproduction.* In press is an edited anthology of feminist film theory, *Feminism and Film.* Her new project is on trauma, cinema, and witnessing.

DEBRA J. LIEBOWITZ is an assistant professor of women's studies and political science at Drew University, New Jersey. She received her Ph.D. from Rutgers University in 2000. Her research focuses on gender and transnational political organizing with emphasis on debates in international political economy and Latin American politics. She has published articles about gender, transnational political mobilization, and the North American Free Trade Agreement, as well as articles on gender and U.S. foreign policy. She also has extensive experience developing experiential educational programs that emphasize issues of gender, leadership, and public policy in the United States, Costa Rica, Mexico, and China.

RAJESWARI SUNDER RAJAN was a senior fellow at the Nehru Memorial Museum and Library in New Delhi, India. She is the author of *Real and Imagined Women: Gender, Culture, and Postcolonialism* and *Of Women/In India: Towards a Better State?*; she is editor of the collections *The Lie of the Land: English Literary Studies in India* and *Signposts: Gender Issues in Post-Independence India.* She is joint editor of *Interventions: International Journal of Postcolonial Studies.*

CYNTHIA SALTZMAN is an anthropologist who has taught at Barnard College and Rutgers-Camden. She has also been a visiting scholar at the Rutgers Institute for Research on Women, a postdoctoral fellow in Judaic studies at Yale University, and a visiting fellow at Yale's Institute for Social and Policy Studies. Most recently, she has done applied work in institutional research. Her writing has focused on feminism and Judaism and on women and unions at Yale.

LYNNE SEGAL is anniversary professor of psychology and gender studies at Birkbeck College, London University. Her latest book is *Why Feminism? Gender, Psychology, Politics*. Her other books include *Is the Future Female? Troubled Thoughts on Contemporary Feminism; Slow Motion: Changing Masculinities, Changing Men; Sex Exposed: Sexuality and the Pornography Debate;* and *Straight Sex: The Politics of Pleasure.*

Index

gender identity, 155; and identity, 78, 98–99; and labor, 94, 96; and material-discursive relationship, 100; media representations and national culture in India, 152, 154, 155; and space, 78–80, 94; and technology, 94
Clifford, James, 147
Clinton, Bill, 42, 44
Coalition against Free Trade, 174
coalition politics, 62–64
Cohen, Marjorie Griffin, 173–175
Commission on Global Governance, 168
commodity, commodification: and nation, 153, 155–156; and sexuality, 163
Common Frontiers (Canada), 171
community, 79–80, 94, 100
CONAMUP (Coordinadora Nacional del Movimiento Urbano Popular, Mexico), 176
Convention on the Rights on the Child, 143
Copenhagen World Summit for Social Development (1995), 135, 137
Cornell, Drucilla, 286
Correspondencia, 180
Cossman, Brenda, 160
Covenant on Social, Economic, and Cultural Rights, 143
Crenshaw, Kimberle, 121
CRM (Consejo Regional de Mujeres/ Women's Regional Council), 177
Cuba, 257
cultural feminism, 117
"Cultural Feminism versus Post-Structuralism: The Identity Crisis in Feminist Theory" (Alcoff), 117
cultural studies: 50, 51–52; Birmingham, 52; and globalization, 18, 21; and space, 16, 18;
cultural tourism: 257–258
culture: and class, 45; and difference/ diversity, 64–65; and gender, 133–134, 149–150; and nation, 150–151, 158–160; and politics, 61, 78; and religion, 214–215; *see also* cultural feminism, cultural studies, cultural tourism
cyberspace: as metaphor for identity, 21; and globalization, 75
cyborg, 80, 90, 101

Das, Veena, 160
Davila, Rosaura, 180
DAWN (Development Alternatives with Women for a New Era), 135
Dawson, Michael, 238
deconstruction, 64
de Courtivron, Isabelle, *New French Feminisms*, 13
de Lauretis, Teresa, 22
D'Entrèves, Maurizio Passerin, 237
dependency, 41–42
Derrida, Jacques, 13
deterritorialization, and globalization, 147, 149
development: and global feminism, 135; and modernization, 68
Devi, Phoolan, 215
Dietrich, Gabriele, 221
difference, 14, 46, 47–49; axes of, 23; and binary structures, 1–3; biology and, 114; vs. diversity, 64–65; and feminist theory, 13–14, 67, 118–119, 124; and politics, 118–120; and post, 69; and time, 67–69; and transnational advocacy, 183–184; in U.S. history, 119
Discipline and Punish (Foucault), 86
discrimination, 113, 121–122, 142–143, 183
diversity: vs. difference, 64–65; and feminism, 2, 6, 13–14, 38, 129–130, 144–145; and activism, 138, 191–207
dynamics, 82, 90, 92, 97

Eagleton, Terry, 52
Eastern Europe, 132
Ehrenreich, Barbara, 43–44
Eisenstein, Zillah, 44
Elsaesser, Thomas, 305
Elshtain, Jean Bethke, 55
ERA, 143
ethnicity: and labor, 79–80; and multipositionality, 23
Etzioni, Amitai, 42
Euclidean geometry, *see* geometry
Europe, 116

family: and feminism, 42–43; and household, 230–232; and human

Questions of Travel (Kaplan), 104n.2

race, 201–204; 318–323; and feminism,
    98, 124; and identity, 98–99; and
    location, 29–30; and free trade debate,
    183–185; theory, 121
Rajan, Rajeswari Sunder, 6, 8, 294, 297
Ransby, Barbara,
rape: and human rights, 142; representa-
    tions of, 160
Rapp, Rayna, 283
Rashtriya Swayamsevak Sangh (RSS), 221
Rathbone, Eleanor, 40
Ray, Satyajit, *Devi*, 215
Reagan, Ronald, 42, 173
Rebuilding the Nest (Blankenhorn et al), 43
Regulska, Joanna, 230, 234, 236
religion, 212–223; and body, 8; and
    feminism, 8, 133; and materialism, 8;
    and postcolonialism, 219
"Report from the Bahamas" (Jordan), 22–
23
reproduction, 39; and agency, 114, 284,
    293, 294; and body, 9, 283; and
    choice, 15; cultural meanings, 283;
    gender politics and identity, 284, 292;
    and labor, 180, 284; and space, 294;
    politics in India, 282–298; rights, 134
Réseau Canadien d'Action, 171
reterritorialization: 149–150, and gender,
    body, 157–158
Rich, Adrienne, 195; "Notes toward a
    Politics of Location," 24; "When We
    Dead Awaken: Writing as Re-Vision,"
    and Anglo-American feminism, 19, 24
rights, hierarchies of, 141; *see also* human
    rights
Rio Earth Summit on the Environment
    (1992), 135
Ritchie, Laurel, 174
Robertson, Roland, 30
Roe v. Wade, 124
Romanticism, and second-wave femi-
    nism, 19
Rome World Food Summit (1997), 135
Romito, Patrizia, 46
Room of One's Own, A (Woolf), 30–31,
Rose, Gillian, 71–72
Ross, Andrew, 48

Rwanda, 134, 142

Said, Edward, 31; "Traveling Theory," 16
Salinas, 177
Saltzmann, Cynthia, 6, 7–8
Sandoval, Chela, 22
Sangari, Kumkum, 220
Sarakar, Tanika, 221
Sartre, Jean-Paul, 308
Scale, 101–102
Scattered Hegemonies (Grewal and Kaplan),
    25, 26
Schor, Juliet, 56
science: feminist science studies, 4, 101;
    history and philosophy of, 76, 92; as
    practice, 86; theories of, 85
Scott, Joan, 37
second wave feminism: black feminism,
    and development of
    multipositionality, 22; developments
    in, 110, 112–113; and history, 115;
    and modernism/Romanticism, 19, 67;
    and postmodernism, 66–67; and
    power, 115; and temporal rhetoric, 18;
    and third-world feminist theory, 113
Sedgwick Eve Kosofsky, 22
Segal, Lynne, 4–5
sex tourism, 257–281
sexuality, 257–281; and
    commodification, 163, 257–281; and
    culture, in India, 158–160; globaliza-
    tion as threat, in India, 157–158,
    161–163; and identity, 98–99,
    113–114; and nation, in India, 149,
    156–163; and representation of gender
    violence, 160; rights, 134
Shange, Ntozake, 19
Shortell, Mary, 179
Shiv Sena (Bombay), 158, 162, 163
Shiva, Vandana, 219
The Shock of Arrival (Alexander), 29
Signs, 49, 120
Sisterhood is Global (Morgan), 25
Sjolander, Claire, 183
Smith, Anna Marie, 44
Smith, Barbara, 22
Smith, Dorothy, 292
Smith, Geoffrey-Nowell, 305
Smith, Neil, 102

www.ingramcontent.com/pod-product-compliance
Lightning Source LLC
Chambersburg PA
CBHW071833270326
41929CB00013B/1979